Break and Flow

New World Studies
Marlene L. Daut, Editor

Break and Flow

HIP HOP POETICS
IN THE AMERICAS

Charlie D. Hankin

University of Virginia Press
Charlottesville and London

University of Virginia Press
© 2023 by the Rector and Visitors of the University of Virginia
All rights reserved
Printed in the United States of America on acid-free paper

First published 2023

9 8 7 6 5 4 3 2 1

Library of Congress Cataloging-in-Publication Data
Names: Hankin, Charlie D., author.
Title: Break and flow : hip hop poetics in the Americas / Charlie D. Hankin.
Description: Charlottesville : University of Virginia Press, 2023. | Series: New World studies | Includes bibliographical references and index.
Identifiers: LCCN 2023002578 (print) | LCCN 2023002579 (ebook) | ISBN 9780813949819 (hardcover) | ISBN 9780813949826 (paperback) | ISBN 9780813949833 (ebook)
Subjects: LCSH: Rap (Music)—Cuba—History and criticism. | Rap (Music)—Brazil—History and criticism. | Rap (Music)—Haiti—History and criticism. | Rap (Music)—Political aspects—Cuba. | Rap (Music)—Political aspects—Brazil. | Rap (Music)—Political aspects—Haiti.
Classification: LCC ML3531 .H344 2023 (print) | LCC ML3531 (ebook) | DDC 781.64/9—dc23/eng/20230203
LC record available at https://lccn.loc.gov/2023002578
LC ebook record available at https://lccn.loc.gov/2023002579

Cover art: Photo by author.

*To the memory and spirit of
Malcoms "Justicia"*

Contents

	Acknowledgments	ix
	Introduction	1
1.	Yearning: "Nan lòt dimansyon"	19
2.	Raplove: "Es lo que hay"	48
3.	Uprooting: "Qué importa si sonamos americano hermano"	71
4.	Scale: "Rap é meu lugar"	92
5.	Writing: "Enraizados da letra"	110
6.	Violence: "Sou fèy blanch"	142
	Epilogue: En-/un-gendering Hip Hop	171
	About the Artists	173
	Selective Timeline of Brazilian, Cuban, and Haitian Hip Hop	179
	Permissions	183
	Notes	185
	Discography	229
	Bibliography	235
	Index	265

Acknowledgments

I AM deeply grateful to the artists who taught me about this practice from the perspective of their communities and shared their wisdom in conversation and collaboration: Malcoms "Justicia," Rubén Marín, Anderson, Bárbaro "El Urbano," Carlito, David "D'Omni," DJ Leydis, Etián "Brebaje Man," Isaac "El criminal del flow," La Fina, Lourdes "La cimarrona," Osmel Francis, Prófugo, Yimi "Konclaze," Temba, Charly Mucharrima, Maykel "Osorbo," El Funky, Keren Kmanwey, Raudel "Escuadrón Patriota," Padêro MC, Carolina Rebouças, Preto Zezé, Carlos "Nego" Gallo, Pedro Vilão, Andrézão GDS, Lesivo MC, Coro Emissi, Erivan "Produtos do Morro," Lenny, Brisa Flow, Débora Garcia, Luana Hansen, Preto Aplick CH, Rappin' Hood, Rincon Sapiência, Sharylaine, Tiely "Queen," Xis, Bocafloja, K-Libr, D-Fi Powèt Revòlte, Blay'Z, Kameleyon, 35 Zile, Ed, Bob Montinard, Fabris, Jota C, and Mil Maneras. Fieldwork would not have been possible without the welcoming reception I received from these artists, as well as the friendship and insights of Juan Carlos Averhoff Mena, Lia Leite, Lucas Rozzoline, Ephesien Bury, Fernanda Sofia, Rodrigo Brandão, Mélanie Montinard, Bertha Abreu, Valmir de Souza, and Alexandre Pereira.

This book took shape as a doctoral dissertation under the caring guidance of Rachel Price and Bruno Carvalho and the mentorship of Gabriela Nouzeilles. Comments from Gavin Steingo, Nick Nesbitt, Fred Moten, Richard Aldersley, and two anonymous readers of the manuscript were invaluable. I am especially grateful to Eric Brandt and Marlene Daut of UVA Press for their enthusiasm and belief in this project since I first proposed it. Thanks also to Minori Cohan for careful reading and comments on an earlier draft and to Lunine Pierre-Jerome for meticulously reviewing my transcriptions and translations of Kreyòl. My debts extend to mentors and colleagues from the University of Oregon, Princeton, and Colby:

Pedro García-Caro, Lanie Millar, Alejandro Martínez, Berta del Río, Pedro Meira Monteiro, Serge Gruzinski, Gustavo Rossi, Tiffany Creegan Miller, Karen Gillum, Betty Sasaki, Nicolás Ramos Flores, Dámaris Mayans, Brett White, Lola Bollo-Panadero, Ana Almeyda-Cohen, Sandra Bernal, and Dean Allbritton. None of this would have been possible without the unconditional love and support of my family Nancy, David, Dorae, and Ariana.

Fieldwork was supported by Fulbright, the University of Oregon Center for Latino/a and Latin American Studies, the Princeton Center for African American Studies, the Princeton Program in Latin American Studies, and the Princeton Department of Spanish and Portuguese. Costs of publishing and permissions were generously offset by the Office of the Provost at Colby College, for which I extend personal thanks to Provost and Dean of Faculty Margaret McFadden.

A small portion of chapter 4 is derived from an essay published as "*La Aldea:* Martí, McLuhan y marginalidad en el hip-hop habanero," in *Isla diseminada: ensayos sobre Cuba,* ed. Justo Planas et al. (Editorial Hypermedia, 2022), 45–68. © Hypermedia.

Chapter 5 is derived from an article published as "'Enraizados da Letra': Lyrics and the Letter in Brazilian, Cuban, and Haitian Rap," *Journal of Latin American Cultural Studies* 30, no. 4 (2021): 619–40. © Taylor and Francis. Available online at: https://doi.org/10.1080/13569325.2021.2017270.

Lyric permissions are included in the back matter.

Break and Flow

Introduction

WHEN I heard Los Aldeanos perform in early 2009 at the Barbaram music club of Nuevo Vedado, Havana, one of their refrains was "el rap es guerra" (rap is war).[1] Taking on an enemy generally called "el sistema" (the system), the rap duo had gained a large domestic following, received international attention, and raised suspicion from Cuban authorities.[2] After the show that night, audience members continued to recite "el rap es guerra," praising Los Aldeanos for winning a war for words, for saying things that otherwise couldn't be said. The verse mobilized a shared yearning to change the world.

The call was answered (albeit in less bellicose terms) across the bay in East Havana by rapper and graffiti writer Nono, who recorded the opening lines of the song "Rendición de cuenta" (Accountability) over a rumba beat in the converted bedroom studio of Malcoms "Justicia":

> Digo yo: hip hop no necesita mayores explicaciones
> Aspiraciones comunes que aún no tienen nombre
> . . . .
> Haremos un diccionario de esta actividad.[3]

> (I say: hip hop doesn't need greater explanations
> Common aspirations that don't yet have names
> . . . .
> We'll make a dictionary of this activity.)

Taking the floor to speak as if in public address, Nono names hip hop, calling out to it. Her verses invoke the still-undefined "common aspirations," the poetic and political possibilities, that unite hip hop artists across distance. Part of the practice of hip hop, in Nono's terms, involves the collaborative, community-forging work of defining that practice:

creating a hip hop dictionary ("haremos un diccionario de esta actividad"). This is poetic work because, like "el rap es guerra," "haremos un diccionario de esta actividad" is a rap lyric about the power of rap.

Break and Flow is concerned with how and why rap sounds in the Americas. It is a work of hip hop poetics because it attends to the lyrical qualities and poetic features of rap songs. And it is a work *about* hip hop poetics because it considers how rappers in Cuba, Brazil, and Haiti elaborate a shared poetic project that echoes across geographic and linguistic borders. While I have built the archive of songs and lyric transcriptions through ethnographic fieldwork and recording collaborations, I focus less on artists' intentions than on the demands and actions of their songs. My aim is not to uncover meaning but to identify the conventions and "techniques that make meaning possible," the effects that rap lyrics have on their listeners.[4] One of my central claims is that rap songs themselves, as acoustic objects, wield the force of community-building and world-making.

Hip hop is mythologized to have begun at a block party in the Bronx of New York City in August 1973, when residents uprooted by Robert Moses's recently completed Cross Bronx Expressway gathered to dance to the breakbeats of funk and soul tunes.[5] As a cultural practice, hip hop encompasses four basic elements: graffiti writing, breaking or breakdancing (by B-boys and B-girls), turntabling and beat-making (by disc jockeys or DJs), and rapping (by masters of ceremony or MCs), to which a fifth element, knowledge, is sometimes appended. Hip hop emerged in major cities across the Americas amidst the global rise of neoliberalism in the early 1980s, typically first as breakdance and then as rap.[6] Three decades later, the genre of Latin urban or *urbano* music (which incorporates rap, trap, reggaeton, Brazilian *funk,* and other popular Latinx and Latin American musical traditions) became one of the most consumed genres worldwide.[7] Though my focus is on rap lyrics, I have retained "hip hop" in the book's subtitle and throughout because of the frequency with which rappers use the term. Rap and hip hop are neither identical nor distinct. Instead, they are involved in a part-whole relation or metonymy: rap, a verbal art form, is the musico-poetic expression of hip hop culture.

With the objective of tracing hip hop poetics in the Americas through rap, *Break and Flow* is set from the mid-1980s to the late 2010s, during which time the cities of Havana, São Paulo, and Port-au-Prince functioned as important nodes for rap in their respective languages.[8] By focusing on Cuba, Brazil, and Haiti, I do not pretend to be exhaustive or representative of hip hop in the Americas. Instead, I follow Alexandra Vazquez's call for approaching (Cuban) music by "listening in detail," that is, treating granular "flashes, moments, [and] sounds" as sites for excavating creative genealogies and histories of colonial and racial oppression.[9] Listening in detail to rap songs in Cuban Spanish, Brazilian Portuguese, and Haitian Creole (*Kreyòl*) reveals hip hop poetics to be a multilingual practice rooted in neighborhood empowerment and worldly yearnings.

Hip hop's emergence in Brazil, Haiti, and Cuba corresponds to cultural and political openings: the end of the Brazilian military dictatorship in 1985; the popular overthrow of the Duvalier dictatorship in Haiti in 1986; and the beginning of Cuba's "Special Period" in 1990. My journey between these spaces began with my 2009 introduction to Los Aldeanos, which years later inspired multiple return trips to Havana to carry out interviews, record violin tracks, and participate in concerts and workshops.[10] During these visits, younger Havana-based artists lamented the fact that, apart from Los Aldeanos, Cuban rap was better known abroad than on the island.[11] Older generations of Cuban hip hoppers waxed nostalgic about 1980s dance gatherings to US funk and soul music known as *moña*, a word that refers to the Afro hair style. They taught me that hip hop had provided a space to comment on everyday scarcity, confront racism, and critique closely regulated and highly bureaucratic culture institutions. It is no coincidence that Cuban rappers were among the catalysts for a wave of protests in July 2021.[12]

Brazilian hip hop garnered comparatively less international attention but established a significant role in the domestic cultural sphere. I resided in Fortaleza, Brazil, through most of 2015 and learned from hip hop artists there that, just as in Cuba, Brazilian rappers took inspiration from neighborhood dances known as *bailes black* (Black dances), where US and Brazilian soul and funk music was played. Having emerged out of the bailes, Brazilian rap captured national attention with the 1997 release of the album *Sobrevivendo no inferno* (Surviving in hell) by São Paulo group Racionais MC's. References to the album were still frequent two decades later, when I carried out interviews, attended high- and low-profile concerts, and participated in recording collaborations with artists in São Paulo. For at least thirty years, hip hop remained a forceful voice of empowerment for residents of disadvantaged neighborhoods, the majority of whom are Afro-descendent, and an inspiration for the vibrant *literatura periférica* (peripheral literature) movement, which encompasses a wide range of writing practices associated with urban precarity.[13]

Rap would also play a significant role in Haiti, a country with a long history of musical intervention in politics, from militarized *rara* street bands to Jean-Bertrand Aristide's use of musical refrains in his presidential campaign.[14] The experience of teaching an intensive summer course in the outskirts of Port-au-Prince while conducting research there in 2017 revealed to me that while Haiti's revolutionary triumphs have been systematically ignored by Western notions of progress, Haitians take great pride in their national history.[15] With limited access to the global music industry, Haitian rappers have attained little international recognition, excepting Brooklyn-based Wyclef Jean (who raps primarily in English). But rap groups such as the infamous Barikad Crew, whose 2007 album was entitled *Goumen pou sa w kwè* (Fight for what you believe in), have served as acute historians of the emancipatory potential of their country's past and the way it reflects on the present and future.

Hip hop resonances between Brazil, Cuba, and Haiti derive in part from historical parallels. Cuba and Haiti both faced US military occupation during the early twentieth century, which promoted anxieties over foreign cultural influence. Haiti and Brazil hosted dictatorships during the second half of the twentieth century that put Afro-diasporic symbols to the service of repressive nationalism.[16] In Brazil and Cuba, notions of racial democracy or a post-racial society led to the criminalization of public debate concerning racism.[17] Musically, Afro-Cuban influences in the popular genres of *danzón* and *contradanza* have direct ties to late-eighteenth-century Haitian immigration,[18] while Cuban *son* strongly influenced Haitian music in the 1930s.[19] Furthermore, Brazilian samba and bossa nova follow clave patterns closely related to Afro-Cuban rhythms.[20] These connections suggest that the history of a "national music" is rarely, if ever, contained within a national history.

Historians of the Atlantic world demonstrate the urgency to tell global history through local actors rather than nation-states.[21] Julius Scott, for example, traces the way enslaved people throughout the Caribbean transmitted clandestine information about the Black revolution on the French colony of Saint-Domingue and the founding of Haiti through, in the words of one Jamaican proprietor, "some unknown mode of conveying intelligence amongst Negroes."[22] Rebecca Scott and Jean Hébrard use one family's itinerary to uncover a transnational history of the nineteenth-century circum-Atlantic. They describe their project as "an experiment that might be characterized as micro-history set in motion," which "may reveal dynamics that are not visible through the more familiar lens of region or nation."[23] *Break and Flow* takes the invitation of these scholars to listen to the way rap lyrics scale between the micro-historical and the world-historical as they reflect on and intervene in Atlantic cultural history. I focus on a constellation of micro-histories of hip hop while highlighting how rap songs echo each other's poetics across distance in a process Rio de Janeiro–based rapper MV Bill dubbed "traficando informação" (trafficking information).[24]

Given the limited circulation of artists between the three countries, Brazilian, Cuban, and Haitian rap have remained relatively nonintersecting phenomena.[25] As the portable MP3 format developed and, later, through online streaming platforms such as SoundCloud, Spotify, and YouTube, rap songs attained greater mobility than the artists who created them. Nevertheless, most of the lyrics featured here are not known to artists and listeners of the other two countries. This makes the comparison all the more salient: rap songs from Brazil, Cuba, and Haiti point to a common, sophisticated understanding of what hip hop can and should do. If the content of the lyrics tells a comparative history, their form and function suggest a shared poetics.

When hip hop artists in the Americas translate rap to local contexts, they typically preserve a set of assumptions about the practice. Key concepts such as *underground* and *freestyle*, and sometimes *break* and *flow*, are commonly retained in English.[26] These words' resistance to translation reflects the global reach of US Black culture and what has been called "Hip Hop Nation Language."[27] Furthermore, although hip hop does not constitute a consolidated social movement, the concept of a hip hop movement (*movimento, movimiento,* or *mouvman*) is ubiquitous across Brazil, Cuba, and Haiti. Haitian rapper Blay'Z puts it best when he idiosyncratically employs "movement" in the singular and without article: "hip hop se mouvman" (hip hop is movement).[28] Emphasizing process over product, the verse suggests that what counts is not searching for or participating in *the* hip hop movement, but rather *moving* hip hop. What is it, then, that moves hip hop and what moves with it?

The "ingredients" of rap are much the same as those once described by Cuban *nueva trova* singer-songwriter Silvio Rodríguez: poetry, music, and history.[29] Rap's relationship to history and music is described in the chapters that follow, but its connection to poetry merits additional emphasis. One of the recurrent tropes that cuts across rap songs in Brazil, Cuba, and Haiti is the convention of writing—not only the notion of songwriting, but the practice of producing a written text. Album titles such as Los Aldeanos's *Guerreros de la tinta* (Ink warriors), Port-au-Prince-based D-Fi's *Rev ak plim* (Dream with a pen), or Brasília-based

GOG's track "Escrevo demais" (I write too much), suggest that even though "rap's primary force is sonic," these artists see themselves as authors of poetic texts.[30]

A convenient though probably spurious etymology commonly disseminated by hip hop artists in Brazil treats "rap" as an acronym for "rhythm and poetry."[31] What is distinctive about rap, the acronym suggests, is its pairing of poetry with rhythmic accompaniment. Unlike written poetry, rap makes audible a dynamic tension or "dual rhythmic relationship" between the repeated, lightly syncopated beat of the break and the unpredictable rhythms of a rapper's lyrical flow.[32] Where rhythm in print poetry is inferred by a reader, rap's beat and cross-rhythms are audible and felt in the body.[33] However, meter (a regular rhythmic pattern imposed on the irregular cadence of speech) has characterized poetry for centuries, probably for as long as poetry has existed.[34] And poetry was sung before it was read on the page, a relationship maintained by some African languages that do not differentiate between poetry and song.[35]

For many hip hop artists, rap's status as poetry represents an urgently literary enterprise. As São Paulo–based rapper Sharylaine puts it, "Não quero ser apenas objeto de pesquisa / Idealizo um novo panorama de ignorado na literatura" (I don't want to be only an object of study / I idealize a new panorama of the ignored in literature).[36] A critique of ethnographic or sociological approaches to hip hop, this set of verses expresses a desire for rap to be considered not only as a social phenomenon rooted in popular culture but also as a poetic project of equal merit to "high" literature.[37] What, then, are the stakes of listening to hip hop poetics in the Americas as a new literary panorama? How does the figure of the "ignored in literature" recall centuries of exclusion of some communities, particularly communities of color, from literary institutions?

Ángel Rama famously argued that urbanization in Latin America created a symbolic order or "lettered city" in which literate elites served as gatekeepers of power, decision-making, and urban planning.[38] While colonial hierarchies surrounding orality and literacy have persisted, a "sonic turn" in literary and cultural studies demonstrates that the lettered city was more porous to sound than Rama's formulation implies. Ana María Ochoa Gautier focuses on a variety of texts from nineteenth-century Colombia to demonstrate how "the uses of the *ear* in relation to the *voice* imbued the *technology of writing* with the traces and excesses of the acoustic."[39] Tom McEnaney examines hemispheric influences between writing and radio technology during Franklin Roosevelt's Good Neighbor policy in a phenomenon he calls "narrative acoustics."[40] Njelle W. Hamilton analyzes the presence of popular music recordings in turn-of-the-millennium Caribbean literature as vehicles for "phonographic memories."[41] Marília Librandi takes Brazilian writer Clarice Lispector's phrase to trace the trope in Brazilian literature of "writing by ear."[42] *Break and Flow* builds on this work by treating rap as an innovative, community-forging writing practice that bridges sound, listening, and various forms of inscription.

Rap in Translation

The emphasis on community writing in hip hop poetics recalls a broader history of cultural practices rooted in the African diaspora. Africans and people of African descent were consistently denied access to letters and devised ways to reappropriate the literary traditions from which they had been excluded.[43] For David Treece, "rap therefore returns us to the idea of a black musical aesthetic in which bodily and linguistic expression, drum and word, rhythm and speech, are not to be counterposed but integrated in a single artistic complex."[44] Rap inhabits what Brent Hayes Edwards calls the "infinitely fertile interface between music and literature" that characterizes Afro-diasporic culture.[45] Thus while hip hop emerged in the specific context of urban deindustrialization in predominantly African American neighborhoods during the 1970s, the techniques employed by rappers in the Americas form part of a longer historical arc.[46] Rap music, borrowing from Cuban musicologist Leonardo Acosta, can only be understood from the perspective of its antecedents.[47]

Hip hop is traditionally received as a "Black [American] thing,"[48] but its emergence must be approached also from an Afro-Atlantic framework. Puerto Ricans living in New York City played an integral role in early breakdancing, and rap music owes as much debt to Jamaican disc jockeys (DJs) as to the US funk and soul tunes they played.[49] Beginning in the 1940s, DJs in Kingston, Jamaica, created sound systems out of rented speakers stacked high in the street to amplify the bass of African American records, using a microphone input to layer rhymed jingles in a precursor to rap.[50] Out of sound system culture came reggae, accompanying the antiracist, negritude-inspired Rastafarian theology that emerged concurrently with the music. By the 1970s, thanks in large part to the international profile of Bob Marley, reggae began in turn to inspire African Americans in New York City's outer boroughs. Hip hop and rap were the fruits of this "extraordinary proletarian cross-fertilization" and the transnational resonances produced across what Paul Gilroy called the Black Atlantic.[51]

Though criticized for de-emphasizing Afro-diasporic communities elsewhere in the world, Gilroy's framework of the Black Atlantic brings together countries such as Cuba, Brazil, and Haiti around common links to the transatlantic slave trade.[52] The French colony of Saint-Domingue (on the island of Hispaniola that would become Haiti and the Dominican Republic) once housed the richest plantation economy in the world, supported by three-quarters of a million enslaved people forcibly brought from Africa between 1676 and 1800. In 1804, Haiti became the hemisphere's first independent republic to guarantee freedom to all citizens. Cuba and Brazil, characteristic slave societies, were the last two countries in the western hemisphere to abolish slavery, in 1886 and 1888 respectively. Most enslaved people arrived after Haitian independence (in total, more than two million people to Brazil and 800,000 to Cuba).

The African diaspora, a product of the violent displacement of people from their homelands to provide human capital for European colonialism, has been described as a counterculture to modernity or even a force that produced modernity.[53] However, as Stuart Hall points out, diaspora "does not constitute a common *origin,* since it was, metaphorically as well as literally, a translation."[54] Given the diversity of languages and nations of enslaved people and their descendants as well as the distinct colonial languages of their oppressors, Edwards cautions that diaspora "forces us to articulate discourses of cultural and political linkage only through and across difference in full view of the risks of that endeavor."[55] To account for the mistranslations and misrecognitions characteristic of diasporic exchange, he suggests that "diaspora can be conceived only as the uneasy and unfinished *practice* of such dialogue."[56] In turn, Robert Stam and Ella Shohat have dubbed diasporic identity formation in the hemisphere a process of "race in translation."[57]

Martinican poet and politician Aimé Césaire famously declared that it was in Haiti "where negritude rose for the first time and stated that it believed in its humanity."[58] Following a successful revolution led by enslaved African and Afro-descendent people, the 1805 Haitian Constitution declared that "all Africans and Indians, and those of their blood, born in the colonies or in foreign countries, who come to reside in the Republic [of Haiti] will be recognized as Haitians."[59] By linking nonwhite skin color to citizenship, a newly independent Haiti institutionalized Black internationalism a half-century before Abraham Lincoln's Emancipation Proclamation and a century before the first Pan-African Congresses. Given Haiti's overwhelmingly Afro-descendent population, several political leaders continued to define citizenship around a positive identification with Blackness (the persistence of colorism notwithstanding). Even the violent and repressive Duvalier dictatorship (1957–1986) advocated a nationalist politics of racial identity surrounding the "Black class," called *noirisme*.[60]

In Brazil and Cuba, in contrast, ethnologists and politicians encouraged national narratives of racial mixture (*mestiçagem* or *mestizaje*).[61] In Brazil, notions of miscegenation consolidated into a myth of "racial democracy," while in Cuba they manifested as *transculturación* (transculturation) and colorblindness.[62] One of the things that moves with hip hop is a disavowal of these discourses of harmonious racial mixture and the political agendas of whitening (*branqueamento* or *blanqueamiento*) they typically disguise.[63] Rappers decry abiding racisms and deconstruct racial myths, connecting the resistance of enslaved people of previous centuries to contemporary struggles against racialized violence by predominantly darker-skinned residents of urban slums, which were expanding at unprecedented rates at the turn of the millennium.[64]

Rap's rise in popularity in São Paulo in the late 1990s coincided with a sharp spike in urban violence concentrated in the favelas, where Afro-Brazilians are more than twice as likely to reside than whites.[65] In Cuba, the post-1959 revolutionary government made unprecedented gains in racial equality in its early years and significantly reduced slums. But when the first rap songs were recorded in the early 1990s, "traditional residential patterns that combined race with poverty and marginality" were reemerging as a result of the bourgeoning tourist industry that followed the collapse of the Soviet Union.[66] In Haiti, when *rap kreyòl* (Kreyòl rap) reached national attention in the early 2000s, more than 90 percent of the urban population lived in slums.[67] According to Halifu Osumare, part of the "Africanist aesthetic" in global hip hop involves the creation of "connective marginalities" that articulate these common experiences.[68] Hip hop provides rappers from Cuba, Brazil, and Haiti a "diasporic resource" to engage with local and transnational forms marginal belonging.[69]

It must be acknowledged that the relative proximity of Latin American rappers to the center of global capitalism is fundamentally distinct from that of their US counterparts. Nor is rapping in São Paulo, among the richest cities in the hemisphere, equivalent to rapping in Port-au-Prince, among the poorest. However, artists in São Paulo, Port-au-Prince, and Havana consistently rhyme that they are involved in a common struggle against imperialism and various forms of oppression. Songs such as Cuban rapper El B's "América," Brazilian rapper GOG's "Sonhos latinos" (Latin dreams), and Haitian rapper Blaze One's "Dekolonizasyon" (Decolonization) speak to a hemispheric impulse.

At the same time, hip hop artists from these countries almost unavoidably—even strategically—conceive of their work in dialogue with that of rappers from the United States. Because of the United States' privileged position in the West, US Black culture tends to occupy an asymmetric, even hegemonic position in diasporic exchange.[70] British cultural theorists in particular have argued that the global circulation of African American culture has, at times, operated as a form of cultural imperialism, a "decidedly unidirectional transnational flow of iconography and ideas, ideologies and inspirations."[71] Reflecting on his experience teaching at the University of Chicago, Haitian anthropologist Michel-Rolph Trouillot warned "that the African connection was more complex and tortuous than [his students from the United States] had ever imagined, that the U.S. monopoly on both Blackness and racism was itself a racist plot."[72] In this sense, Marina Terkourafi and Tricia Rose have independently suggested that US imperialism represents a key for understanding the global circulation of hip hop.[73] Does the presence of hip hop outside the United States feed back into the US monopoly on Blackness? How do global hip hop artists disrupt the "African American exceptionalism,"[74] or "American imperial privilege,"[75] that contributed to hip hop's global popularity in the first place?

Taking a hemispheric approach to race in the Americas, Petra Rivera-Rideau, Jennifer Jones, and Tianna Paschel demonstrate that the movement of ideas about Blackness can both reinforce racial hierarchies and contribute to the possibility of social transformation in local communities.[76] Juliet Hooker examines critically the role of comparison in transnational approaches to race. Even when mobilized in anti-imperialist projects, she argues, comparison commonly becomes "an exercise in ranking" that can produce insidious misreadings about the way other nations construct race.[77] For example, after traveling to Cuba, Harlem poet Langston Hughes asserted that Cuban "Negro musicians," unlike their US counterparts, "somehow have saved—out of all the centuries of slavery and all the miles and miles from Guinea—the heartbeat and songbeat of Africa."[78] Such exercises of ranking, Hooker contends, fail to account for differences in scale (for example, between a relatively small island nation and a rising global superpower) and the way power asymmetries condition comparison. As an alternative, Hooker proposes a methodology of juxtaposition or counterpoint, where two objects are placed together not to establish a relation between the two but rather to reveal something in their side-by-side presentation that would not otherwise be apparent.[79] In this spirit, my comparative analysis endeavors to hear contrapuntal juxtapositions, rather than rankings, between expressions of rap from three countries of widely varying scales.

Hip hop's differing scales are further complicated by academicization, which carries its own set of hierarchies. In the United States and abroad, university departments have begun to embrace rap music, particularly when it appeals to social justice agendas or avant-garde sensibilities. In May 2018, for example, the Universidade Estadual de Campinas (UNICAMP), one of Brazil's most prestigious universities, included the lyrics to the rap album *Sobrevivendo no inferno* by Racionais MC's on students' required reading list.[80] Researchers and professors openly collaborate with hip hop artists, sometimes co-teaching.[81] Hip hop artists, in turn, have written anthropological and sociological dissertations.[82] The entry of hip hop into the academy raises the question of how to write about a practice that no longer generates moral panic nor necessarily constitutes a marginal or marginalized activity.[83] In writing about hip hop or bringing it into the classroom, are we doing something for it, or merely doing something to it?[84] As H. Samy Alim puts it, "How have we as scholars reproduced the hierarchies that we are trying to dismantle? How has our methodology silenced and disempowered the very folks we claim to be giving voice to and empowering?"[85]

I write about hip hop in the Americas with acute sensitivity to and anxiety over blind spots and biases derived from my privileged position as a white male–identifying researcher from the United States. Once when discussing race with a rapper in Port-au-Prince, he explained to me wryly that hip hop cannot only be about Blackness, because rap is widely popular in Japan and there are no Black people there. This perhaps begins to explain why I encountered no resistance when engaging in musical collaborations and conversations with predominantly nonwhite artists. When artists did invoke aspects of my identity, they focused not on my whiteness but on my Americanness (which represented an implicit link to US hip hop). Differences in class and access to hard currency were more salient than differences in race. But what seemed most important to artists was my identity as a musician, my interest in collaboration, and my belief in the transformative power of rap.

Furthermore, the writing of *Break and Flow* took shape in a privileged historical context where, given a large body of prior work on hip hop by scholars and practitioners, I was able to circumvent older debates about whether hip hop constitutes a legitimate object of academic study.[86] My aim was to take a fundamentally descriptive approach and to acknowledge whenever possible that "the music is theorising itself quite well."[87] How should we hear, for example, Nono's ambivalent self-presentation: "Nono no es mi nombre de guerra" (Nono is not my nom de guerre)?[88] Why does she equivocate on her name, negating what has already been twice negated? How might Nono's negation of name point to a broader refusal to take a position, a radical appositionality that draws on the "magical power" of "tarrying with the negative"?[89]

A set of verses by Dukes, a rapper from São Bernardo do Campo, São Paulo, begins to respond: "Não ofereço a saída, mas tudo bem / as perguntas que faço não têm respostas mas me levam além" (I don't offer a way out, but it's all good / the questions I ask don't have answers but they take me beyond).[90] The rhyme of *além* with *bem,* displaced two beats from its anticipated arrival, signals a "beyond" (*além*) or "way out" (*saída*), that seeks not to provide answers but "to render unanswerable."[91] Speaking to the construction of meaning in rap, Dukes echoes a principle of Afro-Brazilian Macumba religions: "manter-se fiel à dúvida" (to remain faithful to doubt).[92] It is faith in rap's capacity to restore doubt, to ask unanswerable questions, that carries rapper and listener além.

Responding to the abiding legacies of slavery and imperialism, rappers in the Americas demonstrate a "conscious and collective refusal" to reproduce externally imposed aesthetic and political structures.[93] Stefano Harney and Fred Moten ground such work in the refusal of enslaved people and their descendants to accept the individuating liberal order that was imposed on and simultaneously withheld from them. As a practice of institutional critique, the refusal motivates what they call Black study: "Can this being together in homelessness, this interplay of the refusal of what has been refused, this undercommon appositionality, be a place from which emerges neither self-consciousness nor knowledge of the other but an improvisation that proceeds from somewhere on the other side of an unasked question?"[94] The work of Black study is audible in the consistent refusal by rap lyrics to choose between alternatives. As Daniel Levin Becker puts it, "rap takes the easy inherited categories, starting with *good* and *bad,* and atomizes them into something as complex and contradictory and shapeshifting as the world itself."[95] *Break and Flow* examines the way rappers engage in an ongoing "process of self-analysis and reflection" that Brazilian Black radical Abdias do Nascimento saw as essential for the construction of new inaugural myths or "mythopoetry" outside national and imperial frameworks.[96] Hearing rap songs as improvisatory, mythopoetic exercises in Black study maintains the centrality of Blackness while allowing for the varied genealogies and multiple origins invoked by rappers in the Americas. Nono's dictionary of hip hop poetics becomes a search for undercommon, appositional solidarity "irrespective of race, class, gender, religion, nation."[97] The building blocks of this practice are break and flow.

Break and Flow

Rap songs are constructed out of two dualistic elements: the break (a repeated rhythmic pattern that constitutes the hip hop beat) and the flow (a rapper's lyrical delivery).[98] "Breaking" is a dance term with origins in West Africa.[99] The hip hop breakbeat was codified when Bronx-based, Jamaican-born DJ Kool Herc, observing that dancers responded most emphatically to drum solos, isolated and looped these instrumental breaks using two turntables.[100] The syncopated drum solo, pushing or pulling against the beat in a break from the song's main section, became the "unifying force" of hip hop.[101] The break's repeated syncopations link rap genealogically, through funk and soul, to the polyrhythmic construction of African and Afro-Caribbean musical traditions, whose rhythmic pulses are often felt as asymmetric patterns known as claves (literally, keys).[102] The break is rap music's rhythmic key.

Flow refers to the "rhythmic fluidity" of a rapper's delivery.[103] Kyra D. Gaunt relates flow to African American notions of play, particularly as practiced by Black women and girls. Drawing a parallel with the verbal game that accompanies double Dutch jump rope, she observes that verbal play "is considered an act that is performed for its own sake, for pleasure or reward known as *flow*."[104] In rap, the pleasure of flow depends on the timbre of the voice, the creation of satisfying rhymes, and the elaborate cross-rhythms that emerge in the interaction between voice and beat. Syncopated against the break but always partially subservient to it, "flow is an MC's lyrical fingerprint."[105] It describes a rapper's "ability to exploit the rhythm, rhyme around the rhythm, and yet be able to faithfully return to the rhythm on time."[106] If the break is a syncopated yet stable and repeated rhythm, flow creates the unpredictable, improvisatory feel that gives rap music its polyrhythmic texture.

Despite their dualistic relation, break and flow are constructed using related techniques. Breaks typically derive from fragments of preexisting music that are cut, spliced, and looped in innovative ways in a technique known as sampling. Similarly, the lyrics comprising rap flows commonly emerge in an analogous sampling practice, as artists incorporate sounds and quotations from eclectic sources: poetry, music, politics, television, cinema, everyday speech.[107] A twelve-line set of verses by São Paulo–based rapper Criolo in the song "Duas de cinco," for example, contains no fewer than five samples: Brazilian singers Tom Jobim and Cazuza, Brazilian poets Carlos Drummond de Andrade and Manuel Bandeira, and French film director Patrice Chéreau.[108] What sort of history is woven into this intertextual web of references, which spans multiple media, decades, and continents? Here, the pleasure of flow derives from returning to and revising preexisting material. This infinite regress gives rap its sense of movement, always in medias res. There is no point of origin or originality, no clear borders demarcating where this practice begins and where it ends. "If you're reading this," writes Becker in the preface to his book *What's Good: Notes on Rap and Language,* "it's already too late. Rap has moved on."[109] However, given the recursive construction of sampling and intertextuality, rap is also always moving backward. My notion of break and flow is meant to capture the feedback loop between repetition and innovation constitutive of rap.

I also propose break and flow as a metaphor to describe the repetitions and innovations audible at the level of rap's transnational circulation. As rap roots in new places, some version of the break inevitably returns (commonly syncretized with local rhythms). Flows, on the other hand, shift with the specificity of language, place, and an artist's poetic decisions. If the break is the axis of repetition that connects hip hop with history and genealogy, flow is the axis of improvisation and substitution, of "history telling itself in real time."[110] Break and flow account, respectively, for the diachronic and synchronic axes of hip hop's circulation, a process that includes breaks with traditions and flows through, around, and in between them. The framework I am proposing resonates with Hall's description of Black Atlantic culture as a process driven by two vectors, "the vector of similarity and continuity; and the vector of difference and rupture."[111] In rap music the vector of continuity turns out to be rupture itself: the break. What was once a rupture in the song's structure becomes the repeated rhythmic pattern that gives new iterations of rap continuity across time and space.

To account for the way hemispheric resonances emerge within the local granularities of rap in three distinct national spaces, the structure of *Break and Flow* is recursive rather than chronological. Many of the same characters, scenes, and songs return multiple times over the course of the six chapters, evocative of the iterative development of break and flow and the nonlinear accumulation of culture, race, and memory. I begin by listening in detail to self-reflexive rap lyrics to consider how poetic innovation produces social effects (chapters 1 and 2). Surpassing the boundaries of the contexts in which they emerge, the social aspirations and poetic conventions of rap songs link neighborhood histories of hip hop to Afro-diasporic modes of belonging (chapters 3 and 4). By using hip hop to create local-global connections and remake history and place, rappers forge new genealogies, elaborate a community writing practice, and produce decolonial forms of knowledge (chapters 5 and 6). Immediately following the epilogue is a section entitled "About the Artists," which contains names and brief descriptions of the rappers whose voices are featured in *Break and Flow*.

Each chapter takes its title from a rap verse and corresponding poetic convention or technique. Chapter 1, "Yearning: 'Nan lòt dimansyon,'" explores the capacity of rap lyrics to produce material effects in what Port-au-Prince-based rapper Princess Eud calls "another dimension." Focusing on lyrics that point to and seek to intervene in specific contexts outside hip hop, I demonstrate how rap's poetic work draws on Black feminist theories of yearning. The yearnings expressed in outward-pointing lyrics, I argue, engage with past, present, and future in relation to the experience of economic and political history. In one direction, rap yearnings mirror or parody the speculative ethos of the neoliberal moment of hip hop's globalization. In another, they engage with the subjunctive to revisit occulted histories and point to alternate modes of inhabiting the world. Despite the hypermasculinity associated with hip hop, rap yearnings reveal that a feminist practice undergirds hip hop poetics.

Outward-directed yearnings are commonly accompanied by inward-pointing lyrics that define or describe the practice. "Hip hop cubano, es lo que hay" (Cuban hip hop, it's what there is), a Cuban rap slogan playfully asserts. Chapter 2, "Raplove: 'Es lo que hay,'" turns to the widespread practice of rapping about rap, an act I call raplove. I trace possible genealogies for this recursive invocation of form in content, from Afro-diasporic techniques of improvisation to Afro-Caribbean musical structures to European ars poetica to Indigenous epistemologies of listening. In its most developed form, raplove manifests as a love song to hip hop, a prayer-like apostrophe to the practice, with Afro-Caribbean and Judeo-Christian overtones. Inward-directed, quasi-religious expressions of raplove reinforce rap's community-forging potential and compliment outward-directed yearnings to intervene in the social sphere and remake the world.

Part of the poetic work of yearning and raplove is to rewrite histories of nation and neighborhood. In chapter 3, "Uprooting: 'Qué importa si sonamos americano hermano,'" I explore the politics of importing a cultural practice from the United States and "sounding American" (following the verse from Havana-based rapper Bárbaro "El Urbano"). During the first half of the twentieth century and again under mid- to late-century authoritarian-leaning governments, Haiti, Cuba, and Brazil all experienced campaigns that consolidated national identity around Afro-diasporic musics amidst anxieties over US cultural imperialism. Cubans and Brazilians used dances to US soul and funk music (out of which rap emerged) as a space for consciousness-raising and racial empowerment. In Haiti, the first rap songs were released during *dechoukaj,* the political uprooting that followed the overthrow of the Duvalier dictatorship. Rappers in all three national spaces documented hip hop's new routes as a history of uprooting by the uprooted, complicating origin stories and narratives of importation and nationalization.

This shared sense of uprooting is counterbalanced by affirmations of neighborhood belonging. São Paulo–based rapper Sabotage affirms in a verse that "rap é meu lugar" (rap is my place). Chapter 4, "Scale: 'Rap é meu lugar,'" traces the role of placemaking in hip hop poetics by considering three local signifiers of neighborhood: the Haitian *baz* (base), the Brazilian *periferia* (periphery), and the Cuban *aldea* (rural village). Drawing on the urban histories of Port-au-Prince, São Paulo, and Havana, I demonstrate how rappers use territorial markers to scale from the hyperlocal to the translocal, as in the verse "periferia é periferia em qualquer lugar" (periphery is periphery in any place).[112] Despite their connection to urban space (evidenced by artistic names such as El Urbano, "The Urban One"), rappers in Cuba, Brazil, and Haiti also scale the neighborhood to invoke historically grounded notions of the rural. Their multi-scalar approach between neighborhood and world exposes a cosmopolitan yearning typical of postcolonial writers since at least the turn of the twentieth century.

Rappers' placemaking and use of scale relies, in turn, on the capacity of lyrics to build community. Chapter 5, "Writing: 'Enraizados da letra,'" explores the way rappers "root" themselves in lyrics and the letter, as Brasília-based rapper GOG's verse asserts. I propose that one of the dominant tropes connecting rap lyrics from Brazil, Cuba, and Haiti is the reception of rap as community writing. This practice expands traditional notions of literacy through an emphasis on listening, community-building, and multiple sites of inscription—textual, aural, physical, spiritual. Rappers sample traditions as diverse as *repente* improvisation, *pixação* graffiti, samba, jazz, and lyric poetry. I argue that performing rap as community writing is not only a product of shared oral and aural traditions but also a response to the colonial history of letters in Latin America.

Given this history, rap writing entails a corollary: the entanglement of writing with violence. Port-au-Prince-based rapper D-Fi rhymes that his verses take shape "sou fèy blanch" (on a blank page). Chapter 6, "Violence: 'Sou fèy blanch,'" demonstrates how rappers sample traditions of poetic protest and rewrite hip hop by deploying rap as a critique of violence. I highlight artists' promotion of consciousness-raising as they reflect on legitimate and illegitimate uses of violence. Self-reflexive lyrics foreground a metonymical proximity and, at times, complicity of the rapper vis-à-vis the structures of violence being addressed. Rooted in the histories of militancy and militarization of each country and the revolutionary struggles of Afro-descendent peoples, rap songs expose colonial legacies as contemporary forms of racial, class, gender, and urban violence, including stereotypes commonly associated with hip hop. The critique of violence also reveals the unfinished work of hip hop poetics, particularly with respect to gender and genre.

Some urgently activist, some strategically capitalist, all highly self-reflexive, the verses contained in *Break and Flow* range from commercially successful to mostly unknown, from songs whose YouTube videos boast view counts in the billions to MP3s that remain unreleased. These artists possess widely varying access to global markets and economic capital. Some are amateurs in the etymological sense of the word (from the Latin *amare*, meaning to love) and earn their income primarily from other work. Some create their own informal markets through the distribution of songs and albums. Others rely on frequent touring, though few enjoy the type of financial success of high-grossing commercial rappers in the United States. In Cuba, the situation is further confounded by the fact that, during the 1990s and into the 2010s, amateur musicians could generally earn more money from foreign tips and informal remittances than could professional musicians pertaining to official government cultural agencies. These distinct economies and their social relations influence rap songs, as they do all art.[113] Yet similar poetic features (albeit with crucial differences) are audible at distinct levels of market insertion. Resonances between songs suggest that the relative proximity to or distance from national and international markets—either by choice, contingency, or necessity—is a difference of degree rather than kind.

Since textual transcriptions are inadequate for capturing the sonic (and increasingly visual) materiality of rap, I have curated a YouTube playlist that includes all referenced songs available for streaming (http://tinyurl.com/breakandflow), and you are encouraged to listen along.[114] These cultural artefacts share in a practice of articulating new foundational myths—like the Haitian Revolution or dechoukaj, Cuban moña, Brazilian bailes black, a Bronx block party in 1973.

1 Yearning
"Nan lòt dimansyon"

PRIOR TO its collapse in 1991, the Soviet Union accounted for 80 percent or more of Cuba's imports, exports, and foreign investments. Between 1989 and 1993, Cuba's economy contracted by more than one-third, and citizens faced extreme scarcity of food and other commodities. To cope with what Fidel Castro called the Special Period, the government rewrote the constitution, eliminated the state monopoly on foreign trade, legalized foreign currency, and promoted new openings to tourism.[1] As inequality rose, disproportionately affecting darker-skinned Cubans with more limited access to tourist dollars, Havana-based rappers recorded the first Cuban rap songs in home studios. Early Havana rappers united around the slogan "hip hop revolución" (hip hop revolution).[2] Though they critiqued the government's handling of the crisis, most artists did not initially reject the idea of the Cuban Revolution outright. By calling for "hip hop revolución," they returned to the source, proclaiming themselves the vanguard of a new revolution that must replace the old.[3]

Another Cuban rap slogan emerged somewhat later, transplanted from concurrent Special Period cultural practices and everyday life: "hip hop cubano, es lo que hay" (Cuban hip hop, it's what there is; it's where it's at).[4] The second slogan playfully disavows the optimism of the first, casting rap as subsistence music. Confronting scarcity with irony, it hails hip hop as a "cultural resource,"[5] the only resource rappers possess. Where "hip hop revolución" asserts the possibility of transformation, the ironic, tautological "es lo que hay" affirms that hip hop is all there is. Where the first slogan points outward into the future, the second points inward, closing in on the present and the creative process of making rap. How are these opposing modes of signaling time and context related? In what way is the impulse to transform the world bound up with the recursive return to rap as an end in itself? What are the social implications of using rap to point at what is and at what could be?

I propose that these two directional vectors—the outward-facing or transformative and the inward-facing or recursive—constitute opposing poles of rap deixis. Deictic words are words whose meaning is conditional on the time, place, or context of the speaker: demonstrative adjectives such as *here* and *this,* personal pronouns such as *they* and *you,* adverbial markers of time such as *now* and *then.* Most linguistic constructions of tense are deictic, designed to communicate the "pastness, presentness or futurity of an event with respect to some transient 'now.'"[6] By pointing to specific unfoldings of pastness, presentness, and futurity, I argue, rap deixis expresses the social force of hip hop poetics.

The inward- and outward-pointing deixis of rap lyrics from Cuba, Brazil, and Haiti carries out poetic work that resonates with Édouard Glissant's reading of Caribbean culture. Glissant identifies in Caribbean poetics the persistence of two overlapping engagements with time: a "yearning for history" (*désiré historique*) characteristic of peoples whose world-historical significance has been consistently denied, and a repetition or return of ideas that conceals a form of resistance in opacity.[7] These same temporalizations are constitutive of rap. The "yearning for history" resounds in the impulse for rap to be "mucho más que música" (much more than music), to forge new communities and imagine alternative worlds.[8] Such yearning draws on the centrifugal force of hip hop poetics, the possibilities that extend outside the rap song.

Conversely, the playful recursion of "lo que hay" retreats into what Roman Jakobson called language's "poetic function," a "focus on the message for its own sake."[9] Rapping about rap (an act I call raplove) affirms admiration, faith, even veneration of hip hop. If yearning expresses a desire based on absence and lack, raplove expresses a desire based on presence and redundancy. How, then, is rap's pointing capacity or deixis related to the work of hip hop poetics? What "structures of longing" are imbedded in rap music?[10] Is the music "attempting to prompt us to do something . . . or is it modeling that doing, striving to address that imperative—sounding that task in more than one sense—in its achieved form"?[11] This chapter considers the poetic and political implications of the yearnings expressed in rap lyrics from Cuba, Haiti, and Brazil.

O direito de sonhar: Rap Utopias and Yearning

When Brazilians went to the polls in 1985 for their first democratic elections in two decades, residents of São Paulo's outer neighborhoods, predominantly Afro-Brazilian, were congregating regularly in the city center to breakdance.[12] Rappers added their rhymes to the mix during a moment of "anseio musical" (musical yearning) that accompanied the return to democracy.[13] Hip hop had begun to circulate around the globe a few years earlier,[14] propagating what Cornel West calls rap music's "utopian aspirations . . . violently juxtaposed with lyrical hopelessness of the oppressed poor people of Afro-America."[15] In the Americas, as Paul Gilroy suggests, hip hop derives from a broader tradition of Afro-diasporic music united around the utopian impulse of a "politics of transfiguration."[16]

By the time Long Island–based Black Power rap group Public Enemy performed in São Paulo in 1991, its single "Fight the Power" had become an international rap anthem.[17] Yet even as Chuck D of Public Enemy famously called rap "Black America's CNN," hip hop was moving west and, with the rapid commodification of Los Angeles gangsta rap, ideologies were shifting.[18] West coast rappers found new ways to fight the power that challenged the "East Coast utopians."[19] If hip hop's migration west in the United States and toward the center of global popular music brought it farther away from Public Enemy's countercultural rallying cry, its concurrent and continued migration south and to the Global South brought it, at least for a time, closer. Protest rap became one of the dominant threads of hip hop poetics in the Americas, as it did elsewhere in the world.[20]

One form of protest in rap lyrics from Brazil, Cuba, and Haiti is the affirmation of what Brasília-based rapper GOG calls "o direito de sonhar" (the right to dream).[21] Recovering the right to dream, to imagine utopian alternatives, constitutes a primary form of resistance for marginalized communities whose material realities tend to foreclose this possibility. Yet the objects of the rap utopia range so widely and change so frequently—from a better world to a better ride, from the right to the city to the right to party, from nostalgic return to messianic redemption, from the recovery of history to the expediency of global popular culture—that utopia may no longer be the most useful category. Coined by Thomas More in the early sixteenth century and inspired by European colonialism in the New World, utopia referred to an ideal island nation.[22] While More's neologism invokes no place, or a nonexistent place, by the time of the Industrial Revolution, utopia had been displaced to the future, a "journey in time rather than space."[23] Utopians, explains Robert Cover in an essay about the reliance of legal order on narrative, are unable "to bear the dissonance of the lawfulness of the intolerable"; hence utopianism is, "like all nomic eschatology, extremely unstable."[24] Somewhat paradoxically, utopianism points toward arrival at a future that its own internal logic has indefinitely deferred.

Without denying the "utopian dreams" central to "diasporic aspiration,"[25] Tina Campt suggests that for Afro-diasporic peoples, the potentiality of such expressions lies not in the point of arrival but in the aspirational quality itself, "in their persistent striving for futurity."[26] Campt advocates for a Black feminist practice involving the "performance of a future that hasn't yet happened but must."[27] This future is not a question of hope, but rather a demand of tense, "the tense of possibility that grammarians refer to as the future real conditional or *that which will have had to happen.*"[28] Rejecting the Western teleology of progress, the Black feminist future real conditional approximates what C. L. R. James called "the future that is in the present" or Ashon Crawley names "otherwise" possibilities, "infinite alternatives to what *is.*"[29] Rap yearnings engage urgently with these "otherwise" possibilities or this "future *now.*"[30] Yet where Campt locates the temporality of what will have had to happen in the grammatical imperative, rap songs point also to the imperative for retaining subjunctivity: what could have happened or might (still) happen.[31] It is this strand of hip hop poetics that I take up here.

In a foundational book, Tricia Rose describes hip hop's emergence at the intersection of "social alienation, prophetic imagination, and yearning."[32] Yearning expresses absence or lack: we yearn for what we don't have, something lost or never possessed. At the beginning of Homer's *Odyssey,* only Odysseus "still yearned to go home."[33] But what if rather than seeking the reconstruction of a lost home (nostalgia), yearning could provide, as bell hooks suggests referring to Black feminist yearning, a "common psychological state" or a home in itself?[34] What if yearning could remake the world while also "refus[ing] participation in the upkeep of a fabricated world . . . to aspire to social arrest, to stop making the world"?[35] What if instead of a return home, yearning could capture the impulse that Minkah Makalani calls the "politically unimaginable" of Black Marxist thought, "a refusal of any utopia, of any pursuit of a specific vision of the future"?[36]

Isabelle Stengers and Philippe Pignarre find in Black feminist yearning a source of protection against what they call "capitalist sorcery."[37] Yearning does not signal a "fixed point to which one must stick," they argue, but represents a set of strategies for "disarticulating the putting of backs against the wall" (*mises au pied du mur*).[38] Where the concept of utopia points to a fixed yet unattainable vanishing point, yearning resides in the power of pointing or deixis. Inhabiting process rather than product, it eschews commodification. But if yearning can cultivate sensitivity against commodification—and much of rap yearning is indeed anticapitalist—yearning is also, and under neoliberalism primarily, fed by capitalist sensibilities. How are rap yearnings bound up with the industry, with rap earnings?

Not by coincidence, hip hop's globalization in the early 1980s coincided with the economic philosophy typically called neoliberalism. Politicians such as Augusto Pinochet, Margaret Thatcher, and Ronald Reagan encouraged an ideology "that human well-being can best be advanced by liberating individual entrepreneurial freedoms and skills within an institutional framework."[39] Part of the success of neoliberal rhetoric was its ability as a political project seeking to restore power to economic elites in the wake of the 1960s to masquerade as a utopian ideal for wealth redistribution through the advocacy of individual liberty and market freedom. The "theoretical utopianism of neoliberal argument," David Harvey argues, "primarily worked as a system of justification and legitimation for whatever needed to be done" to realize the goal of reconsolidating political power among economic elites.[40] Neoliberalism combined the liberalist utopia of individual freedom and the capitalist drive of producing surplus value.

One of the effects of neoliberal economic policy was the development of financial capitalism, which became so pervasive that Randy Martin describes a "financialization of daily life."[41] Financialization, Martin argues, rejects older philosophies of saving money and embraces a "new psychology" where "money is not to be left untouched, but constantly fondled, minded daily like a well-stocked refrigerator."[42] Anyone who has seen a commercial US rap video made since the early 1990s will have no doubt observed a great deal of money being fondled—although it is worth noting that hip hop artists tend to fondle fake bills: "real" fake money as opposed to the speculative "real" money of finance capital. The endless supply of paper bills in rap videos from the 1990s and 2000s (and I will return to parallel examples in Cuba and Brazil) gives the impression that "money seemingly comes from nowhere, from the depths of quotidian experience itself . . . sheer communion with money for nothing is the only cost of admission."[43] What rap videos repurpose from financialization is the "thrill of speculation."[44] To speculate, which bears the etymological trace of seeing or looking (*specere*), means to predict or hypothesize. Money "establishes itself as a sign able to signify its own future . . . a sign which creates itself out of the future."[45] Though distinct from Black feminist futurity in its mode of world-making, financialization shares the demand for a "future *now*."

My aim is to trace some of the yearnings in Haitian, Cuban, and Brazilian rap, as products of economic and political history.[46] What

Glissant called the postcolonial "yearning for history" takes on a particular significance in Haiti, the world's first free Black republic and the only nation-state founded on a successful revolution of enslaved people.[47] Received in the West as an act of "barbarism and unspeakable violence" and hence "an excessive event,"[48] the Haitian Revolution was systematically excluded from bourgeois metanarratives of liberalist progress, despite Haiti having been the first country in the hemisphere to abolish slavery.[49] In response to this history, Haitian rap kreyòl artists consistently evince a world-historical consciousness. Their yearnings point backward (recovery and restitution) and forward (prophecy and projection), "exploiting the capacities of the subjunctive" in an "an ongoing exploration of *what might be*," as Saidiya Hartman puts it.[50] They express "unyielding hunger and thirst for the *promise* of the future—what bell hooks calls 'Yearning'—coupled with a bitter awareness of the *presence* of 'past' oppressions."[51] This subjunctive yearning for history harmonizes with the trope of the Sankofa bird from Ghanaian Akan philosophy of "returning to the source," which has been commonly mobilized by Afrodiasporic communities.[52]

In Cuba, the world-historical significance of revolution similarly shapes rap lyrics. Following the Cuban Revolution of 1959, the government projected the continuation of a teleology indefinitely into the future by numbering and commemorating each successive year, a practice that continued throughout the period covered in this book. Given the revolution's "monopoly over time's meaning,"[53] Cuban rap yearnings seek either to revolutionize further ("hip hop revolución") or to escape from revolutionary time ("es lo que hay"). Access to foreign currency surfaces as one path out of revolution—generally into neoliberal, financializing logic—and rap lyrics reflect this and reflect on it. The defense of the party emerges as another path out of revolution, into a suspended temporality. Popular genres such as reggaeton and *trapton* echo developments in US trap and global Latin urban music by expressing a yearning bound up with intoxication from drugs and alcohol (although "hard" drugs are less common in Cuba). In the drug-induced redundancy of desiring more of the same, yearning folds in on itself. The escape from revolutionary time by means of a constant re-embedding in the present belongs to what François Hartog identified as the presentism characteristic of the post–Cold War era: the suspension of historical time in favor of an ever-expanding present.[54]

In Brazil, among the most unequal countries in the world, rap yearnings commonly take the form of what São Paulo–based "peripheral poet" Sérgio Vaz calls "sede de hoje" (thirst for today).[55] Sometimes manifesting as the visceral desire to conjure neoliberal excess, "sede de hoje" expresses a consumption-based model of citizenship that derives subjecthood from the right to accumulate commodities.[56] Music videos of the São Paulo genre *ostentação* (ostentation) affirm this right by performing a speculative logic wherein rappers become the heroes of their own rags-to-riches stories. In an extension or parody of financial speculation, these videos are "about what [the artists] didn't even have yet, what they were aspiring to."[57] Through the speculative alchemy of ostentation, some artists literally rap themselves rich.

While this cursory typology of rap yearning suggests that the subjunctive predominates in Haiti, the tautological in Cuba, and the speculative in Brazil, all forms of yearning permeate all three spaces, layering together in the same song or sometimes even the same verse. It is no coincidence, finally, that many of the songs in this chapter come from musical genres that may not strictly be classifiable as what in Brazil is called "rap de raiz" (roots rap). These adjacent genres or subgenres of rap are indebted to hip hop such that they cannot be dissociated from it, but it must be acknowledged that they possess their own internal trajectories and names: *proibidão*, ostentação, and *ousadia* in Brazil; reggaeton and traptón in Cuba; and trap in Haiti. My intention in listening across these subgenres to two of the predominant shapes of rap yearning—the Black feminist and the neoliberal—is neither to moralize nor to propose a synthesis. Instead, detailed listening reveals that both vectors of yearning are generative of hip hop poetics.

Rap yearning is a mode of world-making. Princess Eud came to dominate the Port-au-Prince rap scene in the late 2010s, a sentiment expressed in her appropriately entitled album *Eudomination* (2017). In the title track she boasts that she "voye tèt grenn nan lòt dimansyon / M prezante Ayiti nan bon kondisyon" (commits Afro-textured kinky hair to another dimension / I present Haiti in a good condition).[58] Invoking her African roots, Eud uses rap "to write a new story," as Hartman puts it, "beyond what could be thought within the parameters of history."[59] Eud's *lòt dimansyon*, or other dimension, echoes a verse recorded a year earlier by fellow Port-au-Prince-based rapper D-Fi Powèt Revòlte: "Sou fèy blanch, m vin refè mond lan avan l refè m" (On a blank page, I come to remake the world before it remakes me).[60] Recovering the etymology of the Greek *poiēsis* (to make), D-Fi's *fèy blanch* (blank page) and Eud's lòt dimansyon signal the power of rap to reshape the world.

The reference to remaking in rap kreyòl perhaps invokes the Vodou *lwa* (divinity) of love, Ezili. With no African precedent, Ezili was born in

Haiti: an equivocal embodiment of love in the violent, exploitative context of chattel slavery. She appears at night as a pale virgin, but in songs she is sung as married or prostituted, abandoned or betrayed, jealous or loving. Ezili is "a spirit of love who forbids love," giving herself away in sexually ambiguous marriage to her devotees (who can be either male or female) in such a way that prods memory rather than fantasy while she "demands that the world be reinvented."[61] As if mounted by Ezili, D-Fi rhymes himself in the position of coming (*m vin*) to make the world. This interval between coming and becoming—the opening of Eud's lòt dimansyon—prepares a quasi-messianic arrival of hip hop.

Among the foremost theorists of Judeo-Christian messianism, Walter Benjamin identified messianic time (the time of the "now" or the filling of "empty time") as the site of history, the moment when past and present converge dialectically in a revolutionary leap toward a classless, stateless society.[62] For Benjamin, the Messiah is not sent by heaven, but is reactivated by each generation in a "weak" messianic force wielded by the collective subject of oppressed humanity.[63] Messianic time, explains Giorgio Agamben in a rereading of Saint Paul via Benjamin, emerges at the moment when the Messiah heeds her calling and a caesura opens up between chronological time and the end of time, marked by the fulfillment of the promise, the promised land.[64] The messianic moment is a calling and a coming, the temporality of revolution immediately prior to its triumph (or the poetic verse suspended by enjambment prior to its resolution, as Agamben has argued elsewhere).[65] Rap songs yearn to fill the "empty time" of the musical or poetic caesura, the convergence of words and actions where a verse's calling, its lòt dimansyon, could achieve its (sonic) realization in the world.

This is the subjunctive mood of the yearnings of São Paulo–based artist Dina Di (born in Campinas). Dina, who became something of a Brazilian rap messiah herself following her unexpected death in 2010, prophesizes a new beginning:

Independente do lugar, deixa o bonde levar
. . . .
Logo mais, tá no mundão
Pra gente se acertar, recomeçar.[66]

(Independent of the place, let the train take you
. . . .
Soon you'll be in the world, in the crowd
For us to set things right, to begin again.)

The verses reassure and encourage the listener to have faith in the possibility of beginning again, to follow the proverbial train that will *logo mais* (very soon) disembark in the *mundão* (the crowd, the vast expanse, the world). The final verse inaugurates a new beginning through being together in community, part of the *amor* (love) that echoes throughout Dina's lyrics. Rap becomes "an invocation, rebellious return to the blessedness of beginning again, wandering free in pure process of forgetting and finding."[67] This is where rap lyrics reside for Brisa de la Cordillera (born in Chile and based in São Paulo): "Jogo ainda não virou, mas vai virar / Mundo gira, tempo dirá" (The game still hasn't flipped, but it will / The world turns, time will tell).[68] The homophonic slippage between *virar* (turn over), *gira* (rotate), and *dirá* (will tell)—between the messianic temporality of logo mais and the subjunctive possibility of the lòt dimansyon—is where rap yearning produces its effects.

Tan pou tan: Past Subjunctives

Master Dji recorded the first Haitian rap kreyòl songs in the waning years of the Duvalier dictatorship. "Tan pou tan" (Time for time) was released in 1988, two years after Baby Doc's fall and amidst liberation theologist Jean-Bertrand Aristide's incipient populist movement: "Nou la nouvèl jenerasyon d'Ayiti / Fòk nou met tèt ansanm pou nou ka rekonstwi" (We are here, the new generation of Haiti / We must put our heads together to be able to reconstruct).[69] Expressing a yearning to remake during a period of both instability and possibility, the lyrics inscribe rap kreyòl in the *nouvèl jenerasyon* (new generation) movement. Nouvèl jenerasyon musicians met dismissal from the left as bourgeois and irrelevant and from the right as drug users and party goers.[70] However, these verses echo a common jingle from the period to "mete tèt ansanm" (put our heads together), adopted by Aristide (regarded as Haiti's first democratically elected president) in his successful 1990 campaign.[71]

Master Dji's song builds around the repeated refrain "tan pou tan" (time for time), which is sung with a stutter, reinforcing a homophonic ambivalence between the noun *tan* (time), the verb *tann* (wait), and possibly the possessive *tan n* (our time). The connection between time and waiting reinforced by these homophones recalls a 1964 speech by Dr. Martin Luther King Jr., where King described what he called the "myth of time." In the speech, King critiqued "those individuals who argue that only time can solve the problem of racial injustice in the United States, in South Africa, or anywhere else; you've got to wait on time."[72] Invoking this insidious myth of time, a set of verses from "Tan pou tan" rhymed by Papash evinces a tension between the urgency of the present time (*tan*) and the necessity of waiting (*tann*) for the right moment:

> Nou konn tout sa k te pase
> Nou pa ta vle rekòmanse
> Nou gen anpil travay pou n fè
> Pou nou rive fòk nou pa gad dèyè
> E menm si fòk nou pran san tan, zafè, zafè!
> Sa k vin apre yo va pwofite
> Va kontinye sa nou te kòmanse
> Car se nou menm ki tout fòs yon nasyon
> E n ap fè bak si nou nan divizyon
> Fòk nou ka tann avan nou gen satisfaksyon.[73]

> (We know everything that's happened
> We would not want to start over
> We have a lot of work still to do
> For us to get there, we can't turn back
> And even if it takes one hundred years, so what, so what!
> Those who come after will benefit,
> Will continue what we started
> Because we are the force of the nation
> And we'll go backward if we're divided
> We've got to be able to wait before we can get satisfaction.)

Here, Papash juxtaposes present *divizyon* (division) with future *satisfaksyon* (satisfaction). He calls on his listeners to remember the past and continue "what we started." The lyrics express both a yearning to avoid going backward and a desire to return to the emancipatory potential of the Haitian Revolution. Filtered through the past, the present instability of post-Duvalier dechoukaj (uprooting) dissolves into the forward movement of an ensemble-to-come.

These are subjunctive verses in that they point to "events that have not happened."[74] As Samuel Delany points out, "were English a language with a more detailed tense system, it would be easier to see that *events that have not happened* include past events as well as future ones."[75] Kreyòl marks the past and the subjunctive with *te* and the conditional with *ta*. Perhaps the proximity of past and conditional and the homophonic double meanings that Kreyòl facilitates make it better equipped to account for the subjunctivity of the past. For rappers in Haiti, a nation whose leaders have consistently failed to live up to its promise of radical equality, subjunctivity offers a mode for engaging with the world-historical.[76]

José Esteban Muñoz locates in the subjunctive a "critical affect and a methodology" of hope that lays the groundwork for a queer future always in process of becoming.[77] To invoke or reanimate the past wields the emancipatory potential of heretofore unimagined futures: "it is important to call on the past, to animate it, understanding that the past has a performative nature, which is to say that rather than being static and fixed, the past does things."[78] In this sense, Papash's conditional verse "nou pa ta vle rekòmanse" (we would not want to start over) invokes the past to bypass the present and recover the future of revolution. Returning to the past wields, in Campt's terms, "the power to imagine beyond current fact and to envision that which is not, but must be."[79] However, in the final line, Papash instructs his listeners to be patient, to wait for satisfaction. The time will come when they can fulfil their messianic calling and become the "force of the nation," but for now it is too early for the future. "Tan pou tan" inhabits the "space of the interval, between too late and too early, between the no longer and the not yet."[80] This subjunctivity is part of what makes the yearnings of Haitian rappers resonate with the "as-yet-incomplete project of freedom" of enslaved people and their descendants.[81]

Little had changed two decades later when the rap crew Rockfam released one of its most popular songs "Jodi pa demen" (Today is not tomorrow). The uplifting, gospel-inflected track opens with Stevenson Théodore on the violin while the music video cuts between takes of the Rockfam crew wearing smart black suits and scenes of everyday life in Port-au-Prince. The lyrics echo Papash's call to wait on time: "Aksepte soufri jodi / demen pou w ka rejwi" (Accept suffering today / Tomorrow is for you to be able to rejoice).[82] The prophetic track transports the listener to a future reached through the sacrifice of the present.[83] Is there something emancipatory, then, about waiting for the future? Can the call to "wait on time" that King critiqued resound prophetically outside of time? How does rap begin the process of "ending the grip of Time" in such a way that "restores the World anew, from the position Blackness registers"?[84]

The subjunctive remaking of the world from the position of Blackness is the subject of Fantom's rap song "Si Desalin te la" (If Dessalines were here).[85] The music video begins in a sugarcane field, depicting scenes of slavery and torture, and then transitions to a church plaza, the camera placed on the ground so the sky gleams in the background, illuminating the church and evoking divinity. A piano melody traces soft minor seventh arpeggios while collaborating artist Solis sings a melodic line of *ooo*'s reminiscent of gospel. Strings enter during the chorus, accompanying the repeated refrain of the song's title, which adds to its prayer-like quality. In the introduction, Solis tells a subjunctive history of revolutionary leader Jean-Jacques Dessalines, author of the 1805 constitution that formally abolished slavery and guaranteed equality and citizenship for all Blacks.

A leader of the Haitian Revolution, Dessalines served briefly as emperor of the fledgling republic but was betrayed by Haitian generals led by Alexandre Pétion and assassinated in 1806.[86] Once president, Pétion would accept an agreement with France that Haiti pay indemnities to former plantation owners as reparations for losses sustained during the revolution, which Haiti was not able to pay off in full until 1947.[87] The song's intro casts the assassination of Dessalines, a result of Pétion's betrayal, as Haiti's original sin. At a moment when anything was possible, when enslaved people had successfully overthrown plantation owners to found a free nation, Haitians killed their messiah, precipitating the country's subsequent crises as if part of divinely ordained castigation. The opening verses of the song ask the listener to consider how Haiti might be different if Dessalines had lived longer, if Dessalines were here.

In the final rapped verse Fantom alternates between historical and subjunctive narrations of the past. His lyrics bring together major points of Haiti's colonial, revolutionary, and postrevolutionary history: its status as the richest sugar-producing colony in the western hemisphere; the inauguration of the revolution with the *bwa kayiman* (Bois Caïman) ceremony led by maroon leader Dutty Boukman; the revolution's triumph led by Dessalines in the Battle of Vertières; Pétion's betrayal of Haiti in his ambush plot against Dessalines; and the militarized agriculture of postrevolutionary leaders. Taking these events as a point of departure, the lyrics trace a subjunctive yearning for Dessalines's survival and the continuation of the revolution. Rap yearning, borrowing from Glissant, becomes "a kind of future remembering" that refuses the linear structure of time.[88] "Conjuring a future full of pasts," the song describes both what was and what might be.[89]

Laurent Dubois notes that the ambush and assassination of Dessalines "has become a legendary historical moment, a tragic testament to the way that Haiti's glorious independence so rapidly collapsed into violence."[90] Dessalines even gained the status of a lwa, syncretized with the warrior spirit Ogou, supporting the possibility of hearing Fantom's rap as an invocation to Ogou Desalin. It must be noted, however, that in his brief reign as Emperor, Dessalines presided over a militarized government and fought

Album cover to *Realismo sucio y arte pop*.

to maintain large-scale plantation agriculture.⁹¹ For a majority of Haitians, the Dessalines regime did not represent a significant break with oppressive labor practices.⁹² As such, the veneration of Dessalines stems from his leadership in the revolution and his betrayal by Pétion: he is reborn as a martyr of what Haitian independence could have been. Yet the recurrent figure of Dessalines as a sort of deus ex machina does not signal a way out of Haiti's present. Rather than projecting utopian arrival or revolutionary rupture, "Si Desalin te la" dwells in its yearning and reminds Haitians that they can imagine future redemption only by reanimating the past.

Fantom closes his verses by calling for a new revolution, in a sense echoing the Cuban rap slogan "hip hop revolución," insofar as both imagine a new revolution coming out of the old. With his 2015 album *Realismo sucio y arte pop* (Dirty realism and pop art), Havana-based rapper and producer Malcoms "Justicia" sought to establish a dialogue with trends in international art. During the 1990s, several Cuban artists had emulated Andy Warhol: for example, Alexis Esquivel's 1995 painting "Pop revolution," which features a series of images of José Martí and Ernesto "Che" Guevara on labels of Cuban Hatuey beer. When describing *Realismo sucio y arte pop* to me, Malcoms evoked the pop art aesthetic and compared his lyrics to the use of images in advertising.⁹³

The first part of the album title alludes to the *realismo sucio* (dirty realism) literary movement of Cubans writing from abroad during the 1990s. In this literary genre, novelists such as Pedro Juan Gutiérrez promised an "authentic," quasi-ethnographic experience of everyday scarcity and hypersexuality in an underbelly of Havana otherwise unavailable to tourists.[94] The protagonist of Gutiérrez's 1999 novel *El Rey de la Habana* (The king of Havana), among the best-selling realismo sucio novels, expresses repeatedly one possible slogan of the literary movement in the phrase "me da igual" (it doesn't matter, I don't care).[95] Like "es lo que hay," Gutiérrez's "me da igual" expresses little regard for the future. Indeed, *El Rey de la Habana* forecloses futurity entirely, ending with murder and death in a makeshift house atop a garbage heap. Gutiérrez leaves his protagonist to be devoured by rats in an anonymous, all-consuming present in which "nadie supo nada jamás" (nobody ever knew anything).[96] The novel speaks to "the collapse of the communist ideal as the future of the revolution," triggered by the fall of the Berlin Wall in 1989.[97]

Cuban realismo sucio drew inspiration from North American dirty realism of the 1980s, which Malcoms explained to me was characterized by its use of direct language to address everyday events. The songs comprising *Realismo sucio y arte pop* seek to say things, as he put it, "in ways they haven't been said in Cuba."[98] In clear dialogue with realismo sucio, his song "La ciudad no duerme" (The city doesn't sleep) includes a mention of lust (*lujuria*), the smell of garbage ("mal olor debido a la basura"), and collapsing houses ("tu casa se derrumba").[99] The song's later verses, however, depart from the genres named by the album title by decrying Havana's dancing residents as "Dementes sin lógica / Que bailan tristemente" (Crazy lunatics without logic / Sadly dancing).[100] Here, dance occupies a state suspended between "me da igual" and "es lo que hay." Malcoms's pessimistic rereading of dance reanimates denigrations of dance by intellectual elites almost a century earlier.[101] The depiction of somnambulant Havana dancers recalls, moreover, one of the most recurrent clichéd representations of Cuba throughout the Special Period and its aftermath of an island suspended in time.[102] The lyrics assert that Havana suffers from insomnia: the city cannot sleep, and as a result, it cannot wake up.[103]

By the end of the song, Malcoms's patience for waiting has run out. He calls for

> La toma del Palacio de la Revolución en radio reloj
> Los universitarios pa' la calle con ideas de otra revolución
> No nos quitan la alegría y la satisfacción de ponernos de pie
> Vamos a hacer lo que hizo Fidel
> La Revolución se está acabando, es lógico
> Y tiene que empezar otra vez.[104]

(The taking of the Palace of the Revolution in *radio reloj*
University students to the street with ideas of another revolution
They can't take from us the joy and satisfaction of standing up
We're going to do what Fidel did
The revolution is ending, it's obvious
And it must begin again.)

With dance in Cuba generally understood to be a national pastime bringing *alegría* (joy) and *satisfacción* (satisfaction), Malcoms reserves these emotions for the revolutionary act of collective protest (illegal in Cuba except in highly ritualized contexts).[105] Unlike Gutiérrez, he ends his narration by evoking the figure of revolution as eternal return: one revolution ends and another begins. In a gesture that sounds curiously at odds with Cuban realismo sucio, Malcoms calls for students to gather in the Plaza de la Revolución and follow Fidel's example, resuscitating the ethos of "hip hop revolución." The radio allusion reinforces the reference to the Cuban leader by invoking the "capacity for instantaneous uprising" that Castro saw as both the danger and power of the radio.[106] Malcoms's "failure" to translate the ethos of realismo sucio into rap reflects a latent yearning for history and for the future of revolution.

Dopados de la mente: The Right to the Present

If realismo sucio had a soundtrack, it would have been *timba* music—the upbeat, highly syncopated, clave-based dance music played by big bands of predominantly Afro-Cuban university graduates trained as musicians.[107] Fusing rumba and son with the "tropical" sound of salsa, timba emerged in Cuba in the 1980s and gained popularity in the 1990s.[108] Lyrically, timba singers elaborated social chronicles not unlike those of Special Period literature and rap.[109] Like rappers, timba singers recovered a discourse about race and racism that had been rendered unspeakable by an official policy of colorblindness.[110] Ariana Hernández-Reguant suggests that timba musicians performed a "disidentification with the racial status quo" by naturalizing Blackness, inverting a long-standing colonial hierarchy by casting Black male hypersexuality as superior.[111] Anticipating trends in reggaeton, timba artists frequently sang about money and sex.

Timba was controversial both because artists circumvented the socialist doctrine of racelessness and because they embraced international markets. Unlike many Cuban rappers, timba artists welcomed commercialization, mobilizing Blackness to acquire wealth.[112] NG La Banda's 1994 song "Santa palabra" (Santo words), for example, playfully syncretizes commodification with African-inspired Regla de Ocha (also known as Santería): "No escondas los collares ni los santos por temor al qué dirán / Oye, porque los santos lo malo te quitan y muchas cosas buenas que te dan" (Don't hide the necklaces or the saints for fear of what they'll say / Listen, because saints rid you of the bad and give you many good things).[113] In a critique of the Revolution's censorship of Afro-Cuban religions, as well as its disapproval of individualistic displays of wealth, NG La Banda links the *collares* (necklaces) worn by initiate *santeras* and *santeros* to ostentation, perhaps even alluding to the bling-bling culture of contemporaneous gangsta rap.[114] Timba's commercial success in Cuba is one example of the way, as George Yúdice puts it, "culture is increasingly wielded as a resource for both sociopolitical and economic amelioration."[115]

At timba concerts, what Yúdice calls the "expediency of culture" seems also to have manifested as sexual expediency. Performances foregrounded dance and placed the female body at center stage. Departing from partner dance, women would perform sexualized *despelote* and *tembleque* pelvic movements onstage and in the audience to stimulate men, who would remain relatively stationary.[116] Much has been critiqued about timba's machismo, but Vincenzo Perna suggests that for some women who performed "the *despelote* at the request of musicians, singing sexist lyrics did not represent an act of submission, but the demonstration of an equal-to-equal relationship between two interdependent economic subjects."[117] Drawing a parallel with Cuba's dual currency system of the time, Jan Fairley interprets the female body in timba as "convertible currency." She suggests that timba performances rehearsed "a symbolic exchange of Cuban women by Cuban society, represented by the Cuban musicians on stage and dancers in the audience, with non-Cubans, represented by the foreigners in the dancing audience."[118] Highlighting Black male hypersexuality and women as expedient resources available for exchange, timba artists reinforced clichéd representations of Cuba and Cubans. If social critique is to be redeemed here, it is perhaps in the quasi-parodic performance of these highly asymmetric contractual relationships.

Given extreme austerity measures and free trade agreements implemented in economies throughout the hemisphere during the 1980s and 1990s, Marc Perry describes in his book on Cuban rap an emergent "neoliberal Cuba."[119] The growth of the Cuban tourist industry and relaxation of restrictions on *empresas mixtas* (mixed enterprises) during the 1990s, coupled with an expanding market of *cuentapropismo* (self-employed small businesses), can be cited as evidence of a neoliberal turn. Furthermore, the place of the female body in timba music in the 1990s seems to have been driven by market imperatives and the exchange of currency (foreign and domestic), reminiscent of neoliberal free trade. However, Cuba's economic transformations of the 1990s and 2000s were significantly more regulated than the neoliberal policies adopted elsewhere in the Caribbean, such as in Puerto Rico and the Dominican Republic.

Moreover, the Cuban musical genre that would come closest to embracing neoliberalism was not rap but reggaeton (*reguetón*). With Afro-Panamanian origins, reggaeton crystallized in marginalized Black communities of San Juan, Puerto Rico, in the 1990s, where it was originally called *música negra* (Black music) or *underground* (a term taken from hip hop).[120] As the dance genre commercialized, it pushed the expediency of bodies further, maintaining the collares but mostly abandoning the *santos* and other elements of Black empowerment characteristic of timba. Lyrics increasingly turned to sex and bordered on the pornographic.[121] Not unlike the despelote and tembleque in timba, the signature *perreo* dance move of reggaeton simulated and stimulated sex, its relationship to pornography explicit (*perreo* refers to "doggy style").[122] Fairley even cites an interview with a male concertgoer who explained that "real" sex could occur during dance.[123] Reggaeton's expediency, then, lies in the proximity between ritualistic courtship and sexual intercourse. The means were in the end, like the simulacrum of sex that could become the real thing. Given Special Period scarcity, the body represented one of the few renewable resources available (accounting, in part, for the prevalence of prostitution). In reggaeton, the "way out" did not lead to an eternal return to revolution. The collapse of teleology puts off deferral: rather than a mating ritual, dance becomes the thing itself.

As reggaeton was beginning to enter Cuban airwaves in the early 2000s, a rap subgenre associated with prostitution, drugs, and money emerged in Atlanta, Georgia.[124] Where an anxiety of "selling out" had permeated hip hop's commercialization in the 1980s, rappers of the subgenre known as trap begin from a posture that might better be called "selling in." As Jesse McCarthy puts it, trap provided a "soundtrack of the dissocialized subject that neoliberalism made . . . the funeral music that the Reagan revolution deserves."[125] In the verses of Dominican American trap artist Belcalis "Cardi B" Marlenis Almanzar: "Look, I don't dance now, I make money moves / Say I don't gotta dance, I make money move."[126] A former stripper, Cardi B's successful music career permitted her to transition from the necessity of strip-dancing to make money, to the possibility of making lucrative "money moves," and finally, to the ability to "make money move." Her body's commodification is continually abstracted into the music, and the lyrics pass through a parallel stripping-down. The replacement of end rhyme with epistrophe suggests that Cardi B is also tacitly affirming: "I don't have to *rhyme* now." Though trap music videos commonly exude excess, trap lyrics economize language.

The trap breakbeat "sounds like a downtempo hip hop track," while an artist's flow (the words at times so economized as to be indecipherable) typically features verses in triplet meter, almost evocative of limerick in their circularity, which gives trap a double-time feel.[127] Hi-hats in double or triple time imbue the beat with the bellicose quality of a marching band, while a pumped-up, syncopated base skips the primary beats, knocking the marching band off-kilter.[128] A sonic expression of the interplay between the drugs being sold (typically uppers such as crack cocaine) and the drugs being consumed (primarily opioids such as "lean," a mixture of soft drink and prescription-strength codeine or promethazine cough syrup),[129] trap music feels at once too fast and too slow—and this is no doubt part of its appeal.

Justin Burton argues that trap artists carry out an "ironic performance of blackness in a post-race society."[130] For Burton, one ironic signifier of Blackness lies in the use of digital voice enhancement software such as Auto-Tune (a practice referred to in general as "autotune"), sometimes employed to detune the voice intentionally.[131] Autotune gives trap a *posthuman* quality that Afro-diasporic thinkers such as Kodwo Eshun and Sylvia Wynter have mobilized to question the universalist claims of Western humanism.[132] For nonwhite and nonmale communities of people, for whom the category of the human was withheld, the posthuman can serve as a mode of critique. In this sense, the posthuman quality of autotune in trap performs historical work, invoking a longer genealogy in Afro-diasporic performance.

In 1990s R & B, for example, the voice was commonly distorted by a vocoder machine, a digital technology that produces the analog effect of a robotic voice.[133] Focusing on R & B group Jodeci's 1993 track "Feenin," Alexander G. Weheliye draws attention the use of the vocoder each time the word *feenin'* (as in drug fiend) is sung. The song draws a parallel between the chemical mediation of drugs in the body and the technological mediation of the singer's voice, both gesturing toward the posthuman. The effect, Weheliye argues, is the expression of an "all-encompassing desire," but "always already a desire of the second order: the performance of desire rather than desire as such."[134] Similarly mediated by drugs and digitally distorted voices, trap artists perform a related "desire of the second order." Their lyrics express a yearning for something presumably already attained: "No longer motivated by hip-hop's drive to conspicuously consume—they long ago acquired anything they could have wanted—[they] instead dissolutely cycle through easily available pleasures, feeling a combination of frustration, anger, and self-disgust, aware that something is missing, but unsure exactly what it is."¹³⁵ This Faustian bargain of selling in perhaps accounts for the minor modes and dark visuals that undergird even the most ostensibly celebratory iterations of trap.

In 2015, Cuban duo Yomil y el Dany fused trap-inspired beats, autotuned flows, and reggaeton's upbeat danceability in the self-styled genre of traptón. Although I have encountered no evidence of the drug lean in Cuba, Yomil y el Dany referenced drugs in two consecutive album titles, *Sobredosis* (Overdose; released in 2016) and *Dopados de la mente* (Drugged in the mind; released in 2018).¹³⁶ Nominated for the *Billboard Latin Music Awards* and one of Cuba's most successful musical acts of the late 2010s, Yomil y el Dany remind their listeners of a humble upbringing: "salimos de barrios marginales" (we come from marginal neighborhoods).¹³⁷ At their US debut in Miami, they put on the most expensive concert on record for a Cuban act, with some spectators paying up to nine hundred US dollars for tickets.¹³⁸ The song "Sacrifice" describes their speculative rise to fame: "Todo comenzó por una ficción / Y terminó siendo nuestra profesión" (Everything began with a fiction / And ended being our profession).¹³⁹ Elsewhere, they sing of money as a facile panacea: "To' está bien, hay money" (It's all good, there's money).¹⁴⁰ All are tropes familiar to reggaeton as well as trap.

Yomil y el Dany's self-presentation song "Evolutions," however, displays a greater degree of self-reflexivity. In heavily autotuned vocals and sparse lyrics characteristic of trap, they advocate a "doped" state of mind:

> Vinimos pa' hacerte sentir, yeah, yeah, yeah
> . . . .
> Dopados de la mente, pensando diferente
> Con un ritmo convincente
> Que le gusta a to' tipo de gente.¹⁴¹
>
> (We came to make you feel, yeah, yeah, yeah
> . . . .
> Doped in the mind, thinking differently
> With a convincing rhythm
> That all types of people like.)

Trapton's "convincing rhythm" contains a universalizing, even democratizing power. Significant is the absence of an object for the transitive verb *sentir,* the series of "yeah, yeah, yeah" taking the place of the object. This music is not meant to make the listener feel something in particular, but rather simply to feel: a "biologic of thought" available to all people.[142] While providing an escape from the present, the music induces its own inescapable present, coaxing the listener into a recursive state of pure feeling, a caesura outside of time. To borrow from Anthony Reed's description of jazz, trapton elaborates a "rhythmic feeling for life . . . within which official notions of Time appear in distorted ways."[143] What experiences of time open up when listeners are asked to "pensar diferente" (think differently), in a state "dopados de la mente"? If trapton circumvents Cuban revolutionary time, does it also escape the suspended temporality characteristic of post–Special Period Cuba?

While they insist, in the song "Evolutions," on supplying continually more trapton, Yomil y el Dany also reveal a yearning for history that sounds curiously at odds with the presentism of "dopados de la mente":

> Dale trapton, somos lo que está de moda
> La nueva historia de la música cubana
> Sin pare y sin coda
> La nueva generación, soy la evolución.[144]
>
> (Give them trapton, we're what's in style
> The new history of Cuban music
> Without stop and without coda
> The new generation, I'm the evolution.)

It is difficult not to hear the word "evolution" as "revolution" without the *r*. The inventors of trapton profess to occupy an ever-expanding present and, in an almost Hegelian move, they proclaim arrival at the end of history: a synthesis of Cuban music "without stop and without coda."[145] Their hybrid of trap and reggaeton blends the familiar reggaeton beat with trap syncopation, combines autotune singing and rapping, and asserts musical historicity. Unlike the subjunctive yearning of Malcoms's renovated revolution, Yomil y el Dany emphatically rhyme that the future is now and it is them. In doing so, they express the presentism that Hartog associates with the period after the fall of the Berlin Wall, where "a permanent, elusive, and almost immobile present . . . nevertheless attempts to create its own historical time."[146] What, then, could come after trapton?

"Evolutions" was released the same year as what became one of the most successful US trap songs of the decade, the 2016 Migos song "Bad and Boujee." The Migos track reached number one on the *Billboard* Hot 100 list and had registered more than one billion views on YouTube as of March 2021. The music video depicts an extended scene of the group dining at an ostensibly upscale restaurant. Instead of plated meals, the rappers drink champagne in plastic cups and share a tub of fried chicken; one member of the party has an instant Cup Noodles bowl on her plate. Released on the 2017 album appropriately titled *Culture,* "Bad and Boujee" asserts that "the cosmopolitanism of the underclass is good enough for them. In this, everyone wins. The fetish of class and racial transgression is given a smooth membrane across which to exchange approving glances."[147] "Bad and Boujee" questions whether there is anything left to yearn for when confronted with all the new money the artists could have imagined.

The same year, eighteen-year-old Haitian rapper Asap Fresh and his G-Shytt crew released a Haitian remix of "Bad and Boujee" entitled "Balèn bouji" (White candles, colored candles). Among the most popular songs heard on the radio that summer in Port-au-Prince, "Balèn bouji" recycles the Migos beat and adopts Migos's stripped-down, economized language.[148] Obviously lacking the Migos budget, the music video alternates between two frames filmed on a single street corner, where members of the G-Shytt crew drink beer and move their arms up and down to the beat, underscoring the track with parody: these rappers are anything but boujee.[149] Nevertheless, the song transforms the "capitalist sorcery" of the Migos lyrics into Vodou magic,[150] Migos's frequent use of extralinguistic sounds becoming Vodou incantations:

> Balèn bouji
> Genlè w poko janm fè maji
> Lè w zonbi w pa gen souf ooo
> Rezon, sa se fason m aji yeah
> Bilolo hoo bilolo bilolo bilolo bilolo ayibobo
> Ou di w pa konn sa k vodou
> Ou pran nan vodou
> Ou wè lougawou
> Zonbi nan kay ou
> Oungan pran vwa w
> Kounya gad tray ou, han![151]
>
> (White candles, colored candles
> You probably have yet to do magic

When you're a zombie, you don't breathe
The reason: that's how I act, yeah
Bilolo hoo bilolo bilolo bilolo bilolo ayibobo[152]
You say you don't know what Vodou is
You're trapped by Vodou
You see the werewolves[153]
Zombies in your house
Vodou priests taking your voice
Now, look how you are suffering, yeah!)

The song's title is a pun on the candles used in Vodou ceremony and its lyrics substitute Migos's new money with Vodou zombie cultural capital.[154] In light of the dictatorship's appropriation of peasant symbols, the recovery of cultural patrimony such as Vodou is significant.[155] Furthermore, by performing national clichés, Fresh gave listeners what they wanted. The formula of taking a US-made trap anthem and inserting recognizably Haitian elements proved fruitful: the success of "Balèn bouji" granted the G-Shytt trio several high-profile concerts in Haiti, and the group began work on its first mixtape.[156] Thus Asap Fresh launched his career through the speculative performance of remixing a popular US trap tune, announcing that he, too, could be "bad and boujee," and in a distinctly Haitian way.

Quem imagina levanta a mão: Speculative Futures

The speculative mode has permeated Brazilian popular music as well. The genre of proibidão (strongly prohibited) emerged in Rio de Janeiro during the 1990s.[157] The rapped lyrics of these songs, which were at times literally banned, paid homage to favela gangsters.[158] Drug traffickers and cartels would finance weekly dances and personally attend them, displaying arsenals of machine guns to transform community gatherings into spectacles for promoting cohesion by reinforcing their hegemony.[159] Given the literal connection of proibidão to drug trafficking and gang violence, some Brazilian rappers joined the media in vilifying the genre as morally reprehensible and responsible for inciting violence.[160]

However, Cidinho e Doca's hit "Rap da felicidade" (Happiness rap), which became a sort of anthem and was still widely played more than twenty years later, displays none of the above criticisms.[161] The chorus expresses a modest plea, a yearning not for speculative accumulation but simply for the right to exist: "Eu só quero é ser feliz / Andar tranquilamente na favela onde eu nasci" (All I want is to be happy / To walk around in peace in the favela where I was born).[162] The eminently catchy melody and eloquent verses are memorizable upon first listening, encouraging the listener to sing along. The lyrics affirm a right to place in a city where the poor have been systematically excluded, something like what Henri Lefebvre called the "right to the city."[163] "Rap da felicidade" rehearses an occasion to be proud of being from the favela. In contrast to the subjunctive yearnings of Master Dji, Fantom, and Malcoms, this song does not reach into the past or future, instead conjuring an alternate present.

When "Rap da felicidade" was released in 1995, 45 percent of Brazilians made less than the equivalent of six US dollars per day, and homicide rates were climbing sharply.[164] Over the next decade, during President Luiz Inácio Lula da Silva's first tenure as president (2003–2011) as well as in the first few years under President Dilma Rousseff, poverty and homicide rates declined significantly.[165] Following the late arrival of the 2008 global economic recession in Brazil and a mounting political crisis that culminated in the impeachment and removal of Rousseff and the conviction and imprisonment of Lula, poverty and violence again began to climb. These transformations influenced the experience of what Sérgio Vaz calls the "sede de hoje" (thirst for today) of residents of disadvantaged neighborhoods.[166] The yearnings expressed in Brazilian rap and adjacent genres archive the way "sede de hoje" shifted with changing economic and political conditions: the increasing urban violence of the 1990s, the reduction of poverty in the 2000s, the mounting global crisis of the 2010s. The zeitgeist of each period can be traced in this music through narratives of what is called *superação* (overcoming), the ability to overcome or surmount difficult circumstances despite coming from a disadvantaged background. Superação ranges from the Public Enemy–inspired Black Power ethos of the Racionais MC's verse "a fúria negra ressuscita outra vez" (Black fury rises again; see chapter 6), to self-improvement narratives, to the flaunting of capital accumulation, to creative and strategic engagement with markets.[167]

When I met Padêro MC in Fortaleza in 2015, the global recession had arrived and the city was ranked as the most violent in Brazil and in the top ten worldwide.[168] Padêro, who had worked as a *padeiro* (baker), began his rap show "Um novo dia pela paz, pela vida" (A new day for peace, for life) by presenting his personal story of superação as a parable for his audience.[169] He addressed an enthusiastic crowd (mostly comprised of residents of his neighborhood, Barra do Ceará, whom the rapper had personally invited) as if a preacher delivering a sermon:

Boa, boa noite... Só quero dizer para vocês, que se falarem para vocês, que você não é capaz, lute até o fim. Tem um ditadozinho aí que diz que pau que nasce torto morre torto. Na verdade chapa, eu mostrei o contrário. Vários já mostraram o contrário, deram a volta por cima. Se alguém falar para você que você não é capaz, mano, use isso como energia. Vença as barreiras, as dificuldades, seja mais você, chapa. É por você, pelo amor que você tem aos seus filhos, sua família, lute pela paz, pela vida! Padêro MC está na casa, te trouxe pra vitória, irmão.[170]

(Good evening! . . . I want to say to you, that if people tell you you aren't capable, struggle until the end. There's a saying that says that a tree trunk that's born crooked dies crooked. But I proved the opposite, man. Many proved the opposite. They came out on top. If someone tells you you aren't capable, man, use this as energy. Break down the barriers, the difficulties, be more yourself, man. It's for you, for the love you have for your children, your family. Struggle for peace, for life! Padêro MC is in the house, he brought you to victory, brother.)

At this point, Padêro's sermon-like introduction gave way to the breakbeat of the first song. The a cappella spoken introduction narrates Padêro's ascent to community leadership, overcoming the social determinism expressed by the Brazilian proverb "a tree trunk that's born crooked dies crooked." He explained to me later that rap was one of the principal forces to propel him out of involvement in crime.[171] Rap also granted him the opportunity to learn to read and write, a story to which I return in chapter 5. In rap, Padêro leads by example, deploying his personal story of superação to inspire his listeners to overcome their own struggles and imagine "a new day." Yet while hip hop led to the accumulation of social capital, rap did not make him rich.

In this sense, Padêro's self-improvement narrative contrasts sharply with the neoliberal iteration of superação that had emerged in São Paulo a few years earlier. The musical genre known as ostentação (literally, ostentation) not only highlighted the overcoming of difficult circumstances but embraced the neoliberal order that had exacerbated income and wealth disparity in the first place.[172] The slogan of upstart media mogul Konrad "KondZilla" Dantas, ostentação's most important producer, reflects a newfound purchasing power and upward mobility of underclasses: "a favela venceu" (the favela won out). The videos produced by KondZilla project limitless paper bills, motorcycles, cars, planes, and helicopters, exaggerating to the point of parody the image of "liberal individualism" that MTV and television more broadly had disseminated in previous decades.¹⁷³ KondZilla would obtain more than 65 million subscribers in his YouTube channel, and aspiring São Paulo MCs saw the production of a video by KondZilla as a necessary first step to their success.¹⁷⁴

Some ostentação songs simply flaunt wealth, such as MC Guimê's 2012 track "Plaque de 100" (meaning 100 Brazilian *reais*), which features the MC in an empty room fondling paper bills and posing alongside a variety of motorcycles and cars—tropes familiar in US rap.¹⁷⁵ The video rehearses a sort of magical conjuring that Anna Tsing associates with global neoliberalism. Tracing the dramatic narrative performances of speculative startups, Tsing demonstrates the way such enterprises conjure or call into being the extractive profits they hope to attain.¹⁷⁶ Ostentação is perhaps one such speculative conjuring trick, conjuring a world where the MC can appropriate neoliberal accumulation.¹⁷⁷

Produced by KondZilla, MC Boy do Charmes's 2013 track "Nóis de nave" (We're in the ship) begins with images of a man mixing concrete and sweeping the ground. A narrator introduces Charmes as if before a concert: "Ele já foi pedreiro, faxineiro, porteiro . . . e agora é MC!" (He was a bricklayer, a cleaner, a doorman . . . and now he's an MC!).¹⁷⁸ Alexandre Pereira notes that the introduction mobilizes Charmes's humble origins to teach spectators that not only is Charmes one of them but they could be just like him.¹⁷⁹ Reproducing a reality television logic of superação, the announcement casts the MC as the hero of his own rags-to-riches story. The music video splices together "real" scenes of Charmes surrounded by residents of his favela and "dream" sequences of motorcycles, cars, and helicopters. The lyrics mirror these oscillations, beginning with the yearnings of Charmes in the favela and turning to his speculative achievement of purchasing an XT 1100 motorcycle. Crucially, as Pereira notes, artists would typically rent the expensive vehicles featured in the music videos.¹⁸⁰ In this sense, "Nóis de nave" reinforces what Reed calls "the discrepancy between the dream and its realization."¹⁸¹

As Gavin Steingo describes of a different musical context, the song performs a "*willful* ignorance born from the desire to see or hear from the perspective of someone whose attention is not entirely concentrated on actual oppressive conditions."¹⁸² Performance of this type is "not an illusion that hides reality; on the contrary, it *doubles reality*."¹⁸³ In the doubled reality of the music video, Charmes pledges allegiance to the favela and scales his dreams to the shared yearning of his spectators: "Vou imaginando e quem imagina levanta a mão / Por ser humilde eu tenho um sonho e não é em vão" (I'm imagining, and if you imagine raise your hand / For being poor, I have a dream and it's not in vain).¹⁸⁴ Here, yearning returns to GOG's "direito de sonhar" (right to dream).[185] The temporality of the song pivots between the MC's mythologized past (a poor favela resident, dreaming himself rich) and imagined future (a commercially successful singer). Movement between the two poles relies on a speculative logic: Charmes displays the capital he yearns to accumulate by means of the commodification of his music and, by doing so, participates in that process of commodification. Like financial speculation (investing money one doesn't yet possess), ostentação sells videos about a future not yet attained, and the performance conjures that future.

While ostentatious narratives of superação seem to reify the commodity fetish that Marx saw as inherent to capitalism, Krista Thompson suggests that in Black performance, the "ostentatious display of things" can retain a subversive potential.[186] Drawing on the art historical phenomenon of surfacism (the emphasis on texture within the image plane), Thompson argues that the "spectacle of stardom" reimagines materialism and has "the potential to disrupt notions of value by privileging not things but their visual effects."[187] Given the pervasive commodification of Black culture, with origins in chattel slavery, ostentation can perhaps offer protection, a refraction or parody of the fetishizing white gaze on Black subjects.[188]

Brasília-based Flora Matos demonstrates the subversive potential of ostentation: "Eu vou ficar milionária, milionária / Sem nunca depender de um homem pra ter minhas parada" (I'm going to become a millionaire, millionaire / Never depending on a man to have my things).[189] Provocatively stroking a guitar and piano in the music video, Matos transforms her accumulation of capital into feminist critique, her insertion into the market granting independence, autonomy, and the ability to be heard in a male-dominated industry. Furthermore, given that she addresses this and other erotic songs to female lovers,[190] her call of "never depending on a man" acquires (borrowing from Muñoz) a certain "queer futurity."[191] In financial and sexual superação from institutional patriarchy, Matos insightfully circumvents would-be criticisms of "selling out," by financializing queer feminist yearning. Upholding ostentação's market-driven ethos, her yearnings and her earnings become mutually constitutive.

Amidst mounting economic and political crises in the second half of the 2010s, artists began to turn away from the speculative promise of ostentação. The cultural magazine *Veja São Paulo* announced that because of the crisis, ostentação was "on the brink of death," quoting a producer who observed that "the culture of consumerism of the whole society" had become "frustrated by the decrease of money in the pockets of the people."¹⁹² KondZilla explained further: "There was this false illusion that everyone had access to everything. It was a time of celebration and conquest and all these material goods, and people wanted to flaunt them. . . . Now the songs are about dreams and love—people even sing a lot about their moms. It's not the gratuitous display of material goods. If you've got something, you worked hard. It's something you deserve."¹⁹³ KondZilla's description signals an opposition between perceived "false illusions" of commodities (almost a Marxian "false consciousness"), on the one hand, and apparently genuine "dreams and love," on the other.¹⁹⁴ Where ostentação artists emulate or parody the speculative conjuring logic of finance capital—making money out of nothing—motifs of "dreams and love" in the genre known as ousadia (literally, daring) replace the "celebration and conquest" of money with the celebration and conquest of women. In this sense, ousadia feels like a return to some earlier iterations of rap, fetishizing bodies instead of bills. Furthermore, KondZilla's narrative of "working hard" and becoming successful because of "something you deserve" reproduces older Brazilian narratives not only of superação, but also of meritocracy.

Whatever its merits, MC Fioti's 2017 ousadia song "Bum bum tam tam," produced by KondZilla, became the first Brazilian music video to register more than one billion views on YouTube.¹⁹⁵ Instead of paper money and fancy cars, the video features a young, blue-haired Fioti seducing women with a flute in alternating scenes of Orientalized ancient Egypt and innocuous encounters with women on the street. The track samples Johann Sebastian Bach's 1722 Partita in A Minor for Solo Flute (BWV 1013) while the lyrics mostly revolve around the repeated rhythmic phrase "bum bum tam tam." What sort of temporality resonates in this departure from language: the retreat of voice into rhythm, of rap into late-Baroque flute? How should we approach the video's disjunctive takes between the ostensibly mythic space of the sacred flute and the quotidian reality of a young, awkward kid yearning for female attention? Alternating between the benign street scenes and the queer fantasy signified by the flute (a wind instrument that in the West is commonly associated with femininity), the music video recalls the intercalated dream and reality sequences in Charmes.¹⁹⁶ Yet where "Nóis de nave" links dreams to reality through a speculative teleology, "Bum bum tam tam" does not suggest any temporal bridge between the "Egyptian" scene and the "street" scene. If Charmes's "Nóis de nave" signals the possibility of capital accumulation just on the horizon, Fioti's magic flute promises nothing other than the circular refrain of "bum bum tam tam."

Other Brazilian rappers, however, held on to the subjunctive. Belo Horizonte–based Djonga developed a national reputation during Michel Temer's interim presidency following the impeachment of President Rousseff. The dissonance between the audio and video tracks in Djonga's "Junho de 94" (June of '94) reflects this political instability. The lyrics contain familiar hip hop tropes: an anxiety of selling out, speaking on behalf of the oppressed, affirmation of the transformative potential of hip hop. Djonga even boasts of mobilizing protest *as* commodification: "Antigamente eu só queria derrubar o sistema / Hoje o sistema me paga pra cantar, irmão" (Before all I wanted to do was overthrow the system / Today, the system pays me to sing, brother).[197] While acknowledging that rap's antiestablishment discourse can be compromised by the industry, Djonga mocks the "system" for paying him to critique it, acknowledging that he now benefits from the same order he once hoped to overthrow. As with Matos, protest and profit become two sides of the same coin.[198]

About two-thirds of the way through the song, the audio track transitions abruptly and layers or superimposes samples of several Brazilian rap songs (including one of Djonga's own) in a recapitulation, even a sort of elegy, for Brazilian rap.[199] The dissonant, superimposed layers of the musical track are "dramatically out of tune" with each other, their incommensurability evoking what Adam Krims calls the "hip-hop sublime."[200] The song's final seconds, in a prolonged fade-out, invoke Blackness: "Deixa eu devolver o orgulho do gueto e dar outro sentido pra frase: tinha que ser preto" (Let me return pride to the ghetto and give another meaning to the phrase, it had to be Black).[201]

Not unlike the doubled realities of Charmes and Fioti, the music video features alternating sequences of Djonga at two dinner parties, one with a Black family and one with a white family, in both cases being slowly strangled by a rope.[202] At the moment of the audio transition, the video abruptly cuts to a sort of purgatory: a bemused Djonga wearing only underwear serves as a bathroom attendant for a woman sitting on the toilet reading a magazine. Here, rather than offering the promise of money, sexual conquest, or the right to the present, Djonga retreats to the opacity of what Fred Moten calls the Black avant-garde: "He is out of the unit/s of performance, the song form, the song and its collection, the tune and the normal lineup of tunes, the 'standards' (of performance); out of the set, which is to say the party, the jam, the get-together, the gathering."[203] If the lynching scene evokes the history of racial oppression and animates the "performative nature" of the past,[204] the bathroom scene opens a lòt dimansyon, a sort of queer heterotopia, in the way Michel Foucault used the term.[205] What futures emerge in Djonga's outro? How might the queerness of this hip hop afterlife undermine the hypermasculinity common in much of Black radicalism and pervasive in hip hop?[206] What legacies will rap leave? The next chapter turns inward to explore the way rappers define, describe, and theorize this practice.

2 Raplove

"Es lo que hay"

WRITING ABOUT popular music, Simone Lenzi observes that in a certain sense "all songs are love songs."[1] This chapter hypothesizes that rap songs are love songs to hip hop. Listen, for example, to the following verse by Port-au-Prince-based rapper D-Fi: "M te vin fè rap / Ofinal se rap ki fè m" (I came to make rap / In the end it's rap that made me).[2] The chiasmus of these lyrics shrinks the distance between subject and object in a gesture of rapping about rap that I call raplove. Raplove dates at least to the earliest commercially successful rap song released in the United States, "Rapper's Delight" (1979), where in lyrics supposedly written by Grandmaster Caz and performed by Wonder Mike, the subject of the verse unfolds recursively as the verse being rapped: "Now, what you hear is not a test, I'm rapping to the beat."[3] Raplove is expanded into a raplove song (a love song to hip hop) in the song "Act Too (The Love of My Life)" by Philadelphia-based group the Roots: "Hip hop, you the love of my life and that's true."[4] This song addresses hip hop in lyric apostrophe, calling on or invoking the practice to carry out poetic work.

The tendency toward mise en abyme in rap lyrics has not been lost on hip hop scholars, who observe a prevalence of "rappers who rap about rapping,"[5] "metarhyme,"[6] "reflexive circularity,"[7] even ars poetica.[8] As Alexs Pate notes, "examples abound of rap/poets who openly write about writing."[9] I return to the trope of writing and its implications for community-building in chapter 5. The question guiding the present chapter is *why* do rappers rap about rap? How does this centripetal deixis or self-referentiality (using rap to point to itself) counterbalance the yearnings of the previous chapter, the desire for rap to intervene in the world? I will suggest that there is something potentially transformative in the seemingly redundant or tautological act of rapping about rap.

Self-referential rap forms part of a broader tradition in Afro-diasporic music and poetics. Henry Louis Gates Jr. characterizes African American literature as "a meta-discourse, a discourse about itself."[10] Édouard Glissant similarly calls Caribbean poetics a "discourse on discourse (the reexamination of self)."[11] The recursive poetics of musicians and writers from the Caribbean is evident in the phenomenon of "versioning," remixing, or rewriting previous works.[12] For example, Haitian writer, mathematician, and visual artist Frankétienne is well known for releasing palimpsestic revisions of his novels that, as Rachel Douglas observes, draw attention to their compositional process.[13] If Frankétienne's novels are palimpsestic, his poetry is recursive in another sense, featuring frequent repetition of words and sounds at the ends of successive lines. End repetition, the rhetorical figure of epistrophe, performs the writing process by returning recursively to what has already been written. It is no accident that epistrophes are so prevalent in rap that repetition of the same word at the end of successive verses is considered rhyme.[14]

In mathematics and computer science, recursion is a technique of problem-solving, in which a program is made to execute or "call" smaller instances of itself. Recursion is more efficient than iteration (the execution of a series of commands a fixed number of times), because recursive programs build on themselves. Where iteration presents information in a linear fashion, recursion unfolds as a "three-dimensional spiral," as mathematician Fernando Zalamea puts it, evoking the figure that Frankétienne (who also taught mathematics) used to describe his writing.[15] The spiral is one way to bring together the overlapping shapes of raplove that concern me here: the epistrophic (return to rap) and the apostrophic (poetic address to hip hop).

Presente em qualquer canto: Recursion and Epistrophe

São Paulo rapper Xis recorded the highly recursive rap song "Fortificando a desobediência" (Fortifying disobedience) in 2001 during a brief visit to Havana—a rare collaboration between Brazilian and Cuban rappers (Xis, MC White, Telmary Díaz, Papo Record, and 100% Original). The song has a distinctively Cuban feel, featuring a trumpet riff, which was recorded by a musician Xis saw perform at Havana's National Hotel, over a jazz progression paired with a breakbeat. Excited to document the relatively unusual phenomenon of a rap recording featuring artists from the two countries, the rappers devote their lyrics almost exclusively to describing the song being sung. Their recursiveness stems also from the fact that the lyrics were improvised or jotted down quickly, as Xis explained to me, due to time constraints and the spontaneity of the recording session.[16]

Without the time to elaborate a narrative arc, freestylers often rhyme about "what is happening, usually in present tense."[17] Freestyling, in other words, is a poetics of epistrophic return, a turning about on "lo que hay" (what there is). MC White begins his first verse with a sound check, a common gesture used to intone the beginning of a rap verse and something he has presumably just done:

> Chequeando el micrófono una vez más y sin cansarme
> Lo que traigo es mucho, no pienses que voy a pararme
> A mí me sobran las razones por las cuales expresarme
> Impartiendo en cada frase un pensamiento
> Mis ideas fructíferas, la base de conocimiento
> Donde mi procedimiento es fundamento y clave
> Haciendo influencia en ti
> Porque todo lo que digo está en el libro de mi mente
> Que es mi materia aquí para que creas en mí
> Yo como Van Van que estoy aquí, sigo así, no me caigo.[18]

> (Checking the microphone one more time, I don't get tired
> What I bring is a lot, don't think I'm gonna stop
> I have plenty of reasons to express myself
> Giving in each phrase a thought
> My fruitful ideas, the base of knowledge
> Where my method is reason and key
> Influencing you
> Because everything I say is in the book of my mind
> Which is my material here, so you believe in me
> Like Van Van, I'm here, still here, I don't stop.)

In these verses, MC White affirms what he understands to be doing by rapping and, hence, what he is doing at the moment he recites the words. Describing his rap writing process (*escritura*), White invokes a "libro de mi mente" (book of my mind). His description closely echoes nineteenth-century Cuban poet Juan Francisco Manzano, who was born enslaved. Manzano explains in his autobiography that since his owners forbade him from learning to read and write, he "siempre tenia un cuaderno de versos en la memoria y a cualquier cosa improvisaba" (always had a notebook of verses in my memory and at any occasion would improvise).[19] MC White's "libro de mi mente" similarly describes a process of elaborating new verses by returning recursively to old rhymes that have been previously conceived, recalling the compositional techniques of preliterate oral poets (see chapter 5).[20]

In the Cuban context, the notion of rhymes emerging from a mental book takes on religious overtones. White's description of his writing is not unlike the divination practices of Afro-Cuban Ifá high priests (*babalawos*), who translate palm nut arrangements into words by "drawing out" (*sacar*) divinities.[21] In a process that has been explicitly associated with writing, *babalawos* access the virtual archive of Ifá through "recursive recollection" of previous readings that "sustain multiple interpretations of the past."[22] White's lyrics similarly use recursive recollection to access "fruitful ideas" from his mental book—which is perhaps also an echo of the Judeo-Christian Bible. The "base of knowledge" is available to the rapper as if by divine revelation. Read in this key, the song's title, "Fortifying disobedience," seems to parody the ascetic emphasis on obedience in many monotheistic religions, particularly the resurgent Neo-Pentecostalism in Latin America.[23] With Afro-diasporic and Judeo-Christian overtones and a preference for the irregular rhythms characteristic of charm and incantation, raplove is imbued with a certain religiosity.[24] I return to this hypothesis in the second half of the chapter.

The third verse of "Fortificando," which feels more hastily improvised, intensifies the song's recursive structure, singing the conditions and objectives of the song being sung:

> Vengo a mil pa' la gente de Brasil
> Esto es candela, te lo digo a ti, my man, sí!
> Improvisado freestyle, me da la gana
> Canto pa' to' la gente buena de La Habana
> Hip hop cubano, esa es mi canción
> Y estas cosas, mira, salen así del corazón
> Freestyle, my man, solo para ti
> Pa' que te sientas bien bien y feliz
> Que esta es la canción que traigo ahora, sí, mi hermano
> Y estoy cantando, yo lo digo para todos los cubanos.[25]

> (I'm coming in fast for the people of Brazil
> This is hot, I'm telling you, my man, yes!
> Improvised freestyle, it's what I want
> I sing for all the good people in Havana
> Cuban hip hop, this is my song
> And these things, you see, come from the heart

Freestyle, my man, just for you
So you feel good good and happy
Because this is the song that I bring now, yes, my brother
And I'm singing, I say, for all Cubans.)

These verses rely heavily on stock phrases and contain multiple references each to Cuba (where the song was recorded) and Brazil (where the song would be released). The explicit references to freestyle invoke the always-recurring present progressive tense of song, the "continuous present tense of art."[26] Each time the song is heard, whether by a Brazilian or a Cuban, it will indeed be "the song that I bring now."

The capacity of an audio recording to transcend time and space is developed by Xis in a string of metaphorical verses:

Dizem que o mundo é um gueto
Então o rap é nosso continente
Estou presente em qualquer canto.[27]

(They say the world is a ghetto
Then rap is our continent
I'm present in any song.)

The geographical metaphors evoke the archipelagic framework commonly used to describe ghettos, appropriate here as Xis affirms this international rap collaboration.[28] The material link between Cuban and Brazilian hip hop existed only during Xis's short trip to the island and two subsequent visits to São Paulo by Papo Record, Rubén Marín, and a small group of Cuban rappers.[29] Yet the audio recording recovers this link during each playback. Sound, as Salomé Voegelin observes, creates "contingent and mobile connections that defy geographical mapping."[30] When Xis sings himself "present in any song," he calls attention to the capacity of audio recording to offer the listener apparently unmediated access to the moment of artistic creation. Where a poem is "the iterative and iterable performance of an event in the lyric present,"[31] audio playback is iterable in a material sense, recovering the acoustic presence of the event.

However, Xis's ability to be "present in any song" is bound up with his inability to be present in any particular song. As Jonathan Sterne notes, recording technology possesses its own temporalities: "the geologic decay of the medium; the linear sense of historical time and an immutable and inevitable break with the past; and a cyclic notion of time based on the fragment, the sonic element of an event."[32] Xis's emphasis on presence in and through hip hop foregrounds the rap event and brackets the geologic decay of the medium as well as the evolution of recording media and the historical development of hip hop. The invocation of rap's presence is meant to be heard outside of time, casting rap as a sort of transcendental force that can be conjured to do work. Given this, I would venture an additional hearing of "Estou presente" in which the lyric "I" points not to the rapper Xis but to the subject of the previous line, rap: "*Rap is our continent / I* [says rap] *am present in any song.*" In other words, it is rap that creates the spatialized metaphor of a shared continent that transcends geographic borders. To paraphrase Gary Tomlinson, raplove is not only a rap song about rap, but also the singing of the song being rapped about.[33]

Raplove is the process through which artists embody hip hop, rendering it recursively present in their lyrics and communities. This is the sense in which Havana-based rapper El B affirms in a verse "soy hip hop" (I am hip hop), or São Paulo–based Sabotage raps that "rap é minha alma" (rap is my soul).[34] Through this process of embodiment, the rap "I" merges with the personified voice of hip hop. In São Paulo–based Sharylaine's "Livre no mundo" (Free in the world), rapper and hip hop speak through and on behalf of each other:

> Vivo em Portugal, África, Brasil, nesse contexto
> Eu que visualizo e elaboro o texto
> Movimento a mente, o pensamento da sociedade
> Resgato origens, doo o meu corpo aos descendentes
> Me viro uma diversidade social e intervenção
> Elevo minha identidade e nacionalização
> A mim cabe a ingestão, preservação e resistência
> Nasci pluralizada em meio a muita treta
> Onde moro, os povos têm sua ciência
> Que não está dentro da Academia de Letras.[35]
>
> (I live in Portugal, Africa, Brazil, in this context
> I visualize and elaborate the text
> I move the mind, the thought of society
> I recover origins, I give my body to my descendants
> I become social diversity and intervention
> I elevate my identity and nationalization
> I can handle ingestion, perseverance, and resistance
> I was born pluralized in the midst of many hardships
> Where I live, the people have their science
> That isn't inside the Academy of Letters.)

The lyrics emphasize the elaboration of an Afro-diasporic text outside the "Academy of Letters."[36] When I spoke with her, Sharylaine encouraged hearing the song as hip hop culture expressing itself in its own words through rap.[37] Though she insisted that the song's first-person subject is "a cultura hip hop" (hip hop culture)—hence the feminine ending on *pluralizada*—I can't help but hear the feminine ending also in relation to the rapper herself. It would have been simpler for the grammatical subject to be simply "o hip hop" (a masculine term), but then she would have spoken only from the perspective of hip hop and not also from her own. When Sharylaine rhymes "Eu que visualizo e elaboro o texto," rapper and rap speak together. But why the continual need to affirm and embody this practice?

The politics of recursion in Brazilian and Caribbean rap may be elucidated further by Trinidadian steel pan music, where songs are created through the interaction between instrument and voice. While pan singers at times exercise a narrative function and provide social commentary, their voices serve primarily "as another instrument in a rhythmic and timbral 'groove.'"[38] Shannon Dudley identifies in pan an "interactive rhythmic feel" that a singer enlivens "by anticipations and delays, reinforcements and elaborations and expected accents and patterns."[39] Similar to other African and Afro-diasporic song traditions, music and language reach for each other as "independent but overlapping semiotic systems."[40] This "dynamic and unstable condition" of "language striving to become music" creates a recursive feedback loop.[41] In effect, pan musicians traditionally would demonstrate their craft by referring back to a common archive of recognizable tunes, typically played in major modes.[42]

Aldwin "Lord Kitchener" Roberts's "Pan in A minor" breaks with this structure. Responding to critics who "say to me they want a musical change in pan," Kitchener cites a minor key in the song's title.[43] The naming convention inscribes pan in the long-standing tradition in Western classical music of referring to songs by their tonic or home keys.[44] Kitchener's self-reflexive lyrics narrate his performance as if in real time. He sings himself walking onstage and boasts of the song's harmonic innovation:

> I know I had to prove to them I have the ability
> I there and then decide the minor should dominate
> If not entirely for most of the melody.[45]

The lyrics go on to describe the use of a chord progression ubiquitous in Western tonal harmony: the resolution of the dominant seventh to the minor tonic. Kitchener even goes so far as to rap a few verses, accelerating his rhythmic delivery to syncopate with the beating of the pans in three short, percussive verses strung together. How are these recursive lyrics—singing the song being sung—related to the song's harmonic innovation?

The reciprocity between music and lyrics extends throughout the African diaspora, including in Puerto Rican *bomba,* where the voice becomes "an instrument that foregrounds tonality and rhythm," and in Brazilian samba.[46] For example, Jorge Ben Jor's classic 1963 samba "Mas, que nada!" begins with an incantation, a rhythmic incipit addressed to the Afro-Brazilian *orixá* (divinity) of Obá. After invoking the power of "enchantment of words" with an address to Obá,[47] Ben animates the samba by singing (to) it: "Pois o samba está animado, o que eu quero é sambar / Esse samba que é misto de maracatú" (Because this samba's animated, what I want to do is dance / This samba that's mixed with *maracatú*).[48] The lyrics name the rhythm (samba mixed with the slow, regal *maracatú* from Brazil's Northeast), singing the samba that will animate the dance (*sambar*).

An analogous recursive unfolding of song enters the lyrics of Brazilian rappers, who consistently cite samba as a primary influence.[49] In the song "Viagem na rima" (Rhyme trip), pioneer rapper Thaíde begins by vocalizing the breakbeat a cappella ("hu há, hu-hu há") before his collaborator DJ Hum drops the drum track. Here, break and flow emerge reciprocally: first the rapper's voice establishes the rhythm, then the beat joins the voice, then the lyrics describe the practice of hip hop, then the rapper's flow returns to the break. Thaíde's chorus affirms:

> A qualquer dia, qualquer hora, em qualquer lugar
> H-i-p-h-o-p, não tem como parar
> Hu há, hu-hu há.[50]
>
> (Any day, any time, any place
> H-i-p-h-o-p, there's no way to stop it
> Hu há, hu-hu há.)

The verses reassert hip hop's ability to transcend space and time, going so far as to name the practice, literally spelling it out. By calling out the letters of *h-i-p-h-o-p* in sync with the break—singing to the break and along with it—Thaíde ensures hip hop's continuation. It is through his epistrophic return to the breakbeat ("hu há, hu-hu há") that he makes hip hop present "any day, any time, any place." Where the yearnings of the previous chapter point outward toward rap's capacity to produce material effects, here, the poetic work of raplove resides in the desire to be present with rap, to affirm and inhabit the temporality of the rap song from within its acoustic presence.

Una frase que me cause escalofrío: Ars Poetica

When I first traveled to Cuba in 2009, the leaders of the Havana rap scene were Aldo (Al2 El Aldeano) and El B, cofounders of Los Aldeanos. That year, Aldo and frequent collaborator Silvito "El Libre" circulated the song "Manual para hacer una canción" (Manual for how to make a song) on MP3 flash drives. Aldo's lyrics serve as both explanation and exemplification of his capacity to rap:

> Solo necesito odio, tinta, melancolía
> Una historia ajena o personal cual transformar en poesía
> Mirar de manera fría el primer renglón vacío
> Hasta que nazca una frase que me cause escalofrío
> Otro desafío total: colocar las palabras en su lugar
> No es tan fácil rimar, eso se adquiere con el tiempo
> . . . .
> Esto se estudia, lleva dedicación
> Ahora me toca poner algo que termine en "ón"
> Pero si termino en "ón" y nada tiene sentido
> Mejor canto reguetón con cha-cha-chá mal concebido
> Para mí es muy divertido llevar lo vivido al papel.[51]

> (All I need is hate, ink, melancholy
> A story, someone else's or mine, to transform into poetry
> Looking coldly at the first line
> Until a phrase is born that makes me shiver
> Another great challenge: putting the words in their place
> It's not so easy to rhyme, it's learned with time
> . . . .
> This is something that's studied, it requires dedication
> Now I have to come up with something that ends with "ion"
> But if I finish with "ion" and it doesn't make any sense
> It'd be better to sing reggaeton with poorly developed cha-cha-chá
> For me, it's fun to put lived experience to paper.)

The initial verses describe the spontaneous birth ("que nazca") of the perfect verse in an empty line (*renglón vacío*), whose correct execution generates goosebumps (*escalofrío*) when heard by the listener. The closing sequence plays with anticipation and resolution. A metapoetic verse ("Now I have to come up with something that ends with 'ion'") delays the resolution of *dedicación,* exposing the disjunction that rhyme opens between sound and sense.[52] The delay allows the rapper to poke fun at rival genre reggaeton, asserting that the use of poorly conceived rhymes betrays the art of rap. Contrary to reggaeton, rap involves transforming lived experience ("lo vivido") into writing ("al papel").

The referentiality exhibited by "Manual para hacer una canción"—the capacity of words to point to themselves—was for Russian formalist Roman Jakobson the "poetic function" of language.[53] Taking Aldo and Silvito at their word that rapping is a learned skill ("se estudia"), which poetic traditions merit study? To what degree does the recursion characteristic of raplove sample the centuries-old tradition in Western lyric known as ars poetica, that is, self-reflexive poems concerned with the meaning and function of poetry? Written in dactylic hexameter around 19 BCE, Horace's *Ars Poetica* treatise elaborates a writing manual for novice poets covering appropriate uses of meter, diction, the pairing of form and content, and decorum. Horace instructs the reader that a poet must "just now say what ought just now to be said, put off most of his thoughts, and waive them for the present."[54] It is reasonable to assume, given that the treatise is written in verse and its author a poet, that Horace believes he, himself, is saying what ought to be said at the precise moment when it ought to be said. (This certainly seems to be the case for Aldo and Silvito when they describe the execution of their goosebump-inducing rhymes.) But for this to be true, the composition and the reception of the poem would have to be coterminous. Horace's emphasis on the present—on the presence of the poem—is curious given that *Ars Poetica* was an epistolary, written document. How can what the poet has said in the past (or, in this case, written) correspond to "what ought just now to be said"? Only during oral recitation or "dictation" can the poet and the poem inhabit the same time and space.[55] Yet Horace's recursive poem-treatise seems capable of folding time and space, re-rendering what the poet has said as what the poet can just now say. This is perhaps where ars poetica meets MC White's spontaneous writing from a mental book of rhymes.

The most famous Anglophone ars poetica is probably Alexander Pope's "Essay on Criticism" (1711). The "Essay" instructs by performing what it describes, first parodying bad poetry:

> But most by numbers judge a Poet's song,
> And smooth or rough, with them, is right or wrong:
> ....
> These equal syllables alone require,
> Tho' oft the Ear the open Vowels tire;
> While expletives their feeble aid do join;
> And ten low words oft creep in one dull line.[56]

Judging the first line numerically, that is, in terms of the metric rules governing iambic pentameter, confirms that it consists of five metrically perfect iambs. Pope's parody of form demonstrates that metric perfection does not suffice for good poetry; it is precisely the irregular rhythms in words that create "the most valued effects of meter."[57] A few lines later, he illustrates the way repeated assonance produces a cumbersome effect. He then exemplifies how ten monosyllabic words can render a verse metrically sound but aesthetically reprehensible.[58] Subsequent rhyming couplets demonstrate how what Pope calls "expected rhymes" lull a reader to sleep. For Pope, as Jonathan Culler puts it, "to avoid being mere bauble, rhyme should be thematically productive, suggesting an unexpected connection between the meanings of the two words that rhyme."[59]

Pope's "Essay" proceeds to exemplify good poetry in a gesture of boasting so familiar in rap that one wonders whether Pope might have tried his hand in a freestyle battle had he been born three hundred years later:

> True ease in writing comes from art, not chance,
> As those move easiest who have learn'd to dance.
> 'Tis not enough no harshness gives offence,
> The sound must seem an Echo to the sense.
> Soft is the strain when Zephyr gently blows,
> And the smooth stream in smoother numbers flows;
> But when loud surges lash the sounding shore,
> The hoarse, rough verse should like the torrent roar.[60]

These verses perform the way a stream is rendered through rounded vowels and repeated soft, unvoiced consonants, broken up by "loud surges" that "lash" against it: unrounded front vowels and the liquid consonant *l*. The "rough verse" of the torrent is not only fragmented by a comma but indeed "roars" with assonance on the open vowel *o*. The performative lines display a "curious recursion" between "material sound and referential meaning," which is expressed in Pope's famous aphorism "sound must seem an Echo to the sense."[61] The rap song "Manual para hacer una canción" similarly draws the listener's attention to the mutual echoes between sound and sense. Extending the analogy, the rap verse "No es tan fácil rimar, eso se adquiere con el tiempo" almost becomes a sample of Pope's "True ease in writing comes from art, not chance."

The structure of negative/positive ars poetica surfaces also in the lyrics of São Paulo–based Projota, among the best-known rappers in Brazil and featured in the theme song to the 2016 Olympics held in Rio de Janeiro. In a pair of self-reflexive verses, Projota recalls Pope's negative examples: "Tic-tac, tic-tac, onomatopeia / Aqui é clic clac, piripaque, é poucas ideia" (Tic-tac, tic-tac onomatopoeia / Here it's click clack, piripack, not many ideas).[62] Performing and naming onomatopoeia, the rapper disavows its use when the words lack "ideas." Excessively favoring sound over sense, the lyrics suggest, limits the capacity for rap to act. Projota then intensifies his flow to explain in carefully declaimed verses why he raps: "Eu canto porque ainda tenho muito pra falar" (I sing because I still have much to say). Heard alongside adjacent lyrics, this verse also demonstrates the way lines that vary in syllabic length and number of stressed syllables can be made to fit with the break.

Projota's gesture of self-affirmation performs the ubiquitous trope in US rap and Afro-diasporic signifying of boasting.[63] Self-affirmation is so common in rap music that scholars such as Robin D. G. Kelley and H. Samy Alim suggest that boasting of one's ability to "roc the mic" is among the most common subjects of a rap song.[64] Moreover, in all my conversations with artists in Cuba, Brazil, and Haiti, rappers have demonstrated acute familiarity with the history and stylistic features of US rap as a Black cultural practice; no one has mentioned Horace or Pope. Is boasting in Afro-diasporic signifying and European ars poetica connected only by analogy? Where do the poetics of these traditions diverge? Which genealogy would artists prefer? Given the self-reflexive lyrics and frequent references to writing by rappers in these countries, the appositionality or refusal to take a position that I described in the introduction likely applies here.

Tankou m ap rap, m ap bat kata: Apostrophe and Prayer

For some artists, rapping about rap takes on a greater expediency than ars poetica. Among the most popular and commercially successful Haitian rappers of the 2010s, Wendyyy deploys familiar tropes from US rap (boasting, ostentation, bass-heavy trap beats), which he mixes with Latin pop and Haitian *konpa* music. Self-referential lyrics from his album *King rete king* (The king remains the king) elaborate overlapping theories of value. One metric for value is the cultural capital generated by a hit song: "M fè valè m vle . . . Talan m kraze baryè, lè m vle m fè yon hit" (I show the value that I want . . . My talent breaks barriers: when I want to, I release a hit).⁶⁵ The most popular track on *King rete king,* "M'aprann," a family-friendly konpa pop song about losing a lover, lives up to Wendyyy's boasting, having registered more than ten million views on YouTube within just two years of its release.

The album's self-reflexive opening track justifies the production of commercial value in a letter to prospective listeners entitled in French "À qui veut l'entendre" (To whom may wish to listen). The melodic line features piano and strings and avoids the Latin pop sounds and US trap beats audible elsewhere on the album. It sounds like a "conscious" rap song, and the subject of the letter is indeed *rap konsyans* (conscious rap): "Se mwen k pou fè chanjman an oubyen se ou? Hein? Li menm oubyen se nou? . . . M p ap gaspiye tan m albòm mwen an p ap gen rap konsyans" (Is it I who will make the change or is it you? Huh? Is it them, or is it us? . . . I'm not wasting my time on my album to have any conscious rap).⁶⁶ Recalling the truism "time is money," Wendyyy pokes fun at the futility of conscious rap. The lyrics suggest that it is not rap but people that must change the world. If rap's primary value lies in producing capital (exchange-value rather than use-value), there is no time for rap konsyans (which presumably carries less commercial appeal).

The album's final track, "Ayibobo" (a ritual cry in Vodou), boasts only a fraction of the YouTube views of "M'aprann," but its theory of value partially contradicts the disavowal of rap konsyans in the opening track: "M vin raplè w valè w . . . Premye pèp nwa k libere, wi se sa k idantite w" (I've come to remind you of your value . . . First free Black people, yes that's what identifies you).⁶⁷ Here value takes on the meaning of self-worth, even valor, as Wendyyy returns to the tropes of Haiti's revolutionary history and Black liberatory struggle highlighted in chapter 1. The video begins with a television screen of Haitian protest. As iconic images of Wendyyy painted with the blue and red of the Haitian flag are spliced together with scenes of raised Black Power fists and street protest, the message becomes clear: rap kreyòl speaks to and for the Haitian people through hemispheric modalities of Blackness. Thus in addition to the rapper's professed talent in flow and ability to produce a hit song, Wendyyy measures his value through the community-forging, Vodou-inflected potential of Black consciousness-raising.

Vodou rhythms and references have existed in rap kreyòl at least since Port-au-Prince-based rapper 35 Zile codified the genre of Vodou rap in the

Vèvè tracing from a Vodou drum baptism ceremony in Port-au-Prince, July 4, 2017. (Photo by author)

early 2010s. In Haitian Vodou, drumming and singing serve to awaken and bring down lwa (divinities or spirits).[68] A popular Vodou song narrates how the process of "m ap chante pou lwa yo" (I'm singing to the lwa) shifts to "gwo lwa yo reklame mwen" (my great lwa have claimed me).[69] The progressive aspect marked by "m ap chante" ("I'm singing") captures the ongoing present tense of song and ritual. Once the lwa descends, the distinction between subject and object collapses: the singer no longer sings to the lwa, but the lwa sings through the singer. Not unlike Xis's "presente em qualquer canto," the lyrics of this Vodou song affirm the presence of the lwa in the singer by singing the song being sung.

In her song "Vèvè lokal," Haitian American rapper Kanis links a Vodou singer's summoning of the lwa to a rapper's invocation of hip hop. The title refers to the sacred *vèvè* designs traced in cornmeal on the ground by Vodou *oungan* or *mambo* priests—maps designed to guide the lwa's descent. The music video syncretizes scenes of Kanis in a baseball cap (signifying hip hop culture) with visuals of elaborate Carnival masks (signifying Haitianness). Near the beginning, Kanis poses with a carved tree (considered sacred in Vodou ceremony).[70] In a nod to Haiti's musical heritage, the chorus features vocals from Lolo of the well-known *rasin* (roots) band Boukman Eksperyans, the breakbeat giving way to a rasin feel.

Like Wendyyy, Kanis begins the song with an affirmation of Haitian Black Power, an expression of the local-global racial politics that circulate with hip hop: "M reprezante Ayiti pye palmi libète pou pèp nwa" (I represent Haiti, at the foot of a palm tree, liberty for Black people).[71] Later, she samples a verse from a well-known Vodou song, "gen granmoun nan lakou" (there are wise people in the courtyard).[72] The final verses call down a lwa:

> Met tanbou rasin pou lokal e m fè bokal rap santi Ginen
> Mwen bay defi lè m wè m anvi pran yo
> M se sèl fanm nan mitan yo.
> M se zwazo k ap fredone rap ak melodi
> . . . .
> M ba w sekrè ki gen nan vodou
> Lè m rele lwa pou w pa tonbe kriz
> Rap mwen bese zam ki brake, ouvè pòt ki take
> Pipo Beat ap trase vèvè
> Ou ap bezwen rap Niska pou w plake.[73]

> (Root down the drum, I'll make the rap urn feel the spirit of Africa
> I challenge when I see I need to take them
> I'm the only woman among them
> I'm a bird who hums rap with melody.
> . . . .
> I'll give you Vodou secrets
> When I call the lwa so you don't have a seizure
> My rap lowers pointed guns, opens bolted doors
> Pipo Beat is drawing the vèvè
> You need Niska's rap for you to stick.)

Rapping herself a *mambo* (Vodou priestess), Kanis emphasizes that she is "the only woman among them."[74] The metaphor of the bird (*zwazo*) further emphasizes her femininity and the capacity of her voice to ascend, "humming rap with melody," to call down (*rele*) the lwa. Then she reveals a Vodou secret: her rap takes the place of the lwa, making the listener *santi Ginen,* or feel the spirit of Africa.[75] As the song's title suggests, the beat to which she sings (a hip hop breakbeat mixed with Vodou *kata* drumming) becomes the vèvè: a sonic map guiding her rap-cum-lwa to mount the listener.[76]

Explicit links between hip hop and religious worship are widespread in Brazil, Cuba, and Haiti. Gospel rap is popular in Brazil's Northeast, and although less prominent, Christian rap groups exist in Cuba.[77] Cornel West observes that "Black rap music recovers and revises elements of black rhetorical styles—some from black preaching."[78] More recent studies of the role of religion in hip hop highlight the influence of oratory, "soul rap," Christian imagery, and figures of salvation, resurrection, and apocalypse.[79] Also common are references to Five Percenter theology of the Nation of Islam.[80] One scholar calls hip hop a practice of "black liberation theology."[81] In a eulogy to Los Angeles rapper Tupac Shakur on the day of his murder, Baptist pastor Reverend Willie Wilson is said to have affirmed that "hip-hop artists in many instances are the preachers of their generation, preaching a message which, too often, those who have been given the charge to preach prophetic words to the people have not given."[82] For Mark Lewis Taylor, rap is a "spiritual practice" even when lyrics do not explicitly address religious themes, due to its "capacity for conjuring festivals of release and emancipation."[83] Furthermore, the fact that one of hip hop's primary influences was soul music, grounded in gospel traditions of the Black church, suggests that formal resonances between rap and prayer are not only analogical but also genealogical.[84] A latent religiosity undergirds raplove.[85]

In Brazil, where more than 90 percent of the population identifies as religious, hip hop not only takes on characteristics of religion but can become one.[86] For Criolo, "Pra cada rap escrito, uma alma que se salva" (For every written rap, there's a soul that's saved).[87] For Filosofia de Rua, "É o hip hop, minha religião, mantém os meus pés no chão . . . Salvando vidas, a rima é minha oração" (This is hip hop, my religion, keeping my feet on the ground . . . Saving lives, rhyme is my prayer).[88] By offering up rap as a form of salvation, hip hop becomes the form, the content, and the medium. The final section turns to prayer-like apostrophes to hip hop, which I call raplove songs.

Gracias hip hop: Raplove Songs

Havana group Hermanos de Causa released the raplove song "Gracias Hip Hop" (Thank you hip hop) in 2010 during a polemical moment for Cuban rap spearheaded by the antiestablishment discourse of Los Aldeanos. Running counter to the vitriolic critique of the present that characterized many rap songs of the time, "Gracias Hip Hop" looks backward. The song samples the major harmonic progression I–V–vi–IV, widely used in popular music and, appropriately, the changes for the 1960 Ben King tune "Stand by Me." A keyboard repeats an uplifting melodic line in a major key over the "Stand by Me" changes. Professing to carry hip hop within him, Soandres intones a love letter to the practice:

> Gracias hip hop por entenderme
> Los ojos abrirme y permitirme ser
> Un personaje modesto de textos aparte
> Que hoy se nos enorgullece llevarte bajo la piel
> . . . .
> Siempre te agradeceré
> Por estar conmigo cuando te necesité
> Mi fe, la que fue, es y siempre será
> Hip hop, mi áster luz en la oscuridad
> Es mucho más que música
> Es mi libertad, mi credo, mi religión, también mi necesidad
> Mi plan A, mi única bala, mi oportunidad
> Mi última bengala en tierra de nunca jamás
> Mis ganas de rebobinar el tiempo atrás
> Y verme en las mejores épocas del rap
> Gracias hip hop.[89]

> (Thank you, hip hop for understanding me
> For opening my eyes and letting me be
> A modest person with special texts
> Today it makes us proud to carry you under our skin
> . . . .
> I'll always be grateful to you
> For being with me when I needed you
> My faith, what was, is, and always will be
> Hip hop, my aster light in the darkness
> It's much more than music
> It's my freedom, my creed, my religion, also my necessity
> My plan A, my only bullet, my opportunity
> My last flare in never-never land
> My desire to turn back time
> And see myself in the best times of rap
> Thank you, hip hop.)

The poetic address to hip hop takes on religious overtones through a series of abstract epithets commonly attributed to divinity: necessity, light, opportunity, force, and even religion itself. These metaphors are not insignificant given the government's repression of religions, particularly Afro-Cuban religions, prior to liberalizing them in 1991.[90] The lyrics approximate the structure of prayer insofar as they apostrophize or invoke an apparently absent entity (hip hop, in the case of the raplove song; a divinity, in the case of prayer).[91]

In lyric poetry, apostrophes are invocations of an absent power or force. While a real or imagined lover is the most common implied addressee in Western lyric, poets have apostrophized everything and anything: from the sacred to the mundane, from time to the tomato, as Pablo Neruda playfully demonstrated.[92] Such gestures, Culler suggests, perform a certain magic: "to apostrophize is to will a state of affairs, to attempt to bring it into being by asking inanimate objects to bend themselves to your desire. . . . The key is not passionate intensity, but rather the ritual invocation of elements of the universe, the attempt, even, to evoke the possibility of a magical transformation."[93] Deriving from the power of the mythical Orpheus, who used his song and lyre to influence nature and even conquer death, lyric poems "are meant to make things happen, to cause action," to control events "by manipulation of the hidden forces of nature."[94] Magicians, notes Andrew Welsh quoting Aldous Huxley, "are always poets."[95] The magic of apostrophe, however, creates a curious redundancy: apostrophic poems "often tell the addressee something the addressee presumably already knows."[96] Similarly, the rap song that addresses rap (or hip hop) *is*, in a sense, the thing to which it is addressed. Raplove songs become hip hop's quasi-religious love affair with itself.

Here, in the recursive magic of redundancy, raplove approaches what musicologist Steven Feld calls "acoustemology," a mode of knowing entangled with the embodied experience of sound.[97] Feld develops the concept out of fieldwork with Kaluli singers of the Great Papuan Plateau rainforests. Listening to his recording of a woman named Ulahi singing with and to a creek, Feld observes: "Her voice develops a pulsing pattern that densely flows with the sounds of the creek where she sits, and her songs develop different place paths, including one that sings a long succession of places connected to the creek she is singing in. On these selections the performative flow of singing with water and the musicality of singing like water connect deeply to the emplacing poetry of singing about water. Singing about water, with water, and imagining song as water and vocal . . . flow—here the poetry of place meets the sensuality of soundscape and the singing voice."[98] The entanglement of the song's subject and object brings together imitation or mimesis (singing like and about water) with accompaniment or metonymy (singing with water). The singer and the "the creek she is singing in" are engaged in a relationship that might be called recursively metonymic: Ulahi becomes part of the creek of which and to which she is singing. Ulahi sings to the creek, with the creek, accompanied by the creek. She sings from inside the creek and the creek resonates inside her.

Acoustemology provides a model for bringing together the two shapes of raplove: epistrophic return and apostrophic self-address. Both are present in Havana-based rapper Papá Humbertico's raplove song "5,11,83, Hip Hop," which deploys many of the same metaphors heard in "Gracias Hip Hop" to elaborate a series of personal definitions of the practice. Evocative of ars poetica, Humbertico alternates between blocks of positive statements of the form "hip hop is . . ." and negative statements of the form "hip hop isn't . . ." The chorus consists of the words "hip hop" repeated five times and the lyrics proceed as follows:

> Hip hop es valor, rebeldía y cimarronaje
> Hip hop es amor, poesía, mensaje
> Hip hop es ese tatuaje que va marcando mi vida
> Hip hop mi solución, mi escape, mi salida
> Hip hop sanó mis heridas, en la oscuridad fue mi luz
> Hip hop mi religión, mi Dios, mi Jesús.[99]
>
> (Hip hop is value, rebellion and marronage
> Hip hop is love, poetry, message
> Hip hop is that tattoo that's marking my life
> Hip hop my solution, my escape, my way out
> Hip hop cured my wounds, in the darkness it was my light
> Hip hop my religion, my God, my Jesus.)

Citing *cimarronaje* (marronage, or community resistance to slavery), Humbertico presents hip hop as the continued struggle of Afro-descendent peoples. While most verses use the linking verb *is* ("hip hop es . . ."), some omit the verb and become quasi-apostrophes to the practice. The anaphoric insistence on the word "hip hop" creates a chant-like rhythm that supports the religious imagery of the lyrics. In addition to religion, Humbertico grounds his rap in love and rebellion, an urgency clarified by Malcoms Junco Duffay: "We never did it to make money or become famous, or to be heard on the radio or on TV, or to be a part of any commercial institution. We did it for *bomba*, intuition, desire, necessity, entertainment, and hobby. Nor was it a passing fashion, as it was for some others. We weren't playing around; it was our life, our passion."[100] Where Humbertico's lyrics remain emphatically in present tense, Malcoms's invocation of the past introduces a note of nostalgia in the centripetal deixis of raplove. In contrast to the presentism of raplove and the future-oriented yearnings of the previous chapter, this nostalgia echoes Soandres's desire to "rebobinar el tiempo atrás" (turn back time) and revisit the mythologized "mejores épocas del rap" (best times of rap).[101]

Nostalgia is an ubiquitous trope in rap lyrics.[102] Calls of "hip hop is dead" have resounded since at least Nas's 2006 album by that name.[103] Every successive generation of artists lamented the loss of the "old school," wielding nostalgia as "an authenticating device" vis-à-vis "the commodification and commercialization that comes along with mainstream appeal [and] threatens notions of community and authenticity."[104] In *The Future of Nostalgia*, Svetlana Boym outlines two modes of nostalgia: restorative nostalgia, which "stresses *nostos* and attempts a transhistorical reconstruction of the lost home," and reflexive nostalgia, which "thrives in *algia*, the longing itself, and delays the homecoming—wistfully, ironically, desperately."[105] Perhaps the return inherent in the epistrophic shape of raplove is related to the reconstruction of something lost (what hip hop supposedly was), while the redundancy of hip hop's apostrophic self-address evinces a sense of longing associated with what hip hop is ("lo que hay"). Where, then, does the nostalgia sustaining raplove meet the yearnings of the previous chapter?

Performed by Port-au-Prince-based rapper Blaze One, the verses in the song "M ap rap" (I'm rapping) closely resemble the iterative structure of Humbertico's "5,11,83, Hip Hop." The lyrics are built around the anaphora "I'm rapping . . ." and offer a personal manifesto of why the rapper raps. While "M ap rap" does without explicit apostrophe to hip hop, it is nonetheless an implied raplove song: "M ap rap paske se avec sèl zam sa m ka defann mwen . . . M ap rap paske se mwen ki still lidè revolisyon an" (I'm rapping because it's only with this weapon that I can defend myself . . . I'm rapping because I'm still the leader of the revolution).[106] Despite their self-reflexivity, these verses begin to point at something outside the rap song—to continued struggle and revolution—recovering a sense of futurity generally absent in the ongoing present tense of raplove. Similar to when Soandres rhymes that hip hop "es mucho más que música" (is much more than music), here raplove turns out to be less a future of nostalgia and more a nostalgia for the future. For all its inward-pointing deixis, the raplove song yearns to escape its bounds. Nostalgia becomes a sort of asymptotic limit of raplove, the place where its epistrophic turning about and apostrophic redundancy approach the world-making impulse of yearning.

Yearning and raplove converge in the song "Veias abertas" (Open veins) by São Paulo–based rapper Brisa de la Cordillera. The title alludes to Eduardo Galeano's 1971 book *Las venas abiertas de América Latina* (Open Veins of Latin America), a history-from-below of Latin America and a critique of US imperialism. In addition to the Galeano allusion, Brisa samples US rap lyrics, South American protest music, and activist poetry. Her extensive intertextuality performs what rap *can* do while reflecting on what it *should* do:

> A rima não para, é o único que sara
> Terapia, como ouvir a Violeta Parra
> Gracias a la vida que me ha dado tanto
> Si se calla la vida, se calla el cantor
> Seguimos escrevendo sobre os fatos
> Sem cuspir no prato
> Aprendi com Nas de 94
> Que nunca se sabe quando iremos
> Então, é por isso que prosseguiremos
> No estúdio que sobrevivemos visam ampla meta.[107]

> (The rhyme doesn't stop, it's the only thing that heals
> Therapy, like listening to Violeta Parra
> Thank you to life that's given me so much
> If life becomes quiet, the singer will be quiet
> We keep writing about the facts
> Without spitting on the plate
> I learned with Nas in '94
> That we never know when we're gonna go
> So that's why we'll carry on
> In the studio we survive, reach for big dreams.)

The lyrics begin with the affirmation that the rhyme "won't stop," sampled from Grandmaster Flash and the Furious Five's 1979 single "Superappin." The next verses sample South American *nueva canción* (new song) protest music of the 1960s and 1970s, inscribing rap within this tradition. Born in Chile, Brisa cites Chilean singer Violeta Parra (whom she listened to as a child), sampling the refrain of Parra's most famous song: "Gracias a la vida que me ha dado tanto" (Thank you to life that's given me so much).[108] The following verse rewrites Argentine folk singer Horacio

Guarany's verse "Si se calla el cantor, se calla la vida" (If the singer becomes quiet, life becomes quiet).[109] While Guarany's lyrics maintain an optimism that life cannot be quieted as long as the singer sings, Brisa's chiasmus expresses pessimism that the end of life also entails the end of song. A few verses later, Brisa returns to the eschatological motif, sampling New York rapper Nas's verse "you never know when you're gonna go."[110] In Brisa's voice, Nas's redemptive escapism, "nunca se sabe quando iremos," is rechanneled as a reason to carry on ("que prosseguiremos").

In effect, "Veias abertas" affirms the urgency for rappers to continue "writing about the facts." In light of a barrage of "fake news" that aided in the impeachment of President Dilma Rousseff and the 2018 election of far-right former military officer Jair Bolsonaro, the facts were of grave concern to many Brazilians. Brisa's raplove speaks to this urgency: "Rap ainda é fala de quem bota a cara contra quem censura" (rap is still the speech of those who struggle against those who censor).[111] Rather than opting for the more syntactically obvious statement, that rap is the speech of those who still struggle, the verse asserts that rap can *still* voice the efforts of those who struggle. *Still* is a nostalgic adverb. What could still be true was perhaps once more so. It brings to mind the end of a love song by Cuban singer-songwriter Erick Sánchez: "todavía la quiero, todavía la quiero, todavía te quiero" (I still love her, I still love her, I still love you).[112]

"Veias abertas" closes by sampling an audio recording of the poem "Apelo" by Brazilian human rights activist Débora Maria da Silva: "E vocês, vão me ajudar a erguer esses mortos? Vão me ajudar a erguer esses túmulos? Não deixe que meu grito se transforme numa palavra muda a ecoar pela paisagem" (And you, are you going to help me raise the dead? Are you going to help me raise these graves? Don't let my cry turn into a mute word that echoes in the landscape).[113] With the sample of Maria da Silva, Brisa merges the struggles of Brazilian activists against police violence with her own struggle for the past and future of hip hop. Without the commitment of her listener, her *grito*—the cry of the rap song—is transformed into mute words. Mixing nostalgia for hip hop's bygone years with yearning for its still-unfulfilled communitarian potential, Brisa's raplove is indeed a principle of love, "of vulnerability and accountability, of solidarity and transformation."[114]

Finally, the poetic work of raplove and yearning is also prophetic because, as Moten asserts in a different context, it "tells the brutal truth, ... has the capacity to see the absolute brutality of the already-existing and to point it out and to tell that truth, but also to see the other way, to see what it could be."[115] If raplove tends toward the "already-existing" (or "lo que hay"), yearning points at "what ... could be." But to express raplove is to believe in the force of rap yearning, and conversely, to yearn through rap requires the belief—even the faith—in the force of raplove. Thus rather than two opposing vectors, the topology of yearning and raplove is better represented as a Möbius strip or twisted cylinder, a shape that appears to have two sides but only has one.[116] Raplove and yearning are perhaps another name for the poetics of break and flow: the repetition or return of a common set of rhythmic and discursive features against the continual reinvention of context through lyrical innovation. These dualistic forces meet, in Brisa's voice, in the ongoing work of community writing: "O que não tem no livro, tem na comuna inteira" (What isn't in the book, is in the whole community).[117] The transformative solidarity of hip hop poetics in the Americas has much to teach us about the power of words to build communities and other worlds.

3 Uprooting

"Qué importa si sonamos americano hermano"

PORT-AU-PRINCE RESIDENTS began breakdancing and rapping over funk, reggae, and *ragga* beats during a period of violent political upheaval known as dechoukaj (uprooting) that followed the popular overthrow of the Duvalier dictatorship in 1986.[1] A term that evokes the uprooting of a plant, dechoukaj is an apt metaphor for describing the sense of instability but also community cultivation experienced by early rappers in Port-au-Prince. Haitian dechoukaj perhaps shares contextually little with hip hop's mythologized origins a decade earlier in the South Bronx of New York City, where residents were infamously uprooted by Robert Moses's bulldozing of tenement housing.[2] But uprootedness surfaces as a recurrent trope in hip hop across the Americas, as rappers link their material realities not only to those of African American communities but also to Atlantic slavery, which, in Édouard Glissant's terms, entailed violent uprooting (*déracinement*) and the necessity of finding new roots.[3] Through the common experience of uprootedness, artists have found in hip hop new roots that allow them to defy national borders, forge connections between neighborhood communities, and remap their relationship to place.

In chapters 1 and 2, I suggested that rap lyrics carry out poetic work through their prophetic deixis: by pointing inward at what is ("es lo que hay") and outward at what could be ("nan lòt dimansyon"). The yearning for rap to act in the world and for the future of hip hop, I concluded, rests on a recursive return to the source, to raplove for hip hop's past. Here, I turn to that past, to the way rappers in Cuba, Brazil, and Haiti received and represented this practice, and to the historically grounded work of community formation. The imagined and real communities created through rap demand emphasis during an era of resurgent nationalisms around the nostalgic abstraction of idealized pasts.[4] By uprooting and embracing a cultural practice received as African American, rappers in the Americas denationalized hip hop.[5] Their work not only "opens up new avenues of inquiry into the history of U.S. imperialism,"[6] but reconfigures notions of national culture and the place of Afro-diasporic culture within it.

Awad Ibrahim writes that global expressions of hip hop comprise a common language (Hip Hop Nation Language) and sense of belonging that "pays homage to the African American contribution to hip hop but also challenges its American-centricity."[7] This became clear to me in August 2014 when I returned to my apartment from a recording collaboration with Bárbaro "El Urbano" in the neighborhood of Marianao. I began listening to an album that the Havana-based rapper had shared with me on a USB flash drive and encountered the following verse in the middle of the album's middle track: "¿qué importa si sonamos americano hermano?" (what does it matter if we sound American, brother?).[8] Featuring four accented beats, the verse's rhythmic structure and use of assonance and internal rhyme are evocative of US rap.[9] The musical *background* (the English word Cuban hip hop artists use to refer to instrumentals) features a synthesized chromatic melody over a trap-inspired breakbeat.[10] The most prominent accent falls on the penultimate syllable of *importa,* pronounced with a truncated *r* (almost an *l*) characteristic of Cuban Spanish, emphasizing the idea of import yet also betraying an unmistakably Cuban sound in Bárbaro's flow. Given the global prestige of Cuban music, why would a Cuban artist wish to sound American?

Known internationally as "the island of music,"[11] Cuba reached global ears in the 1990s with US guitarist Ry Cooder's Grammy-winning album *Buena Vista Social Club* and Wim Wenders's Academy Award–nominated documentary of Cooder's collaboration with aging Cuban son musicians. In contrast to the international acclaim for *Buena Vista Social Club,* some Cuban intellectuals decried Wenders's nostalgic representation of ruins in Havana and Cooder's lack of engagement with Cuban musical preferences of the period (notably timba, as detailed in chapter 1, but also rap and reggaeton).[12] Bárbaro's provocation "qué importa si sonamos americano hermano" perhaps responds obstinately to the foreign demand for Cuban-sounding music.

More crucially, sounding American means sounding *African* American and thus invokes a long-standing entanglement in Cuba between music and race. No music was more important in this respect than Cuban son (the genre featured in *Buena Vista Social Club*). A Black street genre in the early twentieth century, son was among the first working-class musics in

Bárbaro "El Urbano" performing at the 2014 Cuban Hip Hop Symposium, La Madriguera, Central Havana, August 16, 2014. (Photo by author, used with permission)

Cuba to reach the radio, becoming an object of mass commercialization during the Afrocubanismo cultural movement (1920s to 1940s).[13] Son's musical construction—a hybrid of European-derived poetic forms such as the *décima* and improvisatory *montuno* sections resembling West African music—made it well-suited to symbolize Cuba's mix of races (*mestizaje*).[14]

The concept of mestizaje has been mobilized throughout Latin America to serve varying political and social aims, from notions of cultural exceptionalism (as in José Vasconcelos's *The Cosmic Race* and Fernando Ortiz's *Cuban Counterpoint*), to post-racial colorblindness (as in José Martí's "My Race"), to discourses of whitening (as in the ideas of Antonio Pedreira and Domingo Faustino Sarmiento).[15] Conversely, Afro-diasporic thinkers have reinterpreted mestizaje to signify cultural blackening. When son was reaching national attention in the early 1930s, for example, Afro-Cuban poet Nicolás Guillén famously wrote in the prologue to one of his collections of son-inspired poetry that "the spirit of Cuba is mixed. And from the spirit to the skin the definite color will come to us. Someday, people will say: 'Cuban color.'"[16] While Guillén was revered during the period following the Revolution of 1959, racial policies reverted to a

José Martí–inspired notion of post-racial harmony; racism came to be associated with US imperialism and backwardness, a "national shame" in a socialist country.[17] As this chapter will demonstrate, verses like "qué importa si sonamos americano hermano" challenge official discourses of colorblindness.

Finally, sounding American defies the Cuban Revolution's censorship of foreign musics, a policy that derives not only from Cold War protectionism but also dates to early-twentieth-century fears of foreign influence.[18] The boom of Cuban son followed a series of US military occupations of Cuba and coincided with a burgeoning "circum-Caribbean/transatlantic black press" and trans-Caribbean music-making, with Havana and Harlem figuring as standard stops on the performance circuit.[19] Although son was integral to this process, the jazz age sparked an "anxiety of Americanization," as Jason Borge demonstrates.[20] In this context, Cuban musicologist Alejo Carpentier defended Cuban music as "resistant to all foreign influences that . . . might have been able to dislodge it from its own place."[21] Crucial to understanding the subsequent reception of hip hop, these early-twentieth-century anxieties surrounding foreign cultural contamination extended across Latin America and the Caribbean, including to Haiti and Brazil.

Under the guise of protecting the lives of foreign civilians and upholding democracy, the United States military occupied Haiti between 1915 and 1934, during which time marines brought with them international records and introduced Port-au-Prince residents to jazz.[22] For some, the music brought by US occupiers represented a threat to traditional Haitian music, in particular the *mereng*.[23] One advocate of Haitian music was ethnographer and diplomat Jean Price-Mars, educated in Paris and inspired by primitivist trends of the European avant-garde, who had returned to Haiti in 1902 to carry out ethnographic fieldwork in the countryside.[24] Despite the dangers, Price-Mars continued his research throughout the US occupation.[25] In a series of lectures, he accused Haitian elites of conspiring with US occupiers and betraying their moral obligation to the nation.[26] He encouraged the recovery of Haiti's national identity through a movement of Indigenism (*indigénisme*), advocating the study of Vodou "plainchant" and drumming as the basis for Haitian music.[27] Musicians of the ensuing decades, such as the popular Vodou-jazz group Jazz des Jeunes, would take to heart the invitation to Haitianize, blending Haitian folk traditions with outside sounds.[28]

During a related period of cultural nationalism in the 1930s, Brazilian dictator Getúlio Vargas transformed samba into a national culture industry. Previously associated with Afro-Brazilians, samba—like Cuban son—became a symbol of Brazilian *mestiçagem* (racial mixture).[29] At that time, Afro-Brazilians were envisioning new, collective identities in dialogue with pan-African movements such as negritude, having founded the first Black Brazilian political party, the Frente Negra Brasileira (Brazilian Black Front), in 1931.[30] However, it was not their political organizing but rather their participation in samba (as well as soccer) that was taken to symbolize Brazil's myth of racial democracy, insidious because of the way it obfuscates actually existing inequities and the exclusion of Afro-Brazilians from policymaking.[31]

Not unlike in Cuba and Haiti, the culture wars in Brazil surrounding samba involved decades of debate over the influence of US jazz and African American culture.[32] As early as 1928, public intellectual and musicologist Mário de Andrade asserted that "the reaction against what is foreign must be made slyly by deformation and adaption. Not by repulsion."[33] More cannibalistic of outside influence than Carpentier's notion of musical resistance, Andrade's deformation-adaption model foreshadows the way Brazilian rappers would uproot hip hop, negotiating the conflicting pressures of cultural nationalism and cultural imperialism as they rooted the practice in new contexts and revised what it meant to "sound American" from the perspective of their communities.

O hip hop era o nosso som: Hip Hop before Hip Hop

Following a 1964 coup in Brazil, a military dictatorship again mobilized the country's myth of racial democracy to oppress Afro-Brazilians, adopting the slogan "Brasil, ame-o ou deixe-o" (Brazil, love it or leave it).[34] Residents of Rio de Janeiro and São Paulo opted out of this totalizing logic in a movement that has been called "musical e não contestatário" (musical and not antiestablishment).[35] In community dances known as bailes black (Black dances) or *bailes funk* (funk dances), they embraced a mix of US soul music (by artists such as James Brown, Wilson Pickett, and Kool and the Gang) and Brazilian samba-rock (by artists such as Tim Maia, Jorge Ben Jor, Cassiano, and Gerson King Combo).[36] Although the dictatorship initially allowed cultural production to continue, a more repressive "second coup" precipitated a decade of "cultural void" in the 1970s, during which time the bailes paradoxically flourished.[37]

Born under the dictatorship in 1967, the year US soul music was first heard on Brazilian radio, Thaíde joined the bailes as an adolescent and released the first Brazilian rap recordings in the late 1980s in collaboration with DJ Hum.[38] In "Sr. Tempo Bom" (Mr. Good Times), Thaíde narrates the history of hip hop's introduction in Brazil as a personal story of development, what in literary criticism is called a bildungsroman or in hip hop studies has been labeled "personal narrativizing."[39] The proximity between rapper and hip hop is reminiscent of the expressions of raplove analyzed in chapter 2. "Sr. Tempo Bom" is at once about the coming-of-age of the rapper and hip hop's coming-of-age in Brazil. Emphasizing the cross-pollination of African American and Afro-Brazilian cultures, DJ Hum samples US singer Jean Knight's 1971 soul tune "Mr. Big Stuff," to which the prefix in the Brazilian title alludes. The result is a personal history of Brazilian hip hop rapped over a US musical sample:

> Que saudade do meu tempo de criança
> Quando eu ainda era pura esperança
> Eu via minha mãe voltando pra dentro do nosso barraco
> Com uma roupa de santo debaixo do braço
> Eu achava engraçado tudo aquilo
> Mas já respeitava o barulho do atabaque
> E não sei se você sabe a força poderosa
> Que tem na mão de quem toca um toque caprichado, santo gosta
> Então eu preparava pra seguir o meu caminho
> Protegido por meus ancestrais
> Antigamente o samba-rock, Black Power, soul
> Assim como o hip hop era o nosso som.
> . . . .
> Fui crescendo rodeado pela cultura afro-brasileira
> Também sei que já fiz muita besteira
> Mas nunca me desliguei das minhas raízes
> Estou sempre junto dos Blacks que ainda existem
> Me lembro muito bem do som e o passinho marcado
> Eram mostrados por quem entende do assunto
> E lá estavam Nino Brown e Nelson Triunfo
> Juntamente com a Funk e Cia, que maravilha![40]
>
> (Such nostalgia for my childhood
> When I was still pure hope
> I'd see my mother return to our shack
> Carrying santo clothes under her arm
> I thought all that was funny
> But I respected the sound of the atabaque drum
> I don't know if you know the powerful force

In the hand of the person who plays well, the santo approves
Then I prepared to follow my path
Protected by my ancestors
First it was samba-rock, Black Power, soul
Just like hip hop was our sound.
. . . .
I grew up surrounded by Afro-Brazilian culture
I know I did a lot of stupid things
But I never disconnected from my roots
I'm always together with the Blacks who are still around
I remember well the sound and the choreographed dance steps
That were revealed to those who understood
There was Nino Brown and Nelson Triunfo
Together with Funk and Cia, what a wonder!)

Thaíde's history runs from his mother's veneration of Afro-Brazilian santos, to learning to respect the atabaque drum (associated with Afro-Brazilian religions), to participation in the bailes black as an adolescent, to embracing hip hop culture. Notable are explicit references to Nelson "Triunfo" (credited with introducing breakdance to São Paulo) as well as an invocation of Black Power (in English). Echoing Andrade's call for the incorporation of international sounds by "deformation and adaption," Thaíde locates Afro-Brazilian culture as an antecedent to US hip hop. This interpretation contrasts sharply with the reception of the bailes black in the Brazilian media.

In July 1976, the B section of the *Jornal do Brasil* newspaper bore the headline "Black Rio: O orgulho (importado) de ser negro no Brasil" (Black Rio: The (imported) pride of being Black in Brazil).[41] The article sparked polemics across the political spectrum, including by prominent samba musicians, who saw Pan-Africanism and Black Soul as a threat.[42] Critics on the right denigrated Black Rio as a "model of importation of Afro-American extremism," while some on the left saw it as a guise concealing North American imperialism and cultural colonialism.[43] Even Afro-Brazilian professor and activist Lélia Gonzalez initially condemned Black Rio, though she would later embrace it as an authentic expression of Afro-Brazilian identity and a catalyst for the contemporary Black movement.[44]

The following year, dancer Nelson "Triunfo," from the town of Triunfo, Pernambuco, moved to São Paulo, where he attended a concert by James Brown in the Palmeiras gymnasium. Brown was so impressed with the young Brazilian dancer that he presented Nelson a cape, producing an iconic photograph of Nelson being hoisted into the air by concertgoers.[45] Nelson took the bailes to the São Paulo streets in 1983 after a friend returned from the United States and described the phenomenon of breaking.[46] In addition to several important US-made hip hop films released that year, the Brazilian telenovela *Partido Alto* propelled breakdance to national visibility the following year with an opening sequence featuring Nelson's dance crew.[47] By that time, residents of São Paulo's outer neighborhoods were congregating almost daily to breakdance in the city center, on the Avenue 24 de Maio near the Praça da República and at the central subway station of São Bento.[48] Since São Paulo's outer neighborhoods are distributed among four geographic quadrants (north, south, east, and west), the central subway station provided a natural meeting place.

Though rap would soon replace breakdance as the most widely disseminated element of hip hop in Brazil, dance remained popular. In 1985, the year of the country's return to democracy, Tommy Boy Records released Afrika Bambaataa's song "Planet Rock" in Brazil. "Planet Rock" was a hip hop manifesto, as Jeff Chang puts it, a "polycultural pastiche, framed by swooping, synthesized orchestral stabs . . . hip-hop's universal invitation, a hypnotic vision of one world under a groove, beyond race, poverty, sociology and geography."[49] The Brazilian legacy of "Planet Rock" proved even more enduring than the 500,000 copies it sold in the United States the year of its release.[50] In addition to playing a significant role in hip hop's globalization, "Planet Rock" influenced electro-funk and house music and irreversibly altered the soundtrack of Rio de Janeiro's bailes. Inspired by "Planet Rock" and the electronic, upbeat rhythm of Miami bass, what was called the *pancadão* sound became popular in Rio de Janeiro and throughout Brazil. Thus was born *funk carioca* (Rio de Janeiro funk) or simply *funk* (which I leave in italics throughout to avoid confusion with US funk).[51]

Brazilian rap and *funk* both came out of Bambaataa's freshly packaged hip hop culture by way of the bailes black: a sort of international escape valve for Afro-Brazilian communities alienated by the dictatorship's hypernationalism. Yet where early rap singles such as the Black Juniors dance crew's "Mas que linda estás" (But you're so pretty) shared with *funk* an emphasis on dance, an internal division soon emerged.[52] *Funk* participants in Rio disidentified with the hip hop movement, while rappers in São Paulo rejected the perceived hedonism of *funk*, maintaining closer aesthetic ties to the Black nationalist discourse of radical US rap groups like Public Enemy.[53] Part of the distancing of rappers from *funk* revolved around the refusal of *funk* MCs to espouse a specific politics, which some rappers saw as an abandonment of the bailes' function as a space for *conscientização* (consciousness-raising).[54] *Funk* participants, on the other hand, rejected rappers' claims to cultural citizenship and the traditional "clientelist relationship" between institutions and musicians (particularly in samba).[55] São Paulo hip hop artists probably also defended rap against *funk* as a symptom of the city's long-standing rivalry with Rio de Janeiro (Brazil's "cultural capital"), wishing to emphasize the greater cosmopolitanism of their city (Brazil's "financial capital"). São Paulo's status as the nucleus of Brazilian hip hop was solidified when, a decade after James Brown's São Paulo concert, several prominent US rappers performed concerts there, including Public Enemy.[56]

By that time, the group Racionais MC's (founded by Mano Brown, Ice Blue, Edi Rock, and DJ KL Jay) had formed the independent rap label Zimbabwe Records and released the compilation album *Consciência Black* (Black conscience), featuring several prominent early rappers. One was Sharylaine, whose inclusion in this groundbreaking Brazilian rap album bears emphasizing. Sharylaine's track on the album, which features a US-style funk break, challenges rap misogyny: "Disseram então que eu não podia cantar . . . Não ligue meu bem que isto é prosa / E se tudo se renova Sharylaine está a toda prova" (Then they said I couldn't sing . . . Don't pay attention to that, my dear, this is prose / And if everything's renewed, Sharylaine's up to the test).[57] The reference to prose is curious, given that Sharylaine delivers her rhymes in verse. Perhaps she seeks to draw attention to the distinction of the female voice, uprooting hip hop's hypermasculinity.

Despite a majority-male field, a female and feminist presence continued to grow in Brazilian rap, including artists such as Ieda Hills, Rubia Fraga, Dina Di, and Sharylaine herself.[58] Not yet born when Sharylaine began rapping, Issa Paz acknowledges her predecessors in a song of personal development in the style of "Sr. Tempo Bom." From the 2016 album *Rap Plus Size,* "Agradecimentos" (Acknowledgments) pays homage to Brazilian hip hop in a raplove song:

> Já me senti sozinha, a única da trilha
> Tão distante de tudo, um lobo sem matilha
> Verão sem andorinha, tão fora da quadrilha
> Mas o rap nacional me deu mais que uma família
> Deu irmãos e irmãs, alguns copos de Montilla
> Foi minha força de manhã e maremotos nas pupilas
> Entendimento, noção de espaço e tempo sem apostilas

Conhecimento mais discernimento e eu fui tranquila
Teve algumas armadilhas, mas não foi suficiente
O que a Dina Di dizia já era parte da minha mente
Infelizmente ela se foi, mas deixou sua arte
E seus ensinamentos que me servem de estandarte
Mais uma mártir, mas que sempre será lembrada
Viveu tempo suficiente pra ser eternizada
E eu permaneci aqui por mais que necessidade
Foi por amor, coragem, respeito à comunidade
Essa é por cada MC que vive aqui
Que me inspira, cativa, me dá força pra seguir.[59]

(I've felt alone, the only one of the group
So far away from everything, a wolf without a pack
Summer without swallows, outside of the gang
But national rap gave me more than a family
Gave brothers and sisters, a few glasses of Montilla
It was my force for tomorrow and tsunamis in my pupils
Understanding of the notion of space and time without class notes
Knowledge plus discernment and I was content
There were a few pitfalls, but it wasn't enough
What Dina Di said was already part of my mind
Sadly, she left us, but she left her art
And her teachings that, for me, are standards
One more martyr, but who will always be remembered
She lived long enough to be immortalized
And I remained here for more than necessity
It was for love, courage, respect of community
This is for every MC who lives here
Who inspires and moves me, gives me strength to carry on.)

Born after the bailes black, Paz grounds her self-presentation in the shared sentiment of uprootedness uniting the community that Brazilian rappers call *rap nacional* (national rap). The lyrics highlight the communitarian aspects of hip hop in an elegy to Dina Di that doubles as a general homage to Brazilian women MCs. In the final verse, Paz dedicates her song to "cada MC que vive aqui" (every MC who lives here), the spatial deixis (*aqui*) reaffirming rap's rooting in São Paulo and Brazil.

The elegiac impulse of rap—a solemn effort to preserve the practice and pay homage to its past and present—remained an audible through-line across multiple generations of hip hop artists. While not uncommonly engaging in friendly rivalries with the "old school," and seeking to distance themselves from the work of their predecessors, each new generation of rappers consistently acknowledged its debt to previous generations. This historicist, even conservationist urgency runs counter to popular music's traditional valorization of novelty and the expediency of genres such as Brazilian *funk* or Caribbean reggaeton. It also reflects a commitment to collective authorship and community, scalable from neighborhood to world through a shared sense of uprooting.

Bailando y escuchando música americana: Moña Revolution

During the late 2010s, Cuban hip hop artists similarly expressed a desire to preserve what they called hip hop's "memoria histórica" (historical memory). This led to the curation by Cuban media historian Alejandro Zamora of a hip hop archive at the José Martí National Library, as well as the publication of a collection of essays and testimonials by hip hop artists, coedited by longtime producer and rapper Malcoms "Justicia" Junco Duffay.[60] One of the books Zamora showed me at the library exhibit was an updated edition of renowned Cuban musicologist Cristóbal Díaz Ayala's *Música cubana* (Cuban music; 2003), which bore the new subtitle *del areyto al rap cubano* (from *areyto* to Cuban rap).[61] What is the significance of rap's inclusion in a book on "Cuban music," or the naming of a musical phenomenon called *rap cubano* (Cuban rap)? How did artists of rap cubano respond to the tensions between the genre's imported status and its nationalization?

Following the 1961 announcement of a US trade embargo against Cuba—referred to on the island as *el bloqueo* (the blockade)—Fidel Castro adopted a harsh policy toward what he saw as cultural, political, and economic imperialism, attacking rock music in particular. Any affiliation with rock came to imply a failure to integrate with the revolutionary process and, hence, *desviaciones ideológicas* (ideological drift).[62] The government expressed fear over the political consequences of international exchange, pushing cultural institutions to adopt protectionist policies. Cuban novelist Leonardo Padura reflected that "in the Spanish Caribbean, we were the only ones who lived without knowing that salsa music was being born or that the Beatles (the Rolling Stones and Mamas and the Papas too) were symbols of rebellion and not of imperialist culture, as we were told so many times."[63]

Critical of US imperialism, the Cuban revolutionary government actively supported the struggles of US Black leaders. Fidel Castro offered political asylum to prominent Black activists from the United States, including Black Liberation Army leader Assata Shakur and hip hop activist Nehanda Abiodun.[64] He also supported liberation movements in Africa.[65] Domestically, the early years of the revolution encouraged public debate around racism and sought to eliminate racial discrimination by desegregating public spaces and providing housing and employment opportunities for underrepresented, darker-skinned Cubans.[66] However, to appease white anxiety, and believing that racism would naturally disappear under socialism, Castro abandoned his explicit antidiscrimination agenda by the mid 1960s, closing the Black press and Black clubs and censoring Afro-Cuban religions.[67] Thus while Blacks gained unprecedented opportunities for upward mobility thanks to the revolution, discussion of race and racism became taboo. As Alejandro de la Fuente puts it, "the lack of a public debate about race and racism facilitated the survival and reproduction of the very racist stereotypes that the revolutionary leadership claimed to oppose."[68] Some opposition to racial discrimination persisted, but institutionalized notions of a post-racial society rendered difficult a public debate analogous to "the (imported) pride of being Black."[69]

When the government failed to meet housing demands in the 1980s and residential patterns correlating race, poverty, and marginality reemerged, colorblindness became increasingly difficult to defend.[70] Ironically, darker-skinned Cubans recovered an antiracist agenda in a cultural practice imported from the imperialist enemy to the north. It was common during the time for residents of East Havana to extend and recalibrate their radio receivers using homemade *busters* (booster antennas) to receive US FM radio broadcasts. Cuban rap producer Pablo Herrera recalls a DJ by the name of Elmito in his neighborhood of Santos Suárez, who gained nearly complete access to the Florida WEDR station and the program *99 Jamz*, known for playing Black American music.[71] In the nearby neighborhood of Luyanó, DJ Joseph would also play primarily US funk tunes.[72] Due to their proximity to Florida, residents of East Havana and Matanzas were additionally able to receive US television broadcasts of *Soul Train*, a Black music and dance program that became popular with Cuban youth.[73] The show was instrumental in globally disseminating the 1970s funk style: platform shoes, applejack caps, and bell-bottoms.[74] Listening to US soul and Motown and emulating funk style in neighborhood *bonches* (dance parties), Havana residents soon developed their own practice of US-inspired Black dance while also beginning to improvise rhymes.[75] Attendees of these Havana bonches came to be called "la gente de la moña" or "los moñeros," a name that refers to Afro-textured hairstyles.[76]

Alexey ..el tipo este.. rhymed homage to the moña in the song "Cómo fue" (How it was). Produced by Pablo Herrera, the song's lyrics sample the bolero by that name made popular by Cuban singer Benny Moré. The sample is significant, given Moré's positive reception among Cuban revolutionary intellectuals in the 1960s.[77] The bolero lyrics begin thus: "No sé explicarme qué pasó / Pero de ti me enamoré" (I can't make sense of what happened / But I fell in love with you).[78] Parodying the bolero's nostalgia by eliminating all interrogational inflection and displaying a reticence toward poetic devices like hyperbole and metaphor, Alexey's rap sample responds: "Yo sé explicarme qué pasó / Cómo de ti me enamoré, hip hop" (I know how to make sense of what happened / How I fell in love with you, hip hop).[79] A raplove song, "Cómo fue" substitutes hip hop for Moré's apostrophized lover. Like Thaíde's "Sr. Tempo Bom," the lyrics narrate the rapper's coming-of-age alongside the popularity of African American soul music in Havana:

> Todo comenzó chamaco yo faja'o con una pilé antena
> Alambre de percheros y un Selena
> Sacaba to' el atraso aquel por la ventana y ay, ay, ay
> ¡Loco por coger la 99!
> El Soul Train me entraba sin llovizna ni na'
> ¡Sal del medio, mima!
> ¡'Toy viendo el programa, vieja!
> Mucha vista, mucha oreja
> Copiaba los pasillos y en el barrio luego repartía las cajas
> Y como yo, había muchos en La Habana
> Bailando y escuchando música americana na' ma'
> Papá compró una grabadora pa' mí
> Y mi primer cassette fue de Public Enemy.
>
> Hip hop, hip hop, hip hop, hip hop
> Don't believe the hype
> Do you rememba?[80]

> (Everything started when I was a kid, struggling with a bunch of antennas
> Wire from a coat hanger and a Selena
> I'd throw out all that backwardness through the window and ay, ay, ay
> Crazy to catch *99 Jamz!*
> Picked up *Soul Train* when there wasn't any interference
> Get out of the way, *mima!*
> I'm watching the program, *vieja!*

84 *Break and Flow*

>   Lots of eyes, lots of ears
>   Copied the dance steps and we did even better in the *barrio*
>   And like me, there were many in Havana
>   Dancing and listening to [Black] American music, nothin' more
>   Dad bought a recorder for me
>   And my first cassette was of Public Enemy.
>
>   Hip hop, hip hop, hip hop, hip hop
>   Don't believe the hype
>   Do you rememba?)

The assonance between the words *americana* (American) and *na' ma'* (nothin' more) playfully Cubanizes what had been received as an American practice. When I contacted Alexey to request permission to print these lyrics, the first thing he emphasized was that "música americana" meant "música negra americana" (Black American music). Uprooting hip hop from the US provided a platform for reasserting racial identity and for "throwing out" (*sacar*) Cuba's "backwardness" (*atraso*), presumably a reference to underdevelopment. The lyrics include a sample of Public Enemy's 1988 song "Don't Believe the Hype" layered on a chorus that repeats the words "hip hop," quoting a dead prez song by that name. The pastiche of Benny Moré, Public Enemy, and dead prez captures the early years of Cuban hip hop: a sonic collage of some of the most politically outspoken US rap groups, syncretized with Cuban musical influences. Like Bárbaro would do a decade later, ..el tipo este.. places his emphasis on listening and dancing to (Black) American music.

Havana-based rap group Amenaza had other ideas. Having recently performed at the second annual Cuban hip hop festival in 1996, held in Alamar, founding member Joel Pando asked Pablo Herrera to produce something representative of Cuban popular music of the time.[81] With Herrera, Amenaza recorded its first demos to samples of Cuban *son montuno* (the improvisatory, call-and-response section of a son song). Two years later, Amenaza was invited to travel to France as part of a cultural exchange.[82] The group chose to remain there and released *A lo cubano* on the Spanish label EMI under the name Los Orishas. The new group name invokes the Yoruba-derived sovereigns (*orishas* or *orichas*) of African-inspired Regla de Ocha (Santería). *A lo cubano* sold more than fifty thousand copies globally.[83] And unlike most emigrant artists, Los Orishas managed to maintain close ties to Cuba, receiving airtime on Cuban radio and television and performing at the prestigious José Martí

Anti-Imperialist Platform venue in 2001 for the celebration of the revolution's forty-third anniversary.[84]

The title track of *A lo cubano*, however, is not representative of the lyrics or sound of Cuban rap of the period. Over a tropical-inspired beat, the lyrics describe: "A lo cubano, botella de ron, tabaco habano, chicas por doquier" (Cuban style, bottle of rum, Habano cigar, girls everywhere).[85] The verses perhaps express a yearning for tourist Cuba, which, between 1991 and 2008, was off-limits to most Cubans.[86] At the same time, the "indigenized" Cuban sound and stereotypical lyrics of Los Orishas seem designed to appeal primarily to international audiences.[87] Or perhaps the song practices a form of "strategic exoticism that allows them both to appease and critically undermine demands for clichéd representations of Cuba."[88]

In an ethnography of South African *kwaito* music, which emerged concurrently during the 1990s, Gavin Steingo analyzes a similar tension between local and global pressures. He observes the way the group Bongo Maffin was "pressured into adapting an explicitly—and as [bandmember] Stoan later told me, fictively—'African' sound" as a result of international travel.[89] Drawing on the work of Ackbar Abbas, Steingo differentiates between nonprofessional and commercially successful kwaito musicians by observing two distinct forms of cosmopolitanism: a "cosmopolitanism of dependency," where commercial musicians channeled "highly refracted images and sounds of South Africa to the Euro-American market," and a "cosmopolitanism of extraterritoriality," in which nonprofessional musicians mobilized multiple "outside" sounds for local consumption.[90]

As socialism disintegrated in Eastern Europe and Castro embraced perestroika reforms, Cuban musicians and writers found themselves in high international demand.[91] However, limited access to international travel seems to have produced an impulse, at least for rappers, to incorporate international trends into music made primarily for local audiences—in short, to "sound American." If sounding American resonates with a cosmopolitanism of extraterritoriality, the trajectory of Los Orishas seems to have landed on a cosmopolitanism of dependency, performing Cubanness for primarily foreign audiences—although it is important to recall that their objective to sound Cuban predated their emigration and international popularity.

In any case, the strategy proved fruitful: probably in response to the international success of Los Orishas, Cuban Minister of Culture Abel Prieto is said to have declared hip hop an authentically Cuban cultural expression, paving the way for the formation of the Cuban Rap Agency in 2002 under the auspices of the Cuban Institute of Music.[92] The Agency's goal was "stimulating the consolidation of models that for their characteristics are an expression of the values of our Cuban culture."[93] In the context of a top-down, highly bureaucratic national employment structure, Cuban artists and musicians must regularly audition and present dossiers to belong to agencies and legally earn a salary. As such, hip hop artists broach the subject of the Cuban Rap Agency with ambivalence, understanding its existence between two poles: on one side, as a legitimation of Cuban rap by the state providing a small group of artists minimal infrastructure to work as professional employees and, on the other, as an organized effort to regulate and even suppress hip hop's "American" (that is, imperialist) underpinnings.

The Agency was formed at a time when Cuban hip hop artists were indeed engaging in extensive dialogue, collaboration, and cultural exchange with African American artists and activists.[94] These conversations resulted in US benefit concerts and Havana hip hop festivals featuring prominent US and international artists.[95] The festivals of the late 1990s included appearances by African American activists Abiodun and Shakur, evidence of the importance of US-inspired Black radicalism on the early years of Cuban hip hop.[96] The influence was mutual: when a delegation of Cuban rappers visited New York City in 2001, US hip hop artists praised the Cuban rappers for maintaining the socially conscious "underground" that was supposedly being lost as a result of commercialization.[97] The fruits of these cultural exchanges can be heard in a proliferation of Cuban rap songs from the early 2000s that evoke Blackness: for example, Hermanos de Causa's "Lágrimas negras" (which takes as its pretext the Cuban bolero by that name, "Black tears"), Oye Habana's "Negra" (Black woman), El B's "Negros en TV" (Blacks on TV), and the feminist rap cypher organized by Las Krudas, "Eres bella" (You're beautiful).

The festival in Alamar also functioned as a meeting place for Latin American hip hop artists, who would come together to discuss common struggles against racism, imperialism, and sexism.[98] Mexican rapper Aldo "Bocafloja" Villegas, who attended the festival in the early 2000s, described to me being struck that the event featured concerts as well as academic conferences and debates. Hip hop was used "as a vehicle of connection to open dialogue. But hip hop wasn't the last line of discussion, rather the vehicle, nothing more. So they talked about race, gender, history . . . from a nonhegemonic point of view using hip hop references."[99] However, the growing international exchange taking place in Havana around hip hop culture provoked anxiety in state cultural institutions, leading to the abrupt cancellation of the festival in 2004.[100] The full-scale festival remained suspended nearly a decade later when Bárbaro recorded the verse "qué importa si sonamos americano hermano."

Whose Style Is This? Haitian Rap Kreyòl

In Haiti, state control of culture was intense in the decades prior to the emergence of hip hop. Ethnologist François "Papa Doc" Duvalier led a revolution in 1957 that culminated in a violent dictatorship extending to his son and lasting until 1986. Duvalier consolidated media control almost completely, creating networks with even the most rural peasant communities.[101] By defending negritude and appropriating Vodou symbols through the political tactic of *koudyay* (exuberant street parties designed to garner popular support), he was able to co-opt grassroots leadership.[102] Duvalier also maintained a strict system of patronage over cultural production.[103] An aggressive music patron, he put his strongest support behind the dance genre of *konpa-dirèk,* recognized as the first commercial Haitian genre.[104] Ironically, despite Duvalier's violently enforced cultural nationalism, Haitian konpa derives from Dominican *merengue* and in practice supplanted more Haitianized genres such as Vodou-jazz.[105] When, in the 1960s, US President John F. Kennedy began to increase pressure on Duvalier to step down and American aid and tourism diminished, anti-American sentiment surged; young Haitian artists felt compelled to avoid any foreign cultural "contamination."[106] Gage Averill recounts one musician's description of making a conscious effort to create "nothing serious," in order to avoid political persecution in a context where "everything was politics."[107] This sometimes took the form of *doudouisme* (sweet-sweetism or sweetheartism), where Haitian musicians would strategically deploy nostalgic language about tropical life reminiscent of a "Caribbean postcard"—not unlike Los Orishas's representation of tourist Cuba.[108]

During the late 1970s, artists began to take advantage of cracks in the regime of Jean-Claude "Baby Doc" Duvalier, who had succeeded his father in 1971. The period saw a renaissance of *konsyantizasyon* (consciousness-raising) and stylistic experimentation in the arts. Artists and musicians reclaimed the culture of the Haitian masses that had been "forged in bondage—the Kreyòl language, the Vodou religion, the focus on community, dignity, and self-sufficiency"—the elements that had "ultimately enabled them to destroy slavery and produce something new in its place."[109] *Kilti libète* (liberty culture) groups mixed Vodou songs and rara music with poetry, dance, and theater to recover symbols of peasant culture appropriated by the dictatorship.[110] *Twoubadou* singer-composers of Haitian *mereng* returned to their role as *angaje* (politically committed) musicians, and *sanba* singers developed an interest in *mizik rasin* (roots music), inspired by the political activism of Bob Marley and Rastafarianism.[111] Konpa groups Zèklè, Tabou Combo, and Les Loups Noirs included fusions with US funk, soul, and jazz-rock.[112] The incorporation of new US sounds was paralleled by an interest in breakdance.[113] By the end of the 1980s, some artists had begun rapping in Kreyòl and English, emulating the emergent gangsta aesthetic of US hip hop and the socially conscious lyrics of French protest rap.[114]

Haitian rap kreyòl artists universally attribute the introduction of rap in Haiti to radio DJ Georges "Master Dji" Lys Hérard. The son of Radyo Pòtoprens (Port-au-Prince Radio) owner Antoine Rodolphe Hérard, Master Dji was uniquely situated to introduce the primarily middle-class audience of Haitian radio listeners to rap.[115] As host of the popular radio show *Jungle Tropicale* on Tropic FM, he played some of the first rap and rap kreyòl songs to be heard on the radio in Haiti.[116] His 1986 rap kreyòl song "Sispann" (Stop) features a US-inspired funk break, its lyrics calling on the listener to speak out against the mob violence of dechoukaj in the aftermath of Duvalierism: "Montre m figi w si w pa lach" (Show me your face if you're not a coward).[117] "Sispann" earned Master Dji second prize at the Prix Découvertes RFI competition of Radio France Internationale and gained airtime on French radio. Master Dji tragically died of AIDS in 1994, but rap kreyòl would continue to provide a platform for Port-au-Prince residents to uproot traditions and empower their communities.[118]

Perhaps due to the legacy of Duvalier's cultural nationalism, or part of a conscious return to Price-Mars's Indigenism, some early rap kreyòl artists exhibit a less pronounced tendency to "sound American" than their Cuban and Brazilian counterparts. Master Dji's groundbreaking album *Haiti Rap & Ragga,* for example, mixes rap with Jamaican ragamuffin. And one of the first Haitian songs to feature rap kreyòl was the election song "Veye-yo" (Watch out for them) by popular konpa group Les Frères Parent.[119] The inclusion of rap kreyòl in a popular konpa tune suggests a more rapid creolization of rap with local sounds than in Cuba and Brazil. "Veye-yo" anticipates two tropes that would become commonplace in rap kreyòl: an affirmation that Haiti's present situation must be understood as a consequence of its colonial and revolutionary past, and a vindication of the Kreyòl language.

Kreyòl had emerged during slavery when native speakers of Bantu, Kikongo, and Yoruba, among other African languages, developed forms of resistance within and against French.[120] Throughout the French colonial empire, Creoles opened French vowels, eliminated articles and subject-verb agreement, and mixed French vocabulary with African grammatical structures. Glissant characterizes the operation of Creoles vis-à-vis the colonial language in the following way: "I speak to you in your language, and it's in my language that I understand you."[121] For Glissant, Haitian Kreyòl is the only Caribbean Creole to have developed beyond a tactic of diversion into a full language.[122] A common and uncharacteristically literal Haitian proverb confirms: "kreyòl pale, kreyòl kompran" (I speak Kreyòl, I understand Kreyòl). Spoken monolingually by 95 percent of Haitians, Kreyòl was not declared an official language of Haiti until 1987, the year "Veye-yo" was released.[123] Appropriately, the rap lyrics of "Veye-yo" focus on the politics of Kreyòl and French: "Ka depi ti nèg wè l ka di de mo franse / Li gen tan met an tèt li kapab prezidan . . . Nou fè 1804 sanble ak yon aksidan" (Anyone capable of speaking two words of French / Gets it in their head that they can be president . . . We make 1804 seem like an accident).[124] By focusing on the politics of language and recalling Haiti's legacy of revolution, the lyrics highlight how colonialism continues to plague Haiti's present.

The process of creolization extended to other languages as well. By the end of Baby Doc's regime, more than 400,000 Haitians resided in New York City, a majority in the Brooklyn neighborhood of Flatbush. Coupled with the global dissemination of US Black culture, the large Haitian diaspora (*dyaspora*) led to an increasing incorporation into Kreyòl of English and Hip Hop Nation Language.[125] For example, the 1990 rap kreyòl song "Whose Style Is This?" by Original Rap Staff features mostly English lyrics excepting a few Haitian stock phrases such as "m ap vini" (I'm coming) and "mwen sòti Ayiti" (I'm from Haiti).[126] Money Honey Mike asserts his place in hip hop culture by rhyming in English while using the Kreyòl phrases (pronounced with a New York accent) to draw attention to his Haitianness.[127] The English-language group name Original Rap Staff inverts the teleology of original and copy, positioning the Haitian expression of rap as more authentic than the US rap upon which it was modeled. Like Thaíde in Brazil, Original Rap Staff not only imitates US rap, but establishes rap kreyòl as a precursor. What is at stake in this early rooting of rap kreyòl is not so much the productive mistranslations characteristic of diasporic exchange, but rather a new style: a creolized rap that finds no contradiction in being both African American and Haitian.[128] As Martinican poet Suzanne Césaire wrote of the Creole-speaking Caribbean and the poetry of her country of Martinique, "sera cannibale ou ne sera pas" (it will be cannibal or will not be).[129] For early Haitian rap kreyòl artists, cannibalizing US rap and "sounding American" was bound up at least as much with language as it was with music.

National Rap

Focusing on Haitian dechoukaj and uprooting more broadly, this chapter has traced the way hip hop artists in São Paulo, Havana, and Port-au-Prince confronted opposing forces of nation and world, which pitted historically rooted anxieties over US cultural influence against a desire to eschew cultural nationalism and participate in a global practice associated with African American communities. This field of national and international pressures provided the backdrop for more localized expressions of rap, which are explored in the following chapter. Before turning to these local scales, however, it is worth pausing to reflect on the place of the nation in so-called national expressions of hip hop. Why did Brazilian rappers term their practice rap nacional (national rap)? What are the politics of producing rap cubano (Cuban rap) while aspiring to sound "arrogantly American"?[130] How do these categories map onto global and regional formations such as Latin American rap or hip hop poetics in the Americas?

Scholars and activists of postcolonial contexts have observed a crucial significance of the nation (not the nation-state) in the construction of identity.[131] Defending mid-century decolonization efforts in Africa, Frantz Fanon asserted that "national consciousness, *which is not nationalism,* is alone capable of giving us an international dimension."[132] Similarly, national hip hop does not reinforce the power of the nation-state, but rather expresses a critical longing to represent local communities in a global, Afro-diasporic framework. Rappers in the Americas wield hip hop as cultural capital, a sort of passport for entry into what has been called the Global Hip Hop Nation.[133] In global hip hop the nation is mediated doubly: through a hyperlocal focus on neighborhood place and through transnational yearnings for shared belonging across distance.

Finally, there is the question of the role of music in nation-building and hemispheric solidarity. Pablo Palomino demonstrates that early-twentieth-century musical nationalisms in Latin America, such as those surrounding Cuban son and Brazilian samba, developed largely in parallel with hemispheric ideas about Latin American music.[134] The same dialectical emergence of national and hemispheric communities surrounding music (similarly in response to anxieties over US cultural influence) continues to characterize the circulation of late-twentieth-century practices such as rap. What demands further reflection is how these tensions manifest sonically.

How, for example, did the notion of "qué impota si sonamos americano hermano" influence Bárbaro's decision to ask me to record a violin track for him? There is nothing uniquely American about my training in Western classical and early Baroque violin music. Nor did Bárbaro seem motivated to feature my violin with the objective of making the song sound "more American." Even less desire to sound American was demonstrated by Malcoms "Justicia" when he invited me to co-produce and record violin for the 2017 album *Sentimientos desafinados* (Out-of-tune feelings). Malcoms's idea for each track on the album was to have me create violin melodies based on classic Cuban tunes. He explained to me that while he had Cuban friends who could record violin for him, he was interested in recording with me because "different things could happen," the implication being that those "different things" were a result of my not being Cuban, but not necessarily of my being from the United States.

The interest on the part of these artists in collaborating with me on the violin begins to break down the national/imported binary that is often projected onto hip hop's rooting in the Americas. Geoffrey Baker, for example, has documented a widespread interest in string melodies and minor modes in Cuban hip hop, a sound that he describes as neither African American nor Cuban.[135] String instruments are also popular with rappers in Haiti (Rockfam, Fantom, D-Fi, Wendyyy) and Brazil (Projota, Djonga), although Cuban, Haitian, and Brazilian hip hop artists know little of each other's music. What, asks Baker, "are we to make of the prevalence of classical music samples . . . ? What sort of history is being constructed here?"[136] Instead of signaling a history, these preferences suggest that musical decisions are not necessarily ideological. The next chapter continues to examine the cross-pollination of outside pressures and local imperatives by focusing on the way rappers used scale to root their neighborhood communities in translocal forms of belonging.

4 Scale
"Rap é meu lugar"

ONE OF Brazil's most virtuosic rappers, Mauro "Sabotage" Mateus dos Santos would sonically sign his songs by hailing his favela of Canão (in the neighborhood of Brooklin, São Paulo) during a career tragically cut short by the violence he commonly denounced in rhyme. The marginal neighborhood was not the only territory Sabotage marked when he rapped, however. He also carved out a poetic territory, as he affirmed in the verse "rap é meu lugar" (rap is my place).[1] Where chapter 3 focused on the history and positionality of artists in Brazil, Cuba, and Haiti in relation to pressures of cultural nationalism, hip hop's imported status, and Afro-diasporic belonging, here I zoom in on the place most represented in rap lyrics: the neighborhood. How, I ask following Sabotage, does hip hop provide rappers a technology for placemaking?

Since the 1970s, most of the world's urban population growth has taken place in slums and shantytown communities of Global South cities.[2] While rap was increasing in popularity in the Americas during the 1990s, the World Bank labeled urban poverty the "most significant, and politically explosive, problem of the next century."[3] Hip hop artists, many of whom reside in or identify with marginalized urban communities, scale their experiences of life on the margins of their built environments to horizons of shared marginal belonging. As Verónica Gago puts it, describing the informal economies emergent in disadvantaged neighborhoods of Global South cities, this "capacity to re-scale, to jump scales and connect them . . . challenges the globalized partition between local and global but also national geometry."[4] The "scalar model" of the neighborhood,[5] I argue, allows Sabotage and other rappers to make rap their place.

This chapter centers around three local signifiers of neighborhood: the Haitian baz (base), the Brazilian *periferia* (periphery), and the Cuban *aldea* (rural village). Connected to notions of sovereignty and jurisdiction, the Haitian military metaphor of baz is used to delineate and defend neighborhood zones. The Brazilian notion of periferia derives from the colonial center-periphery model of urban development that tended to push disadvantaged, nonwhite communities to the outskirts. The Cuban aldea imagines quasi-rural solidarity in the context of an urban network created through the circulation of USB flash drives. Each scalar marker relates to the history of its respective built environment in specific ways. Furthermore, and in contrast to US hip hop's urban ethos and the predominantly urban contexts of Brazilian, Cuban, and Haitian rappers, each signifier conjures a historically grounded notion of rurality. These indices of neighborhood belonging function as techniques of "spatial sampling," a concept Ali Coleen Neff develops to describe the modes through which hip hop artists reconfigure space to make local-global connections that complicate notions of origin.[6]

A Cuban rapper once commented to me that hip hop was "our little piece of modernity."[7] This cosmopolitan yearning expresses what Mariano Siskind calls a *desejo do mundo* or *deseo de mundo* (desire for the world).[8] Focusing on the early twentieth century, Siskind demonstrates the way Latin American writers expressed cosmopolitan subjectivities by articulating their position of marginality vis-à-vis Western modernity through a literary form universalized *in* modernity, the novel.[9] Less mobile than early-twentieth-century Latin American intellectuals, rappers in the Americas at the turn of the millennium articulated their own desires for the world through a recently globalized medium, the rap song. In Havana, São Paulo, and Port-au-Prince, artists rerouted and rerooted hip hop (to sample Paul Gilroy),[10] scaling their neighborhood mythologies to worldly forms of belonging. What I call "world hip hop" is meant to describe rap songs that are about the world. The term also evokes a B side, or delayed reaction, to early-twentieth-century "world literature" and late-twentieth-century "world music," in which Cuba, Brazil, and Haiti were important players.[11]

How can the scalability of neighborhood account for the vast differences in scale and power asymmetries between Cuba and Haiti (Caribbean island nations), Brazil (South America's largest economy), and the United States? What role does globalization, "the encroaching of the there on the here," play in the circulation of hip hop poetics?[12] In what ways do hip hop artists respond to the unprecedented expansion of urban peripheries in the second half of the twentieth century and neoliberal "'overurbanization' . . . driven by the reproduction of poverty"?[13] How does world hip hop show that "the global is, in fact, the same as the local; space becomes place"?[14] How, as Gilroy asks, "is black life in one 'hood connected to life in others? Can there be a blackness that connects, articulates, synchronizes experiences and histories across the diaspora space?"[15] The multi-scalar approach of rappers in Haiti, Brazil, and Cuba recalls Aimé Césaire's dualism of the particular and the universal: "My conception of the universal is of one rich in all the particular, rich in all the particulars, the deepening and coexistence of all the particulars."[16] While "universally" true and commonly applied to diverse contexts, Césaire's formulation, like the poetics of break and flow, is born of the particular context of the Caribbean: the point of entry into the New World, an area conditioned by mass forced migration, near annihilation, and centuries-old jockeying for power. It is by scaling their neighborhood particularities that rappers point toward a translocal and transnational convergence of hip hop poetics in the Americas.

Ghetto love ak respè: Defending Baz

When Master Dji began recording the first rap kreyòl singles in the mid 1980s, Haiti's urban population was only around 20 percent, and 90 percent of urban residents lived in slums.[17] Between the early 1980s and the late 2010s, Haiti became a majority-urban country for the first time, its city-dwelling population increasing from 20 to around 55 percent.[18] During that time, grassroots organizing (aggressively repressed under Duvalier) reemerged in Port-au-Prince around the concept of baz (base or zone). Indexing neighborhood jurisdiction, baz allowed community groups to exercise what Chelsey Kivland calls "street sovereignty."[19] In the 1990s, baz took the form of neighborhood defense groups that mobilized around Jean-Bertrand Aristide's Lavalas movement.[20] When President Aristide was ousted by a coup in 1991, militant baz in the neighborhood of Bel Air advocated for his return.[21] Following a second coup against Aristide in 2004, pro-government baz known as *chimè* launched a series of violent protests that Aristide's opponents pejoratively dubbed "Operation Baghdad," the name referencing the US invasion of Iraq.[22]

By that time, Port-au-Prince hosted a vibrant local rap scene. The first recording studio dedicated exclusively to rap kreyòl opened in 2001; in 2003, Radio Planèt Kreyòl sponsored the first Haitian rap festival, Rap'Rocher Haiti.[23] The eleven-member rap kreyòl group Barikad Crew (BC) soon rose to national prominence as a result of a third-place finish in the popular Konkou Chante Nwèl (Christmas song contest) sponsored by the TV station Telemax.²⁴ As a journalist for the newspaper *Le Nouvelliste* put it, by sampling popular konpa dance tunes and mixing "vulgarities and good advice," BC reached poor and rich alike: "Poor kids, as much as the well-nourished ones of the best schools, sang their lyrics. . . . The most inspired texts of Haitian music in recent years, all categories taken together, are signed Barikad Crew."²⁵ In 2006, the group was recognized as the best Haitian musical act of the year in any category with a prestigious Ticket d'Or.²⁶

Rap groups such as BC organized into local cliques to represent and defend their neighborhood baz in a performance that sampled Haitian modes of rural alliance and the posses associated with US rap.²⁷ When additional rap crews developed, each adopted a different *mouchwa* (handkerchief) color, modeled after Haitian Carnival flags and US gangs.²⁸ The handkerchief colors ushered in an era of "beef" between different hip hop crews, again a hybrid of the ritualized violence characteristic of Haitian rara street bands and the East Coast–West Coast rivalry commercialized in US gangsta rap.²⁹ In this sense, Dade of BC affirms in the song "Se konsa l ye" (That's how it goes): "Barikad Crew met chalè / San ezitasyon nou p ap pè pa vin wouze baz ou" (Barikad Crew brings the heat / Without hesitation we're not afraid to come beat up your baz).³⁰ As Kivland puts it, while different baz "reflect the democratic hopes of the Haitian underclass, they are also tied to the novel forms of violence and insecurity that have arisen in the wake of the Duvalier dictatorship" and, I would add, to the violence linked to certain iterations of hip hop culture.³¹ I return to this (hypermasculine) trope of violence and its critiques in chapter 6.

One of the opening lines of "Se konsa l ye" invokes the ghetto: "Dèske yo wè m se nèg geto yo panse kè m pa gen nivo" (Once they see I'm from the ghetto, they think I don't have heart). Ubiquitous in global hip hop communities, the "racialized urban ghetto" functions "as a site of power and prestige."³² As Marcyliena Morgan observes, the *ghetto* trope is constructed "in relation to local culture and history that is seen as particular, but through which other neighborhoods and the world are also evaluated."³³ For Haitian rappers residing in urban slums such as Cité Soleil and Bel Air, the baz framework grafted nicely onto US hip hop's "ghettocentricity."³⁴

D-Fi raps "pou di w nan geto nou tout pa bandi" (to tell you that in the ghetto we're not all criminals).³⁵ Through rap, he maps his neighborhood of Castro in Delmas 33, Port-au-Prince:

On dreamer pa gen limit
Nan rap, m pa sot nan on blòk ki mitik
M pran blòk mwen m fè l mitik
Castro we go hard, D-Fi is yours
100% benefis kòm si n te envesti nan on biznis bòz
Pèsòn pa ka di m pa kite anyen rap la
Yeah! M met Castro sou map la.[36]

(A dreamer has no limits
In rap I don't come from a mythic block
I take my block and I make it mythic
Castro we go hard, D-Fi is yours
100 percent beneficiary as if you'd invested in a business boss
Nobody can tell me I've left anything out in rap
Yeah! I put Castro on the map.)

An expression of raplove is audible in this self-reflexive description of rap's placemaking. With the verse "Castro we go hard, D-Fi is yours," the rapper offers up his rap persona in ritualistic sacrifice to his neighborhood. His cartographic metaphor captures the indexical relationship that the lyrics establish between rap and ghetto as he mythically (*mitik*) transforms his block and puts Castro "on the map." By scaling down from ghetto to Castro, D-Fi inscribes his neighborhood place within a global hip hop framework. His colleague Blay'Z similarly combines a transnational notion of the ghetto with the particularity of the Haitian experience by creolizing Hip Hop Nation Language: "Ghetto love ak respè ke n ap pataje" (ghetto love and respect that we share).[37] This verse syncretizes the "ghetto love" popularized by US rappers and R & B artists with rural Haitian socialization codes of *onè ak respè* (honor and respect).[38] Blay'Z expresses a "'local cosmopolitanism,' a cosmopolitanism from the ground up."[39] Urban "ghetto love" embraces Haiti's historically rural majority.

Despite their urban context, rap kreyòl lyrics also point to the countryside, perhaps because while forests once covered nearly 60 percent of Haiti, by 2006 that number had fallen to less than 2 percent.[40] Barikad Crew addresses the problem of deforestation in "Pa koupe bwa" (Don't cut down trees), a rap song whose title samples the popular song "Ayiti Demen" (Tomorrow Haiti), written by Haitian poet Jean-Claude Martineau. The eminently catchy melody and extensive repetition of the refrain "pa koupe bwa" encourage singing along as didactic lyrics call on Haitians to listen to rap kreyòl as their nation's collective conscience (*konsyans*) and to preserve their forests: "An n fè souple rebwazman, se fòs l ap pote / Tout jèn kou vye an n monte nan mòn n al plante" (Let's please work on reforestation, it will bring force / All the young and the old, let's go up the mountains to plant).[41] The song does not appear to have changed policy, since Haiti has continued to rely on coal burning as a fuel source, and soil erosion exacerbated by topsoil removal from logging has remained common.[42] However, BC's message reached a large listening public.[43] This ecocritical song suggests that in Haitian rap kreyòl, place-making involves not only establishing one's place in hip hop and scaling notions of the urban ghetto, but preserving the literal ground or soil (tè) of the Haitian countryside.

Periferia é periferia: Translocal Marginality

In Brazil, urban peripheralization similarly has rural roots. During the nineteenth century, popular settlements known as *cortiços* provided housing to poor workers in Rio de Janeiro, including recent rural immigrants to the city, freed persons, and people who had escaped slavery.[44] In light of European notions about the "origins" of poverty and anxieties over hygiene and public health, cortiços were perceived as "unclean" areas of violence and delinquency, a "locus of poverty" or "social hell" housing a "dangerous class."[45] They were later renamed favelas. The word *favela* comes from a plant that grows in the area of Canudos in northeastern Brazil, which was the site of a separatist settlement during the late nineteenth century. As republican forces moved to overthrow the Portuguese monarchy, the Canudos community, whose residents followed the teachings of messianic leader Antônio Conselheiro, represented a threat to republican unity. In his classic book *Os sertões* (1902), Euclides da Cunha describes Canudos's strategic hillside position and threatening lack of order, comparing it to the "first barbarous groups" (*primeiros agrupamentos bárbaros*).[46] These characteristics were transplanted onto a Rio de Janeiro hillside community, the Morro da Favela, when soldiers from the War of Canudos (1893–1897) returned to the city to reside there. One antagonism (rural vs. urban) was superimposed onto another (poor, hillside communities vs. affluent, urban centers).[47]

While there were efforts to limit favelas to Rio—administrators once envisioned São Paulo to be "the great Brazilian metropolis without favelas"—the 1930 Plano de Avenidas (Avenues Plan) codified a center-periphery organizational model in São Paulo that precipitated the rapid expansion of slums.[48] During the next decade, São Paulo became the fastest-growing city in the world and by mid century, nearly half of São

Paulo residents lived in suburban areas with inadequate infrastructure.⁴⁹ One was Afro-Brazilian writer Carolina Maria de Jesus, who resided in São Paulo's Canindé favela when her memoir *Quarto de despejo* was published in 1960. In it, she ruminates on the scalability of the favela: "I redirect my thoughts toward the heavens. I think: could it be that there are inhabitants above? Could it be that they're better than us? Could it be that the majority there supplants ours? Could it be that the nations there are equally varied as ours, here on earth? Or is there only one nation? Could it be that favela exists there? And if favela exists there, when I live there, will I live in the favela?"⁵⁰ Carolina's writing delineates a marginal territory grounded in her favela but eminently scalable to others. Throughout her memoir, she refers to favela in the singular rather than the plural. The idiosyncratic absence of an article almost gives *favela* a partitive character, as if an uncountable part of a whole. However, (the) favela did not provide for Carolina a sense of community (as it would for Brazilian rappers a few decades later), and she was eventually able to move to a wealthier neighborhood.⁵¹

Carolina resided in São Paulo during a moment of transition in its urban form. Teresa Caldeira identifies at least three periods of sociospatial segregation in the development of São Paulo: first, the concentration of multiple social groups into small, densely populated enclaves (late nineteenth century to 1940s); second, center-periphery development segregating different social groups by large distances (1940s to 1980s); and third, a neoliberal moment in which "different social groups are again closer to one another but are separated by walls and technologies of security" (beginning in the 1980s).⁵² When rappers from São Paulo deploy the concept of periferia, they are responding to the latter two modalities of urban form: the large distances separating some disadvantaged neighborhoods from the city's center and the increasingly close proximity between rich, gated condominiums and centrally located favelas (a result of gentrification, among other factors).⁵³

Between 1980 and 1993, during which time the first Brazilian rap songs were released, the percentage of São Paulo's population residing in favelas increased from around 5 percent to almost 20 percent.⁵⁴ In 1988, São Paulo–based Mano Brown rapped that "Não é gueto americano, é Brasil, periferia" (It's not the American ghetto, it's Brazil, periphery).⁵⁵ In this early use of scale to invoke urban marginality, Brown rejects the term *ghetto* (associated with US hip hop) in favor of the Brazilian *periferia*. The verse maps the "anxiety of Americanization," analyzed in the previous chapter, onto neighborhood geography.⁵⁶ When Mano Brown was born in 1970, urban race riots across US cities had contributed to a rapid increase in the use of the term *ghetto,* particularly when applied to African American urban communities.[57] References to the ghetto entered popular music, for example, in Elvis Presley's "In the Ghetto" (1969), Donny Hathaway's "The Ghetto" (1970), and California funk band War's *The World Is a Ghetto* (1972).[58] Brown was clearly aware of these references, evidenced by the sample of War's song "Slippin' into Darkness" in one of the most famous Racionais MC's tracks, "Capítulo 4, Versículo 3." The War sample suggests a more complex relation between the US ghetto and the Brazilian periferia than the binary logic of "Não é gueto americano." Rather than rejecting one term in favor of the other, the transformation of the US ghetto into the Brazilian periferia follows Andrade's formulation of deformation and adaption rather than repulsion (see chapter 3).[59]

Brazil's modernist capital city of Brasília (founded in 1960) was envisaged to resist socioeconomic segregation.[60] However, as migrants moved there to work on its construction, Brasília's poor came to reside primarily in unplanned *cidades satélites* (satellite cities) that sprung up in the capital's outskirts. Genival Oliveira Gonçalves (GOG) was born in one of these satellite cities five years after Brasília's founding. In 1993, he opened the independent rap label Só Balanço, among the first in Brazil.[61] The 1994 album *Dia a dia da periferia* (Day to day of the periphery) established GOG as one of Brazilian rap's foremost theorists of urban marginality and neighborhood scale. The song "Brasília periferia," for example, documents the expansion of Brasília's satellite cities in a litany of neighborhood references highlighting the spatialized marginality of poor favelas vis-à-vis rich enclaves. In the middle of the song, GOG intones a verse that would become one of Brazilian rap's most important slogans: "periferia é periferia em qualquer lugar" (periphery is periphery in any place).[62] Racionais MC's would sample the verse a few years later in the title and chorus of the song "Periferia é periferia."[63] While continuing to highlight the specificity of Brazilian urban life, "periferia é periferia" scales the Brazilian periferia beyond the scope of any particular neighborhood. Hip hop is put to the service of what Anna Tsing calls a "scale-making project,"[64] conjuring the periferia as a space that inevitably reproduces the marginality of other disadvantaged neighborhoods, even in other built environments.

Derek Pardue suggests that the discourse of Brazilian rappers revolves around "ideologies of marginality," the assertion of marginal cultural citizenship to disrupt the "semiotic and geographic control" that overdetermines the periferia as violent and criminal.[65] The verse "periferia é periferia" imagines a horizontal peripheral community or "brotherhood,"[66] the stakes of which Mano Brown establishes in "Fórmula mágica da paz" (Magical formula for peace): "Ensinamento da favela foi muito bom pra mim / Cada lugar um lugar, cada lugar uma lei, cada lei uma razão e eu sempre respeitei" (The favela education was good for me / Each place a place, each place a law, each law a reason, and I always respected).[67] Here, Brown "pays homage not only to his own community, but to the favela in general."[68] The verses describe a mutually constitutive relationship between place (topos) and legal order (nomos), recognizing a distinct (extralegal) order corresponding to each neighborhood-jurisdiction. His "favela education" has taught him to respect the co-constitution of topos and nomos as he moves through the neighborhoods of São Paulo's *zona sul* (southern zone).[69]

Brown's lyrics also imply the existence of a generalized periferia nomos around what is sometimes called the *mundo do crime* (world of crime),[70] the "emergence of 'crime' as a legitimate normative instance" or "pillar of a central community."[71] Where outside the periferia crime denotes the absence of order, Brown inverts the order/disorder paradigm from the point of view "Da ponte pra cá" (From this side of the bridge). In this song, the figure of the bridge (*ponte*) indexes the literal bridges above the Pinheiros and Tietê Rivers that divide much of São Paulo's periphery from its center. The bridge—a structure that joins while separating—is an apt metaphor for describing hip hop's "connective marginalities."[72] Furthermore, with the verse "cada favelado é um universo em crise" (each favela resident is a universe in crisis), Brown scales up the São Paulo referent of ponte to a generalized favela universe, even a sort of ghetto archipelago.[73] As São Paulo "peripheral poet" Sérgio Vaz puts it, "para nós, a periferia é um pais" (for us, the periphery is a country).[74]

Racionais provided a marked contrast to white middle-class rapper Gabriel "o Pensador" Contino, the son of a *Rede Globo* journalist in Rio de Janeiro. Released by Sony, Contino's 1993 album *Gabriel o Pensador* sold 200,000 copies in its first few months and earned the rapper three MTV music videos and appearances on dozens of television programs, including on *Rede Globo* (where Racionais MC's adamantly refused to appear).[75] Not unlike white New York–based rap group the Beastie Boys or white rapper Robert Matthew "Vanilla Ice" Van Winkle (whose 1990 song "Ice Ice Baby" spent sixteen weeks as number one on the *Billboard* pop charts), Contino faced criticism for gentrifying the genre.[76] However, his lyrics address structural racism and social issues and, while catering to a middle-class audience, they contributed to rap's growing popularity in Brazil.[77] What is germane to placemaking is that Contino's raps are not generally grounded in the periferia. In contrast to Racionais, Contino's use of scale involves, for example, the song "Retrato de um playboy" (Portrait of a playboy), where he mocks the daily beach life of a resident of one of Rio de Janeiro's affluent neighborhoods.[78]

Two decades later, GOG returned to his theorization of the periferia in the song "ISO 9000 do gueto" (ISO 9000 of the ghetto), which begins, appropriately, with a sample of "Da ponte pra cá" by Racionais MC's. The refrain from the original asserts: "Não adianta querer, tem que ser, tem que pá / O mundo é diferente da ponte pra cá" (It's not enough to want, you have to be and such / The world is different from this side of the bridge).[79] GOG parodies: "De que lado você tá? / Não adianta afirmar nós que tá, citar uma pá de nomes" (What side are you on? / It's not enough to affirm "we're here," list some names). GOG's deconstruction of Racionais suggests that it no longer suffices simply to affirm on which side (of the bridge) one resides and to recite a litany of neighborhood references (a gesture not unfamiliar in GOG's own early lyrics). GOG now offers a digitally enhanced ghetto snapshot through the metaphor of ISO, a measure of camera lens sensitivity to light. High ISOs—and nine thousand is extremely high—let in more light and increase shutter speed, augmenting the grain of the photo while allowing for the capture of fast-moving objects.

The metaphor implies GOG's ability to capture the fast-moving ghetto in all its granularity, a vision that paradoxically allows the rapper to see past local detail. The interchangeability of rap, ghetto, and periferia encourages a slippage between the Brazilian periferia and the world:

> O rap é o gueto; o gueto pode ser o mundo
> A gueto-visão unida a informação, elo fecundo
> Radicais livres, livros de vários calibres
> Quanto vale? Se não sabe, pergunte ao ourives
> Sarau Bem Black emplaca a importância da aliança
> Sarau Bem Legal, recital só com crianças
> Combato o estresse lendo a obra de Ferréz
> Samba da Vela, já fisgou, salvou dez vezes dez
> Cooperifa, quem decifra o peso dessa casa?
> Periferia soberana, Opa Soul, Sarau da Brasa.[80]

> (Rap is the ghetto; the ghetto can be the world
> Ghetto-vision unified information, a fertile link
> Free radicals, books of various calibers
> How much is it? If you don't know, ask the jeweler

Sarau Bem Black supplies the importance of alliance
Sarau Bem Legal, a recital with only children
I combat stress reading a book by Ferréz
Samba da Vela, already hooked, solved ten times ten
Cooperifa, who can make sense of the strength of that house?
Sovereign periphery, Opa Soul, Sarau da Brasa.)

The first verse introduces a peculiar syllogism linking rap, ghetto, and world through "ghetto-vision," evocative of a TV broadcast. The following verse plays on the term "radicais livres" (free radicals), a pun between the chemistry phenomenon of unpaired valence electrons (which result in highly reactive compounds) and the notion of a free radical people whose weapons, in this case, are multiple-caliber books. GOG then provides evidence for the scalability of the ghetto: the *literatura periférica* (peripheral literature) movement spearheaded by Ferréz; the *saraus* (literary circles) that emerged around hip hop in São Paulo's periphery and subsequently spread to other cities; the legendary Sarau da Cooperifa, opened in São Paulo's zona sul in 2001.[81] He lands on a formulation that inverts historically received notions of the marginalized neighborhood as a place in conflict with the normative legal order, proclaiming a *periferia soberana* (sovereign periphery). By folding the hyperlocal into a ghetto world, GOG transforms "the land of the ghetto into the land of myth and the future."[82] What futures could emerge in a "sovereign periphery"? How might a "ghetto universe" offer alternative and more inclusive models for citizenship?[83]

La aldea: Rural Solidarity and the Global Village

The ghetto trope does not figure prominently in Havana hip hop, probably as a result of the Cuban Revolution's nationalization of housing and the relative absence of slums, or what are called *barrios insalubres*.[84] Many of the most active early rappers of the 1990s hailed from the revolution's flagship housing development, the newly constructed city of Alamar in East Havana. Not unlike Brasília, Alamar followed a future-oriented utopian vision and residents emigrated there to build the city, promised housing in exchange for labor.[85] The urban form of Alamar was designed to facilitate the creation of Ernesto "Che" Guevara's *hombre nuevo* (new man). In his famous 1965 letter "El socialismo y el hombre en Cuba" (Man and Socialism in Cuba), Guevara emphasized a Marxian dialectic between individual and society, advocating individual sacrifice for a common cause and calling on the masses to follow their party vanguard toward a communist horizon.[86] In this sense, Alamar's functional organization was intended to leave "no place for distraction."[87] To ensure maximal efficiency, the city featured Soviet-style segmented square towers separated into numbered zones with goods, services, and cultural centers (many of which remained unfinished) in each zone.[88] Ironically, instead of promoting homogenization, Alamar's diversity of residents (who had come from all over Cuba), coupled with its status as a new city lacking established cultural traditions, precipitated the opposite: an artistic avant-garde.[89]

While Alamar was initially the center of Havana hip hop, rappers hailed from all across the city: from more distant peripheries such as La Lisa and Guanabacoa to some of the most central neighborhoods of Centro Habana, Habana Vieja, and El Vedado. Given the food shortages and precarity of the 1990s, early Havana rappers framed their city as a new South Bronx.[90] For a brief period, they emulated the East Coast–West Coast rivalry of US gangsta rap, verbally defending the territories of "Costa Este" (East Coast) in Alamar, "Costa Norte" (North Coast) in El Vedado, and "Costa Oeste" (West Coast) in the neighborhoods of Playa and Marianao.[91] But this animosity was more performed than real: artists would share the scant instrumentals they could get their hands on (generally acquired from foreigners or Cubans returning from abroad).[92] As independent rap studios formed, mostly through the help of foreign remittances and gifts from foreign artists and anthropologists, the necessity to collaborate only increased.[93] Although Alamar was unquestionably a periphery of Havana, since hip hop artists were distributed geographically throughout the city and because scarcity impacted all residents during the Special Period (albeit unevenly), the notion of "periferia é periferia" would not have made sense.[94]

The relative absence in Havana rap of a discourse surrounding urban peripheralization is curious, however, given the documented presence of what is known as *reparterismo*. *Repartero* is a pejorative term that refers to residents of Havana's outer municipalities (*repartos*). During the 1990s, it was used to refer to partner-less dance in timba music.[95] A decade later, the term became associated with reggaeton, drawing on and precipitating a stereotype about the genre's underclass audience members.[96] Repartero eventually became a popular subgenre of reggaeton when artists such as Chocolate MC reappropriated the term associated with urban marginality as a marker of Blackness.[97] Cuban rappers, however, mostly disavowed reparterismo—although on more than one occasion I heard rappers, themselves residents of the repartos, refer to reggaeton artists pejoratively as reparteros.[98] While marginality and scale were central to the discursive placemaking of Cuban rappers, the ghetto trope was conspicuously absent.

Cuban rappers turned instead to the revolution's history of suppressing dissent. When the earliest participants of moña dances to US funk and soul music were still children, Cuban poet Heberto Padilla discovered the difficulty of revolutionizing art under a socialist government. An early supporter of the revolution and collaborator with the literary magazine *Lunes de Revolución*, Padilla befriended Yevgeny Yevtushenko, one of the screenwriters for the 1964 Soviet film *Soy Cuba*. Padilla and Yevtushenko attended Fidel Castro's National Library speeches in June 1961, where the revolutionary leader proclaimed that "el artista más revolucionario sería aquel que estuviera dispuesto a sacrificar hasta su propia vocación artística por la Revolución" (the most revolutionary artists would be those willing to sacrifice even their own artistic vocation for the Revolution).[99] Having experienced the Soviet progression toward totalitarianism, Yevtushenko expressed concern to Padilla that Cuba might follow the Soviet Union's example.[100] Soviet Central Committee Secretary Andrei Zhdanov, for example, had rejected musical innovation as an expression of decadent bourgeois individualism, paradoxically aligning the creation of "new Soviet music" with the rigorous maintenance of cultural patrimony.[101] As Susan Buck-Morss observes, in spite of the Party's emphasis on self-criticism to improve society, the political vanguard's protectionist framework ironically limited the self-reflexive critique characteristic of an artistic avant-garde.[102]

After returning from a trip to the Soviet Union, Padilla published the book of poems *Fuera del juego* (1968), which praises revolutionary sacrifice and contains references to scarcity.[103] *Fuera del juego* won a competition of the National Union of Writers and Artists of Cuba (UNEAC) and the judges, including the revered José Lezama Lima, praised the book as an exemplary work of self-criticism.[104] Less than a month later, however, the UNEAC changed its mind and added a famous disclosure restricting the future publication of Padilla's work. In what came to be known as the Padilla affair, the poet faced censorship, interrogation, imprisonment, and even psychotropic drug treatment.[105] As Lillian Guerra puts it, while the Padilla affair "proposed that doubt, debate, and criticism—true nonconformity—were intrinsic and necessary for the Revolution to grow and succeed," it also triggered one of the worst instances of government repression.[106]

The censorship of rappers has included detention and imprisonment, temporary relocation to the countryside, and the closing of venues.[107] In 2021, rappers at the center of a hunger strike organized by the Movimiento San Isidro in Old Havana were indefinitely detained for protesting, inviting comparisons with Padilla.[108] However, censorship more often took the form of the relatively benign but remarkably specific substitution of words or phrases. For example, for the song "Sentimientos desafinados" (Out-of-tune feelings) to be approved for radio and television play, Malcoms "Justicia" was required to alter the verse "sistema programado y caducado" (programmed and expired system) to "*circuito* programado y caducado" (programmed and expired *circuit*).[109] In this sense, Geoffrey Baker argues that the censorship of Cuban rap, rather than a cycle of repression and compliance, more closely resembles a "cat and mouse" game.[110] It was this constantly shifting marginality vis-à-vis state cultural institutions, rather than the more traditional hip hop notion of urban marginality, that provided Cuban rappers a scalable trope.

Aldo and El B of Los Aldeanos entitled their 2003 debut album *Censurados* (Censored). Although they had not yet faced significant censorship, the album title expresses a shared sense of alienation.[111] The group solidified an antiestablishment discourse with the polemical 2007 compilation album *La comisión depuradora* (The cleansing commission), which parodies the purges presided over by Guevara during the revolution's early years. Ironically, rather than facing censorship, the album earned high-profile performance opportunities for the artists and inspired a new generation of social critics.[112] At the height of their popularity in 2008 and 2009, Los Aldeanos hosted weekly rap *peñas* (shows with invited guests) that were labeled "counterrevolutionary" and commonly shut down, but they were typically allowed to reopen elsewhere.[113]

In August 2008, Pablo Milanés, one of the Cuban Revolution's most beloved singers, invited Los Aldeanos to perform at the end of his concert at the José Martí Anti-Imperialist Platform.[114] Unbeknownst to the artists, the festival was underwritten by United States Agency for International Development (USAID) contractors hoping to use Cuban rap to spread "new ideas" (US notions of democracy).[115] However, even in the Cuban-made documentary film about Los Aldeanos entitled *Revolution*, Milanés attests that the group was "doing excellent work" and that, despite musical differences, they shared a common objective with nueva trova singer-songwriters (the artists most closely associated with the revolution) of innovating Cuban music and "expressing something new."[116] While the challenges of performing as a musician in the context of a highly bureaucratic and regulatory cultural apparatus should not be understated, it is worth highlighting the ability of Cuban rap groups such as Los Aldeanos to continue performing throughout the late 2000s despite their antiestablishment discourse.

The group name Los Aldeanos (the villagers) introduces a pun between Aldo and *aldea*, a small rural village generally lacking its own jurisdiction and a word rarely, if ever, used in Havana.[117] "La aldea" became a slogan and sonic signature for Los Aldeanos, also giving name to Aldo's independent record label. The aldea evinces an additional marker of scale not unlike the periferia, with the crucial difference that *aldea* does not derive from everyday speech, nor does it index urban space. Nevertheless, Aldo and El B consistently used *aldea* as a proxy for "mi barrio" (my neighborhood) or "mi gente" (my people), signifying a community united around an imagined rural ethos.[118] Los Aldeanos's neighborhood territory of Nuevo Vedado is less gridded than its counterpart El Vedado (Havana's best-known example of planned urbanization), but Nueva Vedado is centrally located and exhibits few rural characteristics.[119] Why, then, did Aldo and El B cast their community in rural terms? As El B explains in *Revolution*, "we live in a small country, in a small city, in a small neighborhood, and for us the principle of the aldea is this: a place where all people—even if it seems like a utopia—collaborate with each other, have the same objective."[120] Thus rather than referring to urban space, the aldea was intended as a metaphor for a worldview.

In one of Los Aldeanos's earliest songs, El B defined the group name thus: "Aparte de aldeano, revolucionario man / Aparte de ser cubano, amo mi patria también" (Besides being an aldeano, revolutionary man / Besides being a Cuban, I love my motherland too).[121] This ambivalent expression of nationalism syllogistically links the figures of aldeano, revolutionary, and patriot. It is difficult to ignore an echo here—ironic or genuine—of Cuba's national hero José Martí, whom El B would have studied in secondary school. In Martí's writings, the figure of the aldea functions as a metaphor for the autochthonous state of nature, a fairytale land separate from and prior to modernity.[122] Among his most famous works, Martí's "Nuestra América" (Our America; published in 1891) begins with the aldeano: "The vain aldeano believes that his village is the entire world, and as long as he remains mayor, or can torment the rival that stole his girlfriend, or his piggy bank grows, he takes the universal order as a good thing—without knowing about the giants whose boots extend for seven leagues and can crush him, nor the quarrel of the comets in the sky, which move through the air asleep, devouring worlds. What remains of the aldea in America must awake."[123] Martí's aldeano evokes a prior temporality rather than a physical location: an imagined premodern innocence, albeit inflected with the barbarism of Latin America that was famously described by Domingo Faustino Sarmiento.[124] This equivocal first paragraph of "Nuestra América" establishes the aldea as both the root of Latin America's backwardness and the motor for its future development, an escape from the modern city.[125]

Tendentially evoking Martí, Fidel Castro used the word *aldea* in speeches defending development and urbanization. In a 1974 speech in Matanzas, for example, he celebrated the edification of multistory buildings: "We see that soon the first twelve-story building will be built in Matanzas, for which reason Matanzas will lose that appearance of aldea it sometimes has; the same for the city of Santa Clara, which will also begin to have a few tall buildings. The earth must be economized, because we need it to produce food; we must grow upward and make tall buildings."[126] Here urbanization precipitates a loss of "that appearance of aldea," responding to the imperative to "economize" or "save" (*ahorrar*) the earth by "growing" (*crecer*) upward. Crucially, though the appearance of aldea may disappear, its essence (the earth, or *tierra*) will be preserved. While rejecting its developmentalist impulse, Los Aldeanos's neo-Arcadian vision of the aldea reproduces the revolution's Martí-inspired agrarian utopianism.[127]

However, technological innovation was central to the formation of the aldea of Los Aldeanos. At a time when few Cubans had internet access, Aldo and El B distributed their music as MP3s on USB flash memory drives.[128] Lacking (and, at times, refusing) institutional support, they took personal responsibility for the dissemination of their music (aided by foreign anthropologists and producers such as Melisa Rivière).[129] The role of technology in the circulation of their songs and albums points to an additional understanding of the aldea: as a digital network linked by USB drives and ports primarily unplugged from the internet. As Aldo puts it: "Que yo me llevo todos los temas en un MP3 / Por si allá arriba en las nubes tienen puerto USB después" (I'll bring all my songs on an MP3 / In case later, up there in the clouds, there's a USB port).[130]

This digital dimension of the Cuban "underground" hip hop network invites hearing aldea not only as an invocation of the rural but also as a sample of the phrase *aldea global* (global village), a term introduced in the 1960s by media theorist Marshall McLuhan and debated in Havana during the 1990s.[131] For McLuhan, the invention of electricity brought the world into instantaneous interconnectivity, altering the traditional center-periphery structure of human societies.[132] The speed of electricity was so fast that the "fragmented civilization of center-margin structure is suddenly experiencing an instantaneous reassembling of all its mechanized bits into an organic whole . . . the global village."[133] The homogenized, hyperconnected unity of McLuhan's quasi-mystic global village sounds diametrically opposed to Martí's premodern Latin American aldea, but the digital network curated by Los Aldeanos brings the two together.

The Cuban hip hop aldea was indeed going global: by the mid 2000s, Los Aldeanos had gained international notoriety because of the online dissemination of their work by unknown third parties.[134] Their international reputation increasingly posed a challenge for their career on the island. The 2009 song "La naranja se picó" (The orange is rotten) attacked the government explicitly for denying foreign visas to artists—which El B had personally experienced for two consecutive years, prevented from participating in the Red Bull–sponsored international freestyle competition the Batalla de los Gallos.[135] The release that year of the antigovernment album *El atropello* (The accident) coupled with the presence of USAID in Havana (although Aldo and El B fervently deny having been infiltrated) eventually proved too much for state representatives to turn their heads the other way. By 2014, Aldo and El B, along with colleague Silvito "El Libre," had taken advantage of foreign touring opportunities to relocate permanently to Florida, and Aldo claims the group was banned from all performance venues in Cuba.[136] This was around the time I began conducting ethnographic research in Havana, and Los Aldeanos had left a large void in the Havana rap scene.

In yet another iteration of the "cat and mouse" game, during one of their first media appearances in Miami, Aldo and El B ironically defied the Cuban American audience's expectations by refusing to attack the Cuban government. This earned them a highly favorable write-up in Cuba's periodical *Caimán Barbudo* by renowned Cuban music critic Joaquín Borges-Triana. The article went so far as to quote former Cuban Minister of Culture Abel Prieto calling Los Aldeanos "gente revolucionaria" (revolutionary people).[137] Now that the aldea had gone global and ceased to echo as a rallying cry of translocal solidarity in Havana, Los Aldeanos no longer represented a threat, and Cuban cultural institutions could reclaim them. By the end of the 2010s, rappers still residing in Cuba were increasingly learning that the only way forward was through state institutions.[138] To sample José Martí, what remains of the aldea in Cuban hip hop?

After Rap

This chapter has traced the way the grounded signifiers of baz, periferia, and aldea—at once a product of and a contribution to the globalization of hip hop—are tied to urban form and historically conditioned scales of marginality in Port-au-Prince, São Paulo, and Havana. Idiosyncratic invocations of rurality derive from a historically rural majority (Haiti), a long-standing association between urban precarity and rural backwardness (Brazil), and a renovation of nineteenth-century idealizations of pre-modern sociability (Cuba). By scaling their specific experiences of marginality, rappers elaborate translocal, even cosmopolitan spaces of belonging. Yet if their worldly yearnings enact a "networked territoriality," it must be emphasized, as Rita Segato observes, that the "constitutive elements of a territorial experience are not fixed but rather historically defined."[139] Thus when rappers began to cede space to new trends during the 2010s, their use of scale shifted. Future work could further historicize the role of scale in rap and global popular music more broadly.[140]

How, for example, did the fusion of rap with more mainstream genres such as jazz and timba in Cuba, samba in Brazil, or rara and rasin in Haiti affect the idea that "rap is my place"?[141] In what ways did offshoot genres such as Brazilian ostetanção, Cuban traptón, or Haitian trap (see chapter 1) rescale or recalibrate the hip hop trope of marginality? How did the temporary reestablishment of diplomatic relations between the United States and Cuba in 2014 influence what it meant to "sound American"? How did Brazilian rappers respond to the increase in cultural repression following the 2019 election of Jair Bolsonaro? To what degree did the 2021 assassination of Haitian President Jovenel Moïse influence the baz framework of Haitian rap kreyòl artists? How did these new breaks and flows interface with the global wave of Latin urban or urbano music?[142] What, to return once more to Bárbaro's question from chapter 3, did it matter to sound American? Rather than reifying categories such as national and imported, the history of hip hop's rooting in the Americas exposes some of the fallacies and dangers of (musical) essentialism. Bárbaro, who himself emigrated to Finland in the mid 2010s, completed his couplet thus: "¿Qué importa si sonamos americano hermano? / Yo y mi DJ priorizamos sonar como nos salga del ano" (What does it matter if we sound American, brother? / My DJ and I prioritize sounding however it comes out of our ass).[143] There is perhaps no better mission statement for world hip hop.

5 Writing
"Enraizados da letra"

IN A well-known anecdote from his memoir of anthropological research in the Brazilian Amazon, Claude Lévi-Strauss recounts observing a Nambikwara leader trace nonsensical symbols on paper to assert his power by appropriating the anthropologist's writing technology. Having understood the "function of writing," the nonliterate Indigenous leader causes Lévi-Strauss to reflect on the way writing has been used as an instrument of subjugation and empire building.[1] In Latin America, colonizers imposed a hierarchy between alphabetic and oral communication, wielding letters as a precondition for participating in Western modernity.[2] While literacy was commonly withheld from enslaved people of African descent, it was imposed on Indigenous people as an instrument of colonization and Christianization. Upon arrival in a new territory, colonizers would read aloud the *Requerimiento,* a written document whose oral recitation or staged reading established their divinely ordained authority to convert natives into Christians (hence, Spanish subjects) and provided legal justification for enslaving those who disobeyed.[3] The written word was a source of authority for this colonial performance of sovereignty and subjugation.

Ángel Rama famously described the colonial urbanization of Latin America through the metaphor of a "lettered city," proposing that colonial cities developed not only around ethno-racial and socioeconomic patterns of segregation but also through a symbolic order delineated by the ability to read and write.[4] A small group of lettered elites excluded the nonliterate majority from involvement in city planning and policy-making by regulating literacy, linking the "right to the city" to the "right to literature."[5] As Antonio Cornejo Polar puts it, writing entered the region "not so much as a system of communication but rather within the limits of order and authority, almost as if its only possible meaning were power."[6]

The connection between writing and power not uncommonly enters the lyrics of rappers—and perhaps no artist more than GOG, Brazilian rap's "poeta nacional" (national poet). In 2018, I attended a performance by GOG in a public plaza of São Paulo's zona sul (southern zone).[7] The event was sponsored by the Lula Livre (Free Lula) campaign calling for the release of Brazil's incarcerated former president; at one point, event organizers presented GOG with the white-starred red flag of the Worker's Party (PT), and the rapper led the crowd in a call-and-response of "Lula livre." GOG's lyrics, however, focused not on Lula but on the politics of rap itself. Halfway through the concert, GOG descended from the stage and joined the crowd. His verses describe rap's community poetics thus:

> Agita, grita, pela poesia na escrita
> Sinfonia transformada em partitura, acredita
> Nós na fita, em CD, vinil, livro, DVD
> No formato que tiver que ser, ah, vai ser
> Oxigênio que faltava, nosso amuleto
> Enraizados da letra, ISO 9000 do gueto.[8]

> (Agitate, yell, for the poetry of writing
> Symphony transformed into a musical score, believe it
> We're in the area: on CD, vinyl, book, DVD
> In whatever format it has to be, ah, it'll be
> Oxygen that was lacking, our amulet
> Rooted in lyrics and the letter, ISO 9000 of the ghetto.)

An acoustics of the voice (*grita*) and bodily inscription (*agita*), rap is also written poetry (*poesia na escrita*). Not only a symphony (among the most prestigious compositional forms of Western classical music), rap transforms music into a graphic score (*partitura*). Not just a collective expression of "Nós na fita" ("we're in the area" or "it's about us"), rap is the inscription of acoustic data on recording media (*fita* literally means "tape"). At once oxygen (a bodily necessity), documentary photography (a high-ISO ghetto snapshot), and amulet (religious charm), rap is physical, graphic, spiritual inscription—a writing process forged out of centuries of exclusion of Afro-descendent communities from letters.

GOG encourages his listeners, as H. Samy Alim puts it, to interpret "Hip Hop lyrics/poetics as literature."[9] The etymological root for the word *literature* is the Latin word for an alphabetic letter, *litera*. Drawing on this etymology, Walter Ong rejects the "strictly preposterous" term "oral literature," which fails to account for the absence of written residue in the "primary orality" of preliterate poet-singers prior to the near-universal introduction of some form of alphabetic technology throughout the world.[10] Where literature comes into being as text, oral poetry can only be transcribed as text; the oral tradition "was precisely not a literature; literature was what might survive oral tradition, or emerge from it."[11] But oral literature, or what Haitian psychiatrist Ernst Mirville called *oraliture,* captures the interface between orality and literacy audible in GOG's lyrics.[12] Singing with and to Grajaú residents, GOG modeled a community "enraizados da letra," rooted in lyrics and the letter (playing on the dual meaning of *letra*). Where rooting in hip hop culture provided for rappers in Cuba, Brazil, and Haiti the ability to undermine notions of national culture (chapter 3) and to scale between local and global forms of belonging (chapter 4), rooting in lyrics and the letter describes a practice of community writing through lyric ensemble and sharing rhymes. To what degree does GOG's lyric ensemble extend across the Americas? How does his rhyming triad of *agita, grita,* and *escrita* capture a larger articulation in rap of embodiment, listening, and writing?

Affirming community around the "right to write" is significant given the history of Atlantic slavery,[13] which typically pitted "black cultural traditions that favored speech" against "white laws that restricted literacy."[14] In the United States, slaveholding states strongly restricted or outright prohibited literacy for free and enslaved African Americans in an effort to impede the desire for social mobility.[15] In Brazil, though laws of the Portuguese empire did not forbid teaching enslaved people to read and write, local regulations restricted their access to public education.[16] In response to these policies, many Afro-diasporic writers have inscribed traces of orality in literature, attempting to represent textually, as Henry Louis Gates Jr. puts it, the "oral within the written."[17]

The earliest known Latin American example is Afro-Cuban poet Juan Francisco Manzano, who was born enslaved. Manzano wrote his 1835 *Autobiography,* which he entitled *La verdadera istoria de mi vida* (The true story of my life), at the request of white reformer and humanist Domingo del Monte, who planned to use the document as anti-slavery propaganda.[18] In exchange, del Monte's literary circle promised to purchase Manzano's manumission. Though the del Monte group significantly altered the manuscript, corrected its orthography, and granted Manzano no editorial control, Manzano's narrative reveals a specific literary enterprise. In response to his owners' efforts to withhold literacy, Manzano recounts surreptitiously composing décimas (ten-line poems) in his mind: "cuando yo tenia dose años ya abia compuesto muchas desimas de memorias causa pr. qe. mis padrinos no querian qe. aprendiese a escribir" (when I was twelve I had already composed many décimas by memory, since my owners didn't want me to learn to read).[19] Not yet able to read or write, Manzano would have developed this technique of virtual writing by listening to performed décimas, which were commonly improvised. Writing by ear provided for Manzano an entryway into the "lettered city" and, simultaneously, a mode of decolonizing received notions of literacy.

A sonic or aural turn in Latin American cultural studies has revealed some of the voices and sounds to which the "lettered city" had always been porous.[20] Much of this work emphasizes aurality, "the sounding of the *writing*" or its "embodied acoustic performance."[21] In *Aurality: Listening and Knowledge in Nineteenth-Century Colombia*, Ana María Ochoa Gautier analyzes the acoustics of travel writing, novels, and grammar books to emphasize the role of communities that have traditionally been considered "nonliterate" in the construction of various texts.[22] Indebted to this work, my aim is somewhat different. Rather than analyzing how rap as a verbal art form has influenced textual practices, I listen to rap itself as inscription. I do not treat rap as a synthesis or mediation between orality and literacy, but rather as a practice of "writing by ear,"[23] or *aural* literacy. The aural techniques of rap writing begin to break down the orality/literacy binary, questioning whether such a binary ever existed in practice.

Aurality resounds not only in the sonic materiality of writing, but also clears space for a relational, embodied ethics of listening. Jennifer Lynn Stoever observes that Afro-diasporic writers have consistently deployed "listening as a form of agency, a technique of survival, an ethics of community building, a practice of self-care, a guide through racialized space, a site of racialization, and a mode of decolonizing."[24] By emphasizing listening and rereading hip hop through the particularities of their languages, places, and histories, rappers in the Americas elaborate a community writing practice in dialogue with older musico-poetic traditions. This chapter traces how rappers in Cuba, Brazil, and Haiti ground their work in Afro-diasporic performance practices such as *pwen,* samba, and jazz and cultural traditions as diverse as *repente* improvisation, *pixação* tagging, lyric poetry, and journalism. Listening to how and why Latin American rappers write also points to larger questions about the function of poetry at the turn of the millennium and the capacity of words to produce material effects.

Escucha calle piensa: Listening to the News

As detailed in chapter 4, many of the earliest raps of Los Aldeanos were about neighborhood life in Nuevo Vedado, Havana. In "El periodista" (The journalist), El B rhymes himself a journalist-chronicler. With pervasive near-rhyme and incessant assonance, he offers his listener a

> Subterráneo diario del barrio y escenarios sumarios
> De necesarios comentarios sin horarios, de MCs
> De un país donde se muestra un matiz que nunca ves
> Y lo que dura una semana llega una vez al mes.
> Escasez de respuesta aumenta el flujo de porqués
> Es el resultado de una encuesta, puesta la paciencia
> Penitencia de un pueblo que lucha, escucha calle piensa
> En sobrevivir sin temor a prescindir de vergüenza.
> . . . .
> Periódicos son letras, letras no son periódicos
> Diagnósticos recetados por un MC, no médico
> Incrédulos aquellos que nos siguieron la pista
> Desde el cronista realista El B, el periodista
> El liricista mencionado, no publicado
> La voz del barrio: Santa María, Nuevo Vedado
> El mal mirado pues lo único que sabe hacer
> Es publicar verdades no memorias del ayer.[25]

> (Subterranean neighborhood diary and summary scenes
> Of necessary commentaries without a schedule, from MCs
> Of a country where there's a nuance that you never see
> And what arrives once a month lasts for a week.
> Scarcity of response, the flow of *why*s increases
> It's the result of a survey, challenging patience
> Penitence of a people who struggle, listen street, think
> About living without fear and avoiding shame.
> . . . .
> Newspapers are letters/lyrics, letters/lyrics aren't newspapers
> Diagnostics prescribed by an MC, not a doctor
> Incredulous those who follow our track
> From the realist chronicler, El B, the journalist

The lyricist mentioned, not published
The voice of the neighborhood: Santa María, Nuevo Vedado
Shunned because the only thing he knows how to do
Is to publish truths, not yesterday's memories.)

El B's self-fashioning as a *cronista* (chronicler) perhaps evokes the hybrid literary-journalistic genre of the *crónica* (chronicle), popular among Latin American fin-de-siècle writers such as José Martí and associated with the representation of quotidian life in the city.[26] More directly, "El periodista" samples contemporaneous Cuban musical genres such as timba in its presentation of rap as an "oral newspaper."[27] The word *diario* carries the double meaning in Spanish of daily newspaper and diary, and El B deploys both, characterizing his rap as a collective journal and independent free press, a foil to state-controlled periodicals. Echoing GOG by drawing on the double meaning (in Spanish, as in Portuguese) of *letras* as letters and lyrics, he proclaims that "Periódicos son letras, letras no son periódicos" (Newspapers are letters/lyrics, letters/lyrics aren't newspapers). The implication is that rap lyrics constitute a more accurate newspaper than the letters comprising party-run periodicals such as the daily *Granma*.[28] With the apostrophe to his listener "escucha calle piensa" (listen street, think), El B distances his song from the print technologies it critiques by advocating listening as consciousness-raising. The terse dictum instructs an implied listener to hear rap as an alternative to print media.

However, Robin D. G. Kelley argues that the "assumption that rappers are merely street journalists does not allow for the playfulness and storytelling that is so central to Hip Hop specifically, and black vernacular culture generally."[29] Part of a larger set of Afro-diasporic signifying practices, rap songs are less often modes of "street journalism" than expressions of a rapper's ability to "rock the mike."[30] Indeed, "El periodista" is not so much a journalistic account as a second-order journal about El B's function as a rap journalist. The rapper's self-reflexive boasting of his capacity to do the work of a journalist recalls the recursive presentation of raplove which, as I demonstrated in chapter 2, resonates with Western lyric poetry. For centuries, lyric poetry has been understood as an "antigenre to the news."[31] When poetry tells the news, Jahan Ramazani suggests, it does so by "mediat[ing] contemporary history through a transnational thicket of long-memoried aesthetic structures that entwine the news with alternative temporalities."[32] This is perhaps the sense in which El B delivers not the news per se but rather his self-fashioning as a news bearer (a process he presumably carries out elsewhere).

In Haiti, popular music has long served as an important alternative to, and source of, the news. Rara street bands register the history and present of the disenfranchised.[33] Musicians and poets of diverse genres, among them urban *twoubadou,* rural *sanba,* and Vodou *oudjenikon,* are expected to critique important people and document community events and grassroots struggles.[34] Many Haitian rappers follow the chronicling impulse of traditional popular music and consider themselves exponents of *mizik angaje* (politically committed music). Port-au-Prince based PIC, for example, rhymes himself coming into being as a documentary writer: "M ekri m, paske m pale de vi m e de mizè m" (I write myself, because I speak of my life and my misery).[35] His creation of the rap "I" (*m*) through writing (*ekri*) draws authenticity from observations of daily life.

Similarly, BIC deploys autobiographical realism to document the everyday:

Mwen la chak jou m ap gade
Pyeton k ap pase, machin k ap pase
Mwen la chak jou m ap gade
Sivil k ap pase, leta k ap pase
Mwen la chak jou m ap gade
DG k ap pase, ONG k ap pase
Mwen la chak jou m ap gade
Sirèn k ap pase, lespwa k ap pase
Men pesonn pa mande m kisa m ap fè la
Bonjou sa k vle koute
Non pa m se kokorat
Sivouple.[36]

(I'm there every day watching
Pedestrians passing through, cars passing through
I'm there every day watching
Lambda citizens passing through, state officials passing through
I'm there every day watching
CEOs passing through, NGOs passing through
I'm there every day watching
Sirens passing through, hope passing through
But nobody asks me what I'm doing there
Hello is all anyone wants to hear
They call me a cockroach
Please.)

The anaphora of "I'm there every day watching" captures the sequential rhythms and cyclical return of daily life in Port-au-Prince as BIC observes the passing of pedestrians, cars, state officials, NGO representatives, even hope. He raps himself waiting and watching, ignored by passersby, seeking some form of acknowledgment other than *kokorat* (a pejorative term referring to a pilferer or homeless person). The recurrent deixis *la* ("here" or "there" in Kreyòl) leaves the song's place undefined, allowing BIC to align his lyric "I" with the disadvantaged majority. Through the anonymity of place and the universality of daily life, he scales a first-person rap chronicle to a collective archive of mundane, quotidian experience that would almost certainly be ignored by the news cycle. The lyrics emphasize a proximity between the rap "I" and the rapper's "eye." Again, however, the anaphora "Mwen la chak jou m ap gade" is a second-order account: the verse documents the rapper documenting the everyday.

The meta-journalistic structure of these lyrics derives from the fact that, unlike journalism, rap's truth claim has less to do with demonstrable facts and verifiable sources than with representation: how well a rapper *presents again* (mimetic representation) and *speaks on behalf of* (political representation) a community.[37] In Brazil, the genre of rap and the "peripheral literature" movement it inspired have been called "experiential realism: what we read are precisely lived experiences, above all when they are recreated fictitiously."[38] When I attended a June 2018 concert by São Paulo–based rapper Bia Doxum at the Reação Hip Hop cultural center in São Paulo's *zona leste* (eastern zone), she deployed experiential realism as a framing device for one of her songs. To introduce "Culpa minha?" (My fault?), which narrates the story of a young woman blamed for a sexual assault committed against her, Doxum described the song as not "her story" but the untold story of "so many women"—an anonymous autobiography of collective trauma or what Fumi Okiji calls a "plural event."[39] This framing suggests, as several hip hop scholars have observed, that rap's emphasis on the "I" is not necessarily egocentric and can serve to affirm community by expressing collective experience.[40] While commonly the subject of braggadocio and self-aggrandizement,[41] the rap "I" can also become a "collective 'We.'"[42]

For many Brazilian rappers, the communal poetics of experiential realism derive from samba, which is consistently cited as one of Brazilian rap's most important antecedents.[43] Those who draw links between samba and rap emphasize that both are "black peripheral forms of sociability and conscience."[44] As rapper Marcelo D2 put it, "Rap is a re-reading

Bia Doxum performs at the Reação Hip Hop cultural center in São Paulo, June 26, 2018. (Photo by author, used with permission)

of samba. If you can't see that, you don't understand a thing about rap, or about samba."⁴⁵ Without question, the most significant samba singer for Brazilian rappers is José Bezerra da Silva, who chronicled favela life between the 1970s and 2000s. A resident of the Morro do Cantagalo favela in Rio de Janeiro, Bezerra rejected the themes of love and loss that had pervaded popular samba up to that point: "I can't sing of love when I never had it. I'm a realist, I sing reality."⁴⁶ Echoing and anticipating Brazilian rappers, he sang himself a "poeta operário" (working-class poet),⁴⁷ part of a larger practice in which samba musicians "not uncommonly sang themselves as poets."⁴⁸ Possibly a nod to the incipient phenomenon of US gangsta rap, Bezerra's 1990 album *Eu não sou santo* (I'm not a saint) features a cover image of the singer tied to a cross wearing an ammunition belt and brandishing a pistol in each hand.

Brazilian rappers grafted Bezerra's favela realism onto hip hop's characteristic "ghettocentricity,"⁴⁹ but what they took most from Bezerra was the *malandro,* a literary type. According to Antônio Cândido, the malandro is an ambivalent trickster and foundational figure of Brazilian literature that moves between a dialectic of order and disorder, law and transgression, ultimately being absorbed positively as a symbol of Brazilianness.[50] Cândido traces the malandro to the Spanish "golden age" *pícaro,* a narrator-protagonist of humble beginnings who would improve his socioeconomic position through dubious means.[51] *Malandragem* (qualities relating to the malandro) has also been associated with Afro-Brazilian Macumba religious cults, and the Brazilian malandro likely derives from the divine trickster or outlaw in Yoruba mythology known as Exu (Echu-Eleguá in Cuba or Papa Legba in Haiti).[52] By performing the malandro, Bezerra and the rappers he inspired mark a transition from Cândido's "dialectic of malandragem" to what João César de Castro Rocha calls a "dialectic of marginality." Here, rather than a synthesis or conciliation between the malandro's positive and negative polls, what emerges is a direct and sometimes violent confrontation surrounding social inequalities, a topic developed further in chapter 6.[53]

Yet Bezerra cast himself as a "good *malandro,*" an ambassador for the favelas and Robin Hood–like companion who would take only from the rich.[54] For Black Brazilian musicians, as David Treece puts it, *"malandragem* posed the option of 'performing' a certain kind of marginalized social identity as art, of aestheticizing that identity, of transforming it into a style."[55] Thus in Brazilian rap, malandragem has less to do with *what* is being represented than with *how* it is represented. Thaíde, for example, makes malandragem a formal maneuver: "Na verdade, a malandragem tá na maneira como vou rimando contra a maré" (In truth, malandragem is in the way I go rhyming against the tide).[56] The verses carry out the malandragem they describe: making *maré* rhyme with *malandragem* is indeed an exercise in "rhyming against the tide" (as well as a play on the saying "remar contra a maré," rowing or fighting against the current).

Padêro MC's appropriately named rap group Relatos de Fortaleza (Fortaleza stories) arrives at a related formulation by asserting "criminality" in style only: "meu estilo é de bandido, mas é só o estilo" (my style is of a criminal, but it's only the style).[57] Padêro's colleague Carolina Rebouças similarly cites malandragem as a lifestyle of learning: "Ainda tenho muito que aprender / Afinal, malandragem é viver" (I still have a lot to learn / In the end, malandragem is living).[58] Rebouças's verse in turn samples GOG, whose song "A verdadeira malandragem" (True malandragem) transforms a probably fictionalized testimonial into a didactic lesson: "um dia a vida mostra pra você que a verdadeira malandragem é viver" (one day life shows you that true malandragem is living).[59] Thus a literary trope, filtered through samba, is transformed into a hip hop (life) style to be cited, recited, distributed, and shared among artists.

Elsewhere, GOG elevates rap's testimonial function to the level of parable to elaborate a structural critique of crime. The song "Mais uma história" (Yet another story) transmits the side of the story that would likely be left out of a journalistic account:

> Aqui moleque é perseguido pela fome desde o berço
> Não suportou, traz o terço, o terço
> O moleque saia, saia, não ouvia conselho
> Só ele e o espelho, faz tempo que não vejo
> Na ânsia de realizar seu desejo
> Vacilou na fita, história escrita
> Realidade cruel no dia de visita
> Um senhor chega no distrito pra depor
> A queixa contra seu neto, o agressor
> Quebrou o barraco inteiro, bang bang
> Sangue do mesmo, sangue dividido
> E é só o início, é bom começar a rezar
> Olhar pro lado, ver, sentir como o outro está
> Eu sei é difícil no luxuoso edifício
> Uma cadeira de chefe seu objetivo
> Mas se eu disser que não foi feito pra você
> Por melhor que você fizer.
> Não acredita maldita praga capitalista
> Ter poder, estar, manter-se em primeiro lugar
> Já prevejo onde vai terminar
> É hora de acordar, de acordar, de acordar.[60]

> (Here's a kid pursued by hunger from the cradle
> He couldn't bear it, bring the rosary, the rosary
> The kid would go out, go out, he didn't hear advice
> Just him and the mirror, it's been a while since I saw him
> Eager to realize his desire
> He messed up in the act, story written
> Cruel reality on visiting day
> An older man arrives to the district to testify
> The grievance against his grandson, the aggressor
> He destroyed the entire house, bang bang
> The same blood, blood divided
> And this is just the beginning, it's time to start praying.
> Look to the side, see, feel how the other's doing
> I know it's hard, in the luxury building

A CEO's chair your objective
But if I said it wasn't made for you,
No matter what you do.
Don't believe it, damn capitalist plague
Having power, being there, staying in first place
I see where this is going to end
It's time to wake up, wake up, wake up.)

Here, GOG's storytelling approaches the Afro-diasporic oral tradition of testifying, "a ritualized form of black communication in which the speaker gives verbal witness to the efficacy, truth, and power of some experience in which all blacks have shared."[61] Or to sample Rio de Janeiro rapper MV Bill, GOG engages in the practice of "traficando informação" (trafficking information).[62] "Mais uma história" testifies in two sections: one narrates the parable of a poor boy tempted into crime and imprisoned for it; the other transforms the parable into structural critique. The first verse establishes the scene of the parable with the indefinite deixis *aqui* (here)—an unnamed, generic location in Brazil's urban margins—and proceeds to describe a boy who is made to pray the rosary when he misbehaves. What the boy needed and never had was a mentor, the absence of which led him to rob his grandfather and destroy the family home. Emphasizing the factors that led to the boy's crime, GOG's rap critiques the police report or journalist account, the *história escrita* (written story).

The transition from parable to critique is completed by the word *olhar* (look), which apostrophizes a hypothetical resident of a luxury building who dreams of running a company. The "capitalist plague" blinds the would-be CEO to his complicity in the boy's fate and blames the boy for the structural conditions that led to his crime, a vicious circle perpetuated by the *história escrita*. Rap seeks to break this (news) cycle wherein "nasce um homen pobre / seu destino é sofrer" (a poor man is born / his destiny is to suffer).[63] Unlike the ritualized writing of police reports and the expediency of news articles, GOG uses enjambment liberally and employs frequent echoes, making it difficult to summarize, condense, or reduce his rap to text. The only adequate summary of the song is the song itself—hearing "mais uma história" one more time. The final, echoed word, *acordar* (wake up), which becomes an implicit command, emphasizes the aural dimension of rap literacy. GOG's rap aims to awaken the listener: "not only to inform, but to form,"[64] to produce knowledge through the movement from "in/formation to trans/formation."[65]

Rap's objective, as GOG puts it in a different song, is to "transformar em poesia o dia a dia da periferia" (transform into poetry the day-to-day of the periphery).[66] Coming full circle, this song contains a sample of none other than Bezerra da Silva.[67] And samba would return the favor: when I attended a performance of Samba do Congo in downtown São Paulo in 2018, the group invited a rapper onstage to perform. The cross-pollination between the two musical genres suggests that not only is rap a rereading of samba, but samba can become a rereading of rap. The Samba do Congo anthem appropriately echoes GOG: "Unindo a letra com a melodia / Transformando em poesia com muita satisfação" (Uniting lyrics with melody / Transforming in poetry with a lot of satisfaction).[68] Professing to elevate daily life to the level of poetry through the union of lyrics and melody, these verses resonate with Louis Zukofsky's description of his poetry as an integral function whose lower limit is speech and upper limit is song.[69] Tracing the samba anthem through Zukofsky and back to GOG, rap comes to represent an integral function that extends from a lower limit of material reality to an upper limit of poetry.

This section has contended that one way to listen to rap is as an "antigenre to the news." While professing to offer "eyewitness testimony" (*testemunha ocular*), rap songs more commonly take the form of second-order testimonials in which the rap "I" represents itself representing reality.[70] One of the primary effects of this self-referentiality (which is reminiscent of raplove) is that the information trafficked by rap turns out to be mostly the sonic poetics of hip hop. This is the sense in which El B's imperative "escucha calle piensa" withholds the news it promises to deliver. Rap does not deliver the news but rather an injunction to listen. It is a mode of listening in community, thinking through listening, listening to the street, and making the street listen.

Embromation: Intertextuality, or Writing by Ear

Rappers also listen attentively to other rappers. During a 2014 recording session in his home studio in San Miguel del Padrón, East Havana, Malcoms "Justicia" played for me one of his recent beats and proceeded to improvise a flow of nonsensical phonemes inspired by New York–style rap, demonstrating what the track might sound like with the addition of a rap flow. He paused to explain that for it to be "real rap," it would need to be sung in English (by which he meant Hip Hop Nation Language).[71] A few years later during fieldwork in São Paulo, a Brazilian

Malcoms "Justicia" at work in his converted bedroom studio, 18A16 Producciones, in San Miguel Del Padrón, East Havana, December 20, 2016. (Photo by author)

rapper described to me an early step in his writing process as improvising a flow without words to establish a rhythmic architecture prior to filling it in with semantic meaning.[72] He glossed the process using the anglicized neologism *embromation* (from the Brazilian verb *embromar*), meaning to deceive, joke, procrastinate, or beat around the bush, to pretend to say something important while ostensibly not saying anything at all. Rincon's writing process derives from a broader tradition in which the earliest Brazilian raps were imitative embromations of US-style flows.[73] By citing this tradition, the Brazilian rapper clarified for me what Malcoms had meant: that rap begins "as a rhythm without words."[74] Rappers develop literacy in part through mimicry, a quasi-parodic rooting in received notions about how rap sounds. Grounded in parody, embromation is a citation of English, "reducing it to the mere quality of being English-like," as Constantine Nakassis puts it in a different context.[75] Analogous to the way rap producers construct the break by sampling (citing, reusing, and recontextualizing) fragments of other songs, embromation draws on aural samples achieved through studied listening.[76]

The sound of US rap is arguably the first intertext for rappers in the Americas, but (as previous chapters have made clear) it is by no means the only intertext. When I attended the February 2019 Potaje Urbano hip hop festival in the Cuban provincial town of Colón, Matanzas, the opening night featured a battle (*batalla*) between rappers and *repentistas*. Cuban repente is a form of rural poetry sung by verbal artists who improvise décimas, ten-line lyric poems dating to Spanish colonialism. Following the expansion of the European printing press, published décimas became widely popular among lettered elites on the Iberian Peninsula, where they were also performed and improvised by the nonliterate majority.[77] The décima proved an enduring colonial institution, becoming the most prevalent form of poetry in rural Cuba (as well as Puerto Rico) during the nineteenth century, and employed as a source of periodical information by soldiers leading up to and during the Cuban wars of independence against Spain.[78] Performers of décimas constituted, as Jadiel Díaz Frene puts it, a "mass media of public expression."[79] Thus nineteenth-century rural poets in Cuba repurposed an Iberian lettered tradition for their own revolutionary objectives.

At the Colón hip hop festival, repente entered a new register. Each battle pitted a repentista against a rapper, the repentista accompanied by a three-piece son band and the rapper by a DJ. One repentista would improvise a décima around a *pie forzado* (forced poetic foot) suggested by the audience.[80] A rapper would respond in kind. Although in their improvisations, rappers and repentistas emphasized unity more than difference, the performances were competitive, and the audience determined the winner at the end of each round. Repentistas consistently won greater crowd approval despite the context of the hip hop festival. Multiple rappers in attendance agreed that the verses of the repentistas were more syntactically complex and semantically creative. Rappers had much to learn from the repentistas, they told me. The fact that repente is melodic (following a fixed melody) also seemed a welcome relief from rap's "extreme narrowing of melodic amplitude."[81]

In the final round, the rapper and repentista exchanged places, the repentista rapping over a recorded hip hop instrumental and the rapper improvising a décima accompanied by the son ensemble. The role reversal signaled continuity across these improvisatory verbal art forms: the former, a rural expression originating in the Iberian Peninsula and popular in the nineteenth-century Caribbean; the latter, an urban expression of primarily Black youth originating in marginalized neighborhoods of late-twentieth-century US cities. The willingness of repentistas to share the stage with rappers and try their hand at rapping completed the circle, demonstrating that these two lyrical practices could trace intertextual paths toward shared "poetic citizenship."[82]

A related practice of repente is common in Northeastern Brazil, also derived from the Iberian décima and similarly used to comment on history, social problems, and daily life.[83] Unlike the fixed melody of Cuban repente, Brazilian repente features a rhythmic declamation of improvised verses over a recitation tone, with the voice typically dropping a third on each main beat and descending a fifth stepwise at the end of a phrase. Brazilian repente shares with rap a preference for repeated assonance and near-rhyme, and like their Cuban counterparts, Brazilian rappers cite repente as a precursor to rap.[84] The comparison extends to improvisatory battles. In the *cantoria* song duels or *desafios* between repentistas in Brazil's Northeast, which originally took place in private homes and small bars but subsequently entered large festivals, improvisers are judged on their ability to conform to fixed metric and rhyming patterns while critiquing their opponent.[85]

Fortaleza-based rapper and producer Erivan "Produtos do Morro," originally from Juazeiro do Norte in the rural *sertão* (backlands), emulates the style and sound of repente. He performs in rural attire, incorporates rhythms from the Northeast such as the *baião,* and raps references to repente's characteristic *embolada* flow, for example, in the song "Embolada, repente e baiao."[86] Fortaleza-born RAPadura Xique-Chico (whose rap name evokes a hard candy made from the evaporated sugarcane juice ubiquitous in Brazil's Northeast) also samples the sound of repente, transducing his rap flow into repente embolada. In the song "Norte Nordeste me veste" (North Northeast adorns me), RAPadura begins in prose, then transitions to a rap flow marked by repeated assonance, and finally arrives at the percussive, consonant-heavy two-tone recitation style of embolada. The opening verses establish the sertão as God-given recipient of poetry, significant given the widespread denigration of Brazil's Northeast as impoverished and underdeveloped. The rap verses combine the boasting and assonance characteristic of both repente and rap while maintaining the traditional resolution of rap into end rhyme. In the repente-style embolada verses, the breakbeat falls away to the rhythm of handclaps, and RAPadura abandons end rhyme, embodying motifs of Brazil's Northeast:

> Cortando o céu da estrada, do nada eu faço de tudo
> Com a enxada aro esse mundo e no estudo faço morada
> Sou doce lá dos engenhos e venho com essa doçura
> Contenho poesia pura, a fartura de rima tenho.[87]

(Cutting the sky from the roadway, out of nothing I make anything
With the hoe I till this world and in study I make a home
I'm sweet from the sugarmills and I come with this sweetness
I contain pure poetry and have an abundance of rhyme.)

Here RAPadura performs a repente flow with references to the landscape and history of Brazil's Northeast, which he syncretizes with hip hop tropes of rocking the mic and making something from nothing.[88]

These examples demonstrate the way rappers write: by listening to and incorporating musical and poetic intertexts. Mikhail Bakhtin famously made a similar observation of novelistic discourse (albeit at the exclusion of poetry), calling it *heteroglossic,* that is, an amalgamation of the multiple social registers circulating at a given place and time.[89] Criolo of Grajaú, in São Paulo's zona sul, masterfully performs the dialogic, intertextual construction of rap in a series of verses that is almost entirely citational:

> É o cão, é o cânhamo, é o desamor
> É o canhão na boca de quem tanto se humilhou
> Inveja é uma desgraça, alastra ódio e rancor
> E cocaína é uma igreja gringa de le Chéreau
> Pra cada rap escrito, uma alma que se salva
> O rosto do carvoeiro é o Brasil que mostra a cara
> Muito blá se fala, e a língua é uma piranha
> Aqui é só trabalho, sorte é pras crianças
> Que vê o professor em desespero na miséria
> Que no meio do caminho da educação havia uma pedra
> E havia uma pedra no meio do caminho.[90]

> (It's canine, cannabis, lovelessness
> It's the cannon in the mouth of the person who was so humiliated
> Envy's a disgrace, it spreads hate and resentment
> And cocaine's a foreign church in le Chéreau
> For every rap written, there's a soul saved
> The coalminer's expression is Brazil showing its face
> A lot of *bla* is spoken and the tongue's a piranha
> Here it's only work, luck is for kids
> You see the professor in despair and misery
> In the middle of the road of education there was a stone
> And there was a stone in the middle of the road.)

Criolo uses a medial stop dividing each verse to jump liberally between different registers and intertexts. The first verse samples Tom Jobim's 1972 bossa nova hit "Águas de março": "É pau, é pedra, é o fim do caminho / É um resto de toco, é um pouco sozinho" (It's a stick, it's a stone, it's the end of the road / It's part of a stump, it's a little alone).[91] Maintaining Jobim's parallelism, Criolo substitutes "canine" and "cannabis" for "wood" and "stone" while intensifying Jobim's benign loneliness with the absence of love (*desamor*). Cutting "road" and "stone" out of Jobim's verses, he returns to them later in a sample of Carlos Drummond de Andrade's well-known 1928 poem: "No meio do caminho / tinha uma pedra" (In the middle of the road / was a stone).[92] By inserting the word *educação* into the circular motion of Drummond's stone, Criolo resignifies these famous verses as a metaphor for Brazil's failing education system.

Between the bossa nova musician and the modernist poet, Criolo alludes to French film director Patrice Chéreau, out of whose name he creates a pun with the past tense of *cheirar,* meaning to sniff (cocaine).[93] The "coalminer's expression" a few verses later samples Manuel Bandeira's 1921 poem about child labor and exploitation, "Meninos carvoeiros" (Boy coalminers),[94] which Criolo would have studied in secondary school. The invocation of the Bandeira poem is meant to display the true face of Brazil, as Criolo pairs "Meninos cavoeiros" with the verse "Brasil mostra tua cara" (Brazil show your face) from the 1988 Cazuza pop hit "Brasil."[95] Amidst this dense intertextuality, Criolo affirms that rap is "só trabalho" (only work). To whom, or at what, is the prolonged, sinister, rhythmic laugh that closes the verses directed? How does Criolo's intertextuality act not only on the sampled texts, but on the listener receiving the samples? What kind of work does the rap song perform?

By far the most common intertextuality in Brazilian rap is among rappers, who constantly sample, cite, and rewrite each other's verses. Racionais's well-known rap aphorism "periferia é periferia" samples GOG (see chapter 4).[96] Sabotage's "rap é compromisso" has been repeated by hip hop artists throughout Brazil. DMN's "homem de aço" (steel man) was sampled by Rappin' Hood and Atitude Feminina, among others.[97] Rappin' Hood's "sujeito homem" (male subject) has been sampled by several rappers, including Belo Horizonte–based Djonga.[98] Additional examples abound. By continually returning to a common repertoire of verses, Brazilian rappers build community through a shared sense of hip hop literacy. As with samba, rap lyrics commonly enter the everyday speech of broader urban communities in an intertextuality that Jennifer Roth-Gordon calls "conversational sampling."[99] The "collaborative nature" of conversational sampling, Roth-Gordon suggests, allows youth to "(re)define themselves and highlight shared aspects of their sociopolitical context" within a local-global framework.[100] The sampling of lyrics becomes a re-citation machine, a continuous act of citing (again) and reciting out loud upon which to forge community.[101]

Finally, the intertextual practice of re-citing verses in Brazilian rap can, itself, be heard as the sample of an older tradition, the Afro-Brazilian verbal game known as *pontos* (points). Sung verses of collective authorship, pontos are improvised in competitive settings while participants decipher them and throw or launch (*atirar, lançar, jogar*) additional ones at their opponents.[102] In *rodas de jongo* (circular dances accompanied by two drums), pontos take the form of the call-and-response of short phrases invoking *orixás* (Yoruba-derived Afro-Brazilian divinities).[103] Rap's citationality differs from that of pontos in that it does not necessarily reach the religious dimension of pontos (although it sometimes does; see chapter 2), and it often (though not always) preserves the individual authorship of the sampled verse, as opposed to the anonymous, collective authorship of a ponto. But like pontos, rap re-citation is a "communal and competitive discourse" that builds community around deciphering and retransmitting a message.[104]

As Alexs Pate puts it, "rap/poets study each other" and "challenge each other to grow."[105] The words *study* and *studio* share an etymology, maintained in the Spanish word *estudio* (which refers to both), and it is no coincidence that the recording studio is a primary locus for collaborative rap writing. The studio functions as "a research centre" for experimentation,[106] including embromations over newly made beats. With parallels in blues and jazz, as well as salsa, rappers' intertextual writing draws on the "individual/collective cultural agency" of Afro-diasporic exchange.[107] Through community writing, rappers develop aural literacy around a shared and ever-expanding repertoire of breaks and flows.

Nan tèt mwen: Freestyle, or Writing in the Mind

When I met D-Fi in his neighborhood of Delmas 33, Port-au-Prince, in July 2017, I asked him to clarify a verse. He responded wryly that he didn't have the lyrics written out; they were "nan tèt mwen" (in my head).[108] I was reminded of MC White's formulation of bringing out verses from "el libro de mi mente" (the book of my mind),[109] or Manzano's description from almost two centuries earlier of improvising décimas by compiling a "cuaderno de versos en la memoria" (notebook of verses in my memory; see chapter 2).[110] However, D-Fi's response also came as a surprise, given that the title of the mixtape is *Rev ak plim* (Dream with a pen) and most of his songs reference writing explicitly. I suspected that even if D-Fi was no longer in possession of his written lyrics or didn't want to share them with me, he had written them down. My suspicion was confirmed when, after we had collaborated and knew each other better, I asked him to clarify a verse from a newer album and he generously shared a typed Word document over WhatsApp. When I requested permission to print longer lyric excerpts for a few of his songs, he meticulously corrected my written transcriptions. Reflecting on our first encounter, I came to hear the phrase "nan tèt mwen" as an encoded message about how D-Fi writes rap.

By playfully displacing his lyrics from the written page to the virtual realm of "nan tèt mwen," D-Fi perhaps engaged in the Haitian practice known as *voye pwen* (sending or throwing points).[111] Common in everyday speech, music, and Vodou ritual, pwen (points, like Brazilian pontos) are encoded messages about an individual or group that are spontaneously sent out. Haitian pwen carry "magical energy" or "power that symbolically captures the essence of a relation or an entity."[112] Their power is transferred when a listener *ramase pwen* (picks up a point), collects or deciphers the message, and reflects on its implicit critique. Where the simplest pwen are *pwovèb* (proverbs), more complex pwen take the form of *chan pwen* (point songs). It should come as no surprise that Haitians voye pwen to comment on political turmoil and to chastise, mock, or critique a person or group.[113] Heard as a pwen, D-Fi's phrase "nan tèt mwen" pokes fun at my reliance on written text to decipher some lyrics.[114] However, "nan tèt mwen" also points to a crucial technique of rap composition in which writing and improvisation are involved in a constructive feedback loop.

The same year of my first collaborations in Havana with Malcoms, I participated in a recording session with rapper Etián "Brebaje Man" and producer Prófugo in the outer Havana neighborhood of La Lisa. I layered a few violin tracks on one of Prófugo's beats before Etián entered the booth. Without picking up a pen, Etián employed the technique known in the Black oral tradition as "narrative sequencing," writing a story in his mind.[115] When his improvisation derailed, Prófugo would stop the recording and back up, at which point Etián would begin again from where he had left off, building on previous ideas and rhyme schemes. This is an extreme example by an unusually talented improviser, but it demonstrates the way freestylers create structures and rhymes recursively, drawing on ideas that have been previously tested out.[116] Freestyling requires the maintenance of a "mental bank" of rhymes and grammatical structures that fit with the break.[117] This seemingly spontaneous exercise is performed through the masterful repetition or citation of learned formulae or "rules shared by the community."[118]

In the early twentieth century, scholars of epic poetry such as Milman Parry and Albert Lord made the groundbreaking observation that Homeric verse (previously received as the literary product of a single poet) in fact represented a performative oral tradition based on highly formulaic verse structures designed to facilitate memorization. As Lord suggests, the structures of oral poetry are learned and internalized by listening. The oral poet "does not 'memorize' formulas, any more than we as children 'memorize' language. He learns them by hearing them in other singers' songs, and by habitual usage they become part of his own singing as well. Memorization is a conscious act of making one's own, and repeating, something that one regards as fixed and not one's own."[119] By listening to and mastering an analogous rap "grammar" of syntactic formulations, shared references, ritualized practices, and rhyming conventions, rappers similarly develop the oral and aural skill of writing in the mind.[120] Given the proliferation of texts and screens in the urban environments of most hip hop artists in Cuba, Brazil, and Haiti, rap does not emerge in the preliterate context of what Walter Ong calls "primary orality," but instead represents an expression of "secondary orality" or "mediatized orality."[121] Tricia Rose notes in this sense that rap is a "dynamic hybrid of oral traditions, postliterate orality, and advanced technology."[122] However, like the structure of preliterate oral poetry, the sonic grammar governing rap flows provides an aural "technology for the storage and retrieval of cultural memory."[123]

In the early 2000s, Aldo of Los Aldeanos codified a distinctive flow that played with the boundary between freestyle and writing and became widely popular among Havana hip hop artists. The song "Vereda tropical" (Tropical path) takes its title and chorus from the bolero popularized by Cuban singer Tito Gómez's Riverside orchestra.[124] Aldo rewrites the bolero's opening verses, but his "Vereda tropical" bears no musical resemblance to the big-band sound of its musical pretext, in spite of Aldo having studied the saxophone.[125] If sampling has been described as "a conscious preoccupation with artistic continuity and connection to Black cultural roots," how should we hear Aldo's antisample?[126] Recalling the cultural nationalism detailed in chapter 3, perhaps the inaudible bolero—invoked in name but not in sound—disavows institutional pressures to create Cuban-sounding music.[127]

Aldo's verses are a tour de force of what Geneva Smitherman calls "tonal semantics," "the use of voice, rhythm and vocal inflection to convey meaning in black communication . . . a kind of acoustical phonetic alphabet."[128] Repeated assonance takes advantage of the relatively few vowel sounds in Spanish, to establish a "multirhyme matrix."[129]

> Desfile de miles misiles, fusiles fusilen al killer
> Para que no aniquilen a débiles giles ni a hábiles viles
> Y dile que el flow recopilen, vacilen y afilen
> Que al final alfileres hay
> En sus pupitres sus nalgas peligran
> Lo mismo escribiendo que haciendo freestyle
> Ninguno de ustedes conmigo se libra.[130]

> (Parade of a thousand missiles, guns shoot the killer
> So they don't annihilate simple fools and vile geniuses
> And tell them to recapitulate, falter, and sharpen the flow
> Because in end, there are pins
> In their desks, their asses are in danger
> The same writing as freestyling
> None of you with me gets free.)

Dividing this set of verses into two parts with the enjambed word *hay* (there are), Aldo employs "bridge rhyming technique" to connect two assonant series: the staccato two-syllable *i-le* of *misiles* and the more open *a* of *peligran*, with the *i-le* recovered once more in the word *freestyle*.[131] In an onomatopoeia of the guns described, the rapid-fire delivery, supercharging the beat with as many syllables as possible, simulates freestyle and obfuscates meaning. The effect is that "the closer rhymes appear as adjacent pairs, the stronger the sound play and lesser the stability of meaning in individual words."[132] One has to listen attentively in order to catch the words—so much so that Cuban hip hop artists came to bemoan fruitless attempts by other rappers at imitating Aldo's flow, jamming together so many words that their semantic content would become completely obscured and approach something like embromation, an unintended parody of rap.[133] Aldo's flow draws on what Fred Moten calls "the excessive, out-from-the-outside motion and force with which sound infuses the verbal. Words don't go there; words go *past* there. Bent. Turned. Blurrrred."[134] All the words are there, but they are not all equally audible.

Through the bent, blurred phonemes parade "a thousand missiles," a clear reference to the Cuban Missile Crisis of 1962. Perhaps Aldo seeks to cast rap as a world-historical event on the level of the Bay of Pigs invasion, significant given USAID's attempted infiltration of Cuban hip hop (2009–2011) and the Cuban government's anxieties surrounding foreign influence.[135] Thus while approaching embromation, Aldo's verses nonetheless "capture" his listener by inscribing semantic meaning. To whom does Aldo direct his writing, from which apparently nobody "gets free"? What message does Aldo transmit to government bureaucrats, presumably those seated at desks risking pricking their "asses" on "pins"? Does he sanction or denounce the state's ritualistic displays of militarism? How does his ability to sound "lo mismo escribiendo que haciendo freestyle" relate to his interweaving of sound and sense? Pointing to the word's etymology, Moten notes that *improvisation* "is usually understood as speech *without foresight*. But improvisation . . . always also operates as a kind of foreshadowing, if not prophetic, description."[136] Writing "nan tèt mwen" indeed involves future anticipation, and Aldo's "lo mismo escribiendo" suggests that in rap, freestyle and writing are two sides of the same coin.

Rap literacy typically has more to do with writing lyrics than using letters. However, as John Guillory suggests, literacy is never "a simple matter of knowing how to read or write but refers to the entire system by which reading and writing are regulated as social practices in a given society."[137] In Brazil, almost a third of the adult population is considered functionally illiterate.[138] While most urban rappers have at least a high school education, Padêro MC of Barra do Ceará, Fortaleza recorded his first album as a functional illiterate (*analfabeto*), reciting lyrics to friends who served as scribes. Motivated by a desire to write down his raps, Padêro spent the next four years learning to read and write, skills he used to compose the lyrics for his subsequent albums.[139] Like the English word *literacy*, the Portuguese word *alfabetização* (acquiring literacy) evokes alphabetic letters. Padêro's example requires a different understanding of literacy and alfabetização, for the rapper was certainly literate in rap before he could read and write in Portuguese. Prior to his alfabetização, Padêro's lyrics were written in community.

The communitarian implications of rap literacy are further clarified in the collaborative song "Palavra de luta" (Word of struggle) by Bia Doxum and Ni Brisant. Here, the verses are spoken, rather than rapped, over ethereal yet rhythmic chords on a piano. Doxum recites her verses first, followed by Brisant, with their voices merging at crucial moments. Their call-and-response performs the community literacy they describe:

[Doxum]
A pixação mais alta
Escorrendo do vigésimo andar
Diz o que muitos queriam ser
E poucos puderam se tornar.
. . . .

[Brisant]
Caçando meu papel no mundo
Encontro a palavra que é oração
Mantra que me veste
Nas figuras das nuvens
Na queda dos muros.
Eu não escrevo para dar voz aos oprimidos
Eu sou um deles e estou aqui.

[Doxum and Brisant]
A minha gente nunca se deixou calar.

[Brisant]
Meu povo só nunca foi ouvido
Escrevo e vou
Nessa caligrafia sem tradução
Descubro

[Doxum and Brisant]
Não estou só
Ainda é através dos olhos
Que reconheço os meus.[140]

([Doxum]
The highest pixação
Flowing from the twentieth floor
It says what many wanted to be
And only a few could become
. . . .

[Brisant]
Putting on my worldly role
I find my word in a prayer
A mantra that clothes me
In the figures of the clouds

Falling from the walls
I don't write to give voice to the oppressed
I am one of them and I am here.

[Doxum and Brisant]
My people were never silenced.

[Brisant]
My people were simply never heard
I write and go
In this untranslatable calligraphy
I discover

[Doxum and Brisant]
I'm not alone
It's still through my eyes
That I recognize mine.)

Built around the second inversion of a D minor chord, the piano harmony oscillates between the fifth degree of A minor and the sixth degree of B-flat major. The oscillation mirrors the dialogue between the voices of the rappers. When the song reaches its climax with the verse "Não estou só" (I'm not alone), sung by both rappers in unison, the piano strikes a low D, finally resolving the D minor chord to its root, as if affirming the recognition of community described in the verses.

This community rooting in lyrics, the song suggests, is related to the practice of pixação, signature tags written on the walls of gated high-rise condominiums. Based on the runic alphabet and not directly associated with hip hop culture (although undoubtedly a form of graffiti), *pixos* are written in stylized letters, indecipherable for a majority of city residents.[141] At least one *pixador* even claimed to be able to read and write pixos despite being analfabeto in Portuguese.[142] Describing what a pixador called "knowing how to read the wall," Alexandre Pereira observes that "the stylization given to the letters is an element that only makes sense to those adept in this practice."[143] In other words, content is subsumed into form; pixação is not merely an alternative writing practice, but an alternative mode of reading.

Brisant's lyrics suggest that pixação (and, by analogy, rap) allows a people "never heard" to "recognize" itself in the inscription. The mixed audiovisual metaphor opens a passageway between these distinct yet overlapping community literacies, both rooted in the margins of São Paulo. This is perhaps what Brisant means that he "goes where he writes": his verses materialize into the action of their pronouncement, mediating between pixação's graphic inscription of letters and rap's sonic inscription of lyrics. Sampling Octavio Paz, rap is "not only a verbal object but rather a profession of faith and an act."[144] It is in this sense that Doxum and Brisant's rap becomes *oração*, which can mean either grammatical clause or prayer: a writing practice at once linguistic and spiritual. At stake is an aural, intertextual writing that engages simultaneously with multiple media and sites of inscription. Rewriting style as content, form as function, rappers and pixadores trace the limits not so much of a "lettered" or "written city," but a city to be written on.[145] The invocation of pixação suggests that rap's literary program is not limited to written texts nor the simple affirmation that "Hip Hop is poetry."[146] Here rap becomes calligraphic, jumping between the oral-aural and the visual.

Embodying the verses ("escrevo e vou") grounds rap in what J. L. Austin called illocutionary speech, the capacity to exert a "certain *force* in saying something."[147] Illocutionary speech acts are performatives that do what they say, for example, the pronouncement of marriage. The enunciation of the words carries out the action they describe. Rather than strictly performative, poetry in Austin's sense is "more properly understood as performative utterance aesthetically held in suspended animation."[148] But in community, rappers consistently push verses toward their illocutionary potential as part of "a clear continuum in which African American [and Afro-diasporic] artists have put things learned by listening into action by way of performance."[149] The movement from aurality to action, I will argue in the next section, is related to rap's intertextual cross-pollination with other traditions.

Rapjazz: Action, or Writing across Media

Up to this point, I have analyzed rap as a community-forging writing practice developed at the ear and in the mind through intertextuality with practices such as journalism, samba, repente, pwen, and pixação. I now wish to explore how intertextuality opens up a passage between words and actions, a reflection that continues in the following chapter. To do so, I turn to two explicitly intertextual or intermedial projects, São Paulo–based rapper Tássia Reis's song "Meu rapjazz" (My rapjazz) and Haitian writer Franketiénne's book-length poem *Rapjazz*. These independently conceived notions of rapjazz introduce an analogy between rap and jazz that incorporates jazz as part of rap's prehistory.[150]

Moten and Edwards have analyzed an acute interest in the letter on the part of prominent jazz musicians. In his reading of jazz musician

Cecil Taylor's album *Chinampas,* which combines voice and percussion, Moten describes a poetry that "presents no graphic system" and thus falls outside of conventional definitions of written verse, but nonetheless performs "aural writing."[151] Edwards analyzes how letters written by jazz musicians such as Louis Armstrong and Duke Ellington exhibit "a tendency to jump the track from one medium to another," between textual inscription and musical improvisation.[152] He characterizes the connection between jazz improvisation and the improvisatory writings of jazz musicians using the title of the Monk and Clarke tune "Epistrophy." A literary device meaning "turning about" in Greek, epistrophe involves the repetition of a word or sound at the end of successive phrases (see chapter 2). Fundamental to understanding epistrophe (or epistrophy) in jazz is scat, mythologized to have originated in 1926 when Louis Armstrong is said to have dropped his written lyrics to "The Heebie Jeebies Dance," at which point he began to improvise sounds.[153] Often understood as vocalists imitating instrumentalists, scat "points at something outside the sayable, something seen where it collapses."[154]

Riding a musical track that pairs a jazz piano riff with a hip hop breakbeat, Reis's flow in "Meu rapjazz" begins in scat. Curiously, she pairs her vocal sample of scat with a parody of nonsensical speech, criticizing a common accusation made by the political right of the tendency of the activist left to make facile complaints ("mimimi"):

> Sem mimimi, zumzumzum
> *C'est fini,* aqui é clack bum
> Menos enrolação e mais ação
> Mais participação e mais ação
> Menos falação e mais ação
> Faladores falam muito, eu não.
> Não tenho tempo a perder
> Quero vencer por mim e lutar por você.[155]
>
> (Without the *mimimi, zumzumzum* [of capoeira]
> *C'est fini,* here it's crack boom
> Less waffling and more action
> More participation and more action
> Less ranting and more action
> Talkers talk a lot, I don't.
> I don't have time to lose
> I want to overcome for me and struggle for you.)

Discarding aimless verbosity as meaningless sound, Reis calls for less "waffling" (*enrolação*) and "ranting" (*falação*) and more direct language: "direto e na fuça e sem blá blá blá" (direct and no bullshit, without *bla bla bla*).[156] The epistrophe in her repeated call to action (*ação*) on three successive verses not only evokes jazz but encourages a jump from sound to embodiment. By citing jazz, Reis's verses seek to embody their illocutionary force, to cross the boundary between words and deeds. Where, then, is scat located on the continuum between words, sounds, and actions? Is scat part of the "bla bla bla" that Reis rejects? Or is scat, rather, that place "outside the sayable" where words turn to actions? The pre- or post-linguistic character of scat reinforces the fact that, on a material level, the capacity for words to act on bodies resides in their sound: the epistrophe on *ação*, the onomatopoeia of *clack boom* and *zumzumzum*, the transformation of sonic affect into embodied effect. For Reis, rapjazz indeed points outside the sayable, but not only into sound. Her lyrics move through words and away from them, impelling the bodies in which they resonate to "struggle with her" as she struggles for them.

Conversely, in Haitian poet Franketienne's book-length poem *Rapjazz* (1999), rap is made to "jump the track" in a different direction: from sound onto the page. Having experienced the rise of Duvalierism, Franketienne elaborated a literary movement during the 1960s known as *spiralisme* (spiralism), which aimed to "seize the real in the diversity of its aspects."[157] In language evocative of Duvalierist violence, Franketienne proposed "a method of approach for attempting to seize a reality always in movement. . . . It is the miracle of art: to attempt to capture the real without killing it. Capture: to seize, to immobilize. It is about apprehending without suffocating."[158] *Rapjazz* creates a double helix spiraling through the literary performance of spoken Kreyòl and the oral-aural invocation of written French:

> Mots et rêves
> sont mes repères.
> Mon journal
> n'a pas de dates.
> En rapjazz
> je dis ma ville.[159]
>
> (Words and dreams
> are my landmarks.

My journal
has no dates.
In rapjazz
I speak my city.)

Where rappers access writing through an aural medium, Franketienne makes written words speak through a graphic text. The phrase "I speak my city" exposes the "continual confrontation, within writing, of the phonic and the graphic."[160] Capturing the linear and cyclical rhythms of life in Port-au-Prince,[161] Franketienne writes himself pregnant with his city (in French) and offers a manual (in Kreyòl) on how to raise and nourish dreams, presumably the offspring of his poiesis:

Ma ville ardente
est dans mon ventre.

Fwote rèv
grese rèv.

Reveye rèv
rechofe rèv.

Miyonnen rèv
pouponnen rèv

Netwaye rèv
eskanpe rèv.[162]

(My burning city
is in my womb.

Scrub dreams
grease dreams.

Wake up dreams
warm up dreams.

Caress dreams
nurture dreams

Clean dreams
fold dreams.)

The epistrophe on *rèv* raises dreams from the register of the mechanical ("scrub," "grease," "warm up") to the organic ("caress," "nurture") before transforming them into a sort of external clothing one might wear ("cleaned," "folded," and "neatly ironed"). Though dreams begin in the poet's womb (*ventre*), their materializations act as external protection, practicing spiralisme by capturing Port-au-Prince in movement. The landmarks of *Rapjazz* are words and dreams: virtual spaces within the urban fabric that allow for the rewriting and reimagining of the world.

Frankétienne has explicitly supported rap kreyòl artists, and, in turn, some Haitian rappers have looked to his example, paying homage to one of Haiti's best-known writers.[163] Although Princess Eud does not reference Frankétienne directly, she similarly explores the protective power of poetry in a rap dialogue between French and Kreyòl that is structurally evocative of *Rapjazz*. The music video for "Eudomination" reinforces the French-Kreyòl tension by alternating between celebratory dance scenes and staged anticolonial struggle. In the lyrics, Eud encodes a decolonial message (rapped in Kreyòl) in a song whose self-proclaimed purpose (sung in French) is to make people move:

Lè w konn fè kolonn
Ou antre nan batay
Même si ta vie en dépend.
Mwen toujou saj, m pa awogan
Men m ka tounen yon vòlkan.
An n bliye tout bagay
Kounyeya ban m mizik pou m
Pete tenpan.

On est venu pour vous faire bouger
On est venu pour vous faire danser, danser oh
Ça va chauffer, on avance, on avance
Sauter, sauter, bouger, bouger dans la danse.[164]

(When you are loyal to your friends
You join the battle
Even if your life depends on it.
I'm always wise, I'm not arrogant
But I'm capable of becoming a volcano.
Let's forget everything
Now give me music so I can
Bust eardrums.

We've come to make you move
We've come to make you dance, dance oh
It's gonna get hot, move up, move up
Jump, jump, move, move in the dance.)

Given the anticolonial scenes depicted in the video (and my imperfect ear in Kreyòl), I initially heard the first verse as "Lè w konn fè kolon" (When you learn what the colonizer did). Eud's management team kindly corrected me when I reached out for permission to cite these lyrics. I wonder, however, whether the near-homophonic relationship between *kolonn* (column, similar to *konbit,* here referring to a cooperative team or group of friends) and *kolon* (colonizer) carries out poetic work. I'm reminded of Grada Kilomba's assertion that in postcolonial contexts, "sometimes one would prefer not to remember [the colonial past], but one is actually not able to forget."[165]

Eud's verses introduce a dialectic between struggle or battle (*batay*) and dance (*bouger*) that rejects the commonly attributed escapist function of dance and the centuries-long denigration of "African" dance in Haiti (considered an expression of Vodou "fetishism" and antithetical to productive labor).[166] Dance, writes Njelle W. Hamilton, describing the French- and Creole-speaking Caribbean, "is both embodied freedom and embodied memory."[167] In Eud's formula, "advancing" (*on avance*) through the "eardrum-shattering" break catalyzes the remembrance of anticolonial struggle represented in the video. The rupture of eardrums (hearing loss) paradoxically allows the listener to hear Eud's emancipatory poetics more clearly. Listening functions as "a proto-political, critical practice aimed at what in the past is not yet exhausted, at forms of life still on the horizon."[168] Rap becomes something like socially engaged danced poetry, seeking "to pass along an idea without ceasing to involve the whole body of the listener."[169] Here, movement itself is a decolonial act. Like *Rapjazz,* "Eudomination" expands writing not only between words and sounds but also between words and bodies, listening and acting, dance moves and decolonial movement.

Community Writing

The findings of this chapter suggest that one way to listen to rap is as a remainder of Rama's "lettered city," a practice that would have been *left out* by lettered elites (and, no doubt, Rama himself) and whose defense of the literary is *left over* from the lettered city. Techniques of listening, embromation, "nan tèt mwen," and rapjazz trace a more expansive understanding of letters and lyrics: a writing in freestyle or phono-graphic inscription. While the intertextual, intermedial, and aural achievements of rap songs deserve attention on their own aesthetic merits, it is in the capacity of these poetic features to enact community literacy that hip hop's social and political possibilities reside. Rap is not only about transforming reality into poetry, but also about writing new realities into existence.

Many rappers across Cuba, Brazil, and Haiti understand rap as a form of regeneration through rhyme. Sabotage, for example, claimed that rap saved him from a life of crime: "Atenciosamente eu sigo em frente, tipo assim / Regenerado delinquente" (Attentively I carry forward, like this / Regenerated delinquent).[170] It is not uncommon to find T-shirts and digital memes with some form of the slogan "hip hop saved my life," and scholars and practitioners have acknowledged hip hop's "healing" or "transformative" powers.[171] Only by "pronouncing the world," as Brazilian pedagogue Paulo Freire puts it, can we begin to transform it.[172] The pronouncement of the world confronts the violence inaugurated by those who wield power against those who do not.[173] Rappers participate in this transformative work of pronouncing the world. Through their emphasis on writing, they invoke poetry and music as forms of popular militancy and critique various forms of oppression. One mode of this critique is the critique of violence, the subject of the final chapter.

6 Violence
"Sou fèy blanch"

IN 1941 the American Marxist magazine *New Masses* printed a text by Jacques Roumain, which the Haitian poet had read at a recent poetry forum, entitled "Is Poetry Dead?" The Spanish and French translations, published a few years later, were given the title "Poetry as a Weapon" ("La poesía como arma," *Gaceta del Caribe;* "Poésie comme arme," *Cahiers d'Haïti*). In the text, Roumain argues that the poet "is not free if his thinking is not action. . . . The poet is at the same time a witness and an actor of the historical drama."[1] His call for the weaponization of poetry was echoed more than a half-century later by K-Tafalk of the infamous Haitian rap kreyòl group Barikad Crew: "Lyrics dramatik kòm zam" (Dramatic lyrics like weapons).[2] Several thousand miles away in Brazil, Fortaleza-based hip hop artist Lenny Fernandes recited for me the chorus of an unreleased song: "A minha consciência é a minha arma / A letra do meu rap é a minha bala" (My conscience is my weapon / My rap lyrics are my bullet).[3] How does the rap metaphor of *letras/lyrics* as *armas/zam* (weapons) participate in the *longue durée* of poetic militancy described by Roumain? Under what conditions can rap carry out or incite violence, as mainstream media have not uncommonly asserted?[4] How might verses like "A letra do meu rap é a minha bala" point to a decolonial mobilization of violence, part of what Frantz Fanon called the necessary "praxis [that] enlightens the militant because it shows him the means and the end"?[5]

In disadvantaged neighborhoods of New York City, breaking and rap provided sites for creatively channeling conflicts between rival gangs, with some gangs literally disbanding into dance crews.[6] However, mainstream perceptions of hip hop not uncommonly emphasize connections to gang warfare as well as isolated violent incidents.[7] Around the same time that hip hop culture began to circulate outside the United States in the early

1980s, the infamous "broken windows" theory linked neighborhood signs of "disorder," such as broken glass and graffiti, to the perpetuation of violence and crime.[8] Hip hop's commercialization capitalized on the association of poverty with delinquency, as well as a generalized racialization of urban precarity. The industry commodified an image of rappers as ambassadors of "violent black youth culture" in a vicious circle wherein, at worst, artists became complicit in an insidious form of mimicry by performing the stereotypes historically assigned to Black people across the Americas.[9] In Colombia, for example, violence is "almost a requirement of sorts for entrance into [the] hip-hop world."[10] Critical of the way the industry compels rappers to sell (Black) violence, Tricia Rose suggests that claiming rappers merely represent a violence that is "already everywhere" is not a sufficient apologia.[11]

Judith Butler points out that accusations that rap incites violence return us to the question of whether words can enact bodily harm.[12] One way to approach the issue, Butler suggests, is to analyze hate speech: performative speech acts that, as defined juridically, carry out violence. In hate speech, "the threat begins the performance of that which it threatens to perform; but in not quite fully performing it, seeks to establish, through language, the certitude of that future in which it will be performed."[13] Since hate speech is carried out through the medium of language, it cannot enact per se the violence it pronounces. But hate speech does exert force, inaugurating the performance of the violence it threatens to carry out. Might the same logic apply in reverse for speech acts that denounce violence? That is, can the pronouncement of letras/lyrics as armas/zam somehow counter the violence committed against the urban poor in the Global South? One of the findings of the previous chapter is that rap lyrics wield what J. L. Austin called "illocutionary force" in the social sphere.[14] There, I demonstrated that in rap, illocutionary force—the capacity for words to carry out the actions they pronounce—is bound up with the development of specific forms of literacy surrounding community writing. Here, I argue that the convention of writing in hip hop poetics produces a corollary: the responsibility to critique violence.

For Walter Benjamin, the critique of violence illuminates "other kinds of violence than all those envisaged by legal theory."[15] Condemning the violence sanctioned by written law, Benjamin calls for a "different kind of violence" linked to a different kind of writing.[16] His argument rests on reinterpreting the Ten Commandments of the Hebrew Decalogue, a lawmaking and law-preserving text generally understood as the written representation of a higher authority. For Benjamin, the written text (including the Commandment forbidding murder) should not be taken "as a criterion of judgement, but as a guideline for the actions of persons or communities who have to wrestle with it in solitude and, in exceptional cases, to take on themselves the responsibility of ignoring it."[17] A revolutionary application of writing, the critique of violence identifies instances when violence is the only legitimate recourse for the oppressed to redress the illegitimate violence of the state monopoly on power. The point of departure for any critique of violence, Paulo Freire notes, is the recognition that violence is always inaugurated by the oppressor.[18]

This chapter explores how rappers sample traditions of musical and poetic militancy, asking to what degree they critique physical, political, and symbolic violence. How, by building community around more expansive and inclusive kinds of writing, can rappers elucidate Benjamin's "different kind of violence"? My aim, following Idelber Avelar, is to explore how "rhetorical (symbolic, literary) are to be linked with social (political, juridical) instances of violence in ways that go beyond a functionalist or cause-and-effect scheme."[19] Among the forms of violence addressed in Brazilian, Cuban, and Haitian rap are political oppression, police brutality, official modes of writing, censorship, urban militarization, and pejorative representations of hip hop. By engaging with traditions of Black feminism, musico-poetic militancy, and decolonization, rap songs create historically and locally grounded critiques of violence and reveal forms of oppression faced by disadvantaged urban communities.

It is important, here, to draw a distinction between Brazil, Cuba, and Haiti. Many Brazilian cities have some of the highest homicide rates in the world: during the peak of a crack epidemic in the 1990s, São Paulo reached 52.5 homicides per 100,000 people—more than three times higher than New York City during its violent peak that decade.[20] In contrast, Havana's homicide rates are consistently lower than many US cities. Though homicide rates in Port-au-Prince tend to be lower than those of some neighboring Caribbean nations, political turmoil in Haiti leads to frequent spikes in violence.[21] As a result of varying indices of violence and distinct modalities of urban life, hip hop artists from these countries critique violence in different ways. Brazilian and Haitian rappers commonly decry the militarization of urban space. Cuban and Brazilian rappers denounce militarized government repression and the threat of censorship. Haitian and Cuban rappers disavow symbolic forms of violence associated with the ongoing legacies of revolution. In all three countries, rappers participate in and, at times, critically undermine a generalized militarization of popular culture.

In terms of the function of writing, rap's critique of violence is rehearsed at the level of content as well as form. Following Butler, I aim to listen to the way rappers "do things with language, produce effects with language, and . . . do things to language, but language is also the thing that [they] do."²² As such, each of the following sections evaluates a different figure of *rap-violence* in relation to writing and performative speech. I begin by analyzing the ontological implications of rappers' formalization of violence, a relation of greater proximity than the metaphorical notion that they simply "represent" violence. I then turn to the militancy of Black feminist rap to examine how women artists respond to the violence of hypermasculinity. Finally, by tracing histories of militarization, I demonstrate some of the decolonial implications of rap's critique of violence. Each section listens to "the function, the urgency, the pain, the necessity, and the hope of [rap] writing. Is it necessary to commit life to writing, or is it the inverse? Commit writing to life?"²³ As São Paulo rapper Dukes puts it, "Me recolho para longe do olho que tudo quer ver / Desligo a TV, vou escrever, sobreviver" (I take cover far away from the eye that wants to see everything / I unplug the TV, I'll write, survive).²⁴

Terra de ninguém: Violence and Metonymy

Historian of oral poetry Paul Zumthor argued that in the context of protest, song "takes on a certain violence" and channels and "regurgitates that violence" onto the listening public.²⁵ During the second half of the twentieth century, several musical genres were associated with violence and protest, including punk, heavy metal, and rap.²⁶ In 1995, a US Department of Justice–funded study concluded that "Heavy Metal Rock and Gangsta Rap Music Promote Violence" and "children and teenagers should not be allowed to listen to the violent messages in this music."²⁷ For Mano Brown of the São Paulo group Racionais MC's, however, "o rap não se relaciona com a violência . . . ele vive a violência, ele nasce dentro" (rap isn't related to violence . . . it lives violence, it's born inside).²⁸ Rather than serving as a medium for representing, "regurgitating," or promoting forms of violence external to the music, rap can critique violence from within. Thus the presentation of letras/lyrics as armas/zam is something more than a metaphor (a figurative relation between two distinct objects).

A reticence toward metaphor is widespread in rap lyrics, as evidenced by Tássia Reis's formulation from the previous chapter: "direto e na fuça e sem blá blá blá" (direct and no bullshit, without *bla bla bla*).²⁹ El B similarly rejects rhetorical embellishment: "Por más que quieras estar fuera y hablar con metáforas / Embellecerlo más que los griegos sus ánforas" (As much as you want to be outside and speak in metaphors / Embellish it more than the Greeks did their amphoras).[30] For El B, the quality of rap writing is measured by its capacity to access reality directly, rather than through rhetorical sleight of hand. He calls for mimesis without metaphor, the unmediated expression of a world of which the rapper cannot "estar fuera" (be outside). Despite rejecting metaphor, El B delivers one himself, seeming to fall back into the trap he aims to elide. This paradoxical use of metaphor to disavow metaphor elucidates the distinction between metaphor as a rhetorical device and metaphor as an ontological relation, the latter of which was explored by Roman Jakobson. For Jakobson, human thought exists between two poles: a metaphoric axis based on similarity and a metonymic axis based on contiguity.[31] Affirming the similarity between two objects necessarily establishes their ontological separation (metaphor), whereas objects that are contiguous are entangled in a relation of proximity (metonymy). What El B is rejecting is not the use of metaphors but *metaphorical distance*. Rap is not similar to the social realities it voices but rather contiguous with them (a part-whole relation).

Additional verses may help clarify the rap-violence metonymy. Dina Di describes rap as a form of inscription on the body: "No rap eu me garanto, me adianto e não vai ser em vão / Cada palavra que escrevi na pele eu já senti" (In rap I guarantee myself, I get ahead and it won't be in vain / Each word that I wrote on my skin, I felt).[32] The verses imply that Dina carries in her skin and feels ("já senti") what she raps—scars or wounds derived from the lived experience of everyday survival. By comparing her rap writing to writing on skin (tattoos), she emphasizes a metonymical proximity between writing and its corporeal effects: "Some rap/poems can harm you";[33] there is "no poem that does not open itself like a wound, but no poem that is not also just as wounding."[34]

Belo Horizonte–based Djonga's presentation of a tongue-gun similarly exceeds the metaphorical logic of similarity: "Eu pássaro de alma, preso na arapuca / Viver machuca, talvez por isso que minha língua é uma bazuca" (I, soul of a bird, imprisoned in a trap / Life hurts, maybe that's why my tongue's a bazooka).[35] In a move that recalls Zumthor's formulation of protest song taking on violence, the wound of living ("viver machuca") produces Djonga's tongue-gun and casts the rapper in the role of both receiver and perpetrator of violence, an act necessary for his survival. As the song progresses, the rapper's breath becomes increasingly audible, presumably a result of his strangulation depicted in the music video.³⁶ Djonga's quickened breath, however, is more than performative: it also reflects the physicality of his flow, jamming ever more words into the beat. The tongue-gun leaves the rapper literally short of breath, a physical expression of the capacity of words to exert force on the body (and probably also a reference to the conversations around Black breath galvanized by the 2014 police murder of Eric Garner in New York City and reinvigorated after the 2020 police murder of George Floyd in Minneapolis).³⁷ If the bazooka functions as a metaphor for Djonga's rap, his shortness of breath demonstrates a metonymical proximity with the violence it describes.

This capacity for rap to wound can also turn into a "violence against language."³⁸ A set of verses by Zeca Baleiro on GOG's track "O peso da palabra" (The weight of the word) describes a sonic battlefield of words dismembered: "Quem canta com verdade, pode até sair do tom / Palavra lavra, ara, rara, terra de ninguém, palavra é arma pra luta que se anuncia" (Those who sing with truth can even go out of key / *Palavra lavra, ara, rara,* no man's land, words are weapons for the struggle that is foretold).³⁹ Performing violence on the word *palavra* (word), the lyrics slice palavra into sequentially smaller sonic fragments before affirming "terra de ninguém" (no man's land).⁴⁰ Despite having dismembered *palavra*, Baleiro nonetheless upholds faith in the truth-telling power of words ("quem canta com verdade") irrespective of how they sound ("pode até sair do tom"). Here, it is not rapping in tune, but rather intoning the truth, that makes words weapons. Words constitute at once the ammunition, the opposing army, and the battlefield of a war for "O peso da palavra." As H. Samy Alim observes, "language *is* the revolution, a powerful discourse in and of itself."⁴¹ The struggle for truth is intimately bound up with the struggle for the word.

Guerreiras/Guerreras: Black Feminism, or Writing to Survive

For Carolina Maria de Jesus, who spent her days collecting wastepaper for money in the São Paulo favela of Canindé in the late 1950s, the ability to write—to imagine worlds and to inhabit them in words—was a primary form of resistance. As Beatriz Jaguaribe notes, the "entrance into the domain of the letter is . . . a form of extricating herself from the narrative of sheer survival that emerged from the daily activity of gathering waste paper."⁴² When a São Paulo journalist published her diary in 1960 as the best-selling memoir *Quarto de despejo* (The trash room, titled in

English as *Child of the Dark*), Carolina was exposed to a different mode of earning money in exchange for paper. Her memoir was commodified as the *Diário de uma favelada* (Diary of a favela resident), a label Carolina would never be able to transcend, even when she moved to a more affluent neighborhood soon after its publication.[43] Nevertheless, writing retained an important use-value for Carolina, granting her an outlet for channeling the violence of urban precarity: "Enquanto escrevo vou pensando que resido num castelo cor de ouro que reluz na luz do sol. . . . As horas que sou feliz é quando estou residindo nos castelos imaginários" (When I write, I start to believe I reside in a castle of gold that glimmers in the sunlight. . . . The hours when I'm most happy are when I'm residing in imaginary castles).[44] Writing provides an escape from reality and a mode of insertion into other worlds.[45]

Conceição Evaristo has argued that given the systematic exclusion of women of color from literary institutions, any act of writing by Black women in Brazil is necessarily insubordinate.[46] Evaristo describes the writing of Afro-Brazilian women as a practice of *escrevivência*, a contraction of writing (*escrever*) and survival (*sobrevivência*).[47] Carolina's escrevivência resides in part in the affirmation of a "territory of belonging" in literature.[48] Though her body of work outside her memoir has received limited readership, she continues to serve as an inspiration for marginalized Black women writers throughout Brazil, including "peripheral poet" Tula Pilar Ferreira, whose performance poem "Sou uma Carolina" (I am a Carolina) makes the connection clear: "Feminino e poesia / Pobreza eu não quero nunca mais / Porque agora a caneta é o meu troféu" (Female and poetry / I don't want poverty ever again / Because now the pen is my trophy).[49] Thus in addition to marking an individual act of insubordination, escrevivência becomes a practice of community writing and collective critique.

While hip hop is not itself a social movement, many artists believe it can accompany activism and motivate militancy.[50] Black women rappers take a leadership role in this respect, empowering their communities through hip hop by offering workshops, engaging in outreach, participating in political campaigns, and sometimes circulating transnationally.[51] Brazilian and Cuban rappers frequently sing themselves as *guerreiras* or *guerreras* (warrior women), performing and embodying struggles against intersecting forms of oppression and alienation, including hip hop's hypermasculinity.[52] In Brazil, the guerreira figure invokes a rich history of grassroots struggle and intersectional politics on the part of Black women, who frequently lead community activism.[53] It is this tradition that Dina

Di invokes when she presents herself as "uma mina normal . . . guerreira, solitária, autoritária por nascença" (a normal girl . . . warrior, single, authoritative by birth).[54]

The guerreira emerges also as a central trope for Brasília-based group Atitude Feminina (Feminine Attitude), whose song "Mulher guerreira" (Warrior woman) issues a declaration of war against misogyny. The terms of struggle are defined in opposition to traditional gender roles. The final rapped verses of the song, rhymed by Renan Inquérito (a man), play on the double meaning of *gênero* as both gender and genre:

> Comédia, romance, gênero, não importa mais
> Masculino, feminino, tanto faz
> Preconceito não rola, não cola, não é Durex
> Talento no hip hop é unisex.[55]
>
> (Comedy, romance, genre/gender isn't important anymore
> Masculine, feminine, doesn't matter
> Prejudice doesn't roll, doesn't stick, isn't Durex
> Talent in hip hop is unisex.)

Rejecting the distinction between television genres (*gêneros*) such as comedy and romance, and playfully rhyming *Durex* (condoms) with *unisex*, Renan condemns the perceived gender gap in hip hop. Disavowing both gender and genre, the verses assert both the place of women in hip hop and the place of hip hop in Brazilian popular culture. The last words of the song, appropriately, belong to Aninha (a woman) in self-presentation: "sou mulher guerreira" (I am a warrior woman).

Some Brazilian rapper-guerreiras see themselves as part of an international tradition of Black feminism, as suggested by São Paulo–based Débora Garcia's song "Pretas panteras," whose title plays on the traditional Portuguese translation of Black Panthers (*Panteras Negras*) by turning the adjective black (*preta* or *negra*) into a noun: Black *women* panthers. Appropriately, the song begins with a clip of Angela Davis.[56] Germane for understanding such expressions of transnational Black feminist solidarity is the Combahee River Collective Statement, penned in 1977 by Barbara Smith, Demita Frazier, and Beverly Smith. The manifesto of the Boston-based feminist collective took the experience of Black women to develop "coalition building" around the universal struggle for liberation against all forms of oppression: racial, sexual, socioeconomic, geopolitical, or otherwise. The authors assert: "If Black women were free, it would mean that everyone else would have to be free since our freedom would necessitate the destruction of all the systems of oppression."[57] By foregrounding structural class analysis to draw parallels between economic marginalization (urban peripheries) and geopolitical marginalization (global peripheries), the authors followed the groundwork of Black inter/nationalists of the early twentieth century.[58] In contrast to some male Black radical leaders, however, the Combahee River Collective placed Black women at the center of a coalition, emphasizing the importance of male allies and rejecting what they called white "lesbian separatism."[59] This is perhaps the spirit in which Atitude Feminina invited Inquérito to participate in the song "Mulher guerreira."

The warrior woman trope and its intersectional politics extend to feminist rap in Cuba. Havana-based rapper Odaymara Cuesta of the group Las Krudas, for example, begins the song "Eres bella" (You're beautiful) with what Tanya Saunders calls "a Yoruba call to ancestral warrior women."[60] The rapper intones: "Para todas las mujeres que, como nosotras, están luchando, especialmente a las más negras, especialmente a las más pobres, especialmente a las más gordas, como yo. A todas las campesinas, guerreras, urbanas, a todas las hermanas" (To all the women who, like us, are struggling, especially the blackest, especially the poorest, especially the fattest, like me. To all the countrywomen, warriors, urban women, to all the sisters).[61] Cuesta establishes concentric circles of resistance against patriarchy, racism, classism, and what constanzx alvarez castillo calls *gordofobia*.[62] The opening shout-out or hailing gesture exemplifies the way rapper-guerreras rehearse a discourse of intersectionality among various oppressed groups,[63] emphasizing the importance of, in Nelly Richard's words, "pluralizing the mark" of the feminine "we."[64]

Finally, feminist rap confronts the violence of hypermasculinity that permeates even hip hop's most ostensibly radical wings. While some male rappers are feminist in their own right,[65] others maintain inherited divisions regarding the perceived social roles of men and women. Their performances of masculinity exclude, objectify, or outwardly denigrate women. The Cuban rap anthem "Rap es guerra" (Rap is war), whose title could hardly be more explicit, is illustrative of the former. The lyrics of the all-male crew (including Aldo, El B, Papá Humbertico, El Discípulo, and Anderson) are constructed around a *pie forzado*, with each rapper contributing a sixteen-bar verse ending with the line "el rap es guerra." Papá Humbertico's contribution expresses the masculine militancy characteristic of guerrilla warfare in Latin America:

Y en las filas de este escuadrón me alisto
Con el micrófono en la mano del silencio desisto
Sé que me has visto ametrallando a la mentira
Son balas mis palabras y no mi boca, mi mente las tira.
. . . .
Seré héroe o mártir para mi gente
Nunca traicionaré, siempre tenlo presente
De la guerrilla de los que no mienten, viejo soldado
Traigo un fusil que no se ha encasquillado
Por Dios amparado sobre la faz de la tierra
Ideología kamikaze
El rap es guerra.[66]

(And in the ranks of this squadron I enlist
With the microphone in my hand, from silence I desist
I know you've seen me bombarded with lies
My words are bullets fired not by my mouth, but by my mind.
. . . .
I'll be a hero or a martyr for my people
I'll never betray, always keep that present
From the guerrilla, from those who don't lie, old soldier
I bring a weapon that hasn't gotten stuck
Protected by God on the face of the earth
Kamikaze ideology
Rap is war.)

Humbertico's deployment of the words-as-bullets trope extends to a description of the microphone, symbolic of the projection of the voice, and—significantly—a phallic object that is brandished. The rapper constructs masculinity through a traditional formula: the ritualistic awarding of masculine status by "going through tests and confronting death."[67] Humbertico's rhymes assume the masculine violence of armed struggle, although it is unclear whether he would be willing to take up physical arms like the guerrillas he invokes (clearly a reference to Fidel Castro's 26th of July movement leading to the Revolution of 1959). How does this masculine construction of the rapper-warrior perform violence on women hip hop guerreras? Which forms of sacrifice and martyrdom (politically charged words in postrevolutionary Cuba) are suggested by Humbertico's "kamikaze ideology"? At what point or under what conditions can verbal violence turn into physical violence?

El rap es guerra: Poetry, Song, and Revolution

The linkage of rap to real and symbolic warfare echoes a long-standing militarization of poetry that, in Cuba, dates at least to the nineteenth-century independence wars (1868–1878 and 1895–1898), when it was common practice for soldiers to write poems.[68] Cuba's national hero José Martí, instigator of the Revolution of 1895 and inspiration for the Revolution of 1959, described Cuban poet-warriors in "Los poetas de la guerra" (Poets of war; published in 1893): "their literature wasn't in what they wrote, but in what they did. They sometimes rhymed poorly, but only the pretentious and dishonorable would say so to their face, because they died well. There, the rhymes were men."[69] Here it is not poetry that "takes on a certain violence" (Zumthor's formula),[70] but violence that takes on a certain poetry.

Constructed in Martí's image, the Cuban Revolution of 1959 prompted a generation of militant poets and singer-songwriters who, taking their cue from *nueva canción* (new song) protest singers in Chile, Argentina, and Uruguay, as well as from US and British folk rock, departed from the traditional emphasis in Cuban music on dance to use music for social critique.[71] In parallel with the newly elevated literary status of popular song in Brazil during the 1960s,[72] Cuban nueva trova singers such as Silvio Rodríguez, Sara González, and Pablo Milanés reflected on the revolutionary force of poetry and music and directly influenced rappers three decades later.[73] Nueva trova artists sought to revolutionize their craft by moving away from stock phrases and rejecting the commercialism of foreign music industries.[74]

Innovating song while maintaining commitment to the revolution placed them in a difficult position, as evidenced by the corpus of lyrics written by Silvio Rodríguez.[75] For example, Rodríguez's song "Debo partirme en dos" (I must split myself in two) performs a tension between commitment to revolution (the imperative of a political vanguard) and commitment to song (the imperative of an artistic avant-garde).[76] As Juan Otero Garabís shows, Rodríguez carved out an "identity between art and combat, between singer and soldier."[77] The connection is more than metaphorical: Rodríguez fought as a singer, twice serving in the Angolan Civil War.[78] He recounts the experience in "Canción para mi soldado" (Song for my soldier), recovering a Martí-esque poetic violence: "Si caigo en el camino / Hagan cantar mi fusil" (If I fall along the way / Make my rifle sing).[79] But his songs also express an ambivalence with respect to the possibility of singing the revolution, even an ambivalence toward the revolutionary project itself.[80] While Rodríguez maintained good favor with the government throughout his career, he seems to have been reluctant to accept Fidel Castro's dictum that "the most revolutionary artists would be those willing to sacrifice even their own artistic vocation for the Revolution."[81] In more direct language and in a different generational context marked by Special Period scarcity, Cuban rappers would cast themselves as heirs to this revolutionary ambivalence.

Cuban hip hop artists commonly echoed (or parodied) ideologies of the revolution, particularly with respect to the practice of self-criticism.[82] Several early rap groups, for example, sampled Fidel Castro's call for "dentro de la Revolución, todo; fuera de la Revolución, nada" (inside the Revolution, everything; outside the Revolution, nothing),[83] by defining hip hop as a "revolución dentro de la Revolución" (revolution inside the Revolution).[84] The slogan also echoes French philosopher Régis Debray's 1967 essay ¿Revolución en la Revolución? (Revolution in the Revolution?), which describes Castro's guerrilla warfare, rather than the Communist Party, as the true expression of Latin America's revolutionary vanguard. In the spirit of Debray, even the most explicitly antigovernment rap of the late 2000s rejected not so much the 1959 Revolution's premise or its "guerrilla base," but rather the Party's practice of censoring its own Bolshevik-inspired policy of self-criticism.[85] Representing themselves in the image of the revolution's guerrilla past, rappers cast themselves as a new generation of poet-warriors at war with the revolution's present.

In 2007, Los Aldeanos organized a collective of the most antiestablishment rappers in Cuba and released the album *La comisión depuradora* (The cleansing commission). The collaboration, which participating rappers saw as a zenith of Cuban hip hop, uncovers a darker history of the revolution's early years, its title evoking a series of purges and executions of alleged conspirators held at the Havana fortress of La Cabaña in the immediate aftermath of the revolution's triumph.[86] Proyecto Chardo begins the opening track of *La comisión* with an ironic two-second sample of the 1969 pop song "Para verte reír" (To see you smile) by Spanish-Filipino duo Juan y Junior. The song then shifts abruptly from the pop sample to a loop of minor strings over a bass-heavy breakbeat as lyrics explain that the objective of the album is "ir limpiando poco a poco los cerebros de la gente" (to clean little by little the minds of the people).[87] Thus Chardo redefines the notion of cleansing (the suppression of dissent) to refer to rap's capacity to clean people's minds of government brainwashing, something like an Althusserian demystification of ideology.[88]

Cuban DJs set up for an event at the International Cuban Hip Hop Symposium in Central Havana, August 26, 2019. (Photo by author)

In the follow-up compilation album *Tribu Mokoya* (Mokoya tribe), Los Aldeanos and collaborating artists released a nearly eleven-minute diatribe directed against rap's perceived repression by state-run media. "Háblame" (Talk to me) decries an official policy of scapegoating, as well as the hypocrisy of the CubaDisco music awards having twice recognized Puerto Rican rap and reggaeton group Calle 13 with an International Prize while ignoring or outright censoring hip hop artists involved in analogous work in Cuba.[89] A couplet in the middle of the song expresses the ethos of protest rap: "No es para fiesta lo que yo hago / Es protesta lo que grabo" (It's not for parties, what I do / It's protest, what I record).[90] By juxtaposing party (traditionally known as *pachanga*) and protest, the verse reanimates long-standing debates over the role of pachanga in the Cuban public sphere.

In the 1960s, Ernesto "Che" Guevara famously described the Cuban Revolution as "revolución con pachanga" (revolution with party), a revolution that included or even foregrounded popular merriment. However, pachanga faced skepticism and censorship when it was deemed unproductive for revolutionary ideology. The most notorious example was the documentary film *P.M.* (1961), produced without the approval of the Cuban Institute of Cinematographic Art and Industry (ICAIC), which precipitated a scandal for depicting a popular euphoria ostensibly disconnected from revolutionary progress. Lillian Guerra terms this interpretation "pachanga sin revolución" (party without revolution).[91] In their refusal of the party, the rappers of *Tribu Mokoya* espoused the inverse, something like a "revolutión without pachanga," as Baker puts it.[92]

More directly, "no es para fiesta ..." is a critique of the ubiquitous dance genre reggaeton. Cuban hip hop artists have nearly unanimously decried reggaeton for promoting "a good time even if there's a massacre in their concerts," while rappers "put all their effort into placing difficult reflections in the minds of their contemporaries."[93] Reggaeton foregrounds the body as a "site of pleasure, personal gain, and social mobility rather than productive, collective labor."[94] Given a long-standing hyper-politicization of the public sphere, reggaeton represents an escape from politics.[95] Such an overt rejection of Guevara's "new man" was predictably met with suspicion by cultural institutions. In 2005, for example, the Center for Research and Development of Cuban Music (CIDMUC) released a report criticizing reggaeton for its "vulgar, obscene lyrics."[96] A decade later, the CIDMUC sponsored a book project on the history of Cuban rap, finally published in 2017. As such, Cuban rappers have little basis for complaining that they faced greater censorship than reggaeton artists; if anything, institutions appear to have been even more reticent to accept reggaeton than rap.[97] Yet since reggaeton artists did not profess to be "the voice of a generation,"[98] they could more easily find ways around the state control of verbal discourse.[99] Reggaeton's lasting popularity suggests that some rappers' insistence on protesta instead of fiesta may have been shortsighted. Nor should we take the verse "no es para fiesta" to be necessarily representative of all Cuban rappers. Anónimo Consejo, for example, calls on his listeners to "Procura la pachanga como siempre censuran / Procura ser más consciente en tu escritura" (Look for pachanga, since they always censor it / Look to be more conscious in your writing).[100] The couplet asserts that pachanga is not incompatible with consciousness-raising and rap writing.

Nan hip hop la mwen toujou bay san m: Militarism and Invasion

A collaborating artist in *La comisión depuradora* and *Tribu Mokoya*, Escuadrón Patriota advocates a form of poetic militancy based on nonviolent resistance. Although his artistic name is a military metaphor ("Patriot Squadron"), Escuadrón aligns rap with pacifism:

¿Por qué pensar diferente es una traición ultranza?
¿Por qué a varios sectores se les margina y se rechazan?
Si no se respetan los criterios, esta nación no avanza
Pero entonces se desata la injusticia
Y es un peligro hablar y el miedo te paraliza
Y tu mensaje de paz lo transforman en belicista
Nunca hablé de ponerle una bomba al Ministro de Justicia, nunca
Y a la sociedad civil la militarizan.[101]

(Why is it that thinking differently is a betrayal punishable by death?
Why are some sectors marginalized and rejected?
If they don't respect the rules, this nation doesn't advance
But then injustice is let loose
And it's dangerous to speak and fear paralyzes you
And your message of peace, they transform into something bellicose
I never spoke of putting a bomb in the Ministry of Justice, never
And they militarize civil society.)

The verses critique the way Cuban civil society militarizes perceived counterrevolutionary discourse, casting any voice of dissent—even a peaceful one—as a violent threat to social stability. Despite limited knowledge of each other's work, some rappers in Northeast Brazil and Haiti have taken a similar approach, rejecting the poet-warrior type to insist instead on "rap pela paz" (peace rap).[102] How does this "peaceful message" harmonize with the notion that "rap is war"? What are the possibilities of peace rap amidst cultural militarism and the extreme power asymmetry between the state monopoly on violence and the individual actions of residents of disadvantaged urban neighborhoods?

Arguing for the right of colonized peoples to take up arms against their oppressors, Fanon declared nonviolence a bourgeois invention designed to delegitimate mid-twentieth-century anticolonial wars in Africa.[103] US Black civil rights leader Robert Franklin Williams followed up Fanon's defense of decolonial violence with the book *Negroes with Guns* (1962), which he published in Cuba while residing there in exile.[104] The following year, Black Arts Movement (BAM) founder Amiri Baraka—who also traveled to Cuba and was sympathetic with the Cuban Revolution—wrote that for Black Americans, it was "much too late" for nonviolence, calling later for "poems that kill."[105] I do not mean to suggest that it is too late for peace rap; on the contrary, rap undoubtedly provides listeners and performers a space for creatively channeling violence and voicing injustice. However, some Brazilian and Haitian hip hop artists have taken Baraka's invitation to heart, their lyrics yearning to surpass the realm of the symbolic and intervene in a social sphere already saturated with militarism.[106]

In contrast to the Cuban government's top-down and largely symbolic displays of militarism, in Haiti militarism emerges from below. Haitian popular identity has crystallized around the metaphor of the people as an army since at least the period of organized mass poisonings of slave-owners by *mawon* (maroons), such as those led by François Mackandal (Makandal) in the mid eighteenth century, which catalyzed the Haitian Revolution (1791–1804).[107] Haitian grassroots warfare provides the counterpoint to a long-standing militarism-from-above, which has remained a through-line in Haitian history since the colonial period: from French occupation of the island (1625–1793), to the failed Napoleonic invasion (1802–1804), to the US occupation (1915–1934), to Dominican dictator Rafael Trujillo's massacre of Haitians (1937), in addition to a long series of military coups, including two against democratically elected President Jean-Bertrand Aristide (1991 and 2004), and the 2021 assassination of President Jovenel Moïse.

Music has occupied a central place in Haitian militarism, drawing a dual lineage from eighteenth-century French military music (where the drum was used to communicate commands to soldiers) and military traditions from sub-Saharan African warfare.[108] Ensemble practices known as *kò mizik* reproduce drumming styles and hierarchies characteristic of military bands.[109] Widely popular and extremely hierarchical rara street bands "conceive of themselves as armies connected to imaginary states that move through territory, carry out armed maneuvers, and conduct diplomatic relations with other groups in the process of their musical celebrations."[110] Using military titles like *kolonèl* (colonel), *majò jonk* (drum major), and *pòt drapo* (flag bearer), rara bands patrol their territories and sometimes employ *zam kongo* (spiritual weapons associated with the Kongo peoples), such as the use of powders and charms, to defeat other bands during competition.[111] Under some circumstances, the stylized militarism of raras and other carnival bands can erupt into militant political protest and physical violence.[112]

Chapter 4 detailed the way Haitian rap groups separated into baz (bases), a name that invokes both defense (military base) and governance (political base). The militarism of baz emerged in Port-au-Prince as part of the popular insurgency surrounding Aristide's Lavalas movement. Though Aristide consistently spoke out against violence, he refused to condemn its use against Duvalier's former special forces, known as the Macoutes.[113] In a controversial 1991 speech, Aristide invoked the figure of self-defense against the Macoutes. US human rights and intelligence analysts simplified his message by interpreting it as a justification for murder, but Peter Hallward argues that Aristide was evoking a structural imbalance so great as to necessitate a legitimate use of violence.[114] This logic was endorsed by rap groups such as Barikad Crew in lyrics that describe defending their baz. In the song "Ou pa anyen nan zòn nan" (You're nothing in the area), for example, Izolan brags of the way "Nan hip hop la mwen toujou bay san m / Avèk baz mwen m toujou bay dan m" (In hip hop I always give my blood / With my base I always give my teeth).[115] The rhyming pair of *dan* (teeth) and *san* (blood) brings rap into the realm of Roumain's "Poetry as a Weapon," opening a bridge between verbal and physical violence that is sometimes crossed.

In Brazil, the state is well known for crossing this bridge, entering favelas with military tanks and engaging in armed conflicts that frequently result in deaths. For Benjamin, militarism "is the compulsory, universal use of violence as a means to the ends of the state."[116] Rappers and favela residents consistently denounce the sanctioned use of military force to "pacify" poor communities by labeling such acts *invasão* (invasion). The group Consciência Humana, from the São Paulo suburb of São Mateus, imagines waking up one day with good news: "Sem violência, sem racista, sem polícia / Sem ouvir tiazinha chorando por que invadiram sua goma" (Without violence, without racists, without police / Without hearing the aunt crying because they invaded her house).[117] Cidinho e Doca's "Rap das armas" (Rap of weapons) also denounces the violence of the Brazilian military police (PM) under the rubric of invasão. The chorus consists almost entirely of gunshot onomatopoeia ("Paparrapa parrapa parra clack bum / Parrapapapapapa papapapa"), seeming to imply that shots are being fired by both sides.[118] By deploying a term that ordinarily refers to military intervention by foreign powers, Brazilian rappers cast themselves in direct and violent opposition to the state. As Carl von Clausewitz defined in his famous treatise *On War,* invasion is *"the seizure of enemy territory; not with the object of retaining it . . . neither to conquer the enemy country nor to destroy its army, but simply to cause general damage."*[119] The term *invasion* is apt in the context of Brazilian favelas. What is the *parrapapapapapa* of an MC compared to the invasion of a favela by armed military tanks?

Despite (or as a result of) their critique of violence, some Brazilian rappers have been targets of a resuscitated 1940 Penal Code that renders illegal any *apologia ao crime* (apology of crime), defined as "public apology for a criminal fact or the author of a crime."[120] The title track of the 1998

Dentent os do Rap album *Apologia ao crime* exposes the absence of structural critique behind the criminalization of the apologia: "As portas estão fechadas / Uma oportunidade lhe foi negada" (All the doors are closed / An opportunity was denied to him).[121] A year later, the music video for Facção Central's "Isso aqui é uma guerra" (This here is a war) featured members of the rap group heavily armed, apparently ready for the war to which the lyrics refer: "É uma guerra onde só sobrevive quem atira" (It's a war where only those who fire survive).[122] Both the song and the video were censored for inciting crime.[123]

A few years later, Facção Central responded with a song also titled "Apologia ao crime," providing an additional structural critique of violence: "Saber que pra ter arroz, feijão, frango no forno tem que pegar um oitão e desfigurar um corpo / Entendo o motivo, sou fruto da favela" (Knowing that to have rice, beans, and chicken in the oven you have to pick up a thirty-eight[-caliber gun] and disfigure a body / I understand the motive, I'm the fruit of the favela).[124] Here, marginality and precarity produce crime (and rap), not the other way around. Lest the song be misinterpreted as defending crime, the chorus implores: "Não caia na armadilha, siga a minha apologia" (Don't fall in the trap, follow my apologia). In this way the group resignifies the notion of apologia ao crime to mean precisely the opposite of its legal definition: a second-order apologia or a critique of the defense of crime. The move recovers the lyric root of *apologia*, "a system for proving a general point through examples."[125] As a critique of violence, the rap apologia exposes the state's militarized oppression of the disadvantaged.

A fúria negra ressuscita outra vez: Black Reason and *Quilombismo*

In addition to critiquing present-day violence, Brazilian rappers draw on the militarized resistance or "West African warfare" of fugitive and marooned formerly enslaved people.[126] By calling for a collective, anticolonial, anti-imperialist struggle in the tradition of those who fought against slavery, they follow Abdias do Nascimento's manifesto "O quilombismo."[127] The neologism *quilombismo* profiles a contemporary practice of resistance drawn from the Palmares *quilombo* (maroon community), whose residents defied invasion attempts for nearly a century in Brazil's Northeast (1605–1694) before the community was suppressed by the colonial army.[128] Brazilian rap songs practice quilombismo in various ways. Rappin' Hood's "Us guerreiro" (The warriors) and Sharylaine's

"Rei Zumbi" (King Zumbi) narrate the triumph of Palmares leaders Zumbi and Dandara. In the song "Crime bárbaro" (Barbarous crime), Rincon Sapiência personifies the poetic "I" of an enslaved person revolting: "Escravos apoiam meu desempenho / Foi eu que matei o senhor de engenho" (The enslaved people support my performance / It was I who killed the plantation master).[129] The music video features Rincon, presumably having escaped slavery, running away from a heavily armed white man in military garb. To introduce the song, an off-screen narrator announces that it was "inspired by the fictitious short story by writer Danilo Albert Ambrosio," a reference to Rincon himself.[130] This framing device invites the listener to hear "Crime bárbaro" as the musicalized version of a short story by the rapper (or as the short story itself), redoubling the importance of writing in rap's critique of violence.

Mano Brown, who once suggested that rap participates in the Black radical tradition of "o conceito da violência contra a violência" (the notion of violence against violence), offers an even more fugitive critique of violence in "Capítulo 4, Versículo 3" (Chapter 4, verse 3).[131] The numbers correspond to the third track on the fourth album of Racionais MC's, aligning the group's artistic production with divine scripture:

> Eu tenho uma missão e não vou parar
> Meu estilo é pesado e faz tremer o chão
> Minha palavra vale um tiro, eu tenho muita munição
> Na queda ou na ascensão minha atitude vai além
> E tenho disposição pro mal e pro bem
> Talvez eu seja um sádico, um anjo, um mágico
> Juiz ou réu, um bandido do céu
> Malandro ou otário, padre sanguinário
> Franco atirador, se for necessário
> Revolucionário, insano ou marginal
> Antigo e moderno, imortal
> Fronteira do céu com o inferno
> Astral imprevisível, como um ataque cardíaco no verso
> Violentamente pacífico, verídico
> Vim pra sabotar seu raciocínio.
> . . . .
> E a profecia se fez como previsto
> 1997 depois de Cristo
> A fúria negra ressuscita outra vez
> Racionais, capítulo 4, versículo 3.[132]

(I have a mission and I'm not going to stop
My style is heavy and I make the ground shake
My word's worth a gunshot and I have a lot of ammunition
Falling or rising, my attitude goes beyond
I have a disposition for bad and for good
Maybe I'm a sadist, an angel, a magician
Judge or accused, a bandit from the sky
Malandro or moron, a blood-thirsty priest
A sniper, if necessary
Revolutionary, insane, or marginal
Ancient or modern, immortal
Border of heaven and hell
Unpredictable astral chart, like a heart attack in the verse
Violently pacifist, true
I came to sabotage your reasoning.
. . . .
And the prophecy was fulfilled as predicted
1997 AD
Black fury rises again
Racionais, chapter 4, verse 3.)

In ambivalent self-presentation characteristic of malandragem (see chapter 5), which he directly references, Brown presents himself through a series of dramatis personae he may or may not (*talvez*) represent. He ends the series by describing rap through the aphoristic paradox "violently pacifist, true." The paradox captures the materiality of rap-violence: "Brown's ammunition are the intoned words" and the violence is executed against logic and reason.[133] This is the sense in which Brown addresses his listener in the mission statement "I came to sabotage your reasoning."

Responding to a reporter about the origin of the name Racionais, fellow group member Edi Rock explained that "it comes from raciocínio, no? A name that has to do with the lyrics, with us."[134] The group affirmed elsewhere that the name Racionais pays homage to the influence of Tim Maia's "rational culture" (referring to Maia's record *Tim Maia Racional*), although Brown contradicted this reading on another occasion, insisting that the group might better have been called *Emocionais* (Emotional MCs).[135] The refusal to take a position with respect to the origin and meaning of the name continues the sabotage of reason described in the lyrics. Yet the group clearly intends for rap to be an instrument of critical reasoning: "Eu tô confuso, preciso pensar / Me dá um tempo pra eu raciocinar" (I'm confused, I need to think / Give me some time to reason).[136] The notion of *raciocínio* on their own terms resonates with Achille Mbembe's definition of "Black reason," "the place where writing seeks to exorcise the demon of the first narrative [of Black people as racial subjects and sites of savage exteriority] and the structure of subjection within it, the place where writing struggles to evoke, save, activate, and reactualize original experience (tradition) and find the truth of the self no longer outside of the self but standing on its own ground."[137] For Mbembe, Black reason aims to rewrite Blackness outside the violent structures of subjugation externally imposed upon it. In their critique of violence, rappers participate in this search for the "truth of the self . . . on its own ground." As Brown reaches the penultimate line of "Capítulo 4, Versículo 3," church bells accompany an ethereal chorus of *alleluia*'s. He rhymes himself a prophet and announces the second coming of "Black fury," presumably a reference to Palmares. Practicing quilombismo, Brown's rap moves forward by going back, narrating the present by recovering the occulted history of centuries-old struggles against racialized oppression, to reimagine futures in and through hip hop.

Si nou vle dekolonize mantalman: Decolonization and *Pwezi Filozofik*

During the mid twentieth century, Brazilian scholars and activists cast Palmares as Brazil's "república negra" (Black republic),[138] invoking the founding of Haiti (commonly described as the world's first Black republic).[139] The Haitian Revolution remains the only example of warfare by enslaved people leading to the formation of a nation-state. Trouillot famously contended that the Haitian Revolution was "silenced" from Western history due to its unthinkability.[140] Susan Buck-Morss, in turn, has provided compelling evidence that Friedrich Hegel encountered news of the Haitian Revolution while drafting his theory of the master-slave dialectic (although Hegel's *Phenomenology* avoids mentioning Haiti by name).[141] Thus the Haitian Revolution's "silencing" is even more insidious: it represents the conscious erasure of a world-historical event that was very much the subject of Western thought.

Aristide's postpresidential memoir and poetic treatise, subtitled *Pwezi filozofik pou dekolonizasyon mantal* (Philosophical poetry for mental decolonization), promotes the recovery of Haiti's revolutionary history by bringing together popular philosophy, slogans from the fervent *mizik rasin* (roots music) movement, and Ubuntu ontology. The book's title

Haïti—Haitii? introduces a homophonic slippage between the indigenous Taino word *ayiti,* meaning "land of the mountains" (from which Haiti got its name), and the Swahili contraction of *Hai* (not) and *tii* (obey):

Kisa, kisa mo Haïti a vle di pou nou ?

Pou reponn konenn kesyon sa a,
Nou chwazi itiliza yon fòm langaj
Ki marye 2 fòs : pwezi ak filozofi.
Yo fè lago, ale vini, youn nan lòt.

Pwezi a mouye nan sous enspirasyon
Yon poèm nan lang Swahili—Kreyòl
Ke n kwafwe ak tit sa a: Haïti—Haitii.[142]

(What does the word Haiti mean for us?

To answer this profound question
We chose a style of language
That combines 2 strengths: poetry and philosophy.
One compliments the other in achieving the task.

This poetry draws its inspiration
From a poem in the languages Swahili and Kreyòl
That we titled: Haïti—Haitii.)[143]

By linking Haiti's name to Swahili, Aristide frames the country's founding as a call to disobey: "An Swahili: Haitii / Ki vle di: Pa obeyi" (In Swahili: Haitii / Which means: Do not obey).[144] Not only a revindication of Indigeneity, the naming of Haiti represents a right of refusal: a "refusal to forget,"[145] or a "refusal of what has been refused."[146] For Aristide, refusal takes the form of a poetic address to *manman Lafrik* (mother Africa) and *manman libetè* (mother liberty: Haiti). Africa signifies the origin of philosophy and Haiti the kernel of freedom—concepts more commonly associated with the bourgeois revolution of Haiti's former metropole.

If not in book form, Aristide's *pwezi filozofik* (philosophical poetry) reached the ears of Haitian rappers. Original Rap Staff samples the refrain, popularized by Aristide, "Tout moun se moun" (Every person is a person) in a rap manifesto for equality and autonomy.[147] Released in 1996, the year Aristide's Fanmi Lavalas was officially registered as a political party, the Original Rap Staff song heeds the populist leader's call by deconstructing the hegemony of the power-holding minority: "Ou pa bezwen gran nèg pou w fè yon stil ak tèt w" (You don't need to be a powerful person to have your own style).[148] A decade later, Barikad Crew would similarly reject the powerful person and embrace Aristide's emphasis on cooperation and collaboration: "Non gran moun se sa nou tout dwe di / Nou di non! Nou tout fè youn, se sa k ap bay lavi" (No sir, that is what we all must say / We say no! All of us make one, that's what can give us life).[149] Fantom's couplet plays on the homophone *non*, which can mean "no" or "name," such that the refusal "No sir, that is what we all must say" can also be heard as "The name 'powerful person': that is what we all must say." Thus the communitarian force of the little-man majority deconstructs the *gran moun* and becomes a collective refusal of the status quo.

Aristide's project of pwezi filozofik is most directly echoed in the rap song "Dekolonizasyon" (Decolonization), written by Jiwenrison Guetz Marcena and performed by Blaze One. Didactic lyrics defend the importance of "dekolonize mantalman" (mentally decolonizing).[150] They disavow the pervasive notion "that the Haitian poor are cultural agents of their own immiseration," as exemplified by interpretations of the 2010 earthquake as divine castigation for Haiti's "pact with the devil," which supposedly allowed for the revolution to triumph.[151] The process of mental decolonization opens up a critique of Haiti's colonial past and its present neocolonial relationship with Western countries. The lyrics to "Dekolonizasyon" begin with an invocation of Haiti's "pèp nwa, pèp lib, pèp fò" (Black people, free people, strong people) and proceed to demonstrate the way "si n ap swiv jounen jodi a w ap wè esklavaj kontinye" (if we're attentive, we'll see that today slavery goes on).[152] One contemporary example is Haitian labor in the Dominican Republic:

> Pran rak bwa, janbe fontyè al fouye nan Duarte
> Sa k ka travay, ranje ponyèt al koupe nan batey
> Se pou montre n esklavaj la ap sible yon kalte
> Sa k ban n kout men enperyalis eskwokri gran flatè
> Depi lontan k ap souse san n e k rann fanmi n anba tè
> Oh God! Yo fè n toujou dèyè e eskli n nan lis la
> Yo ban n tranbleman tè e yo di n se Kris la
> Yo maltrete n, yo vyole dwa n, yo pase l anba pye
> Paske nou se yon ti pèp e se sa k fè fyète n son gran istwa.[153]

> (Take to the woods, across the border to the sugarcane harvest in the Duarte
> Anybody who can work: strengthen your arms, come cut cane in the *batey*
> It's to show us that slavery is targeting a specific group
> They're here to help us, but imperialist fraud, big-time flatterers
> For a long time, they've been soaking in our blood, put our families under the earth

Oh God! They still keep us behind, they exclude us from the list
They give us an earthquake and they say it's Christ
They mistreat us, they violate and step on our rights
Because we're just a small people, and that's what makes us proud of our great history.)

The reference to the sugarcane harvest in the Dominican Republic frames recent Haitian migration there not only in relation to *batey* labor camps, but also as a retreat to the *rak bwa* (woods). Severe deforestation visibly distinguishes Haiti's wooded areas from the eastern portion of the island pertaining to the Dominican Republic.[154] Migrating to the Dominican Republic, then, marks a return to the rak bwa—probably an allusion to *mawonaj* (marronage), the formation of maroon communities by formerly enslaved people, under the protection of woods and high mountainous forests.[155] It was in the rak bwa where the *bwa kayiman* ceremony took place, broadly understood as Haiti's foundational event and probably also a consolidating moment for the Vodou religion.[156] During this 1791 ritual inaugurating the Haitian Revolution, maroon leader Dutty Boukman is said to have sacrificed a pig and rejected the white God (*Bondié blancs*) in favor of a true God.[157] Subsequently, mawonaj proved instrumental in the formation of Haiti's rural majority.[158] When Haiti's founding political leaders centralized power, denied autonomy to the rural majority, and proved unable or unwilling to live up to their promise of radical equality, rural Haitians defended their hard-won freedom by cultivating small garden plots and rejecting state power.[159] Thus emerged the *peyi andeyò* (country outside), forged out of maroon communities and the rak bwa.[160]

"Dekolonizsyon" reclaims the revolutionary connotation of bwa: freedom, liberty, and radical autonomy vis-à-vis the slave-like conditions of Dominican plantations, the oppression of rural Haitians by the state, and Haiti's highly uneven relationship with the West. By invoking the Haitian Revolution alongside exploited Haitian labor and the destruction of the rak bwa, the song situates contemporary struggles in the context of abiding colonial asymmetries.[161] What Aníbal Quijano called the "coloniality of power" (the perpetuation of colonial structures following formal independence) is made clear in the rap sample of the proverb "chenn nan tèt pi di pase chenn nan pye" (chains in the brain are harder to break than chains on the foot).[162] Mental decolonization begins with exposing the multiple forms of coloniality that persist to the present day, including what Rob Nixon calls "slow violence" against the natural environment and the poor.[163] These rap lyrics offer a "prophetic vision of the past" that doubles as a yearning for the future reverberations of Haiti's "gran istwa" (great history).[164]

Rap kreyòl takes a more personal form of "prophetic criticism" in the pen of D-Fi,[165] whose mixtape *Rev ak plim* (Dream with a pen) centers around notions of writing, survival, and remaking:

> M ap chache mwen nan mwen
> M ap chache mwen nan ou
> M ap chache mwen nan nou
> M ap chache mwen nan mwen
>
> M ap gad reflè m a travè mond lan kòm si l t on miwa
> Piramid negriye mwen mi-esklav, mi-wa
> Lank pran vijinite fèy mwen
> Pou bay pwezi dous ou anmè.
> Dèfwa m rap ak kè m, dèfwa m rap ak fyè l mwen
> Rim apre rim vi m jwenn ekilib
> Mwen se a travè on plim pa a travè on jwen ke m vin lib
> . . . .
> Plis m ap gen emosyon m ap pèdi mo
> Plis m ap jwenn D-Fi, m ap pèdi Rhod
> M bouke wè dyab la lè m gàd reflè m
> Sou fèy blanch, m vin refè mond lan avan l refè m.[166]
>
> (I'm searching for me in me
> I'm searching for me in you
> I'm searching for me in us
> I'm searching for me in me
>
> I look at my reflection through the world as if it were a mirror
> Pyramid or slaver, I'm half enslaved, half king
> Ink takes the virginity of my page
> To give sweet or bitter poetry.
> Sometimes I rap with my heart, sometimes I rap with my gut
> Rhyme after rhyme, my life finds balance
> It's through a pen, not a joint, that I become free
> . . . .
> The more emotional I get, the more I lose the words
> The more I find a D-Fi, the more I lose Rhod
> And I'm tired of seeing the devil when I look at my reflection
> On a blank page, I come to remake the world before it remakes me.)

As D-Fi's "I"/eye turns back on itself in the mirror's reflection, he sees the past and writes the future. A product of African royalty as well as slavery, the rapper rejects the subhuman construction of the enslaved person with the verse "I'm half enslaved, half king." The wordplay of *miwa* (mirror) and *mi-wa* (half king) recovers Blackness in its revolutionary fullness. D-Fi searches for himself in others and for others in himself, in language evocative of Aimé Césaire: "We cannot give anyone the delegation to think for us; the delegation to search for us" (*chercher pour nous*).[167] The *fèy blanch* (blank page) becomes the "limit-performance of an equalizing tabula rasa in colonial conflict," where rap can unmask the whiteness atop racial hierarchies by darkening the page.[168] Tracing black marks on a blank page, D-Fi rhymes himself and the world anew. Here, rap's critique of violence feeds back into the yearnings of the opening chapter.

D-Fi's nom de plume is a pun on the word *defi* (challenge or defiance), and his re-creation of the world is coeval with his self-fashioning as a rapper: "to declare one's own identity is to write the world into existence."[169] For the rapper, "the more I find D-Fi, the more I lose Rhod." In other words, Rhod D'Jyvens Télémaque's performative act of "stepping into character" as D-Fi entails the risk of dissolution into the rap persona.[170] Such slippage between the rap "I" and the real-life persona recalls the famous example of Los Angeles rapper Tupac Shakur, who acquired a criminal record only after creating his "Thug Life" character. As Adam Bradley puts it, Tupac "rendered such a vivid character in rhyme that people could mistake it for the truth, and yet that identification may have cost him his life."[171] Poets, prose writers, and singers have published under pen names and alter egos for centuries.[172] The danger in rap lies in being so convincing that the poetic "I" can overtake the real-life persona.[173] Though he risks losing himself, it is only through rap that D-Fi finds balance (*jwenn ekilib*). The equilibrium or metonymical proximity between subject and object, between rapper and rap, is what allows D-Fi to "write the world into existence."

Outro: On Commitment

As I suggested in the introduction, hip hop poetics is not merely a description of the formal features of rap; poetics is what rap songs do. While I have traced three overlapping cultural histories associated with the circulation of hip hop poetics in the Americas, these are not so much cultural histories about hip hop as cultural histories *in* hip hop. By articulating and enacting categories of shared poetic belonging through community writing, Haitian, Brazilian, and Cuban rappers demonstrate in their flows the near-limitless potential for revision that accompanies the recursive return to the break. Rap provides a mode of being and knowing together, a way of making sense of the global in the local, the written in the aural, the (rap)love that undergirds yearning. It is a practice that is always grounding but never on firm ground, always emplacing but never in one place, constantly uprooting, perpetually somewhere else.

By foregrounding the poetic work of self-reflexive lyrics, I have largely bracketed the apotheosis of violence and misogyny characteristic of some rappers, particularly mainstream artists in the United States. It must be acknowledged that even groups such as Racionais MC's, for all its raciocínio, released songs like "Mulheres vulgares" (Vulgar women) and "Estilo cachorro" (Doggy style), which Brown publicly denounced in 2017.[174] Describing openly misogynistic or uncritically violent rap songs, Rose explains that a pact exists between artist, consumer, and the industry, where rap music is understood to represent, "despite its extraordinary expansion as a brand, the truth from the streets of the black ghetto, uninfluenced by corporate agendas for profit, by white desire to consume black violence and sexual excess, and by rappers' own desire to feed such desire for their own financial gain."[175] Brazilian, Cuban, and Haitian rappers give occasion not only to deconstruct this pact, but also to reflect on our widespread complacency with respect to the industry's racist, misogynist, and exploitative structures, and on the wildly different standards we use to judge the violence of Black performers as compared to, say, white politicians.

In a 1996 interview, Boots Riley of the Oakland-based rap group The Coup lamented the loss of "political rap" groups in the United States: "Rappers have to be in touch with their communities no matter what type of raps you do, otherwise people won't relate. Political rap groups offered solutions only through listening. They weren't part of a movement, so they died out when people saw that their lives were not changing."[176] Mark Anthony Neal similarly explains that "political hip-hop was undermined by hip-hop's own internal logic that often privileged constant stylistic innovation, both in narrative and musical content, as a response to intense commodification."[177] Whether or not Riley's and Neal's analyses map neatly onto Latin America, I believe they both reveal, by reifying the category of "political rap," that hip hop's appositional internal logic—its sabotage of reason, as Mano Brown puts it—*is* its politics.[178] What does it mean, then, to assert that political rap groups "died out" because they "offered solutions only through listening"? Might not the politics of rap reside, precisely, in this act of listening? Does not any movement from words to actions, any attempt at harnessing the performative and transformative force of words, return to aurality?

Listening is the interface between the politics and poetics of rap: the vehicle for yearning and raplove, for uprooting, placemaking, and community writing. For this reason, I have focused not so much on "political" or "socially conscious" rappers (although most of those included would identify as such), but on self-conscious, self-reflexive artists committed to defining and expanding the possibilities of hip hop poetics in the Americas. These artists write by listening acutely to the texts and spaces that surround them, elaborating letras/lyrics as armas/zam for creating new forms of knowledge and community. At once "enraizados da letra" and seeking to remake the world "sou fèy blanch," they write to survive.

Epilogue
En-/un-gendering Hip Hop

IN AUGUST 2019, the last time I stayed with my dear friend and longtime collaborator Malcoms "Justicia" before his tragic and unexpected death, I was invited to present at the annual Hip Hop Symposium at the Cuban Rap Agency in Central Havana. The theme uniting the presentations, talks, and concerts that year was women in hip hop, so I selected songs by women rappers from Brazil and Haiti to compare their representations of gender. When I presented the songs, the primarily male audience of Cuban hip hop artists largely ignored the question of gender and became fixated, instead, on genre. Some of the songs I presented didn't conform to their preconceived notions of what constituted the genre of rap (a highly specific breakbeat, a nonmelodic recitation style, an aggressive masculine voice). They accused me of focusing on the musical fusion or hybridity that so often appeals to foreign anthropologists.

For example, I played Princess Eud's "Eudomination," which mixes a hip hop breakbeat with Haitian konpa. Although in her lyrics, Eud self-identifies as a rapper, some male hip hop artists in the audience argued that the song could not be considered rap, since it did not conform precisely to their interpretation of rap's generic conventions (dictated in large part by the music industry's commodification of US rap). The conversation was marked by a constant slippage between genre and gender, facilitated by the fact that Spanish (like Portuguese) uses the same word for both, *género*. The single Spanish word reinforces the fact that both gender and genre are forms of regulation, not essentialist categories but performances in which we participate and through which we are interpellated. When we read (texts as well as people), we assign genres and genders; when we write or fashion ourselves, we practice, participate in, and are subjected by genre/gender in specific ways.[1]

I ended my talk suggesting that the exclusion of female voices in rap might stem as much from the fact that they are of a nonmale gender as that they don't conform to the specific conventions of genre predetermined to correspond to rap and hip hop. For many in attendance, the expansion of genre/gender introduced by the presence of women rappers betrayed hip hop's (masculine) roots, a deep-set conservatism derived from anxieties surrounding hip hop's potential to become something else. "Listening in detail" to Black feminist yearnings and critiques of violence can perhaps begin to shake loose hip hop's hypermasculinity.[2] But how much are the other conventions and techniques associated with hip hop poetics in the Americas bound up with the gendering of hip hop as masculine? How will future artists of rap and its derivative genres confront the aporias of gender and genre as they continue to innovate and transform themselves and their craft? What will hip hop become and what poetic and social legacies will it leave? What can these new breaks and flows tell us about our present and future?

About the Artists

BECAUSE THE themes and chapters of *Break and Flow* build on each other, many of the same artists and songs return at different moments throughout the text. I include here an alphabetical list with short descriptions of the primary artists and groups mentioned in the book. Readers who wish to hear the referenced songs or view the corresponding music videos are invited to visit the YouTube playlist I have curated, either by navigating to YouTube and searching "Charlie Hankin Break and Flow" or by direct link: http://tinyurl.com/breakandflow.

35 ZILE: rapper based in Port-au-Prince. Known for mixing hip hop and Vodou rhythms in what he calls Vodou rap.

ALDO OR AL2 EL ALDEANO (THE VILLAGER): Aldo Roberto Rodríguez Baquero. Cofounder of the Havana-based group Los Aldeanos, the best-known Cuban rap group of the 2000s. Emigrated to Florida in the early 2010s.

ALEXEY ..EL TIPO ESTE..: Alexey Rodríguez Mola. Pioneering rapper and cofounder of the group Obsesión.

ANÓNIMO CONSEJO (ANONYMOUS ADVICE): Havana-based rap duo popular in the early 2000s, comprised of Maigel "MC Kokino" Entenza Jaramillo and Yosmel "MC Sekou" Sarrias.

ASAP FRESH: Port-au-Prince trap group featuring rapper Marc Cuvier Daniel. Released a hit Vodou remix of the Migos track "Bad and Bougee" in 2017.

BÁRBARO "EL URBANO" (THE URBAN ONE): Bárbaro Vargas. Rapper from Marianao, Havana. Participated in important rap projects such as *La comisión depuradora* and *Tribu Mokoya*. Emigrated to Finland in the mid 2010s.

174 *About the Artists*

BARIKAD CREW (BC): infamous Haitian rap group, founded in 2002 in downtown *lavil* bordering Rue Nicolas in Port-au-Prince. Recognized in 2006 with a prestigious Ticket d'Or as the Haitian musical group of the year. Members included K-Tafalk, Fantom, and Izolan, among many others.

BIA DOXUM: Beatriz Oliveira. Rapper, singer, and activist based in *zona leste* (eastern zone), São Paulo.

BIC: Roosevelt Saillant. Rapper and poet based in Port-au-Prince, active since 2000. Has performed abroad on several occasions, including a residency in France with the Cité Internationale des Arts de Paris in 2014 and a collaboration with the Massachusetts Institute of Technology in 2017.

BLAY'Z MATIQ: rapper based in Delmas, Port-au-Prince.

BLAZE ONE: Elisé Senora. Rapper based in Port-au-Prince with a strong reggae influence. Commonly raps about themes of decolonization and Haitian history.

BREBAJE MAN: Etián Arnau Lizaire. Pioneer Havana rapper and master freestyler from the municipality of Playa, Havana. Cofounder of the group Explosión Suprema (Supreme Explosion).

BRISA FLOW: Brisa de la Cordillera. Rapper based in São Paulo, daughter of Chilean immigrants.

CAROLINA REBOUÇAS: rapper and singer based in Fortaleza, Brazil.

CIDINHO E DOCA: Sidney da Silva and Marcos Paulo de Jesus Peizoto. Well-known proibidão group based in Rio de Janeiro.

CONSCIÊNCIA HUMANA (HUMAN CONSCIENCE): controversial rap group from São Mateus, São Paulo, founded in 1990 and featuring rapper Preto Aplick. Emulated US gangsta rap.

CRIOLO: Kleber Cavalcante Gomes. From Grajaú, São Paulo, with family from the Northeast, among the best-known Brazilian rappers. Has released several samba albums in addition to rap. His name is a play on *crioulo* (Creole), which in Brazil was used to refer to Black people born in the New World.

D-FI POWÈT REVÒLTE (REVOLTED POET): Rhod D'Jyvens Télémaque. Rapper based in Delmas, Port-au-Prince. The name D-Fi plays on the word *defi* (challenge).

DETENTOS DO RAP (RAP PRISONERS): rap group formed in São Paulo in 1994 by Maurício D. T. S., Daniel Sancy, DJ Culina, and Denílson Vertelo, who were incarcerated at the time. Known for critiquing the apologia ao crime (apology for crime), a belief propagated by media outlets that Brazilian rappers are apologists for violence.

DINA DI: Viviane Lopes Matias. Award-winning rapper from Campinas, São Paulo. Popular in Brazil during the late 2000s.

DJONGA: Gustavo Pereira Marques. Rapper from Belo Horizonte, Brazil. Rose to fame in the late 2010s. Performed with Mano Brown and Criolo on a tour in 2018.

DMN: São Paulo rap group formed in 1989. Known for the song "Homem de aço" (Steel man).

DUKES: self-produced rapper from São Bernardo do Campo, São Paulo.

EL B: Bian Oscar Rodríguez Galá. Cofounder, with Aldo, of Los Aldeanos in 2003. Finalist for the Red Bull–sponsored freestyle competition the Batalla de los Gallos.

ERIVAN "PRODUTOS DO MORRO": Erivan Barbosa Sales. Resident of the Morro do Castelo Encantado favela in Fortaleza, Brazil, where he has maintained a studio for more than twenty years. Born in the interior city of Juazeiro do Norte, Ceará.

FACÇÃO CENTRAL (CENTRAL FACTION): São Paulo rap group founded in 1989. Gained national notoriety when the music video to the 1999 song "Isso aqui é uma guerra" (This here is a war) was censored for inciting violence.

FANTOM: member of Barikad Crew.

FILOSOFIA DE RUA (STREET PHILOSOPHY): São Paulo rap group formed in 1991.

FLORA MATOS: Brasília-based rapper active since 2009.

GABRIEL O PENSADOR (THE THINKER): Gabriel Contino. Successful Rio de Janeiro–based rapper known for socially conscious lyrics and sometimes critiqued for gentrifying the genre given his middle-class upbringing.

GOG: Genival Oliveira Gonçalves. Pioneer rapper and producer based in Brasília, active since 1992. Known as Brazilian rap's "national poet." Released several important rap albums and a book of rap lyrics, *A rima denúncia* (Rhyme denounces; published in 2010).

HERMANOS DE CAUSA (BROTHERS FOR A CAUSE): Soandres (Soandry) del Río and El Pelón. Rap group active in Havana since the mid 1990s.

IZOLAN: member of Barikad Crew.

KANIS: Niska Garoute. Miami-born Haitian American rapper. Attended primary and secondary school in Port-au-Prince.

LAS KRUDAS: Odaymara Cuesta and Olivia Prendes. Black, queer, feminist rap group formed in Havana in 1996.

LENNY FERNANDES: rapper and B-boy dancer, longtime collaborator with Erivan "Produtos do Morro." Resident of Fortaleza, Brazil.

LOS ALDEANOS: founded by Aldo and El B and active in Havana between roughly 2003 and 2011. Responsible for radicalizing Cuban rap in the late 2000s. Performed alongside Pablo Milanés and other notable Cuban musicians.

LOS ORISHAS: Cuban rap group led by Joel Pando. Emigrated to France in 1998 and released *A lo cubano* in 1999, which became a Platinum-certified album in Spain. Previously known as Amenaza.

MALCOMS "JUSTICIA" (JUSTICE): Malcoms Junco Duffay. Longtime producer and rapper based in San Miguel del Padrón, Havana. Founder and director of 18A16 Studios. Formerly producer of the Cuban Rap Agency's recording label.

MANO BROWN: Pedro Paulo Soares Pereira. Leader of the most famous Brazilian rap group, Racionais MC's. Arguably the best-known rapper in Brazil.

MASTER DJI: Georges Lys Hérard. Founder of Haitian rap kreyòl in the 1980s. Radio DJ and son of Radyo Pòtoprens (Port-au-Prince Radio) owner Antoine Rodolphe Hérard.

MC BOY DO CHARMES: São Paulo–based rapper of the subgenre ostentação. Active during the early 2010s.

MC GUIMÊ: São Paulo–based rapper of the subgenre ostentação. Active during the early 2010s.

MV BILL: Alexandre Pereira Barbosa. Longtime rapper and activist based in Rio de Janeiro. Co-author of the book *Cabeça de porco* (Pork's head; published in 2015), which contains interviews about the crack epidemic. The initials MV stand for Mensageiro da Verdade (Messenger of Truth).

NONO: Yanelis Cándida. Rapper from East Havana.

OBSESIÓN (OBSESSION): rap duo formed in 1996 in Regla, Havana, by Alexey Rodríguez and Magia López (former director of the Cuban Rap Agency).

ORIGINAL RAP STAFF: Port-au-Prince-based rap group active since 1994.

PADÊRO MC: Francisco Velto Barbosa Lima. Rapper from Barra do Ceará, Fortaleza. Learned to read and write as an adult to write down his rap lyrics. Left involvement in crime to become a community leader.

PAPÁ HUMBERTICO: Humberto Joel Cabrera Santana. Havana-based rapper and producer, known for running the Real 70 studio, which released several important albums in the 2000s.

PRINCESS EUD: Eunide Edouarin. Successful rapper based in Port-au-Prince, active in the 2010s.

PROJOTA: José Tiago Sabino Pereira. Well-known rapper based in São Paulo. Featured on the 2016 Rio de Janeiro Olympic Games theme song.

PROYECTO CHARDO: Havana-based group. Participated in the legendary album *La comisión depuradora*.

RACIONAIS MC'S (RATIONAL MCS): Mano Brown, Ice Blue, Edi Rock, and DJ KL Jay. Best-known Brazilian rap group, formed in São Paulo in 1988. Their independently released album *Sobrevivendo no inferno* (1997) sold more than 1.5 million copies.

RAPADURA XIQUE-CHICO: Francisco Igor Almeida do Santos. Fortaleza-born Brazilian rapper known for emulating the style and poetic forms of the rural *sertão*.

RAPPIN' HOOD: Antônio Luiz Júnior. São Paulo–based rapper active since 1989. Known for a series of albums entitled *Sujeito homen* (Male subject). Invested some of his earnings to build a soccer complex and training center.

RELATOS DE FORTALEZA (FORTALEZA STORIES): rap group formed in Fortaleza in 2004 by Padêro MC.

RINCON SAPIÊNCIA: Danilo Albert Ambrosio. Rapper based in São Paulo. Commonly rhymes about slavery and racial justice.

ROCKFAM: popular rap kreyòl group based in Port-au-Prince.

SABOTAGE: Mauro Mateus dos Santos. Legendary rapper from the favela of Canão in Brooklin, São Paulo. Made a cameo appearance in the 2002 film *O Invasor* (The Trespasser). Tragically murdered in 2003.

SHARYLAINE: Ildslaine Mônica da Silva. Longtime rapper and activist based in São Paulo. Founder of the first all-female Brazilian rap group, Rap Girl's (1986), and featured on the 1989 rap compilation album *Consciência Black* (Black conscience).

SILVITO "EL LIBRE": Silvio Liam Rodríguez Varona. Florida-based, Havana-born rapper, longtime collaborator with Los Aldeanos. Son of world-renowned Cuban singer-songwriter Silvio Rodríguez.

TÁSSIA REIS: rapper and singer based in São Paulo. Member of the feminist rap collective Rimas e Melodias (Rhymes and Melodies).

THAÍDE & DJ HUM: Altair Gonçalves and Humberto Martins. Pioneer Brazilian rap group, also participated in the bailes black of the 1970s and 1980s.

VISÃO DE RUA (STREET VISION): rap group formed in Campinas, São Paulo, in 1994 by Dina Di, often in collaboration with Negra Li.

WENDYYY: Duvert Wendy. Trap-style rapper widely popular in Port-au-Prince during the late 2010s.

178 *About the Artists*

WYCLEF JEAN: rapper and actor born in Port-au-Prince, moved to Brooklyn at age nine. Known for his work with the group the Fugees as well as for an unsuccessful presidential bid in Haiti (2010). Raps primarily in English.

XIS (THE LETTER "X"): Marcelo Santos. Rapper from Itaquera, São Paulo, active in the 1990s and 2000s. Traveled to Havana in 2001 to record the track "Foritifando a disobediência" (Fortifying disobedience) with Cuban rappers MC White, Telmary Díaz, Papo Record, and 100% Original.

YOMIL Y EL DANY: Roberto Hidalgo and Daniel Muñoz. Founders of the self-styled genre traptón, fusing reggaeton and trap music. Popular in the late 2010s.

Selective Timeline of Brazilian, Cuban, and Haitian Hip Hop

1957	François "Papa Doc" Duvalier elected in Haiti, soon consolidates power as dictator
1959	Guerrilla forces including Fidel and Raúl Castro, Ernesto "Che" Guevara, and Camilo Cienfuegos overthrow US-backed dictator Fulgencio Batista in Cuban Revolution
1964	Brazilian military dictatorship begins
1967	US funk music first heard on Brazilian radio
1967	First bailes black (Black dances) held to US and Brazilian funk and soul in outer neighborhoods of Rio de Janeiro and São Paulo
1971	Jean-Claude "Baby Doc" Duvalier succeeds his father in Haitian dictatorship
1973	Hip hop is born at a block party in the Bronx, New York City
1978	James Brown performs in São Paulo to an audience of more than ten thousand people, including Pernambuco-born breakdancer Nelson "Triunfo"
1980s	Cuban moña dances are held in Havana to US soul and funk music
1982	Afrika Bambaataa gives hip hop its name and embarks on the first international hip hop tour
1983–1984	Three hip hop films are released with wide international circulation, including in Cuba and Brazil: *Wild Style* (Charlie Ahearn, 1983), *Style Wars* (Tony Silver, 1983), and *Beat Street* (Stan Lathan, 1984)

Selective Timeline

1983	Nelson "Triunfo" takes the bailes black to downtown São Paulo (Praça da República and the São Bento metro station) in the first gatherings of Brazilian breaking
1985	Miami bass–inflected *funk carioca* (Rio de Janeiro funk) is born, following the Brazilian release of Africa Bambaataa's "Planet Rock"
	Brazilians force the end of the dictatorship, beginning a transition to democracy
1986	Haitians overthrow Jean-Claude Duvalier, leading to political dechoukaj (uprooting)
	Radio DJ Master Dji records the first rap kreyòl hit, "Sispann" (Stop), receiving second prize in the Prix Découvertes RFI competition of Radio France Internationale
1987	Haitian konpa group Les Frères Parent releases the election song "Veye-yo" with verses rapped in Kreyòl
1987	In a new Haitian Constitution, Kreyòl is finally declared an official language alongside French
1988	*Yo! MTV Raps* program launched in the US, becoming one of MTV's first globally televised shows and airing in dozens of countries: first on MTV Europe, then on MTV Asia, MTV Latino, and MTV Brazil
	First Brazilian rap compilation released, *Hip Hop cultura de rua* (Hip hop street culture)
	US rappers Kool Moe Dee, Whodini, Kurtis Blow, and Run-DMC perform in São Paulo
1989	Spike Lee's *Do the Right Thing* is released, contributing to the international popularity of Long Island–based rap group Public Enemy
1991	Jean-Bertrand Aristide wins the Haitian general election and promptly faces a coup. The popular leader would twice more serve as president (1994–1996 and 2001–2004)
	Following the collapse of the Soviet Union, Fidel Castro announces the beginning of Cuba's "Special Period"
	Public Enemy performs in São Paulo, launching the career of Racionais MC's

Selective Timeline 181

1993	Brazil holds its first Mostra Nacional de Hip Hop (National Hip Hop Showcase) in São Paulo at the São Bento metro station
	GOG founds Só Balanço in Brasília, the first independent rap label in Brazil
1996	Second annual Cuban hip hop festival is held in Alamar, East Havana, receiving attention in *Vibe* magazine
Late 1990s	Reggaeton develops in Puerto Rico and circulates widely in the Caribbean
1997	Racionais MC's releases album *Sobrevivendo no inferno*. The music video of "Diário de um detento" (Diary of an inmate) becomes the first rap song to win the Audience Choice award of Video Music Brazil (VMB), run by MTV
	Black August Collective formed in New York City, involving US-based rappers Black Star, Common, the Roots, and dead prez; begins collaborating with Cuban hip hop artists
	In collaboration with Cuban son musicians, Ry Cooder releases the Grammy-winning album *Buena Vista Social Club*, followed by a Wim Wenders documentary (1999)
	Afrika Bambaataa travels to Brazil
1998	Tony Touch, dead prez, and Mos Def perform in Alamar, East Havana at the international Cuban hip hop festival
1999	Los Orishas releases *A lo cubano* in France on the label EMI and a year later in the US (Universal Latino); the album would go gold in France and Switzerland and become Spain's first platinum hip hop album
	The City of São Paulo sponsors Brazil's first hip hop cultural center, the Casa do Hip Hop in Diadema
	São Paulo's homicide rate peaks at 52.5 per 100,000
2002	Port-au-Prince rap group Barikad Crew forms, while the first designated hip hop studio opens in Haiti
	The Cuban Rap Agency is founded under the auspices of the Cuban Institute of Music
	Brazilian film *O Invasor* (directed by Beto Brant) is released, featuring a soundtrack and cameo by rapper Sabotage

	A Brazil chapter of Afrika Bambaataa's Zulu Nation is formed as an NGO
2003	Luís Inácio Lula da Silva begins as president of Brazil (remaining until 2010); Lula would consistently provide financial support for the arts, including hip hop
	La FabriK (Obsesión and Doble Filo) and other Cuban rappers perform in Harlem alongside the Roots, Common, and Harry Belafonte
	São Paulo rapper Sabotage is murdered
	First Haitian hip hop festival, Rap'Rocher Haiti, is held
2004	International Cuban hip hop festival suspended indefinitely
	Puerto Rican reggaeton singer Daddy Yankee releases the international hit "Gasolina"
2005	Barikad Crew rises to prominence in Haiti, winning third place at the popular Christmas songs contest (Konkou Chante Nwel) put on by the Telemax channel
2006	Fidel Castro transfers power to his brother Raúl Castro
2007	Los Aldeanos lead the most outspoken Cuban rappers in a two-disc album, *La comisión depuradora*
2009	USAID sends a Serbian operative to Havana attempting to infiltrate Cuban hip hop
2010	A catastrophic earthquake strikes in Haiti
2011–2012	Following significant reduction in poverty under President Lula's "bolsa família" (family grant) program, the genre of ostentação (ostentation) emerges in São Paulo
	Los Aldeanos and other prominent Cuban rappers emigrate to the United States
Late 2010s	Upstart Haitian rap group Asap Fresh releases Haitian remix of Migos's popular trap song "Bad and Bougee" (2016)
	Luis Fonsi and Daddy Yankee release "Despacito" (2017), which would become the most-streamed video in YouTube history
	Latin urban or urbano music becomes one of the most popular genres globally, including in the United States

Permissions

THE LYRIC quotations in *Break and Flow* are exclusively for the purposes of criticism and scholarship. Most excerpts are de minimis uses covered under fair-use doctrine as outlined in Title 17 of the United States Code (section 107) of the Copyright Act of 1976. When sustaining the book's argument required the use of longer lyric excerpts, every effort was made to obtain permission from copyright holders. These permissions follow. In a limited number of cases, no administrators of copyright were found. One permission request was unfortunately denied and all direct quotes of the song were removed. Any copyright holder who believes there is an omission or incorrect attribution may contact the author, care of University of Virginia Press.

Al2 El Aldeano, "Vereda tropical," from *Nos achicharraron*. 26Musas/Real70, 2010. © Aldo Rodríguez, La Aldea Production; used by permission.

Al2 El Aldeano and Silvito, "El Libre" and "Manual para hacer una canción," from *Los Kbayros,* La Aldea Production, 2009. © Aldo Rodríguez, La Aldea Production; used by permission.

Alexey ..el tipo este.. (Obsesión), "Como fue," from *Contar el rap: Antología de rap y hip-hop cubanos*, Malcoms Junco Duffay, 2017. © Alexey Rodríguez Mola; used by permission.

BIC, "Kokorat," single, Tizon Dife Recordz, 2018. Used by permission.

Criolo, "Duas de cinco," *Convoque seu buda*, Oloko Records, 2014. © Altafonte; nonexclusive world rights secured.

D-Fi Powèt Revòlte, "Castro sou map la," *R.O.D Rhod over D-Fi,* Evazyon Mizik, 2019. © Rhod D'Jyvens Télémaque; used by permission.

D-Fi Powèt Revòlte, "Reflè m," *Rev ak plim Mixtape,* Powèt Revòlte & Dream Recordz, 2016. © Rhod D'Jyvens Télémaque; used by permission.

Bia Doxum featuring Ni Brisant, "Palavra de luta," from *Máquina que gira*, Periferia Invisível, 2015. © Beatriz Oliveira; used by permission.

GOG, "ISO 9000 do gueto," from *Genival Oliveira Gonçalves, Só Balanço*, 2015. © Genival Oliveira Gonçalves; used by permission.

GOG, "Mais uma história," from *CPI da favela*, Zambia, 2000. © Genival Oliveira Gonçalves; used by permission.

Los Aldeanos featuring Papá Humbertico and El Discípulo, "El rap es guerra," from *El Atropello*, Real 70, 2009. © Humberto Joel Cabrera Santana; used by permission.

Master Dji, "Tan pou tan," from *Politik pa m'*, Bwa Patat Records, 1990. © Kreyol Music; used by permission.

Issa Paz and Sara Donato. "Agradecimentos," from *Rap Plus Size*, 2016. © Jupitter Pimentel Zamboni; used by permission.

Princess Eud, "Eudomination" from *Eudomination*, Teamlimyewouj, 2017. © Eunide Edouarin and TuneCore; used by permission.

Sharylaine, "Livre no mundo," single, Leopapel/Cogumarola Produções, 2012. © Ildslaine Mônica da Silva; used by permission.

Thaíde & DJ Hum, "Sr. Tempo Bom," from *Preste Atenção*, Brava Gente/Dueto Edições, 1996. © Dueto Edições; used by permission.

Xis, MC White, Telmary Díaz, Papo Record, and 100% Original, "Fortificando a desobediência," from *Fortificando a desobediência*, Warner Music Brasil, 2001. © 4P Discos; used by permission.

Yomil y el Dany, "Evolutions," from *Sobredosis*, Jungl Yomil y el Dany, 2016. © Roberto Hidalgo; used by permission.

Notes

Introduction

1. Unless otherwise indicated, all translations are mine. English translations of lyrics are literal and do not generally attempt to reproduce the elaborate rhyme schemes and rhythmic complexity of the verses in the original language. I take full responsibility for any errors in translation or transcription. When transcribing rap verses, I use visual line breaks to emphasize metric divisions (what rappers generally call bars). I have chosen to use as sparse punctuation as possible, except when necessary to clarify the meaning of a verse. The reader is encouraged to consult the YouTube playlist I have curated at http://tinyurl.com/breakandflow, which contains all referenced songs that are available for streaming.

2. See, for example, Marc Lacey, "Cuba's Rap Vanguard Reaches beyond the Party Line," *New York Times,* December 15, 2006, sec. Americas, https://www.nytimes.com/2006/12/15/world/americas/15cuba.html.

3. Nono, "Rendición de cuenta."

4. Culler, *Theory of the Lyric,* 6.

5. Chang, *Can't Stop Won't Stop,* 10–13.

6. Chang, "It's a Hip-Hop World," 62.

7. Contreras, "Meteoric Rise."

8. Studies of other contexts in Latin America will be essential to further our understanding of hip hop in the Americas. Several Latinx and Caribbean rappers have enjoyed wide commercial success in the United States (for example, Cypress Hill, Pitbull, Immortal Technique, Wyclef Jean), and most large Latin American and Caribbean cities host vibrant hip hop scenes.

9. Vazquez, *Listening in Detail,* 4.

10. My participation has included twice presenting at the Cuban Rap Agency's annual International Hip Hop Symposium, an event bringing together academic discussions, conversations, and concerts.

11. Cuban rap's popularity abroad was generated in large part by the 1999 release in France and Spain of Los Orishas's album *A lo cubano*. Around that time,

several foreign documentary-makers, journalists, and anthropologists developed an interest in Cuban hip hop, particularly in Havana.

12. Facing increasing scarcity and limited access to health care during the COVID-19 pandemic, as well as continued economic sanctions from the United States, Cubans took to the streets in July 2021 for the largest protests seen in decades. Sparked in part by a hunger strike earlier that year led by the Movimiento San Isidro, the protests included several hip hop artists. In February of that year, rappers and reggaeton artists Yotuel Romero, Beatriz Luengo, Randy Malcolm, Alexander Delgado, Descemer Bueno, Eliexer Márquez Duany, Maykel Castillo Pérez, and Yadam González had collaborated to release the song "Patria o vida" (Homeland or life). Parodying José Martí's slogan "patria o muerte" (homeland or death), the song lent the July protests one of their most potent slogans. Castillo, who lives in the San Isidro neighborhood of Havana, was incarcerated.

13. Tonani do Patrocínio, *Escritos à margem*.

14. Averill, *Day for the Hunter*, 184–200.

15. Trouillot, *Silencing the Past*.

16. Pires, "Estruturas intocadas," 1058.

17. In March 1969, Brazilian dictator Artur da Costa e Silva's Decreto-lei 510 provided for the criminalization of any public debate surrounding racism, under the guise that it incited "ao ódio ou à discriminação racial" (hate or racial discrimination).

18. Moore, *Nationalizing Blackness*, 25.

19. Averill, *Day for the Hunter*, 15, 39.

20. Vurkaç, "Cross-Cultural Grammar," 43.

21. Scott, *Common Wind*; Scott and Hébrard, *Freedom Papers*; Glissant, *Le discours antillais*; Baucom, *Specters of the Atlantic*.

22. Qtd. in Scott, *Common Wind*, 10.

23. Scott and Hébrard, *Freedom Papers*, 4–5.

24. MV Bill, "Traficando informação"; Pardue, *Ideologies of Marginality*, 38.

25. Several Brazilian rappers and DJs traveled to the annual Havana hip hop festivals in the early 2000s, including São Paulo–based Xis. A delegation of Cuban rappers performed in Brazil during the same decade. When financially feasible, Brazilian and Cuban rappers continued to travel between the two countries sporadically throughout the 2010s to participate in events related to community activism. Cuban rapper Yamay "La Fina" Mejías, in particular, has promoted such dialogues, for example with Brazilian rapper Luana Hansen, who attended the Artwoman International Festival of Women Artists in Havana in 2014, organized by Mejías. The research-activism of Tanya Saunders has also facilitated the circulation of some of these artists, including Mejías herself. I know of only one Haitian rapper, Blaze One, who performed in Brazil (alongside São Paulo–based BNegão in 2017). After the 2010 earthquake, Cuban rapper Escuadrón Patriota composed a song "Por Haití" (For Haiti), affectionately referring to Haiti as Cuba's *hermana* (sister). Cuban producer Pablo Herrera collaborated with Haitian rapper Fila

Mystere. At the time of writing, Haitian rapper D-Fi planned to travel to Havana to participate in a hip hop festival.

26. "Freestyle" can also be rendered as "improvisation" (*improvisación, improvização,* or *enpwovizasyon*), but such an approximation loses the notion of a free style (free of what?) that ties improvisation to the break ("free" time).

27. Alim, "Hip Hop Nation Language"; Ibrahim, "Arab Spring," 106.

28. Blay'Z, "We Run It."

29. Silvio Rodríguez, performance of "Playa Girón," YouTube video, https://www.youtube.com/watch?v=gmOK3NmcDOE.

30. Rose, *Black Noise,* 64.

31. See, for example, Teperman, *Se liga no som,* 13.

32. Bradley, *Book of Rhymes,* 7.

33. Wood, "Understanding Rap," 140.

34. Stewart, "Letter on Sound," 33–34.

35. Zumthor, *Oral Poetry,* 142; Brown, "Relations between Music and Literature," 44; Hollander, "Music and Poetry," 533; Winn, *Unsuspected Eloquence,* 3; Ortiz, *La africanía de la música folklórica de Cuba,* 243; Hale, *Griots and Griottes,* 128. Several scholars have identified African griots as antecedents to rappers. See, for example, Alim, Ibrahim, and Pennycook, *Global Linguistic Flows,* 1; Neff, "Senegalese Hip-Hop," 271; Pardue, *Ideologies of Marginality,* 35; Smitherman, "'Chain Remain the Same,'" 4; Potter, *Spectacular Vernaculars,* 116. In Brazil, the term *griô* (griot) entered into wide usage in the late 1990s, leading to the 2011 Lei Griô or Griot Law (PL 1786/2011), which formally recognized and protected "traditional cultures of oral transmission" as part of Brazilian cultural patrimony.

36. Sharylaine, "Livre no mundo."

37. Garabís, *Nación y ritmo,* 24.

38. Rama, *La ciudad letrada.*

39. Ochoa Gautier, *Aurality,* 7. All emphasis is original unless otherwise indicated.

40. McEnaney, *Acoustic Properties,* 7.

41. Hamilton, *Phonographic Memories.*

42. Librandi, *Writing by Ear.*

43. Gates, *Signifying Monkey,* 131.

44. Treece, *Brazilian Jive,* 190.

45. Edwards, *Epistrophies,* 16.

46. Rose, *Black Noise,* 21.

47. Acosta, *Otra visión de la música popular cubana,* 11.

48. Chang, *Can't Stop Won't Stop,* 229; Perry, *Prophets of the Hood,* 18–21.

49. Rivera, *New York Ricans;* Flores, *From Bomba to Hip-Hop;* Patterson, "Ecumenical America"; Hebdige, *Cut 'n' Mix.*

50. Patterson, "Ecumenical America," 107; Krims, *Rap Music,* 152; George, *Hip Hop America,* 7.

51. Patterson, "Ecumenical America," 108; Gilroy, *Black Atlantic*.

52. See Shilliam, *Black Pacific*.

53. Gilroy, *Black Atlantic*; Casimir, *La cultura oprimida*; Nascimento, *O quilombismo*; Mintz, *Caribbean Transformations*; Williams, *Capitalism and Slavery*; Glissant, *Caribbean Discourse*; Baucom, *Specters of the Atlantic*; Fischer, *Modernity Disavowed*; Palmié, *Wizards and Scientists*.

54. Hall, "Cultural Identity and Diaspora," 228.

55. Edwards, *Practice of Diaspora*, 13.

56. Edwards, 110.

57. Stam and Shohat, *Race in Translation*.

58. Césaire, *Notebook*, 15.

59. Qtd. in Fischer, *Modernity Disavowed*, 238.

60. Averill, *Day for the Hunter*, 55.

61. See, for example, Ortiz, *Contrapunteo cubano*; Freyre, *Casa-grande e senzala*.

62. See Ortiz, *Contrapunteo cubano*.

63. Salles, *Poesia revoltada*, 148.

64. Davis, *Planet of Slums*, 1–37.

65. Pereira, "Brazil: Fiscal Policy," 555.

66. de la Fuente, *Nation for All*, 266, 313–14; Hamberg, "'Slums' of Havana," 86; Perna, *Timba*, 2; Hernandez-Reguant, "Havana's Timba," 350; Farber, *Cuba since the Revolution*, 176–78.

67. United Nations Human Settlements Programme, "Population Living in Slums," The World Bank, 2018, https://data.worldbank.org/indicator/EN.POP.SLUM.UR.ZS?locations=HT.

68. Osumare, *Africanist Aesthetic in Global Hip-Hop*, 63.

69. Brown, "Black Liverpool," 318; Rivera-Rideau, Jones, and Paschel, "Introduction: Theorizing Afrolatinidades," 14.

70. Campt, "Crowded Space of Diaspora," 101.

71. Brown, "Black Liverpool," 317.

72. Trouillot, *Silencing the Past*, 71.

73. Terkourafi, *Languages of Global Hip Hop*, 168; Rose, *Black Noise*, 19.

74. Gilroy, *Black Atlantic*, 4.

75. Lerner and West, *Jews and Blacks*, 70–73.

76. Rivera-Rideau, Jones, and Paschel, "Introduction: Theorizing Afrolatinidades," 15.

77. Hooker, *Theorizing Race in the Americas*, 12.

78. Hughes, *Collected Works*, 42–43; see Guridy, *Forging Diaspora*, 124–26; Kutzinski, "Fearful Asymmetries," 114.

79. Hooker, *Theorizing Race in the Americas*, 13.

80. Kaique Dalapola, "Álbum de Racionais MCs entra nas leituras obrigatórias da Unicamp," *R7*, May 23, 2018, https://noticias.r7.com/sao-paulo/album-de-racionais-mcs-entra-nas-leituras-obrigatorias-da-unicamp-23052018.

The texts written by Mano Brown, Edi Rock, KL Jay, and Ice Blue appear alongside sonnets by Portuguese poet Luís de Camões.

81. Amaral, *O que o rap diz.*

82. For example, rapper and anthropologist Jean Gardy Seide "Kameleyon," along with two other colleagues, wrote a history of Haitian hip hop for his master's thesis. Many US rappers, including Chuck D (*Fight the Power*) and Gucci Mane (*The Autobiography of Gucci Mane*), have published autobiographies.

83. See Hebdige, *Subculture,* 93. Virgílio López Lemus notes that when academic studies begin to emerge about a cultural practice, this typically means the practice is in decline. That said, given the way popular culture can now be disseminated and discussed instantaneously through online streaming services and social media, the gap between a phenomenon and its analysis has been significantly reduced. See López Lemus, *La décima constante,* 65.

84. See Forman, "Introduction," 3.

85. Alim, *Roc the Mic Right,* 12.

86. On hip hop in the United States, see Rose, *Black Noise;* Krims, *Rap Music;* Perry, *Prophets of the Hood;* Chang, *Can't Stop Won't Stop;* Alim, *Roc the Mic Right;* and Kajikawa, *Sounding Race in Rap Songs.* On hip hop in Latin America, see Castillo-Garsow and Nichols, *La Verdad;* Dennis, *Afro-Colombian Hip-Hop;* Fernandes, *Cuba Represent!;* Baker, *Buena Vista in the Club;* Saunders, *Cuban Underground Hip Hop;* Perry, *Negro Soy Yo;* Zamora Montes, *Rapear una Cuba utópica;* Hernández Baguer and Junco Duffay, *Contar el rap;* Teperman, *Se liga no som;* Amaral, *O que o rap diz;* Feltran, "Sobre anjos e irmãos"; Treece, *Brazilian Jive;* Garcia, "Ouvindo Racionais MC's." Geoffrey Baker's *Buena Vista in the Club* (2011) remains the most detailed ethnography of Cuban rap through the 2000s. Alejandro Zamora's collection of interviews with Cuban hip hop artists, *Rapear una Cuba utópica* (2017), and Grizel Hernández Baguer and Malcoms Junco Duffay's compilation of essays and testimonials, *Contar el rap* (2017), are also invaluable resources—and groundbreaking insofar as they are written and published by Cubans rather than foreign researchers. Derek Pardue's *Ideologies of Marginality* (2008) provides a detailed ethnography of rap and urban space in São Paulo, while bossa nova specialist and literary scholar Walter Garcia's essays on the poetics of Racionais MC's bring an often neglected literary angle to the study of Brazilian rap. Haitian rap kreyòl, in addition to receiving mention in ethnomusicological monographs, has been the subject of theses and articles by Port-au-Prince-based anthropologists. See Averill, *Day for the Hunter;* McAlister, *Rara!;* Manuel and Largey, *Caribbean Currents;* Seide, Badiau, and Alexis, "Les causes de l'implantation"; Larose, "Représentation de la femme projetée par les rappeurs."

87. Eshun, *More Brilliant than the Sun,* 183.

88. Nono, "Rendición de cuenta."

89. Hegel, *Phenomenology of Spirit,* §32.

90. Dukes, "Flor de aço."

91. Harney and Moten, *Undercommons*, 49.
92. Simas and Rufino, *Fogo no mato*, 39.
93. Glissant, *Caribbean Discourse*, 163.
94. Harney and Moten, *Undercommons*, 96.
95. Levin Becker, *What's Good*, 264.
96. Nascimento, *O quilombismo*, 75.
97. Morgan, *Real Hiphop*, 48.
98. Bradley, *Book of Rhymes*, 7.
99. Toop, *Rap Attack 2*, 142.
100. Chang, *Can't Stop Won't Stop*, 67–70.
101. Katz, *Groove Music*, 16.
102. Sublette, *Cuba and Its Music*, 168–70; Quintero Rivera, *Salsa, sabor y control!*, 67; Scherzinger, "Mathematics of African Dance Rhythms."
103. Osumare, *Africanist Aesthetic in Global Hip-Hop*, 47.
104. Gaunt, "Translating Double-Dutch," 252–53.
105. Bradley, *Book of Rhymes*, 30.
106. Alim, *Roc the Mic Right*, 96.
107. Rose, *Black Noise*, 88–89.
108. Criolo, "Duas de cinco."
109. Levin Becker, *What's Good*, 1.
110. Levin Becker, 3.
111. Hall, "Cultural Identity and Diaspora," 226.
112. GOG, "Brasília periferia"; Racionais MC's, "Periferia é periferia."
113. See Adorno, "On Lyric Poetry and Society."
114. Use the direct link (http://tinyurl.com/breakandflow) or navigate to YouTube and search "Charlie Hankin Break and Flow." Not on the YouTube playlist but available on SoundCloud: Bárbaro "El Urbano" Vargas, "Se respira" (https://soundcloud.com/cumano/se-respira-b-rbaro-el-urbano); Sharylaine, "Rei Zumbi," (https://soundcloud.com/sharylaine/rei-zumbi-sharylaine); and Blay'Z, *Jis Pou Trip* mixtape (https://soundcloud.com/blayzmatiq/sets/blayz-jis-pou-trip-mixtape).

1. Yearning

1. García, "A economia cubana," 29–31.
2. de la Fuente, *Nation for All*, 315–16.
3. Baker, "¡Hip Hop, Revolución!"
4. The earliest instance of "es lo que hay" in a Cuban rap recording is probably the 1996 Amenaza song "Somos lo máximo," which takes its bass line and chorus from the salsa tune "Somos lo que hay" (We're what there is) by El Médico de la Salsa. See Herrera Veitía, "Producir rap afrocubano," 102.
5. Yúdice, *Expediency of Culture*.
6. Gell, *Anthropology of Time*, 121.
7. Glissant, *Caribbean Discourse*, 81, 4.

8. Hermanos de Causa, "Gracias Hip Hop."
9. Jakobson, "Closing Statement," 356.
10. Thompson, *Shine*, 21.
11. Edwards, *Epistrophies*, 190.
12. Yoshinaga, *Nelson Triunfo*, 209; Angeli and Ramos, *Triunfo*.
13. Peixoto and Sebadelhe, *1976 Movimento Black Rio*, 17.
14. Chang, "It's a Hip-Hop World," 62.
15. West, *Prophetic Fragments*, 186.
16. Gilroy, *Black Atlantic*, 37.
17. Chuck D, *Fight the Power*, 272; Caramante, "Os quatro pretos."
18. Chang, *Can't Stop Won't Stop*, 251.
19. Chang, 319.
20. Morgan and Bennett, "Hip-Hop."
21. GOG, "Sonhos latinos."
22. Cave, "Thomas More and the New World."
23. Frye, "Varieties of Literary Utopias," 326.
24. Cover, "Nomos and Narrative," 39.
25. Campt, *Listening to Images*, 45.
26. Campt, 11.
27. Campt, 17.
28. Campt, 17.
29. James, *The Future in the Present*; Crawley, *Blackpentecostal Breath*, 2.
30. Campt, *Listening to Images*, 17.
31. Campt, 17.
32. Rose, *Black Noise*, 21.
33. Homer, *The Odyssey* I.13, ed. and trans. Rodney Merrill (Ann Arbor: University of Michigan Press, 2002), 85.
34. hooks, *Yearning*, 27.
35. Okiji, *Jazz as Critique*, 55.
36. Makalani, "Politically Unimaginable," 21.
37. Pignarre and Stengers, *Capitalist Sorcery*, 49.
38. Pignarre and Stengers, 48.
39. Harvey, *Brief History of Neoliberalism*, 2.
40. Harvey, 19.
41. Martin, *Financialization of Daily Life*.
42. Martin, 6.
43. Martin, 46.
44. Martin, 52.
45. Rotman, *Signifying Nothing*, 93–96.
46. There is no precise translation of the English word "yearning" into Spanish, Portuguese, or Kreyòl. The Spanish *anhelo* and the Portuguese *anseio* come closest to capturing the longing, craving, and aspirational quality of yearning. The *Freeman Haitian-English Dictionary* renders yearning as simply *aspirasyon* (aspiration).

None of these words, however, commonly surfaces in rap lyrics. Unlike other tropes of hip hop poetics addressed in *Break and Flow* that might be considered grounded theory (that is, elaborated directly out of rap lyrics, slogans, and conversations with artists), yearning is an external analytic category drawn from Black feminist theory, which I use to describe the way rap produces material effects.

47. Glissant, *Caribbean Discourse*, 81.
48. Fischer, *Modernity Disavowed*, 4.
49. Glissant, *Caribbean Discourse*, 81; Trouillot, *Silencing the Past*.
50. Hartman, "Venus in Two Acts," 11; Hartman, *Wayward Lives, Beautiful Experiments*, 228.
51. Potter, *Spectacular Vernaculars*, 3.
52. Temple, "Emergence of Sankofa Practice," 128.
53. Buck-Morss, *Dreamworld and Catastrophe*, 60.
54. Hartog, *Regimes of Historicity*, 17–18.
55. Vaz, "Centralidades Periféricas." World Bank data from 2018 found Brazil to be the most unequal country in Latin America and in the top ten worldwide.
56. García Canclini, *Consumidores y ciudadanos*; Gago, *La razón neoliberal*; Thompson, *Shine*, 30.
57. Mane and Martinez-Belkin, *Autobiography of Gucci Mane*, 257.
58. Princess Eud, "Eudomination."
59. Hartman, "Venus in Two Acts," 9.
60. D-Fi Powèt Revòlte, "Reflè m."
61. Dayan, *Haiti, History, and the Gods*, 58–63. Ezili descends in many forms, including as the goddess of love Ezili Frida and the darker-skinned and "fiercely maternal" Ezili Dantò. See Ramsey, *Spirits and the Law*, 8.
62. Benjamin, *Illuminations*, 261.
63. Löwy, *Fire Alarm*, 32–33.
64. Agamben, *Time that Remains*, 67–68.
65. Agamben, *End of the Poem*.
66. Visão de Rua, "A noiva do Thock."
67. Howe, *My Emily Dickinson*, 98.
68. Brisa Flow, "As de cem."
69. Master Dji, "Tan pou tan."
70. Averill, *Day for the Hunter*, 177.
71. Averill, 162; Hallward, *Damming the Flood*, 28–29.
72. King, Martin Luther, Jr. qtd. in Amy Goodman, "Exclusive: Newly Discovered 1964 MLK Speech on Civil Rights, Segregation and Apartheid South Africa," *Democracy Now!* Accessed February 24, 2019. http://www.democracynow.org/2015/1/19/exclusive_newly_discovered_1964_mlk_speech.
73. Master Dji, "Tan pou tan."
74. Delany, "About 5,750 Words," 11.
75. Delany, 11.
76. See, for example, Nesbitt, "Turning the Tide," 18.

77. Muñoz, *Cruising Utopia,* 4.
78. Muñoz, 27–28.
79. Campt, *Listening to Images,* 17.
80. Hartman, "Venus in Two Acts," 14.
81. Hartman, 14.
82. Rockfam, "Jodi pa demen."
83. See Hartog, *Regimes of Historicity,* 13.
84. Ferreira da Silva, "Toward a Black Feminist Poethics," 90.
85. Fantom and Solis, "Si Desalin te la."
86. Dubois, *Haiti,* 54–87. Unlike revolutionary leaders such as Toussaint Louverture and Jean-Jacques Dessalines, Alexandre Pétion was born free to an upper-middle-class professional mulatto family. Pétion organized the 1806 assassination plot against Dessalines. Inaugurated as Haiti's first president in 1807, Pétion set up a sharecropping system that met widespread approval, but ultimately created a model for oligarchical, exclusivist, and autocratic rule that would be followed by subsequent leaders. Today, Pétion's name is immortalized in the most affluent neighborhood of Port-au-Prince, Pétion-ville.
87. The *New York Times* published a powerful exposé on this subject on May 23, 2022, entitled "The Ransom." https://www.nytimes.com/live/2022/05/23/world/haiti-france-ransom.
88. Glissant, *Caribbean Discourse,* 144.
89. Tsing, *Mushroom,* 79.
90. Dubois, *Haiti,* 50.
91. Trouillot, *Haiti, State against Nation,* 73.
92. Dubois, *Haiti,* 45–47.
93. In conversation with author, June 14, 2019.
94. Whitfield, *Cuban Currency,* 100.
95. Gutiérrez, *El rey de la Habana,* 25.
96. Gutiérrez, 218.
97. Hartog, *Regimes of Historicity,* 3.
98. In conversation with author, June 14, 2019.
99. Malcoms "Justicia," "La ciudad no duerme"; "a bad smell as a result of garbage"; "your house collapses."
100. Malcoms "Justicia."
101. See, for example, Roig de Leuchsenring, "Bailando junto al abismo," 123.
102. Whitfield, *Cuban Currency,* 137.
103. The title is almost certainly a play on New York City's unofficial slogan "the city that never sleeps," presenting Havana as a perversion of New York: a somnambulant, sleepless city.
104. Malcoms "Justicia," "La ciudad no duerme."
105. Article 54 of the Cuban Penal Code criminalizes unsanctioned public protest.
106. McEnaney, *Acoustic Properties,* 134–35.

107. Quiroga, *Cuban Palimpsests,* 164.
108. Quiroga, 166–69; Hernandez-Reguant, "Havana's Timba," 254.
109. Fairley, "Ay Díos, Ampárame," 85–86.
110. Perna, *Timba,* 2; Hernandez-Reguant, "Havana's Timba," 250.
111. Hernandez-Reguant, "Havana's Timba," 251.
112. Hernandez-Reguant, 271.
113. NG La Banda, "Santa palabra."
114. Fernández Olmos and Paravisini-Gebert, *Creole Religions of the Caribbean,* 61–65; Acosta, *Otra visión de la música popular cubana,* 147. Not unlike timba musicians, as Todd Ramón Ochoa notes, Regla de Ocha or Santería practitioners adjusted quickly to the growing tourist trade during the 1990s. See Ochoa, *Society of the Dead,* 6.
115. Yúdice, *Expediency of Culture,* 9.
116. Fairley, "Ay Díos, Ampárame," 92–93.
117. Perna, *Timba,* 154–55.
118. Fairley, "Ay Díos, Ampárame," 93.
119. Perry, *Negro Soy Yo.*
120. Marshall, "From Música Negra," 36.
121. Marshall, 49.
122. Fairley, "How to Make Love with Your Clothes On," 286; Manuel and Largey, *Caribbean Currents,* 114–15.
123. Fairley, "How to Make Love with Your Clothes On," 288.
124. My use of the word *trap* refers to the subgenre of rap music that emerged in the southern United States. "Trap" can also refer to a popular and extremely lucrative form of electronic dance music, or EDM. See Josh Eells, "Night Club Royale," *New Yorker,* September 30, 2013, https://www.newyorker.com/magazine/2013/09/30/night-club-royale.
125. McCarthy, "Notes on Trap."
126. Cardi B, "Bodak Yellow."
127. Burton, *Posthuman Rap,* 80–85. Jeff Chang notes that the tempo of the breakbeat began to slow down and the bass to be "pumped up" as early as the 1980s. See Chang, *Can't Stop Won't Stop,* 241–42.
128. McCarthy, "Notes on Trap."
129. Burton, *Posthuman Rap,* 97.
130. Burton, 72.
131. Burton, 76. Mixing the vocals to sound intentionally out of tune in rap dates at least to Public Enemy in the late 1980s. See Walser, "Clamor and Community," 296.
132. Weheliye, "'Feenin': Posthuman Voices," 26–27. See Eshun, *More Brilliant than the Sun;* Wynter, "Unsettling the Coloniality of Being/Power/Truth/Freedom."
133. Weheliye, "'Feenin': Posthuman Voices," 22.
134. Weheliye, 38.

135. Fisher, *Ghosts of My Life,* 175.
136. In the nineteenth century, the word "dope" was associated with smoking semiliquid forms of opium.
137. Yomil y el Dany, "Evolutions."
138. Mario J. Pentón, "Altos precios para concierto de Yomil y el Dany en Miami causan indignación en las redes sociales," *Miami Herald,* August 4, 2017, https://www.elnuevoherald.com/noticias/sur-de-la-florida/article165546142.html.
139. Yomil y el Dany, "Sacrifice."
140. Yomil y el Dany, "Ni santas ni finas."
141. Yomil y el Dany, "Evolutions."
142. Eshun, *More Brilliant than the Sun,* 54.
143. Reed, *Soundworks,* 87.
144. Yomil y el Dany, "Evolutions."
145. Alexandre Kojève, who introduced Hegel to French readers, conceives of the final chapter of Hegel's *Phenomenology* as marking the triumph of the liberal state and the end of history. See Kojève, *Introduction to the Reading of Hegel.* Francis Fukuyama famously applied similar logic to the fall of the Berlin Wall in 1989, referring to liberal democracy as "the final form of human government" and hence, "the end of History." See Fukuyama, "The End of History?," 4. See also Hartog, *Regimes of Historicity,* 15.
146. Hartog, *Regimes of Historicity,* 17–18.
147. McCarthy, "Notes on Trap."
148. Asap Fresh's achievement of one million YouTube views in G-Shytt's first single is remarkable, given that only around twelve million people globally speak Haitian Kreyòl.
149. Daniel, "Balèn bouji."
150. Pignarre and Stengers, *Capitalist Sorcery.*
151. Asap Fresh, "Balèn bouji."
152. *Bilolo ayibobo* is a ritual cry in Vodou that is used roughly in the sense of "alleluia" or "amen" (*Freeman Haitian-English Dictionary*).
153. *Lougawou* are shape-shifting creatures common in Caribbean mythology; in Vodou they generally take the form of a werewolf and allegedly attack people. See Murrell, *Afro-Caribbean Religions,* 81.
154. For some of the early-twentieth-century mythology surrounding zombies in Haiti, see Hurston, *Tell My Horse,* 179–98; Seabrook, *Magic Island.*
155. Averill, *Day for the Hunter,* 117.
156. Gaspar, "G-Shytt, le nouveau feu du BPC."
157. Sneed, "Bandidos de Cristo," 221–22. The syncopated *tamborzão* breakbeat of Brazilian *funk* emphasizes offbeats, similar to the hip hop breakbeat.
158. Sneed, "Bandidos de Cristo," 222.
159. Sneed, 228–29.
160. Erivan "Produtos do Morro" Barbosa Sales and Lenny Fernandes, personal interview, Fortaleza, Brazil, March 30, 2015.

161. The longevity of "Rap da felicidade" is also due in part to its re-release on the 2007 *funk* compilation album *Elite Squad.*
162. Cidinho e Doca, "Rap da felicidade."
163. Lefebvre, "Right to the City."
164. "Poverty Headcount Ratio at $6.85 a Day (2017 PPP) (% of Population)—Brazil," World Bank Poverty and Inequality Platform, https://data.worldbank.org/indicator/SI.POV.UMIC?locations=BR; "Intentional Homicides (per 100,000 People)—Brazil," UN Office on Drugs and Crime's International Homicide Statistics database, World Bank, https://data.worldbank.org/indicator/VC.IHR.PSRC.P5?locations=BR. In Brazil, the countrywide homicide rate reached 25.7 per 100,000 people in 2003 and, after declining through 2010, rose to over 30 in 2017. In the 1990s, São Paulo's homicide rate consistently doubled the countrywide rate.
165. Ferreira de Souza et al., "Os efeitos do Programa Bolsa Família." Reduction in Brazil's poverty rate was facilitated by the *bolsa família* (family grant) program of the Worker's Party (PT).
166. Vaz, "Centralidades Periféricas."
167. Racionais MC's, "Capítulo 4, Versículo 3."
168. Kenneth Rapoza, "Brazil Is Murder Capital of the World," *Forbes,* January 29, 2016, https://www.forbes.com/sites/kenrapoza/2016/01/29/months-before-rio-olympics-murder-rate-rises-in-brazil/.
169. Hankin, "Rap e conscientização," 139. Padêro and other featured artists performed as part of the Petrúcio Maia Music Festival at the Praia de Iracema, which I had the opportunity to attend in Fortaleza, July 25–31, 2015.
170. Transcription by author, July 31, 2015.
171. Francisco Velto "Padêro MC" Barbosa Lima, personal interview, Fortaleza, Brazil, November 1, 2015.
172. The cover story of the June 27, 2018, edition of *Veja São Paulo* captured the neoliberal version of superação: "Empreendedores do Grajaú: A 35 quilômetros ao sul da Avenida Paulista, uma geração de músicos, cineastas e artistas escanteia dificuldades e se profissionaliza" (Entrepreneurs of Grajaú: 35 kilometers south of Paulista Avenue, a generation of musicians, filmmakers, and artists sweep aside difficulties and professionalize).
173. hooks, *Belonging,* 209.
174. Pereira, "Funk ostentação em São Paulo."
175. Dantas and MC Guimê, "Plaque de 100 (Clipe Oficial)."
176. Tsing, "Inside the Economy of Appearances," 118.
177. Tsing, 119.
178. Dantas and França, "Nois de Nave."
179. Pereira, "Funk ostentação em São Paulo."
180. Pereira.
181. Reed, *Freedom Time,* 177.
182. Steingo, *Kwaito's Promise,* 15.

183. Steingo, 6.
184. MC Boy do Charmes, "Nois de nave."
185. GOG, "Sonhos latinos."
186. Thompson, *Shine*, 33.
187. Thompson, 25.
188. Thompson, 33, 256–57.
189. Matos, "Preta da quebrada."
190. See, for example, Matos, "Ela quer ser minha namorada."
191. Muñoz, *Cruising Utopia*.
192. Deodoro, "O funk ostentação"; "Aquela época refletiu a cultura do consumismo de toda a sociedade, que foi frustrado com a diminuição do dinheiro no bolso das pessoas."
193. Darlington, "How KondZilla Took Funk out of the Favelas and into the Mainstream," *Billboard*, July 18, 2019, http://www.billboard.com/articles/news/magazine-feature/8520345/kondzilla-brazilian-favela-funk-konrad-dantas-interview.
194. See Eyerman, "False Consciousness and Ideology in Marxist Theory."
195. By March 2020, "Bum bum tam tam" had registered 1.4 billion views.
196. In the music video, a background of pharaoh-style coffins evokes ancient Egypt, where end-blown flutes were used in ritual and agricultural ceremonies (although Foiti holds a transverse flute). Egyptian flutes were commonly associated with the god Isis, a motif famously explored in Mozart's opera "The Magic Flute." In the Papua New Guinea highlands, transverse flutes are considered sacred instruments and are used in coming-of-age initiation ceremonies for men, as well as to intimidate women and establish male hegemony. The flute seems to carry a similar function in the video: Fioti uses the flute in modern street scenes as an instrument of ritualistic sexual conquest. In contrast, in the West flutes have traditionally been associated with femininity, in addition to the homoerotic connotation of blowing into a phallic object. Fioti's use of the flute thus creates an ambiguous sexuality, perhaps even a (probably inadvertent) queerness. See Hickmann, "Egyptian 'Uffāṭah Flute," 104; Gee, "Notes on the Egyptian Motifs"; Hays, "Sacred Flutes, Fertility, and Growth"; Halstead and Rolvsjord, "Gendering of Musical Instruments."
197. Djonga, "Junho de 94."
198. See Kellner, *Media Culture*, 189.
199. Brazilian rap songs sampled in "Junho de 94" include Criolo's "Esquiva da esgrima," "Jesus Chorou" by Racionais MC's, Emicida's "Beira de Piscina," and Djonga's own "O mundo é nosso." Identifying samples has become a cultivated skill, reflected by the website Who Sampled: Exploring the DNA of Music, which crowdsources information about the musical intertextuality of genres such as rap.
200. Krims, *Music and Urban Geography*, 111.
201. Djonga, "Junho de 94."
202. Solano and Marques, "Junho de 94."

203. Moten, *In the Break*, 159.
204. Muñoz, *Cruising Utopia*, 27–28.
205. Foucault, "Des espaces autres," 755. For Foucault, heterotopias are ambivalent realizations of utopia: "des sortes de contre-emplacements, sortes d'utopies effectivement réalisées dans lesquelles les emplacements réels, tous les autres emplacements réels que l'on peut trouver à l'intérieur de la culture sont à la fois représentés, contestés et inversés, des sortes de lieux qui sont hors de tous les lieux, bien que pourtant ils soient effectivement localisables" (sorts of counter-sites, of effectively enacted utopias in which real sites—all the other real sites that can be found within the culture—are simultaneously represented, contested, and inverted; the types of places that are outside of all places, even though they may be localizable in reality).
206. Moten, *In the Break*, 215.

2. Raplove

1. Lenzi, *Per il verso giusto*, 19. "Tutte le canzoni sono canzoni d'amore."
2. D-Fi Powèt Revòlte, "Konsidere m beni."
3. Sugar Hill Gang, "Rapper's Delight."
4. The Roots featuring Common, "Act Too (The Love of My Life)."
5. Levin Becker, *What's Good*, 14.
6. Chang, *Can't Stop Won't Stop*, 257.
7. Lapassade and Rousselot, *Le rap, ou, la fureur de dire*, 97.
8. Hernández Baguer and Cué, "Hora de abrir los ojos," 315.
9. Pate, *In the Heart*, 5.
10. Gates, *Signifying Monkey*, xxi.
11. Glissant, *Caribbean Discourse*, 12.
12. Hebdige, *Cut 'n' Mix*, xiii.
13. Douglas, *Frankétienne and Rewriting*, 9–10.
14. Smith and Joshi, *Rhymes in the Flow*, 90.
15. Zalamea Traba, *Filosofía sintética*, 185; Wittrock, "Frankétienne's Spirals"; Kauss, "Le spiralisme de Franketienne"; Douglas, *Frankétienne and Rewriting*.
16. Marcelo "Xis" Santos, personal interview, São Paulo, July 5, 2018.
17. Hernández Baguer and Cué, "Hora de abrir los ojos," 320; "lo que está sucediendo, por lo general en tiempo presente."
18. Xis et al., "Fortificando a desobediência."
19. Manzano, *Autobiografía del esclavo poeta*, 308.
20. See Parry, "Studies in the Epic Technique," 312–24; Lord, *Singer of Tales*, 5–36.
21. Gates, *Signifying Monkey*, 10; Holbraad, *Truth in Motion*, 130–43; Holbraad, "Power of Powder," 203.
22. Adéèkó, "'Writing' and 'Reference' in Ifá," 69–72; Apter, "Recasting Ifá," 43.

23. García-Ruiz and Michel, "El neo-pentecostalismo en América Latina," 59.
24. Welsh, *Roots of Lyric*, 135–44.
25. Xis et al., "Fortificando a desobediência."
26. Lerner, *Hatred of Poetry*, 85.
27. Xis et al., "Fortificando a desobediência."
28. McGrath, "Island as Urban Artifact."
29. Marcelo "Xis" Santos, personal interview, São Paulo, July 5, 2018; Rubén Marín, in conversation with author, Havana, February 10, 2019.
30. Voegelin, *Political Possibility of Sound*, 59.
31. Culler, *Theory of the Lyric*, 226.
32. Sterne, *Audible Past*, 322.
33. Tomlinson, *Singing of the New World*, 87.
34. El B, "Intro"; Sabotage, "Rap é compromisso"; Morgan and Bennett, "Hip-Hop," 177; Morgan, *Real Hiphop*, 20.
35. Sharylaine, "Livre no mundo."
36. Despite a professed rejection of the academy ("não está dentro da Academia de Letras"), this song was written at the request of a friend from a university in Portugal to accompany a monograph on hip hop.
37. Ildslaine "Sharylaine" Mônica da Silva, personal interview, São Paulo, July 23, 2018.
38. Dudley, "Judging 'By the Beat,'" 294.
39. Dudley, 285.
40. Treece, *Brazilian Jive*, 193.
41. Agawu, *African Rhythm*, 181.
42. Dudley, *Music from behind the Bridge*, 40, 164.
43. Lord Kitchener, "Pan in A Minor." I am indebted to Fred Moten for this reference and several other ideas in this chapter.
44. Consider, for example, J. S. Bach's "Partita in A minor" for solo flute, BWV 1013.
45. Lord Kitchener, "Pan in A Minor."
46. Rivera, *New York Ricans*, 39; Treece, *Brazilian Jive*, 194.
47. Simas and Rufino, *Fogo no mato*, 74.
48. Jor, "Mas, que nada!"
49. Treece, *Brazilian Jive*, 195; see chapter 5.
50. Thaíde & DJ Hum et al., "Viagem na rima."
51. Al2 El Aldeano and Silvito "El Libre," "Manual para hacer una canción."
52. Agamben, *End of the Poem*, 34.
53. Jakobson, "Closing Statement," 356–75.
54. Horace, *Art of Poetry*, line 43.
55. In the troubadour tradition of Iberian Provençal poetry, the speaking of the poem was known as "dictation" (*dictamen*). See Agamben, *End of the Poem*, 79.
56. Pope, *Essay on Criticism*, 15, lines 337–47.
57. Welsh, *Roots of Lyric*, 193.

58. Frye, "Introduction," xviii.
59. Culler, *Theory of the Lyric*, 181.
60. Pope, *Essay on Criticism*, 16, lines 361–69.
61. Perloff and Dworkin, "Introduction," 10; see also Wimsatt, "One Relation."
62. Projota, "A milenar arte de meter o louco."
63. Smitherman, *Talkin and Testifyin*, 94; Smitherman, "'Chain Remain the Same,'" 12; Bradley, *Book of Rhymes*, 163; Edwards, *How to Rap*, 25–29.
64. Kelley, "Looking for the 'Real' Nigga," 129; Alim, *Roc the Mic Right*.
65. Wendyyy, "Lè m vle."
66. Wendyyy, "À qui veut l'entendre."
67. Wendyyy, "Ayibobo."
68. Drums are so revered in Haitian Vodou that they are ceremoniously named and baptized, which I had the opportunity to observe in Port-au-Prince in 2017.
69. Hebblethwaite and Bartley, *Vodou Songs*, 1.
70. Delatour and Denis, "Vèvè lokal."
71. Kanis and Lolo, "Vèvè lokal."
72. Averill, *Day for the Hunter*, 183.
73. Kanis and Lolo, "Vèvè lokal."
74. While the grammatical object *yo* probably refers to misogynistic *oungan* (Vodou male priests) wary of female leadership in Vodou, it perhaps also signals the disproportionately male representation in hip hop as well as in Haitian politics. As of 2022, Haiti had had two female prime ministers: Claudette Werleigh (1995–1996) and Michèle Duvivier Pierre-Louis (2008–2009), but female participation in government is disproportionately low. In 2012, the Haitian Parliament passed a quota amendment requiring that at least 30 percent of elected and appointed officials be female, but in 2016, not one of the fourteen newly elected government officials was female. See Jacqueline Charles, "No Women in New Haitian Parliament," *Miami Herald*, January 18, 2016, https://www.miamiherald.com/news/nation-world/world/americas/haiti/article55358850.html.
75. See Ramsey, *Spirits and the Law*, 7.
76. Vodou lwa are said to mount their devotees. See Dayan, *Haiti, History, and the Gods*, 56; Hurston, *Tell my Horse*, 125.
77. Erivan "Produtos do Morro" Barbosa Sales and Lenny Fernandes, personal interview, Fortaleza, Brazil, March 30, 2015; Rensoli Medina, "Visiones paridoras," 44; Zamora Montes, *Rapear una Cuba utópica*, 17–32.
78. West, *Prophetic Fragments*, 186.
79. Toop, *Rap Attack 2*, 47; Pinn, *Noise and Spirit*; Nava, *In Search of Soul*.
80. Perry, *Prophets of the Hood*, 148–54; George, *Hip Hop America*, 68–69.
81. Mendes de Leon, "Poetic Justice."

82. Qtd. in Dyson, *Holler if You Hear Me,* 202.
83. Taylor, "Bringing Noise," 121.
84. See Rudinow, *Soul Music,* 17.
85. Belt, "Rap Music as Prophetic Utterance," 43–54.
86. Pew Research Center, "Brazil's Changing Religious Landscape," July 18, 2013, https://www.pewforum.org/2013/07/18/brazils-changing-religious-landscape/.
87. Criolo, "Duas de cinco."
88. Filosofia de Rua and Sharylaine, "É o hip hop."
89. Hermanos de Causa, "Gracias Hip Hop."
90. Farber, *Cuba since the Revolution,* 173.
91. Ramazani, *Poetry and Its Others,* 128–29.
92. Culler, *Theory of the Lyric,* 8.
93. Culler, 215–16.
94. Cascardi, "Orphic Fictions"; Welsh, *Roots of Lyric,* 144.
95. Huxley qtd. in Welsh, *Roots of Lyric,* 145.
96. Culler, *Theory of the Lyric,* 222.
97. Feld, "From Ethnomusicology to Echo-Muse-Ecology," 5.
98. Feld, 6.
99. Papá Humbertico, "5,11,83, Hip Hop."
100. Junco Duffay, "Esencia y presencia del rap cubano," 105; "Nunca lo hicimos por ganar dinero o fama, ni por salir en la radio o en la televisión, ni por entrar a algún tipo de institución con fines comerciales, lo hacíamos por bomba, intuición, deseo, necesidad, diversión y *hobby,* tampoco fue una moda–como para otros–; no estábamos jugando, era nuestra vida, pasión."
101. Hermanos de Causa, "Gracias Hip Hop."
102. Baker, *Buena Vista in the Club,* 21; Perry, *Prophets of the Hood,* 54.
103. Similar assertions surface in mainstream receptions of poetry, which often voice, as Ben Lerner puts it, "disappointment in poetry for failing to live up to the political power it supposedly possessed in the past." See Lerner, *Hatred of Poetry,* 42.
104. Perry, *Prophets of the Hood,* 55.
105. Boym, *Future of Nostalgia,* xviii.
106. Blaze One, "M ap rap."
107. Brisa Flow, "Veias abertas."
108. Parra, "Gracias a la vida."
109. Guarany's "Si se calla el cantor" inspired a 1973 film by the same name, directed by Enrique Dawi and starring the singer.
110. Nas, "Life's a Bitch."
111. Brisa Flow, "Veias abertas."
112. Sánchez, "Tirado en la calle."
113. Brisa Flow, "Veias abertas"; Ianni and Maria da Silva, "Apelo," 186.

114. Nash, *Black Feminism Reimagined*, 115.
115. Harney and Moten, *Undercommons*, 131.
116. Henle, *Combinatorial Introduction to Topology*, 110.
117. Brisa Flow, "Veias abertas."

3. Uprooting

1. Averill, *Day for the Hunter*, 161.
2. Chang, *Can't Stop Won't Stop*, 11–12.
3. Glissant, *Caribbean Discourse*, 15; in the original French: Glissant, *Le discours antillais*, 29.
4. Balibar, "Nation Form," 349; Anderson, *Imagined Communities*; Baer, *Indigenous Vanguards*, 19.
5. Ibrahim, "Arab Spring," 104.
6. Edwards, "Diaspora," 78.
7. Ibrahim, "Languages of Global Hip Hop," 552.
8. Vargas, "Se respira." In Cuba, the word *americano* refers to someone from the United States. When hip hop artists reference "música americana" (American music), they typically mean African American music.
9. Smith and Joshi, *Rhymes in the Flow*, 4–7.
10. The musical track was produced by Prófugo of La Lisa, Havana.
11. Perna, "Selling Cuba by the Sound," 45.
12. Quiroga, *Cuban Palimpsests*, 149–59; Whitfield, *Cuban Currency*, 30.
13. Moore, *Nationalizing Blackness*, 89; Averill, *Day for the Hunter*, 15.
14. Moore, *Nationalizing Blackness*, 90.
15. See Hooker, *Theorizing Race in the Americas*.
16. Guillén, *Obra poética*, 2:102.
17. de la Fuente, *Nation for All*, 266–78.
18. Moore, *Music and Revolution*, 149–51.
19. Putnam, *Radical Moves*, 151–95.
20. Borge, *Tropical Riffs*, 89.
21. Carpentier, "La música popular," 12; "resistente a todas las influencias extranjeras que . . . hubiesen podido desalojarla del ámbito propio."
22. Trouillot, *Haiti, State against Nation*, 99–106; Averill, *Day for the Hunter*, 31–37. On July 28, 1915, Woodrow Wilson ordered the US occupation of Haiti in response to the assassination of Haitian president Vilbrun Guillaume Sam by an elite-led mob. However, plans had been in the works for the US to assert hegemony in Haiti and neighboring Caribbean nations, particularly over sugar economies, for at least a year prior to the July massacre. The US occupied the Dominican Republic between 1916 and 1924 and maintained a military presence in Cuba during the so-called Sugar Intervention between 1917 and 1922.
23. Manuel and Largey, *Caribbean Currents*, 160. As a result of their exposure to jazz, local big bands began to form in Port-au-Prince during the late 1920s with US- and French-inspired names such as Jazz Hubert, Surprise-Jazz,

and Dynamique Jazz. The genre was eventually identified by the creolized word *djaz*, which came to signify any large dance band.

24. Dubois, *Haiti*, 289–90.

25. Price-Mars was detained by US soldiers during one of his ethnographic excursions in 1918. See Dubois, *Haiti*, 290.

26. Price-Mars, *La vocation de l'élite*, 88.

27. Price-Mars, *Ainsi parla l'oncle*, 121–200. While internationally, Vodou has come to signify an ensemble of spiritual practices that in Haitian Kreyòl are more often referred to by the word *Ginen* (the spirit of Africa), in Kreyòl the word *vodou* denotes a specific mode of dance and drumming. See Ramsey, *Spirits and the Law*, 7.

28. Averill, *Day for the Hunter*, 58–67.

29. Shaw, "São Coisas Nossas," 156–57; Vianna, *O mistério do samba*, 32.

30. Butler, *Freedoms Given, Freedoms Won*, 48–60; Nascimento, "Teatro experimental do negro," 218.

31. Pravaz, "Hybridity Brazilian Style."

32. Borge, *Tropical Riffs*, 94–109.

33. Andrade, *Ensaio sobre a música brasileira*, 26; "A reação contra o que é estrangeiro deve ser feita espertalhonamente pela deformação e adaptação dele. Não pela repulsa." Andrade's formula resonates with the notion of *antropofagia* of his contemporary Oswald de Andrade, whose *Manifesto antropófago* (Anthropophagic manifesto; published in 1928) reclaimed cannibalism as a metaphor for the way Brazilian culture digests international cosmopolitanism.

34. Pires, "Estruturas intocadas," 1058; Peixoto and Sebadelhe, *1976 Movimento Black Rio*, 12–32; Roth-Gordon, *Race and the Brazilian Body*, 164.

35. Batista, "Os Blacks no embalo do soul," 110.

36. Vianna, *O mundo funk carioca*, 24–26.

37. Buarque de Hollanda, *Impressões de viagem*, 100–1; Hanchard, *Orpheus and Power*, 113.

38. Sterling, *African Roots, Brazilian Rites*, 177. US funk music was first broadcast on Brazilian radio in 1967 by white DJ Big Boy as part of the show *Baile da Pesada*, but it subsequently became popular in traditional samba clubs.

39. Alim, *Roc the Mic Right*, 152.

40. Thaíde & DJ Hum, "Sr. Tempo Bom."

41. Lena Frias, "O orgulho (importado) de ser negro no Brasil," *Jornal do Brasil*, July 17, 1976, sec. Caderno B, 1, 4–7. Written by journalist Lena Frias, with an accompanying photo essay by Almir Veiga, the article presented Black Rio as an expression of "soul power, fenômeno social dos mais instigantes já registrados no país" (soul power, a social phenomenon among the most riveting that has ever been registered in the country).

42. Bocskay, "Undesired Presences," 65.

43. Peixoto and Sebadelhe, *1976 Movimento Black Rio*, 17; Dunn, *Contracultura*, 270–71.

44. Batista, "Os Blacks no embalo do soul," 115; Viana, "Lélia Gonzalez," 55.
45. Yoshinaga, *Nelson Triunfo*, 148–50; Angeli and Ramos, *Triunfo*.
46. Yoshinaga, *Nelson Triunfo*, 179–80.
47. Chang, "It's a Hip-Hop World," 62; Hernández Baguer and Cué, "Hora de abrir los ojos," 303. Hip hop films such as Charlie Ahearn's *Wild Style* (1983) and Stan Lathan's *Beat Street* (1984), were becoming popular in Brazil (as well as in Cuba). Films were perhaps most responsible for hip hop's globalization, having a major influence in countries as diverse as Colombia, Japan, Australia, and Germany. See Dennis, *Afro-Colombian Hip-Hop*, 23; Condry, *Hip-Hop Japan*, 62; Maxwell, *Phat Beats, Dope Rhymes*, 79; Brown, "Keeping It Real," 139.
48. Yoshinaga, *Nelson Triunfo*, 209; Angeli and Ramos, *Triunfo*.
49. Chang, *Can't Stop Won't Stop*, 172.
50. *Billboard*, November 27, 2004, 17.
51. Camargos, *Rap e política*, 42–46.
52. Originally a dance crew, Black Juniors was brought together to rap by white Argentine producer Santiago "Mister Sam" Malnati. Their album was appropriately entitled *Break,* paying homage to the street dance practice.
53. Vianna, *O mundo funk carioca*, 34.
54. Vianna, 32, 109; see also Hankin, "Rap e conscientização." In Brazil, the consciousness-raising function of Black social gatherings dates at least to the 1930s, when the Frente Negra would host weekly informative events. See Butler, *Freedoms Given, Freedoms Won*, 116.
55. Yúdice, *Expediency of Culture*, 127.
56. Caramante, "Os quatro pretos"; Yoshinaga, *Nelson Triunfo*, 237. Between 1988 and 1991, São Paulo hosted performances by US rap groups Kool Moe Dee, Whodini, Kurtis Blow, Run-DMC, and Public Enemy.
57. Sharylaine, "Nossos dias."
58. Allucci, Valencio, and Allucci, *Mulheres de palavra*, 4.
59. Paz and Donato, "Agradecimentos."
60. Hernández Baguer and Junco Duffay, *Contar el rap*.
61. The original 1981 edition was subtitled *del areyto a la Nueva Trova* (from *areyto* to nueva trova).
62. Moore, *Music and Revolution*, 149–51.
63. Padura, *The Man Who Loved Dogs*, 67; in the original Spanish: Padura, *El hombre que amaba a los perros*, 100; "en el Caribe hispano fuimos los únicos que vivimos sin saber que estaba naciendo la música salsa o de que los Beatles (Rollings y Mamas *too*) eran símbolo de la rebeldía y no de la cultura imperialista, como tantas veces nos dijeron."
64. Farber, *Cuba since the Revolution*, 21. In a 1960 visit to New York for the United Nations General Assembly, Fidel Castro famously relocated his delegation to Harlem, where he was warmly received by Black leaders such as Malcom X. See Cohen, "When Castro Came to Harlem."

65. Abidde and Manyeruke, *Fidel Castro and Africa's Liberation Struggle.*
66. de la Fuente, *Nation for All,* 266.
67. de la Fuente, *Nation for All,* 185–90; Farber, *Cuba since the Revolution,* 170.
68. de la Fuente, *Nation for All,* 295.
69. Farber, *Cuba since the Revolution,* 180. As Farber indicates, grassroots opposition to racism included a non-elite militant group called the Movimiento de Liberación Nacional (National Liberation Movement), associated with the Afro-Cuban Abakuá religious society, and the Afro-Cuban Study Group.
70. de la Fuente, *Nation for All,* 315–16.
71. Herrera Veitía, "Producir rap afrocubano," 87.
72. Herrera Veitía, 88.
73. Junco Duffay, "Esencia y presencia del rap cubano," 107; Hernández Baguer and Cué, "Hora de abrir los ojos," 303.
74. George, *Hippest Trip in America,* 85; Krims, *Rap Music,* 120. See also Dorian Lynskey, "'An Ad for Blackness': How Soul Train Made America Do the Hustle," *Guardian,* February 20, 2019, sec. Music, https://www.theguardian.com/music/2019/feb/20/american-soul-train-don-cornelius.
75. Junco Duffay, "Esencia y presencia del rap cubano," 107–11.
76. Junco Duffay, 108.
77. See, for example, Guillén, "Benny," 80.
78. Moré, "Cómo fue."
79. Alexey ..el tipo este.., "Cómo fue."
80. Alexey ..el tipo este..
81. Rensoli Medina, "Visiones paridoras," 23; Herrera Veitía, "Producir rap afrocubano," 99. Inspired by radio and television broadcasts of US programs like *Soul Train,* the collective GrupoUno, under the leadership of Balesy Rivero and Rodolfo Rensoli, held the first international festival in 1995 in the *reparto* (municipality) of Antonio Guiteras, or Bahía. The festival moved to Alamar in 1996, where it would remain until 2004.
82. Figueroa Gómez, "Maferefún, Orishas," 273–74.
83. Figueroa Gómez, 275.
84. Figueroa Gómez, 280–81.
85. Los Orishas, "A lo cubano."
86. Simoni, *Tourism and Informal Encounters,* 78.
87. Baker, *Buena Vista in the Club,* 235.
88. Whitfield, *Cuban Currency,* 20.
89. Steingo, *Kwaito's Promise,* 65.
90. Steingo, 148.
91. Cross, "Soviet Perestroika," 144–46; Quiroga, *Cuban Palimpsests,* 149.
92. Baker, *Buena Vista in the Club,* 12.
93. García Amorós, "Agencia Cubana de Rap," 49; "contribuir al desarrollo del género a escala nacional e internacional, estimulando la consolidación

de modelos que por sus características sean expresión de los valores de nuestra cultura cubana."

94. Rivero Nordet, "Crónica de una lengua raspada," 65; Zamora Montes, *Rapear una Cuba utópica,* 54. In 1997, GrupoUno, the group responsible for the Havana hip hop festivals, met with the recently formed New York–based Black August Collective. Black August promoted international cultural exchange between Black musician-activists, focusing in particular on political prisoners in the US and African American prisoners abroad.

95. Rivero Nordet, "Crónica de una lengua raspada," 65. As a result of these conversations, high-profile US rappers and singers such as Mos Def, Common, Talib Kweli, Tony Touch, Sarah Jones, the Roots, Jessica Care Moore, and even Gil Scott-Heron gave benefit concerts in US cities to help fund the Havana festivals, while groups such as dead prez, Tony Touch, and Mos Def traveled to Alamar to perform.

96. Baker, *Buena Vista in the Club,* 250–56.

97. [La delegación?], "De La Habana a Nueva York: El Rap Cubano en la Meca del Hip-Hop," *Movimiento: La Revista Cubana de Hip Hop,* no. 1, 21–25; [Editors of *Movimiento?*], "The Roots en Cuba: Opiniones ofrecidas en conferencia de prensa," *Movimiento: La Revista Cubana de Hip Hop,* no. 1, 36. Cultural exchanges would continue throughout the first half of the 2000s. On June 9, 2003, Obsesión and Doble Filo performed alongside the Roots and Common at Harlem's Apollo Theater.

98. Baker, *Buena Vista in the Club,* 67; Fernandes, *Cuba Represent!,* 15; Suárez de Armas, "El hip-hop"; Hankin, "The (Latin) American Underground."

99. Aldo "Bocafloja" Villegas, personal interview, New York City, May 16, 2018; "como un vehículo de conexión para abrir el diálogo. Pero el hip hop no era la última línea de discusión, sino que era el vehículo, nada más. Entonces se hablaba de raza, género, historia . . . desde un punto de vista no hegemónico utilizando referencias de hip hop." In a chapter for the edited volume *La Verdad: An International Dialogue on Hip Hop Latinidades,* Bocafloja echoes this sentiment: "Decolonize, self-manage, transgress, emancipate. Our redefined version of Hip Hop's four elements." See Bocafloja, "Collective Amnesia," 130.

100. Baker, *Buena Vista in the Club,* 212; Sosin Martínez, "El rap es muchas cosas," 117. Contrary to conspiracy theories, Baker suggests that the festival's cancellation was made mostly because of the imminent threat of Hurricane Charley. One of the incidents that supposedly led to the closing of the festival occurred two years earlier, in 2002, when Papá Humbertico performed in front of a backdrop featuring a sheet with the printed words "Denucia social" (Social complaint). *Denuncia social* was to be the name of Humbertico's forthcoming album, but foreign journalists misinterpreted it as a direct attack on the Cuban government. The incident resulted in several rappers being sanctioned by Cuban authorities.

101. Lewis, "Language, Culture and Power," 46.

102. Averill, *Day for the Hunter,* 72–89.

103. Averill, 58–71.
104. Averill, 78–79.
105. Averill, 78.
106. Averill, 99.
107. Averill, 103–4.
108. Averill, 104. A female type associated with sexual availability, desire, and eroticism derived from the French hyperfeminization of the Caribbean, the *doudou* emerged in French colonial literature during the early twentieth century. On the tradition of *doudouisme* in Francophone Caribbean literature, see Edwards, *Practice of Diaspora*, 159.
109. Dubois, *Haiti*, 17.
110. Averill, *Day for the Hunter*, 117.
111. Averill, 125–33.
112. Averill, 123–25. The 2014 album *Haiti Direct*, released by Strut Records, demonstrates the influence of US soul on Haitian konpa groups of the 1960s and 1970s, such as Les Loups Noirs.
113. Mackendy Jeune, personal interview by phone, June 1, 2020.
114. Jean Gardy Seide "Kameleyon," personal interview, Port-au-Prince, July 10, 2017.
115. Victorin, "Master Dji"; Averill, *Day for the Hunter*, 168. In France, rap won a place almost immediately in the national culture industry thanks in large part to the popularity of Paris-based Claude "MC Solaar" M'Barali, born in Senegal to parents from Chad. MC Solaar's multicultural background met wide appeal across the Francophone world, and France quickly became the world's largest non-Anglophone rap market and an important influence on Haitian rap kreyòl. The global visibility of French rap was solidified with the award-winning 1995 film *La Haine*, which featured a soundtrack of US funk and hip hop artists. On French rap, see Béthune, *Le rap*, 181; Chang, "It's a Hip-Hop World." See also Michael Oliver, "'You're Not Welcome': Rap's Racial Divide in France," *Guardian*, April 22, 2020, sec. Music, https://www.theguardian.com/music/2020/apr/22/rap-music-racial-divide-france.
116. Victorin, "Master Dji."
117. Master Dji, "Sispann," translated by Averill in *Day for the Hunter*, 168.
118. Teddy Fresh, a Haitian-born rapper who grew up in Miami, addressed the HIV/AIDS crisis in his 1992 hit track "Seropozitif" (HIV Positive). The light jazz guitar riff and relaxed flow of "Seropozitif" are reminiscent of contemporaneous New York City groups such as A Tribe Called Quest.
119. Averill, *Day for the Hunter*, 171.
120. Fayer, "African Interpreters," 281–83.
121. Glissant, *Le discours antillais*, 555; "Je te parle dans ta langue, et c'est dans ma langue que je te comprends."
122. Glissant, *Caribbean Discourse*, 19–20.
123. Hebblethwaite, "French and Underdevelopment," 255.

124. Frères Parent, "Veye-yo."
125. Alim, "Hip Hop Nation Language."
126. Original Rap Staff, "Whose Style Is This?"
127. Manuel and Largey, *Caribbean Currents,* 171.
128. Edwards, *Practice of Diaspora,* 14.
129. Césaire, "Misère d'une poésie," 50. Oswald de Andrade's *Manifesto antropófago* had been published fourteen years earlier, in 1928.
130. Perry, *Prophets of the Hood,* 20.
131. Clifford, "Diasporas," 307.
132. Fanon, *Wretched of the Earth,* 179; emphasis mine. The concurrent emergence of nationalism and regionalism holds for nineteenth-century independence figures in Latin America such as Jean-Jacques Dessalines, Simón Bolívar, and José Martí, who called at once for proto-national movements and hemispheric solidarity.
133. Alim, *Roc the Mic Right,* xi; Terkourafi, *Languages of Global Hip Hop,* 5.
134. Palomino, *Invention of Latin American Music,* 46–138.
135. Baker, *Buena Vista in the Club,* 277.
136. Baker, 322.

4. Scale

1. Thaíde & DJ Hum featuring Sabotage, "Vinheta 3."
2. Davis, *Planet of Slums.*
3. Qtd. in Davis, 21.
4. Gago, *La razón neoliberal,* 281; "capacidad de re-escalar, de saltar escalas y vincularlas, de un modo que desafía la partición globalizada entre lo local y lo global pero también la geometría nacional."
5. McEnaney, *Acoustic Properties,* 13.
6. Neff, "Roots, Routes and Rhizomes," 468–69.
7. Carlos "Yimi Konklase" Yussuan, personal interview, Havana, August 18, 2014; "nuestro pequeño pedazo de la modernidad."
8. Siskind, *Cosmopolitan Desires,* 3. Though Siskind does not include a discussion of Haiti, a related phenomenon can be identified, for example, in Emeric Bergeaud's 1859 novel *Stella,* the first published Haitian novel, which narrates the story of the Haitian Revolution guided by French liberalist ideology.
9. Siskind, 9–38.
10. See Gilroy, *Black Atlantic,* 33; Alim, "Translocal Style Communities."
11. Consider, for example, writers such as Nicolás Guillén, Mário de Andrade, and Jacques Roumain and musical genres such as Cuban son, Brazilian samba, and Haitian rasin.
12. Muñoz, *Cruising Utopia,* 29.
13. Davis, *Planet of Slums,* 16.
14. Krims, *Music and Urban Geography,* 35.

15. Gilroy, "It's a Family Affair," 89.

16. Césaire, *Lettre à Maurice Thorez*, 15; "Ma conception de l'universel est celle d'un universel riche de tout le particulier, riche de tous les particuliers, approfondissement et coexistence de tous les particuliers." A native of Martinique, Césaire introduced this formulation in his *Lettre à Maurice Thorez*, in which he broke with the French Communist Party. In the letter, he accuses the French Communist Party of failing to criticize Soviet abuses and highlights the inability of European communism to account for the crucial differences between the formerly enslaved, colonial subjects of the Caribbean and the white proletariat as the supposed universal subject of human emancipation.

17. United Nations Human Settlements Programme (UN-HABITAT), "Population Living in Slums (% of Urban Population—Haiti," World Bank, https://data.worldbank.org/indicator/EN.POP.SLUM.UR.ZS?locations=HT.

18. Department of Economic and Social Affairs, Population Division, "World Urbanization Prospects: The 2018 Revision," United Nations, 2018, https://population.un.org/wup/country-profiles/.

19. Kivland, "Street Sovereignty."

20. Kivland, 142.

21. Kivland, 147.

22. Sibylla Brodzinsky, "Haiti Mob Violence Overwhelms Peace Force," *Guardian*, October 16, 2004, sec. World news, https://www.theguardian.com/world/2004/oct/16/sibyllabrodzinsky.

23. Seide, Badiau, and Alexis, "Les causes de l'implantation du Rap en Haïti," 39.

24. Duval, "Barikad Crew, Respect!"

25. Duval, "Barikad Crew, Respect!"; "Les enfants pauvres, comme les biens nourris des meilleures écoles, chantent leurs lyrics. . . . Les textes les plus inspirés de la musique haïtienne de ces dernières années, toutes catégories confondues, sont signés Barikad Crew."

26. Hall, *Historical Dictionary of Haiti*, 33; Duval, "Barikad Crew, Respect!" The group was comprised of K-Tafalk, Dade, Deja-Voo, Condagana, Fantom, Izolan, Marco, Bricks, Master Sun, Young Cliff, and Brital. See also Erin Wildermuth, "American Hip-Hop in Haiti: Musical Fusion or Cultural Conquest?," *Washington Times*, April 21, 2011, https://www.washingtontimes.com/news/2011/apr/21/us-hip-hop-haiti-musical-fusion-cultural-conquest/.

27. Forman, "Represent," 206; Barthélemy, *Le pays en dehors*, 34–45.

28. Garcia, *Coming Home*.

29. Seide, Badiau, and Alexis, "Les causes de l'implantation du Rap en Haïti."

30. Barikad Crew, "Se konsa l ye."

31. Kivland, "Street Sovereignty," 147.

32. Roth-Gordon, "Conversational Sampling," 64.

33. Morgan, *Real Hiphop*, 53.

34. Kelley, "Kickin' Reality," 209; Robert Montinard, videoconference, August 28, 2020.
35. D-Fi Powèt Revòlte, "Castro sou map la"
36. D-Fi Powèt Revòlte.
37. Blay'Z, "Ghetto"; Alim, "Hip Hop Nation Language."
38. Consider, for example, US R & B singer Jaheim's 2001 album *Ghetto Love*.
39. Voegelin, *Political Possibility of Sound*, 56.
40. Haiti and Armenia Reforestation Act of 2013, S. 1548, 113th Cong. (2013).
41. Barikad Crew, "Pa koupe bwa."
42. Murray, "Wood Tree," 141–42. Several failed attempts have been made at reforestation and transforming logging into a sustainable cash crop.
43. When Barikad Crew released the album *Goumen pou sa w kwè* in November 2007, it sold more than five thousand copies in one day. See Duval, "Barikad Crew, Respect!"
44. Lacerda, "Rio de Janeiro and the Divided State," 77. The formation of these settlements is the subject of Aluísio Azevedo's 1890 novel *O cortiço*.
45. Valladares, *A invenção da favela*, 23–24; Caldeira, *City of Walls*, 79.
46. Cunha, *Os sertões*, 191.
47. Valladares, *A invenção da favela*, 23–26; Oliveira, "Repensando a questão das favelas," 10.
48. Pardue, *Ideologies of Marginality*, 66; Sá, *Life in the Megalopolis*, 14.
49. Cestaro, "A SAGMACS e o estudo da 'Aglomeração Paulistana,'" 7–11. Beginning in the late 1940s and 1950s, Brazilian favelas became a significant area of social and anthropological research, thanks in large part to the influence of French Dominican priest and social scientist Louis-Joseph Lebret, known in Brazil as Padre Lebret, who founded the research and economic action group Économie et Humanisme (Economy and Humanism) in 1942 and the Sociedade para Análises Gráficas e Mecanográficas Aplicadas aos Complexos Sociais (Society for Applied Graphic and Mecanographic Analysis of Social Complexes, SAGMAC) in São Paulo in 1947. A decade later, São Paulo Mayor Toledo Piza signed a contract with the SAGMAC and Padre Lebret to fund the study of development possibilities for the city with a particular emphasis on its rapidly growing periphery. The report was published as the "Estrutura Urbana da Aglomeração Paulistana" (Urban Structure of São Paulo Agglomeration).
50. Maria de Jesus, *Quarto de Despejo,* 45; "Desvio meu pensamento para o céu. Penso: será que lá em cima tem habitantes? Será que eles são melhores do que nós? Será que o predomínio de lá suplanta o nosso? Será que as nações de lá é variada igual aqui na terra? Ou é uma nação única? Será que lá existe favela? E se lá existe favela será que quando eu morrer eu vou morar na favela?"
51. Miranda, *Carolina Maria de Jesus,* 48. Carolina's additional work, which includes novels, poetry, and also musical compositions, has received significantly

less attention than her early memoir. In 2021, Hélio Menezes and Raquel Barreto curated an exhibition on Carolina, including much of her unpublished work, for the Instituto Moreira Salles in São Paulo, entitled "Carolina Maria de Jesus: Um Brasil para os brasileiros."

52. Caldeira, *City of Walls,* 213.

53. Each Brazilian city displays its own idiosyncratic distribution of urban space, but most exhibit some degree of clustering among wealthier residents and concentrated zones of poverty in favelas.

54. Fix, Arantes, and Tanaka, "Case of São Paulo," 3.

55. B. B. Boys, "B. B. Boys é nosso nome."

56. Borge, *Tropical Riffs,* 89.

57. Clark, *Dark Ghetto.*

58. War, "World Is a Ghetto."

59. Andrade, *Ensaio sobre a música brasileira,* 26.

60. Risério, *A cidade no Brasil,* 106–7.

61. Yoshinaga, *Nelson Triunfo,* 270.

62. GOG, "Brasília periferia."

63. Racionais MC's, "Periferia é periferia."

64. Tsing, "Inside the Economy of Appearances," 119.

65. Pardue, *Ideologies of Marginality,* 64. An additional genealogy for marginality in Brazilian hip hop could be drawn with visual artists, writers, and musicians of prior decades. Visual artist Hélio Oiticica, Tropicália musicians Caetano Veloso and Gilberto Gil, and writers of *literatura marginal* (marginal literature) such as Paulo Leminski and Waly Salomão took marginality as the inspiration for a popular avant-garde. Unlike rappers a few decades later, most of these artists did not reside in marginalized neighborhoods. See Faria, Penna, and Tonani do Patrocínio, *Modos da margem,* 24–32.

66. Kehl, "Radicais, raciais, racionais."

67. Racionais MC's, "Fórmula mágica da paz."

68. Salles, *Poesia revoltada,* 118; "homenagear não só a sua própria comunidade, mas a favela de maneira geral."

69. I am following Robert M. Cover's use of *nomos* to refer to a normative universe that we inhabit, a "world of right and wrong, of lawful and unlawful, of valid and void." See Cover, "Nomos and Narrative," 4.

70. Feltran, "O legítimo em disputa."

71. Feltran, "Sobre anjos e irmãos," 46–51; "a emergência do 'crime' como instância normativa legítima nas periferias . . . o esteio de uma comunidade central."

72. Osumare, *Africanist Aesthetic in Global Hip-Hop,* 63

73. Racionais MC's, "Da ponte pra cá"; McGrath, "Island as Urban Artifact."

74. Sarah Fernandes, "'Para nós, a periferia é um país,' diz poeta Sérgio Vaz," *Rede Brasil Atual,* August 16, 2016, https://www.redebrasilatual.com.br/cultura

/2016/08/2018e-hora-da-caca-contar-um-pouco-da-historia2019-diz-sergio-vaz-sobre-cultura-na-periferia-934/.

75. Yoshinaga, *Nelson Triunfo*, 266–67; Teperman, *Se liga no som*, 59.

76. Kajikawa, *Sounding Race in Rap Songs*, 124; Yoshinaga, *Nelson Triunfo*, 267–68.

77. Teperman, *Se liga no som*, 60.

78. Gabriel o Pensador, "Retrato de um playboy (Juventude Perdida)."

79. Racionais MC's, "Da ponte pra cá."

80. GOG, "ISO 9000 do gueto."

81. Partially inspired by the popularity of rap in São Paulo, *saraus* are regular open mics, performance venues, and literary circles typically held in cultural centers or bars of marginalized neighborhoods in major cities.

82. Morgan, *Real Hiphop*, 53.

83. GOG, "Universo gueto."

84. Hamberg, "'Slums' of Havana," 86.

85. Geoffray, "Juan Carlos Flores," 42. See also Regina Cano, "Alamar: City of the Future," *Havana Times,* April 15, 2009, https://havanatimes.org/?p=7485; Milan Alram, "A cidade do futuro meio século depois," *Revista Piauí,* no. 43 (June 2009), https://piaui.folha.uol.com.br/materia/a-cidade-do-futuro-meio-seculo-depois/.

86. Guevara, "El socialismo y el hombre en Cuba." Guevara directed his letter to Carlos Quijano, editor of the Uruguayan weekly newspaper *Marcha,* who published it on March 12, 1965.

87. Morucci, *Alamar, un quartier cubain*, 13.

88. Geoffray, "Juan Carlos Flores," 43; Fornet, *El 71,* 88. Volunteer workers were organized into ten worker collectives known as *microbrigadas* (microbrigades), which became Alamar's numbered zones.

89. David "D'Omni" Escalona Carrillo, personal interview, Havana, August 13, 2014. At the forefront of Alamar's avant-garde was the OMNI-ZonaFranca interdisciplinary arts collective. OMNI-ZonaFranca once staged a performance in Alamar with the effigy of man hanging from a tree in front of a modernist Soviet sculpture covered in *Granma* newspapers and empty cigarette packs, as if to suggest the death of Guevara's "new man" resulting from Special Period scarcity. See Geoffray, "Juan Carlos Flores," 48.

90. Baker, *Buena Vista in the Club,* 218.

91. Junco Duffay, "Esencia y presencia del rap cubano," 115–16.

92. Sosin Martínez, "El rap es muchas cosas," 173.

93. Junco Duffay, "Esencia y presencia del rap cubano," 128; Herrera Veitía, "Producir rap afrocubano," 91.

94. One of the first popular Cuban rap songs was the 1996 Amenaza and Grandes Ligas song "Representando al Vedado" (Representing El Vedado). During the second half of the nineteenth century, El Vedado housed freed and fugitive slaves. By the 1920s and 1930s, it housed some of the city's wealthiest residents,

and its planned urban grid and wide tree-lined avenues became emblematic of Havana's urban modernity. When hip hop emerged in Havana, El Vedado was one of the city's most central neighborhoods, privileged in terms of access to goods and transportation. See Ojeda, "Territorios e identidades," 12–17.

95. Vaughan, *Rebel Dance, Renegade Stance*, 38.
96. Gámez Torres, "Hearing the Change," 248.
97. See Levine, "Sounding El Paquete."
98. At a hip hop festival in Santiago on May 29, 2019, rapper Pedro "El Zulu" Enrique Muñoz Biart held a workshop entitled "Cómo evitar el reparterismo" (How to avoid reparterismo).
99. Prieto, "Heberto Padilla," 120; Castro Ruz, "Conclusión de las reuniones con los intelectuales cubanos."
100. Prieto, "Heberto Padilla," 121.
101. Zhdanov, "On Music," 57–58.
102. Buck-Morss, *Dreamworld and Catastrophe*, 60.
103. Padilla, *Fuera del juego*, 13–16.
104. Cohen et al., "Dictamen del jurado del concurso UNEAC."
105. Prieto, "Heberto Padilla," 125–30; Guerra, *Visions of Power in Cuba*, 354; Fornet, *El 71*, 204–11. Padilla's imprisonment and highly performative, parodic self-incrimination galvanized criticism of the Cuban Revolution from Latin American intellectuals on both the right and the left. See Fornet, *El 71*, 161.
106. Guerra, *Visions of Power in Cuba*, 356.
107. The censorship of rap must be understood in the context of wider policies of strict control of the arts. In 2018, the Cuban government passed the Decreto 349, which criminalized public performance and unsanctioned sales by independent artists not registered with a government agency. In the months leading up to its passage, several rappers, including David "D'Omni" Escalona Carrillo and Raudel "Escuadrón Patriota" Collazo launched a music video and campaign against the decree entitled "#NoAlDecreto349." Both Escalona and Collazo had been detained previously and labeled dissidents or "counterrevolutionaries." In the case of the Decreto 349, an additional rapper, Soandres del Rio, was detained for speaking out. See, for example, María Matienzo Puerto, "Rapero cubano detenido arbitrariamente por el régimen de la isla," *Cubanet*, September 22, 2018, https://www.cubanet.org/noticias/rapero-cubano-detenido-arbitrariamente-regimen-la-isla/; "Seguridad del Estado detiene al rapero Raudel Collazo," *Cubanet*, August 7, 2017, https://www.cubanet.org/noticias/represion-en-camaguey-contra-concierto-de-hip-hop-alternativo/.
108. See Lillian Guerra, "The Return of Cuba's Security State," *New York Times*, May 27, 2021, sec. Opinion, https://www.nytimes.com/2021/05/27/opinion/cuba-artist-luis-manuel-otero-alcantara.html.
109. In conversation with author, June 2018.
110. Baker, "Cuba Rebelión," 13.
111. Baker, 3.

112. Zamora Montes, *Rapear una Cuba utópica,* 80.
113. Bárbaro "El Urbano" Vargas, personal interview, Havana, August 13, 2014; Baker, *Buena Vista in the Club,* 80.
114. Rodríguez, "La aldea, Los Aldeanos, el aldeanismo," 262.
115. Weaver, "US Agency Infiltrated Cuban Hip-Hop Scene."
116. Pedrero, *Revolution.*
117. See Hankin, "*La Aldea.*"
118. Al2 El Aldeano, "Vereda tropical."
119. See Staniski, *Viva el Vedado.*
120. Pedrero, *Revolution;* "vivimos en un país pequeño, vivimos en una ciudad pequeña, vivimos en un barrio pequeño, y para nosotros el principio de la aldea es esta: un lugar donde todas las personas, aunque parezca una utopía, colaboren entre sí, todas tiene un mismo objetivo."
121. Los Aldeanos, "Protestando."
122. See, for example, Lolo, *Lo que quede de aldea;* Ángel, "Defensa de lo local."
123. Martí, *Nuestra América,* 31; "Cree el aldeano vanidoso que el mundo entero es su aldea, y con tal que él quede de alcalde, o le mortifique al rival que le quitó la novia, o le crezcan en la alcancía los ahorros, ya da por bueno el orden universal, sin saber de los gigantes que llevan siete leguas en las botas y le pueden poner la bota encima, ni de la pelea de los cometas en el Cielo, que van por el aire dormido engullendo mundos. Lo que quede de aldea en América ha de despertar."
124. See Sobrevilla, "El surgimiento de la idea," 160. Martí's recourse to rurality bears a well-documented influence from Emerson's transcendentalist notion of "natural man." See Guadarrama González, "El pensamiento integracionista y latinoamericanista de José Martí," 98; Barbosa dos Santos, "Fundamentos políticos de Nuestra América," 137.
125. Ramos, *Desencuentros de la modernidad,* 234.
126. Castro Ruz, "En conmemoración"; "Vemos que ya van a empezar a construir el primer edificio de 12 plantas de Matanzas, con lo cual Matanzas va a perder esa apariencia de aldea que tiene a veces; igual que la ciudad de Santa Clara que va a empezar también a tener algunos edificios altos. La tierra hay que ahorrarla, porque la necesitamos para producir alimentos; hay que crecer hacia arriba y hacer edificios altos."
127. Farber, *Cuba since the Revolution,* 56.
128. By the early 2010s, the sharing of data on USB drives in Cuba had matured into a *paquete seminal* (weekly packet), a one-terabyte physical hard drive containing the most recent national and international audio and video clips, television series, movies, and software, which was updated weekly and circulated in elaborate networks throughout the country. See Grear, "El Paquete Semanal."
129. Rivière facilitated collaborations between Cuban and Puerto Rican rappers, as documented in her doctoral dissertation, "Son Dos Alas: A Multimedia

Ethnography of Hip-Hop Between Cuba and Puerto Rico" (University of Minnesota, 2010).

130. Al2 El Aldeano and Silvito "El Libre," "Una hora de vida."
131. I am indebted to Justo Planas for this detail.
132. McLuhan, *Understanding Media,* 4.
133. McLuhan, 93.
134. Pedrero, *Revolution.*
135. Pedrero.
136. Gámez Torres, "Rap Is War," 14.
137. Borges-Triana, "Yo creo que Los Aldeanos. . . . "
138. In the late 2010s, veteran rapper Rubén Marín took the helm of the Cuban Rap Agency.
139. Segato, *La guerra contra las mujeres,* 67; "los elementos constitutivos de una experiencia territorial no son fijos sino históricamente definidos."
140. McEnaney, *Acoustic Properties,* 13.
141. See, for example, Camacho Moreira, "Confluencias del funk y rap en Cuba," 553.
142. Elias Leight, "Inside Latin Trap, the Viral Sound Too Hot for American Radio," *Rolling Stone Blog,* November 7, 2017, https://www.rollingstone.com/music/music-features/inside-latin-trap-the-viral-sound-too-hot-for-american-radio-255923/.
143. Vargas, "Se respira."

5. Writing

1. Lévi-Strauss, *Tristes tropiques,* 349–55.
2. Rama, *La ciudad letrada;* Ramos, *Desencuentros de la modernidad.*
3. Padrón, "El requerimiento."
4. Rama, *La ciudad letrada,* 40–48.
5. Cândido, "O direito à literatura"; Lefebvre, "Right to the City."
6. Cornejo Polar, *Escribir en el aire,* 41; "no tanto como un sistema de comunicación sino dentro del horizonte del orden y la autoridad, casi como si su único significado posible fuera el poder."
7. An earlier, condensed version of this chapter was published in as "'Enraizados da Letra': Lyrics and the Letter in Brazilian, Cuban, and Haitian Rap" in the *Journal of Latin American Cultural Studies* 30, no. 4 (2021).
8. GOG, "ISO 9000 do gueto."
9. Alim, *Roc the Mic Right,* 127.
10. Ong, *Orality and Literacy,* 11. For critiques of the theological undertones of Ong's notion of "primary orality," see Sterne, "Theology of Sound"; Bernstein, "Introduction," 20.
11. Saussy, *Ethnography of Rhythm,* 9.
12. Govain, "Créolophonie." The neologism *oraliture* is commonly attributed to Paul Zumthor, but Mirville introduced the term in his undergraduate

thesis in Haiti in 1971, a decade before the publication of Zumthor's renowned *Introduction à la poésie oral* (1983).

13. Smith, "Truth of Graffiti," 84; Rose, *Black Noise*, 59.
14. Scott, *Common Wind*, 76–77.
15. Span, "Learning in Spite of Opposition," 27–31.
16. Graham, "Writing from the Margins," 615.
17. Gates, *Signifying Monkey*, 131.
18. Pettway, *Cuban Literature*, 13.
19. Manzano, *Autobiografía del esclavo poeta*, 304.
20. See Ochoa Gautier, *Aurality*; McEnaney, *Acoustic Properties*; Librandi, *Writing by Ear*; Robbins, *Audible Geographies*.
21. Bernstein, "Introduction," 13–14.
22. Ochoa Gautier, *Aurality*, 4.
23. See Librandi, *Writing by Ear*.
24. Stoever, *Sonic Color Line*, 17.
25. El B, "El periodista."
26. Ramos, *Desencuentros de la modernidad*, 126–40.
27. Fairley, "Ay Díos, Ampárame," 85–86.
28. Hankin, "Contrapunteo de Los Orishas y Los Aldeanos," 212–13.
29. Kelley, "Looking for the 'Real' Nigga," 130.
30. Smitherman, *Talkin and Testifyin*; Gates, *Signifying Monkey*; Levin Becker, *What's Good*, 20; Kelley, "Looking for the 'Real' Nigga," 129.
31. Ramazani, *Poetry and Its Others*, 63. In his analysis of poetry and the news, Ramazani cites a famous example by W. H. Auden: "All I have is a voice / To undo the folded lie." El B's declaration of functioning as "la voz del barrio" (the voice of the neighborhood) can almost be heard as a sample of Auden's assertion that the poet's voice serves to demystify the news. See Auden, *Selected Poems*, 88; Ramazani, *Poetry and Its Others*, 72.
32. Ramazani, *Poetry and Its Others*, 71.
33. McAlister, *Rara!*, 4–7.
34. Averill, *Day for the Hunter*, 15.
35. PIC, "Lè m ap ekri."
36. BIC, "Kokorat." Translation provided by artist.
37. See Feltran, "Sobre anjos e irmãos," 51.
38. Faria, Penna, and Tonani do Patrocínio, *Modos da margem*, 20; "realismo experiencial, o que se lê são as experiências vividas mesmo e sobretudo quando reconstruídas ficcionalmente." There is perhaps a comparison worth drawing here with mid-twentieth-century Latin American *testimonio* (testimonial literature). Argentine writer and militant Rodolfo Walsh, for example, used fiction to elucidate eyewitness testimony and solve real cases (such as a 1956 police massacre of *peronista* militants) by narrativizing them in literary fashion. Walsh's testimonio exploded the boundaries of fiction and truth, narrative literature and juridical writing. As Diego Alonso puts it, Walsh "writes the real crime as if it were

a literary crime." See Alonso, "La verdad y las pruebas," 102. Other forms of the Latin American testimonio, such as Rigoberta Menchú's well-known memoir, have sparked polemics surrounding the relation between testimonio, truth, and the institution of literature. See Beverley, *Testimonio*, 7–19.

39. Okiji, *Jazz as Critique*, 68. Doxum's "Culpa minha?" was echoed a few years later in Chile, in November 2019, when a group of hundreds of women with the feminist collective Las Tesis recited the verses "Y la culpa no era mía, ni donde estaba, ni como vestía. El violador, eres tú" (And the fault wasn't mine, not where I was, nor how I was dressed. You are the violator).

40. Lapassade and Rousselot, *Le rap, ou, la fureur de dire*, 90; Kelley, "Kickin' Reality," 194.

41. Barret, *Le rap ou l'artisanat de la rime*, 17.

42. Glissant, *Caribbean Discourse*, 149.

43. Preto, *Emicida*.

44. Garcia, "Um mapa," 218; "samba e rap são formas de sociabilidade e de consciência negras periféricas."

45. Qtd. in Treece, *Brazilian Jive*, 195. São Paulo–based rapper Criolo, who released several samba albums, has on multiple occasions called rap a direct heir of samba.

46. Derraik and Neto, *Onde a coruja dorme;* "Eu não posso cantar o amor quando nunca tive. Sou realista, canto a realidade."

47. Bezerra da Silva, "Poeta operário."

48. Carvalho, *Porous City*, 144.

49. Kelley, "Kickin' Reality," 209.

50. Cândido, "Dialética da malandragem," 77.

51. Cândido, 68–71.

52. Simas and Rufino, *Fogo no mato*, 84–85; Gates, *Signifying Monkey*, 5.

53. Rocha, "A dialética da marginalidade," 36.

54. Lorenz, "Embodying the Favela," 172–79; Derraik and Neto, *Onde a coruja dorme*.

55. Treece, *Brazilian Jive*, 38.

56. Thaíde & DJ Hum, "Febre do hip hop."

57. Relatos de Fortaleza, "Estilo de bandido."

58. Rebouças, "Histórias e sentimentos."

59. GOG, "A verdadeira malandragem."

60. GOG, "Mais uma história."

61. Smitherman, *Talkin and Testifyin*, 58.

62. MV Bill, "Traficando informação."

63. GOG, "Mais uma história."

64. Víctor Fowler qtd. in Zamora Montes, *Rapear una Cuba utópica*, 332; "No solo informar, sino formar."

65. Zalamea Traba, *Filosofía sintética*, 198; "de la in/formación a la trans/formación."

66. GOG, "Dia a dia da periferia."
67. Bezerra da Silva, "Meu bom juiz."
68. Wagner, Loitero and Fernando Ripol, "Hino do Samba do Congo," 3.
69. Zukofsky, *A,* 138.
70. Thaíde & DJ Hum, "Testemunha ocular"; Racionais MC's, "Mano na porta do bar"; MV Bill, "Testemunha ocular."
71. See Ibrahim, "Arab Spring," 106; Alim, *Roc the Mic Right;* Smitherman, "'Chain Remain the Same.'"
72. Danilo Albert "Rincon Sapiência" Ambrosio, personal interview, São Paulo, June 13, 2018.
73. Yoshinaga, *Nelson Triunfo,* 228.
74. Williams, *Marxism and Literature,* 190.
75. Nakassis, *Doing Style,* 119.
76. The practice of citation has a long history that I don't have space to develop here. Borrowing was widespread in Medieval and Renaissance music and poetry and is, as Honey Meconi asserts, "probably almost as old as music itself." See Meconi, *Early Musical Borrowing,* 1. Leo Treitler has demonstrated that contrary to the nineteenth-century written/improvised dichotomy, oral traditions such as Gregorian chant produced stable results over time. Conversely, musical "compositions" (from the Latin *componere,* to put together) drew heavily on improvisation, ornamentation, and borrowing, and performances of a written composition varied widely. See Treitler, *With Voice and Pen,* 11–12. In Medieval Spain, the practice of *contrafacta* (also called *a lo divino* poetry) consisted of quoting and revising secular texts and melodies in religious contexts. See Crosbie, "Medieval 'Contrafacta.'" It was not until the nineteenth century that Western music increasingly came to understand written scores to represent a fixed, stable, iterable, and ideal form of music (something like GOG's *partitura*), as opposed to "live" performance.
77. Dittmar, "Information Technology and Economic Change"; Orta Ruiz, *Décima y folclor,* 7–22; López Lemus, *La décima constante,* 199.
78. Díaz Frene, "Música popular," 34; Pasmanick, "'Decima' and 'Rumba.'" Although sung by both white and Black people, Cuban décimas were considered "música blanca o campesina" (white or peasant music). See Andino Castillo, *Discursos transgresores,* 36.
79. Díaz Frene, "Música popular," 21; "medio masivo de expresión pública."
80. The pie forzado, generally supplied by an audience member or opposing poet in the context of improvisational duels, determines the thematic content of the décima to be improvised as well as its final line. See Fischer, *Modernity Disavowed,* 85; Pasmanick, "'Decima' and 'Rumba,'" 256.
81. Albright, *Panaesthetics,* 237.
82. Ramazani, *Transnational Poetics,* 48.
83. Crook, *Focus,* 195.
84. Teperman, *Se liga no som,* 15; Salles, *Poesia revoltada,* 78; Yoshinaga, *Nelson Triunfo,* 309–10; Rappin' Hood, "Rap du bom—Remix."

85. Crook, *Focus*, 195–99.
86. Erivan "Produtos do Morro" Barbosa Sales and Lenny Fernandes, Personal Interview, Fortaleza, Brazil, March 30, 2015. *Côco de embolada* is the name for the competitive verbal game in which two repentistas exchange rapidly rhymed insults. *Baião* is the rhythmic formula on which embolada—and other popular musics in the Northeast, such as *forró*—are based.
87. RAPadura Xique-Chico, "Norte Nordeste me veste."
88. See Alim, *Roc the Mic Right;* Marrow and Baybutt, *Something from Nothing*.
89. Bakhtin, "Discourse in the Novel."
90. Criolo, "Duas de cinco."
91. Jobim, "Águas de março."
92. Drummond de Andrade, *Antologia poética*, 237.
93. Chéreau's award-winning 1994 film *La reine Margot*, based on the 1845 novel by Alexandre Dumas, depicts the violent sixteenth-century French religious wars between Catholics and Protestant Huguenots; hence Criolo's reference to church.
94. Bandeira, "Meninos Carvoeiros."
95. Cazuza, "Brasil."
96. Salles, *Poesia revoltada*, 60.
97. DMN, "H. Aço"; Rappin' Hood, "Rap du bom"; Atitude Feminina, "Mulher guerreira."
98. Antônio "Rappin' Hood" Luiz Jr., personal interview, São Paulo, July 20, 2018; Djonga, "Esquimó." Similar to the 1968 Memphis sanitation strike slogan "I am a man," Hood's "sujeito homen" implies that hip hop isn't merely youth culture, while also resignifying the "male subject" of a police report.
99. Roth-Gordon, "Conversational Sampling," 67.
100. Roth-Gordon, 69.
101. Levin Becker, *What's Good*, 106.
102. Bilby, "Sonorous Vestiges," 103–5. Both the Haitian pwen and the Brazilian ponto derive from religious song traditions of the Kikongo-speaking region of Central Africa.
103. Simas and Rufino, *Fogo no mato*, 25.
104. Alim, *Roc the Mic Right*, 18; see also Spady, Meghelli, and Alim, *Tha Global Cipha*, 5–6.
105. Pate, *In the Heart*, 34; Marrow and Baybutt, *Something from Nothing*.
106. Eshun, *More Brilliant than the Sun*, 13.
107. Okiji, *Jazz as Critique*, 29; Quintero Rivera, *Salsa, sabor y control!*, 80; Edwards, *Epistrophies*, 78.
108. Rhod D'Jyvens "D-Fi" Télémaque, personal interview, Port-au-Prince, July 12, 2017.
109. Xis et al., "Fortificando a desobediência."
110. Manzano, *Autobiografía del esclavo poeta*, 308.

111. Bilby, "Sonorous Vestiges," 104–5.

112. Ramsey, *Spirits and the Law*, 132; Richman, *Migration and Vodou*, 16.

113. Smith, *When the Hands Are Many*, 48. In the Anglophone world, Afro-diasporic signifying practices often take the form of "playing the dozens," which has been explicitly linked to rapping. See Marrow and Baybutt, *Something from Nothing*; Toop, *Rap Attack 2*, 32. See also Gates, *Signifying Monkey*, 100–101.

114. Several rappers have described the need to include lyric transcriptions with song uploads to clarify words that aren't easily discernible and to correct errors of third-party transcriptions.

115. Smitherman, *Talkin and Testifyin*, 147; Smitherman, "'Chain Remain the Same,'" 12.

116. Danilo Albert "Rincon Sapiência" Ambrosio, personal interview, São Paulo, June 13, 2018.

117. Smith and Joshi, *Rhymes in the Flow*, 82.

118. Moore, *Rock, the Primary Text*, 83.

119. Lord, *Singer of Tales*, 36; see also Parry, "Studies in the Epic Technique."

120. Barret, *Le rap ou l'artisanat de la rime*, 126; Morgan, *Real Hiphop*, 55.

121. Ong, *Orality and Literacy*, 11; Zumthor, *Oral Poetry*, 18.

122. Rose, *Black Noise*, 95.

123. Bernstein, "Hearing Voices," 143.

124. The popular bolero was written in 1936 by Mexican film composer Gonzalo Curiel.

125. Zamora Montes, *Rapear una Cuba utópica*, 73.

126. Smitherman, "'Chain Remain the Same,'" 15–16.

127. See Zamora Montes, *Rapear una Cuba utópica*, 209–34; Baker, *Buena Vista in the Club*, 322.

128. Smitherman, *Talkin and Testifyin*, 134.

129. Alim, *Roc the Mic Right*, 17.

130. Al2 El Aldeano, "Vereda tropical."

131. Alim, *Roc the Mic Right*, 149.

132. Stewart, "Rhyme and Freedom," 43.

133. This sort of critique was common, for example, when I attended the August 2019 Red Bull–sponsored Batalla de los Gallos freestyle competition in Havana.

134. Moten, *In the Break*, 52.

135. Weaver, "US Agency Infiltrated Cuban Hip-Hop Scene." In 2009, USAID sent Serbian operative Rajko Bozic to Havana to approach prominent rap groups, including Aldo and Los Aldeanos, to use hip hop as a platform for disseminating US-sanctioned values. Cuban rappers have categorically denied infiltration.

136. Moten, *In the Break*, 63.

137. Guillory, *Cultural Capital*, 77.

138. Michelino and Macedo, "Consciência fonológica."

139. Francisco Velto "Padêro MC" Barbosa Lima, personal interview, Fortaleza, Brazil, November 1, 2015; Adriana Martins, "A força do rap," *Diário do Nordeste,* March 4, 2017.

140. Doxum featuring Brisant, "Palavra de luta."

141. Lamazares, "São Paulo's Pixação," 201; Pereira, "Quem não é visto," 67; Oliveira, "Visibilidade e identidade"; Siwi, "Pixação."

142. Oliveira and Wainer, *Pixo.*

143. Pereira, "Quem não é visto," 68; "a estilização conferida às letras é um elemento que apenas faz sentido para quem é adepto dessa prática."

144. Paz, *Los hijos del limo,* 92; "un poema no solo es un objeto verbal sino que es una profesión de fe y un acto."

145. Rama, *La ciudad letrada,* 43.

146. Alim, *Roc the Mic Right,* 17.

147. Austin, *How to Do Things,* 120.

148. Ramazani, *Poetry and Its Others,* 133.

149. Bartlett, "Airshafts," 394.

150. Béthune, *Le rap,* 15–71; Perry, *Prophets of the Hood,* 33; Rose, *Hip Hop Wars,* 98.

151. Moten, *In the Break,* 51.

152. Edwards, *Epistrophies,* 22.

153. Edwards, 27.

154. Bauer, "Scat Singing," 303; Edwards, *Epistrophies,* 56.

155. Reis, "Meu rapjazz."

156. Reis.

157. Qtd. in Kauss, "Le spiralisme de Franketienne"; "saisir le réel dans la diversité de ses aspects."

158. Qtd. in Kauss; "une méthode d'approche pour essayer de saisir la réalité qui est toujours en mouvement . . . C'est là le miracle de l'art: essayer de capter le réel sans le tuer. Capter: c'est saisir, c'est immobiliser. Il s'agit d'appréhender sans étouffer."

159. Franketienne, *Rapjazz,* 13.

160. Stewart, *Reading Voices,* 25.

161. Lefebvre, *Rhythmanalysis,* 30.

162. Franketienne, *Rapjazz,* 40.

163. Rap kreyòl songs that reference Franketienne include C-PROJECT's "Hommage à Frank Etienne" (*Nou libre,* 2009) and Blay'Z's "Ghetto" (*Jis pou m di w,* 2016). Franketienne wrote the preface to Haitian rapper BIC's book of lyric poetry *Le Champ MagnéBIC* (2015).

164. Princess Eud, "Eudomination."

165. Kilomba, *Plantation Memories,* 132.

166. Ramsey, *Spirits and the Law,* 96. Drumming and dance have a long history of suppression and prohibition in French colonies (and elsewhere) over fear

that they incite popular revolt. See also Sublette, *Cuba and Its Music,* 9; Tryon, "Friendly Advice," 52; Epstein, *Sinful Tunes and Spirituals,* 29–30.

167. Hamilton, *Phonographic Memories,* 101.
168. Reed, *Soundworks,* 22.
169. Garcia, "Ouvindo Racionais MC's," 176; "o rap quer passar uma idéia sem deixar de envolver todo o corpo do ouvinte."
170. Ivan 13P, *Sabotage;* Sabotage, "Mun-Rá."
171. Travis, *Healing Power of Hip Hop;* Pate, *In the Heart,* 27.
172. Freire, *Pedagogia do oprimido,* 90.
173. Freire, 47–50.

6. Violence

1. Roumain, "Is Poetry Dead?," 22.
2. Barikad Crew, "Nou tout ka pran."
3. Fernandes, "A minha consciência é a minha arma."
4. Toop, *Rap Attack 2,* 58.
5. Fanon, *Wretched of the Earth,* 44.
6. Toop, *Rap Attack 2,* 14.
7. See Chang, *Can't Stop Won't Stop,* 41–66, 299–330; Morgan, *Real Hiphop,* 4, 32–33; Kajikawa, *Sounding Race in Rap Songs,* 71; Mane and Martinez-Belkin, *Autobiography of Gucci Mane,* xi. See also Julie Hinds, "The Famous 1989 Detroit Concert by N.W.A, Then and Now," *Detroit Free Press,* August 13, 2015, https://www.freep.com/story/entertainment/movies/2015/08/13/straight-outta-compton-movie-detroit-ice-cube-joe-louis-arena/31496317/.
8. Wilson and Kelling, "Broken Windows."
9. Rose, *Hip Hop Wars,* 40; Perry, *Prophets of the Hood,* 109–11.
10. Dennis, *Afro-Colombian Hip-Hop,* 65.
11. Rose, *Hip Hop Wars,* 37.
12. Butler, *Excitable Speech,* 13.
13. Butler, 9.
14. Austin, *How to Do Things,* 121.
15. Benjamin, "Critique of Violence," 293.
16. Benjamin, 293; McNulty, "Commandment against the Law," 34–37.
17. Benjamin, "Critique of Violence," 298.
18. Freire, *Pedagogia do oprimido,* 47.
19. Avelar, *Letter of Violence,* 23.
20. Adorno and Nery, "Crime e violências em São Paulo." See also Luiz Malavolta, "'Crack,' uma nova droga invade o país," *O Globo,* September 8, 1991, sec. O País. Violence in the São Paulo metropolitan area peaked in 1999 with a homicide rate of 52.2 per 100,000, with the peripheries of *zona sul, zona leste,* and *zona norte* reporting the highest concentration of homicides. As in New York City, São Paulo's peak in violence coincided with the introduction of crack cocaine to Brazil. In contrast, 2016 data from the World Bank, "International

homicides," https://data.worldbank.org/indicator/VC.IHR.PSRC.P5?locations=BR, placed countrywide murder rates in Cuba at 5 and in Haiti at 9, compared to 30 for Brazil. Brazil ranked in the top twenty in worldwide, while Cuba ranked lower than the United States.

21. Kolbe and Muggah, "Haiti's Urban Crime Wave?," 1–7.
22. Butler, *Excitable Speech*, 8.
23. Evaristo, "Da grafia-desenho de minha mãe," 17; "a função, a urgência, a dor, a necessidade e a esperança da escrita. É preciso comprometer a vida com a escrita ou é o inverso? Comprometer a escrita com a vida?"
24. Dukes, "Eu, a beleza e você."
25. Zumthor, *Oral Poetry*, 219.
26. Marcus, *Lipstick Traces*, 9.
27. Hattemer and Showers, "Heavy Metal Rock and Gangsta Rap."
28. Qtd. in Garcia, "Sobre uma cena," 222.
29. Reis, "Meu rapjazz."
30. El B, "Calles."
31. Jakobson, "Metaphoric and Metonymic Poles," 42.
32. Visão de Rua, "Amor e ódio."
33. Pate, *In the Heart*, 38.
34. Derrida, "Che cos'è la poesia?," 233.
35. Djonga, "Junho de 94."
36. Solano and Marques, "Junho de 94."
37. For theories of Black breath in the United States, see Crawley, *Blackpentecostal Breath*, and Kimberly Bain, "On Black Breath: A Theory and Praxis" (PhD diss., Princeton University, 2020).
38. Agawu, *Representing African Music*, 217.
39. GOG featuring Higo Melo and Zeca Baleiro, "O peso da palavra."
40. The mention of *lavra* is likely also a reference to Mário Chamie's book of poetry *Lavra lavra* (1962), featuring in its afterward a "manifesto didático" (didactic manifesto) or "Poema-práxis" (Praxis-poem). See Buarque de Hollanda, *Impressões de viagem*, 48–49.
41. Alim, *Roc the Mic Right*, 10.
42. Jaguaribe, "Favelas and the Aesthetics of Realism," 332.
43. Miranda, *Carolina Maria de Jesus*, 25.
44. Maria de Jesus, *Quarto de Despejo*, 52.
45. Evaristo, "Da grafia-desenho de minha mãe," 19.
46. Evaristo, 20–21.
47. Evaristo.
48. Miranda, *Carolina Maria de Jesus*, 37.
49. Miranda, 54.
50. Osmel Francis Turner, personal interview, Havana, August 19, 2014.
51. Luana Hansen, personal interview, São Paulo, July 5, 2018.
52. Toop, *Rap Attack 2*, 94.

53. Perry, "Geographies of Power." The term *guerreira* is employed among feminist activists more generally and was used in 2016 as a rallying cry for President Dilma Rousseff, reflected in the refrain "Dilma, guerreira da pátria brasileira" (Dilma, warrior of the Brazilian fatherland).

54. Visão de Rua, "Amor e ódio."

55. Atitude Feminina, "Mulher guerreira."

56. Garcia, "Pretas panteras."

57. Smith, Smith, and Frazier, "Combahee River Collective Statement," 22–23.

58. Smith, Smith, and Frazier, 27; Stephens, *Black Empire*, 1; Bloom and Martin, *Black against Empire*, 3.

59. Smith, Smith, and Frazier, "Combahee River Collective Statement," 19–21.

60. Saunders, *Cuban Underground Hip Hop*, 273.

61. Las Krudas, "Eres bella."

62. alvarez castillo, *La cerda punk*, 30–36.

63. Crenshaw, "Demarginalizing the Intersection."

64. Richard, *Masculino/femenino*, 20; "Hace falta pluralizar esa marca [de 'nosotras']."

65. Malcoms "Justicia" (18A16 Productions) organized and produced the 2012 album *La emancipación* (The emancipation), a two-disc compilation album and accompanying documentary featuring all-female rappers from Cuba. In his own songs, Malcoms often rhymed about machismo, gender equality, and female empowerment. However, such active support for women in hip hop is not the norm. On gender roles, see Smith, Smith, and Frazier, "Combahee River Collective Statement," 24; Davis, *Women, Race and Class*, 30.

66. Los Aldeanos featuring Papá Humbertico and El Discípulo, "El rap es guerra."

67. Segato, *La guerra contra las mujeres*, 113; "atravesando pruebas y enfrentando la muerte."

68. Díaz Frene, "Música popular."

69. Martí, *Martí*, 2:207–8; "su literatura no estaba en lo que escribían, sino en lo que hacían. Rimaban mal a veces, pero sólo pedantes y bribones se lo echarán en cara: porque morían bien. Las rimas eran allí hombres." See also Orta Ruiz, *Décima y folclor*, 35.

70. Zumthor, *Oral Poetry*, 219.

71. Moore, *Music and Revolution*, 137–39.

72. Buarque de Hollanda, *Impressões de viagem*, 41.

73. Feliú et al., "Créeme." The 2012 concert *Créeme* in the Cine Acapulco organized by artist Michel Mirabal, brought together prominent Cuban musicians of multiple genres, including several rappers and nueva trova artists. In the outro to the title track, a collaboration between singer Vicente Feliú and rappers Al2 El Aldeano, Maikel Extremo, Charly Mucharrima, Silvito "El Libre," Bárbaro

"El Urbano" Vargas, and Escuadrón Patriota, Escuadrón announces: "Dos generaciones, dos formas de pensar. Créeme como poetas de este tiempo, con otros argumentos, pero con el mismo amor por los nuestros" (Two generations, two ways of thinking. Believe me as poets of this time, with different arguments, but with the same love for ours).

74. Garabís, *Nación y ritmo,* 181–83.
75. Garabís, 185.
76. Rodríguez, "Debo partirme en dos."
77. Garabís, *Nación y ritmo,* 193–94; "identidad entre arte y combate, entre cantante y soldado."
78. Ribeiro, "'Seremos (otra vez) como el Che?,'" 216.
79. Rodríguez, "Canción para mi soldado."
80. Moore, *Music and Revolution,* 155.
81. Castro Ruz, "Conclusión de las reuniones con los intelectuales cubanos." The militarism of Cuban public speech during the 1960s also manifested in campaigns against illiteracy and idleness. For example, Sara Gómez's 1977 film *De cierta manera* (One way or another) glorifies the importance of work and study and favorably depicts the required military service for all males. The film also shines a positive light on the 1971 *ley contra la vagancia* (law against loafing), designed to increase productivity and eliminate vagrancy. See Gómez, *De cierta manera;* Kennedy, "Cuba's Ley Contra la Vagancia"; see also Whitfield, *Cuban Currency,* 147.
82. Baker, *Buena Vista in the Club,* 55–62; Zamora Montes, *Rapear una Cuba utópica,* 60, 288.
83. Castro Ruz, "Conclusión de las reuniones con los intelectuales cubanos."
84. Mano Armada, "Revolución." See also Zurbano Torres, "Se buscan," 9–12.
85. Debray, *¿Revolución en la revolución?,* 48; Guerra, *Visions of Power in Cuba,* 257–58.
86. Bárbaro "El Urbano" Vargas, personal interview, Havana, August 13, 2014.
87. Proyecto Chardo, "La comisión."
88. Althusser, "Ideology and Ideological State Apparatuses."
89. "Cubadisco premia producción de agrupación Calle 13," *Mesa Redonda,* April 28, 2012, http://mesaredonda.cubadebate.cu/noticias/2012/04/28/cubadisco-premia-produccion-de-agrupacion-calle-13/.
90. Tribu Mokoya, "Háblame."
91. Guerra, *Visions of Power in Cuba,* 319.
92. Baker, *Buena Vista in the Club,* 338.
93. Rensoli Medina, "Visiones paridoras," 58; "Los reguetoneros gozan aunque ocurra una masacre en sus conciertos; los raperos destruyen por poner duras reflexiones en la mente de tus contemporáneos."
94. Baker, *Buena Vista in the Club,* 137; see Zurbano Torres, "¡Mami, no quiero más reguetón!," 520.

95. Baker, *Buena Vista in the Club*, 135–37.
96. Gámez Torres, "Hearing the Change," 229.
97. Zamora Montes, *Rapear una Cuba utópica*, 121; Poole and Chu, *Reggaeton Revolución*; Zurbano Torres, "¡Mami, no quiero más reguetón!," 331.
98. El B, "Intro."
99. Baker, *Buena Vista in the Club*, 137.
100. Anónimo Consejo, "Procura."
101. Escuadrón Patriota, "Decadencia."
102. The notion of "rap for peace" is taken from a 2015 concert I attended by Padêro MC in Fortaleza, later released as the album *Um novo dia pela paz, pela vida* (A new day for peace, for life).
103. Fanon, *Wretched of the Earth*, 23.
104. McEnaney, *Acoustic Properties*, 140.
105. Baraka, "what does nonviolence mean?," 172; Baraka, *Selected Poetry*, 106.
106. See Chang, *Can't Stop Won't Stop*, 396–98.
107. McAlister, *Rara!*, 161; Averill and Yih, "Militarism in Haitian Music."
108. Averill and Yih, "Militarism in Haitian Music," 267–69.
109. Averill and Yih, 178–79.
110. McAlister, *Rara!*, 147–48.
111. Averill and Yih, "Militarism in Haitian Music," 281; McAlister, *Rara!*, 153.
112. McAlister, *Rara!*, 155–56; Averill, *Day for the Hunter*, 46. A similar phenomenon has been documented in New Orleans street bands. See Béthune, *Le rap*, 69.
113. Hallward, *Damming the Flood*, 24.
114. Hallward, 25–26.
115. Izolan, "Ou pa anyen nan zòn nan."
116. Benjamin, "Critique of Violence," 284.
117. Consciência Humana, "Lei da periferia."
118. Cidinho e Doca, "Rap das armas (Original Mix)."
119. Clausewitz, *On War*, 35.
120. Decreto Lei no. 2.848, Artigo 287 (December 7, 1940); "Fazer, publicamente, apologia de fato criminoso ou autor de crime."
121. Detentos do Rap, "Apologia ao crime."
122. Facção Central, "Isso aqui é uma guerra."
123. Teperman, *Se liga no som*, 102; Botelho, Garcia, and Rosa, "Três raps de São Paulo," 190.
124. Facção Central, "Apologia ao crime."
125. Tomashevsky, "Literary Genres," 79.
126. Barcia Paz, *West African Warfare*.
127. Nascimento, *O quilombismo*, 257–61.
128. Sharylaine, "Rei Zumbi"; Rappin' Hood, "Us guerreiro."

129. Rincon Sapiência, "Crime bárbaro."
130. Rincon Sapiência, "Intro." "música que foi inspirada no conto fictício do escritor Danilo Albert Ambrosio."
131. Mano Brown, "Marighella lembra Public Enemy e Racionais, diz Mano Brown," interview by Morris Kachani, *Folha de S. Paulo*, August 18, 2011, http://www1.folha.uol.com.br/ilustrada/961331-marighella-lembra-public-enemy-e-racionais-diz-mano-brown.shtml.
132. Racionais MC's, "Capítulo 4, Versículo 3."
133. Botelho, Garcia, and Rosa, "Três raps de São Paulo," 193; "a munição de Brown são as palavras entoadas."
134. Kehl, "Radicais, raciais, racionais," 98; "Vem de raciocínio, né? Um nome que tem a ver com as letras, que tem a ver com a gente."
135. Garcia, "Ouvindo Racionais MC's," 168.
136. Racionais MC's, "Fórmula mágica da paz." See also Garcia, "Elementos para a crítica da estética," 87; Hankin, "Rap e conscientização"; Preto, *Emicida*.
137. Mbembe, *Critique of Black Reason*, 29.
138. Carneiro, *O quilombo dos Palmares*, 32–33.
139. Robinson, *Black Marxism*, 147.
140. Trouillot, *Silencing the Past*.
141. Buck-Morss, *Hegel, Haiti, and Universal History*.
142. Aristide, *Haïti-Haitii?*, 32.
143. Aristide, *Haïti-Haitii?*, trans. Mildred Aristide, 16.
144. Aristide, *Haïti-Haitii?*, 44.
145. Glick, *Black Radical Tragic*, 1.
146. Harney and Moten, *Undercommons*, 96.
147. Original Rap Staff, "Tout moun se moun"; Aristide and Wargny, *Tout moun se moun*.
148. Original Rap Staff, "Tout moun se moun."
149. Barikad Crew, "Nou di non."
150. Blaze One, "Dekolonizasyon."
151. Ramsey, *Spirits and the Law*, 22; McAlister, "From Slave Revolt." The 2010 earthquake claimed the lives of hundreds of thousands of Haitians, among them several important rap kreyòl artists (including a member of Barikad Crew). Hip hop group Rap N Family and producer Mackendy Jeune eulogized victims in the powerful song "Lè m mouri" (When I die).
152. Blaze One, "Dekolonizasyon."
153. Blaze One.
154. Pellek, "Combating Tropical Deforestation in Haiti."
155. Glissant, *Caribbean Discourse*, 82–83; Price, *Maroon Societies*, 5. Haitian immigration to the Dominican Republic increased significantly following the fall of anti-Haitian dictator Rafael Trujillo in 1961 and throughout the Duvalier dictatorship. As of 2010, there were an estimated 800,000 Haitians living and working in the Dominican Republic, many having migrated there as seasonal

laborers to work in the sugarcane fields, where they lived in *batey* shantytowns. See Simmons, "Structural Violence as Social Practice," 10; Schuller, *Humanitarian Aftershocks in Haiti*, 107; Nunes, "Life," 214.

156. Dubois, *Haiti*, 92.
157. Dumesle, *Voyage dans le nord d'Hayti*, 88; Dubois, *Haiti*, 91.
158. Trouillot, *Haiti, State against Nation*, 44.
159. Casimir, *La cultura oprimida*, 50; Trouillot, *Haiti, State against Nation*, 43–44, 73; Fischer, *Modernity Disavowed*, 270.
160. Barthélemy, *Le pays en dehors*; Fick, *Making of Haiti*.
161. Quijano, "Colonialidad del poder."
162. Blaze One, "Dekolonizasyon."
163. Nixon, *Slow Violence*.
164. Glissant, *Caribbean Discourse*, 64.
165. West, "New Cultural Politics of Difference," 31.
166. D-Fi Powèt Revòlte, "Reflè m."
167. Césaire, *Lettre à Maurice Thorez*, 12; "Nous ne puissions donner à personne délégation pour penser pour nous; délégation pour chercher pour nous."
168. Baer, *Indigenous Vanguards*, 14.
169. Glissant, *Caribbean Discourse*, 169.
170. Kelley, "Kickin' Reality," 190; Levin Becker, *What's Good*, 150.
171. Bradley, *Book of Rhymes*, 168–69.
172. Portuguese poet Fernando Pessoa, for example, used hundreds of different pen names, which he preferred to frame as heteronyms.
173. Perry, *Prophets of the Hood*, 38.
174. Anna Virgínia Balloussier, "'Tem música que não canto mais', diz Mano Brown sobre letras machistas," *Folha de S. Paulo*, December 13, 2017, https://m.folha.uol.com.br/ilustrada/2017/12/1942874-tem-musica-que-nao-canto-mais-diz-mano-brown-sobre-letras-machistas.shtml.
175. Rose, *Hip Hop Wars*, 223.
176. Angela Ards, "Rhyme and Resist," *Nation*, July 8, 1999, https://www.thenation.com/article/archive/rhyme-and-resist/.
177. Neal, "Post-Industrial Soul," 376.
178. Theodor W. Adorno made a similar critique of Sartre's notion of "committed literature," arguing that "committed art" is no better than the notion of "art for art's sake," insofar as both flatten the dialectic between individual and society from which the potentially revolutionary impulse of art derives in the first place. See Adorno, "On Commitment."

Epilogue

1. See Derrida, "Law of Genre"; Butler, *Gender Trouble*.
2. Vazquez, *Listening in Detail*.

Discography

Al2 El Aldeano. "Vereda tropical." *Nos achicharraron*. 26Musas/Real70, 2010.
Al2 El Aldeano and Silvito "El Libre." "Manual para hacer una canción." *Los Kbayros*. La Aldea Production, 2009.
———. "Una hora de vida." *Los Kbayros*, 2009.
Alexey ..el tipo este.. (Obsesión). "Como fue." *Contar el rap: Antología de rap y hip-hop cubanos*. Malcoms Junco Duffay, 2017.
Anónimo Consejo. "Procura." *Hablando de algo*. SAGE, 2007.
Asap Fresh. "Balèn bouji." Single. Interstreet Recordings, 2017.
Atitude Feminina. "Mulher guerreira." *Nossa história*. GRV, 2016.
Barikad Crew. "Banm afem." *Goumen pou sa w kwè*. Sky Production, 2007.
———. "Nou di non." *Goumen pou sa w kwè*. Sky Production, 2007.
———. "Nou tout ka pran." *Goumen pou sa w kwè*. Sky Production, 2007.
———. "Pa koupe bwa." *Goumen pou sa w kwè*. Sky Production, 2007.
———. "Se konsa l ye." *Goumen pou sa w kwè*. Sky Production, 2007.
B. B. Boys. "B. B. Boys é nosso nome." Single, 1988.
Bezerra da Silva, José. "Meu bom juiz." *Alô malandragem maloca o flagrante*. BMG Brasil, 1986.
———. "Poeta operário." *Eu não sou santo*. BMG Brasil, 1990.
BIC. "Kokorat." Single. Tizon Dife Recordz, 2018.
Blay'Z. "Ghetto." *Jis pou m di w*, 2016.
———. "We Run It." *Jis pou trip Mixtape*. Piwo Records, 2013.
Blaze One. "Dekolonizasyon." *Dekolonizasyon*. SME, 2017.
———. "M ap rap." *Federal la*, 2017.
Brisa Flow. "As de cem." *Newen*, 2016.
———. "Veias abertas." *Newen*, 2016.
Cardi B. "Bodak Yellow." *Bodak Yellow*. Atlantic, 2017.
Cazuza. "Brasil." *Ideologia*. Philips Records, 1988.
Cidinho e Doca. "Rap da felicidade." *Eu só quero é ser feliz*. Spotlight Records, 1995.

———. "Rap das armas (Original Mix)." *Rap das armas*. Vidisco, SA, 2008.
Consciência Humana. "Lei da periferia." *Entre a adolescência e o crime*. Zimbabwe, 1998.
Criolo. "Duas de cinco." *Convoque seu buda*. Oloko Records, 2014.
Curiel, Gonzalo. "Vereda tropical." *Música tradicional cubana vol. 4*. Caribe Sound, 2013.
Daniel, Marc Cuvier "Asap Fresh." "Balèn bouji." Music video. Interstreet Recordings, 2017. https://www.youtube.com/watch?v=sFfocUS5qGo.
Dantas, Konrad, and MC Guimê. "Plaque de 100 (Clipe Oficial)." Music video. KondZilla, 2012. https://www.youtube.com/watch?v=gyXkaO0DxB8.
Dantas, Konrad, and Wellington "MC Boy do Charmes" França. "Nois de nave." Music video. CDF Produções, 2012. https://www.youtube.com/watch?v=FVx_t1HbdH8.
Delatour, Xavier, and Babas Denis. "Vèvè lokal." Music video. Lougawou Films, 2017. https://www.youtube.com/watch?v=AFOtwMbRY1E.
Detentos do Rap. "Apologia ao crime." *Detentos do rap*. Fieldzz, 1998.
D-Fi Powèt Revòlte. "Konsidere m beni." *Kwonik on GetoYout*. Evazyon Mizik, 2018.
———. "Castro sou map la." *R. O. D Rhod over D-Fi*. Evazyon Mizik, 2019.
———. "Reflè m." *Rev ak plim Mixtape*. Powèt Revòlte and Dream Recordz, 2016.
Djonga. "Esquimó." *Heresia*. Ceia, 2017.
———. "Junho de 94." *O menino que queria ser Deus*. CEIA, 2018.
DMN. "H. Aço." *H. Aço*. Agaéle Music, 1997.
Doxum, Bia. "Culpa minha?" *Máquina que gira*. Periferia Invisível, 2015.
Doxum, Bia, featuring Ni Brisant. "Palavra de luta." *Máquina que gira*. Periferia Invisível, 2015.
Dukes. "Eu, a beleza e você." *Íntimo*, 2014.
———. "Flor de aço." *Íntimo*, 2014.
El B. "América." *Dr. Jekyll and Mr. Hyde*, 2008.
———. "Calles." Single. Revolution Music, 2018.
———. "El periodista." *Mi filosofía*. Real 70, 2006.
———. "Intro." *Respeto*. Revolution Music, 2014.
Erivan "Produtos do Morro." "Embolada, repente e baião." *A vida é muito boa meu chapa*. Erivan Produtos do Morro, 2009.
Escuadrón Patriota. "Decadencia." *El legado*. Prófugo Productions, 2009.
Facção Central. "Apologia ao crime." *A marcha fúnebre prossegue*, Ouver Records 2001.
———. "Isso aqui é uma guerra." *Versos sangrentos*. 1dasul, 1999.
Fantom and Solis. "Si Desalin te la." *Salute, Vol. 3*. Tapajè Records, 2017.
Feliú, Vicente, Escuadrón Patriota, Charly Mucharrimas, Bárbaro "El Urbano," Silvito "El Libre," Al2, and Hermanos de Causa. "Créeme." *Créeme*. Michel Mirabal, 2012.

Fernandes, Lenny. "A minha consciência é a minha arma." Single, 2015.
Filosofia de Rua and Sharylaine. "É o hip hop." *Era pra ser assim,* 2018.
Frères Parent. "Veye-yo." *Veye-yo.* Michga Records, 1987.
Gabriel o Pensador. "Retrato de um playboy (Juventude perdida)." *Gabriel o Pensador.* Sony Music, 2000.
Garcia, Débora. "Pretas panteras." Music video. Oxalá Produções, July 28, 2017. https://www.youtube.com/watch?v=r-sMK5JL9mc.
GOG. "A verdadeira malandragem." *Das trevas à luz.* Zambia, 1998.
———. "Brasília periferia." *Dia a dia da periferia.* Só Balanço, 1994.
———. "Dia a dia da periferia." *Dia a dia da periferia.* Só Balanço, 1994.
———. "ISO 9000 do gueto." *Genival Oliveira Gonçalves.* Só Balanço, 2015.
———. "Mais uma história." *CPI da favela.* Zambia, 2000.
———. "Sonhos latinos." *Tarja preta.* Só Balanço, 2004.
———. "Universo gueto." *Mumm rá high tech.* GOG, 2017.
GOG featuring Higo Melo and Zeca Baleiro. "O peso da palavra." *Genival Oliveira Gonçalves.* Só Balanço, 2015.
Hermanos de Causa. "Gracias Hip Hop." *Sale a caminar,* 2010.
Izolan. "Ou pa anyen nan zòn nan." Single. OYE OYE Records, 2016.
Jeune, Mackendy, and Rap N Family. "Lè m mouri." Music video, 2011. https://www.youtube.com/watch?v=aqU64mxT1IA.
Jobim, Antonio Carlos. "Águas de março." *Waters of March / Águas de março.* MCA Records, 1973.
Jor, Jorge Ben. "Mas, que nada!" *Samba esquema novo.* Universal Music, 1963.
Kanis and Lolo. "Vèvè lokal." *Enèji.* Kanis Music LLC, 2017.
Las Krudas. "Eres bella." *La emancipación, vol. 1.* 18A16 Producciones, 2012.
Los Aldeanos. "Protestando." *Censurados,* 2003.
Los Aldeanos featuring Papá Humbertico and El Discípulo. "El rap es guerra." *El Atropello.* Real 70, 2009.
Los Orishas. "A lo cubano." *A lo cubano.* EMI, 1999.
Lord Kitchener. "Pan in A Minor." *Forever Vol. 1.* Charlie's Records / VP Records, 2009.
Malcoms "Justicia." "La ciudad no duerme." *Realismo sucio y arte pop.* 18A16 Producciones, 2015.
Mano Armada. "Revolución dentro de la Revolución." *Revolución dentro de la Revolución.* Papá Humbertico, 2006.
Master Dji. "Sispann." Single, 1986.
———. "Tan pou tan." *Politik pa m'.* Bwa Patat Records, 1990.
Matos, Flora. "Ela quer ser minha namorada." *Eletrocardiograma,* 2017.
———. "Preta da quebrada." *Eletrocardiograma,* 2017.
MC Boy do Charmes. "Nois de nave." *Boy do Charmes.* Berber Mobile, 2013.
Moré, Benny. "Cómo fue." *Boleros inolvidables.* Caribe Sound, 2018.
MV Bill. "Testemunha ocular." *Vitória pra quem acordou agora e vida longa pra quem nunca dormiu.* Chapa Preta, 2014.

———. "Traficando informação." *Traficando informação*. Natasha Records / Zambia, 1999.
Nas. "Life's a Bitch." *Illmatic*. Columbia Records, 1994.
NG La Banda. "Santa palabra." *Cabaret panorámico*. BMG International, 1994.
Nono. "Rendición de cuenta." *Contar el rap: Antología de rap y hip-hop cubanos*. Malcoms Junco Duffay, 2017.
Original Rap Staff. "Tout moun se moun." *Ké PóPóz*. Antilles Mizik, 1990.
———. "Whose Style Is This?" *Ké PóPóz*. Antilles Mizik, 1990.
Padêro MC. "Um novo dia pela paz, pela vida." *Padêro MC ao vivo em Fortaleza*. Coletivo Maloqueria, 2016.
Papá Humbertico. "5,11,83, Hip Hop." *Contar el rap: Antología de rap y hip-hop cubanos*. Malcoms Junco Duffay, 2017.
Parra, Violeta. "Gracias a la vida." *Las ùltimas composiciones*. RCA Victor, 1966.
Paz, Issa, and Sara Donato. "Agradecimentos." *Rap Plus Size*, 2016.
PIC. "Lè m ap ekri." *Lè m ap ekri Mixtape Vol. 1*. Fred Hype Prodz, 2015.
Princess Eud. "Eudomination." *Eudomination*. Teamlimyewouj, 2017.
Projota. "A milenar arte de meter o louco." *A milenar arte de meter o louco*. Universal Music International, 2017.
Proyecto Chardo. "La comisión." *La comisión depuradora*. Real 70, 2007.
Racionais MC's. "Capítulo 4, Versículo 3." *Sobrevivendo no inferno*. Cosa Nostra, 1997.
———. "Da ponte pra cá." *Nada como um dia após o outro dia*. Cosa Nostra, 2002.
———. "Fórmula mágica da paz." *Sobrevivendo no inferno*. Cosa Nostra, 1997.
———. "Mano na porta do bar." *Raio-X do Brasil*. Zimbabwe Records, 1993.
———. "Periferia é periferia (em qualquer lugar)." *Sobrevivendo no inferno*. Cosa Nostra, 1997.
RAPadura Xique-Chico. "Norte Nordeste me veste." *Fita embolada do engenho Vol. 1*. 1/4 D'Engenho Produções, 2010.
Rappin' Hood. "Rap du bom." *Sujeito Homen*. Trama, 2001.
———. "Rap du bom—Remix." *Sujeito Homen*. Trama, 2001.
———. "Us guerreiro." *Sujeito Homem 2*. Trama, 2005.
Rebouças, Carolina. "Histórias e sentimentos." Single. Dropout Produções, 2016.
Reis, Tássia. "Meu rapjazz." *Tássia Reis*, 2014.
Relatos de Fortaleza. "Estilo de bandido." *O que eu fui e o que eu sou*. Erivan Produtos do Morro, 2009.
Rincon Sapiência. "Crime bárbaro." *Galanga livre*. Boia Fria Produções, 2017.
———. "Intro." *Galanga livre*. Boia Fria Produções, 2017.
Rockfam. "Jodi pa demen." *Sa w pa ka konprann*. DHAC Records / Rockfam Records, 2007.
Rodríguez, Silvio. "Canción para mi soldado." *Tríptico Vol. 3*. Ojalá, 1984.
———. "Debo partirme en dos." *Días y flores*. Sony BMG Music Entertainment, 1975.

The Roots featuring Common. "Act Too (The Love of My Life)." *Things Fall Apart*. Geffen Records, 1999.
Sabotage. "Mun-Rá." *Trilha sonora do filme O Invasor*. YB Music, 2002.
———. "Rap é compromisso." *Rap é compromisso!* Cosa Nostra, 2000.
Sánchez, Erick. "Tirado en la calle." *Tirado en la Calle (Sobras Escogidas)*, 2014.
Sharylaine. "Livre no mundo." Single. Leopapel / Cogumarola Produções, 2012.
———. "Nossos dias." *Consciência Black*. Zimbabwe, 1990.
———. "Rei Zumbi." Single. DJ Giba, 2013.
Solano, Gabriel, and Gustavo Pereira "Djonga" Marques. "Junho de 94." Music video. Solano Air View and Ceia Ent, 2018. https://www.youtube.com/watch?v=hTUEjPmX0tE.
Sugar Hill Gang. "Rapper's Delight." Single. Sugar Hill Records, 1979.
Thaíde & DJ Hum. "Febre do hip hop." *Assim caminha a humanidade*. Trama, 2000.
———. "Sr. Tempo Bom." *Preste atenção*. Brava Gente / Dueto Edições, 1996.
———. "Testemunha ocular." *Sampa rap*. Sigla, 1996.
Thaíde & DJ Hum, Marcelo D2, Max B. O., MC Kamau, Paulo Napoli, and SP Funk. "Viagem na rima." *Assim caminha a humanidade*. Trama, 2000.
Thaíde & DJ Hum featuring Sabotage. "Vinheta 3." *Assim caminha a humanidade*. Trama, 2000.
Tribu Mokoya. "Háblame." *Tribu Mokoya*. Champion Records, 2011.
Vargas, Bárbaro "El Urbano." "Se respira." *88.01.18,* 2013.
Visão de Rua. "A noiva do Thock." *A noiva do Thock*. Warlok Records, 2004.
———. "Amor e ódio." *A noiva do Thock*. Warlok Records, 2004.
War. "The World Is a Ghetto." *The World Is a Ghetto*. United Artists Records, 1972.
Wendyyy. "À qui veut l'entendre." *King rete king*. Traka Music Group, 2018.
———. "Ayibobo." *King rete king*. Traka Music Group, 2018.
———. "Lè m vle." *King rete king*. Traka Music Group, 2018.
Xis, Telmary Díaz, MC White, Papo Record, and 100% Original. "Fortificando a desobediência." *Fortificando a desobediência*. Warner Music Brasil, 2001.
Yomil y el Dany. "Evolutions." *Sobredosis*. Jungl Yomil y el Dany, 2016.
———. "Ni santas ni finas." *Dopados de la mente*, 2018.
———. "Sacrifice." *Dopados de la mente*, 2018.

Bibliography

Abidde, Sabella Ogbobode, and Charity Manyeruke, eds. *Fidel Castro and Africa's Liberation Struggle.* Lanham, MD: Lexington Books, 2020.

Acosta, Leonardo. *Otra visión de la música popular cubana.* 2nd ed. Havana: Ediciones Museo de la Música, 2014.

Adéèkó, Adélékè. "'Writing' and 'Reference' in Ifá." In *Ifá Divination, Knowledge, Power, and Performance,* edited by Jacob K. Olupona and Rowland O. Abiodun, 66–87. Bloomington: Indiana University Press, 2016.

Adorno, Sérgio, and Marcelo Batista Nery. "Crime e violências em São Paulo: Retrospectiva teórico-metodológica, avanços, limites e perspectivas futuras." *Cadernos Metrópole* 21, no. 44 (April 2019): 169–94. https://doi.org/10.1590/2236-9996.2019-4408.

Adorno, Theodor W. "On Commitment." Translated by Francis McDonagh. *Performing Arts Journal* 3, no. 2 (1978): 3–11.

———. "On Lyric Poetry and Society." In *Notes to Literature,* edited by Rolf Tiedemann, translated by Shierry Weber Nicholsen, 37–54. New York: Columbia University Press, 1991.

Agamben, Giorgio. *The End of the Poem: Studies in Poetics.* Translated by Daniel Heller-Roazen. Stanford, CA: Stanford University Press, 1999.

———. *The Time that Remains: A Commentary on the Letter to the Romans.* Stanford, CA: Stanford University Press, 2005.

Agawu, Kofi. *African Rhythm: A Northern Ewe Perspective.* Cambridge, UK: Cambridge University Press, 1995.

———. *Representing African Music: Postcolonial Notes, Queries, Positions.* New York: Routledge, 2003.

Albright, Daniel. *Panaesthetics: On the Unity and Diversity of the Arts.* New Haven, CT: Yale University Press, 2014.

Alim, H. Samy. "Hip Hop Nation Language." In *The Oxford Handbook of African American Language,* edited by Jennifer Bloomquist, Lisa J. Green, and Sonja L. Lanehart. Oxford, UK: Oxford University Press, 2015. https://doi.org/10.1093/oxfordhb/9780199795390.013.49.

———. *Roc the Mic Right: The Language of Hip Hop Culture.* New York: Routledge, 2006.

———. "Straight Outta Compton, Straight Aus München: Global Linguistic Flows, Identities, and the Politics of Language in a Global Hip Hop Nation." In *Global Linguistic Flows: Hip Hop Cultures, Youth Identities, and the Politics of Language,* edited by H. Samy Alim, Awad Ibrahim, and Alastair Pennycook, 1–24. New York: Routledge, 2009.

———. "Translocal Style Communities: Hip Hop Youth as Cultural Theorists of Style, Language, and Globalization." *Pragmatics* 19, no. 1 (March 1, 2009): 103–27. https://doi.org/10.1075/prag.19.1.06ali.

Alim, H. Samy, Awad Ibrahim, and Alastair Pennycook, eds. *Global Linguistic Flows: Hip Hop Cultures, Youth Identities, and the Politics of Language.* New York: Routledge, 2009.

Allucci, Fernanda, Ketty Valencio, and Renata R. Allucci. *Mulheres de palavra: Um retrato das mulheres no rap de São Paulo.* São Paulo: Governo do Estado de São Paulo; Secretaria da Cultura, 2016.

Alonso, Diego. "La verdad y las pruebas. Cuatro tesis sobre la literatura testimonial de Rodolfo Walsh." *Latin American Literary Review* 39, no. 78 (2011): 95–116.

Althusser, Louis. "Ideology and Ideological State Apparatuses (Notes towards an Investigation)." In *Lenin and Philosophy and Other Essays,* translated by Ben Brewster, 127–88. New York: Monthly Review Press, 2001.

Amaral, Mônica G. T. do. *O que o rap diz e a escola contradiz: Um estudo sobre a arte de rua e a formação da juventude na periferia de São Paulo.* São Paulo: Alameda, 2017.

Anderson, Benedict. *Imagined Communities: Reflections on the Origin and Spread of Nationalism.* New York: Verso, 2006.

Andino Castillo, Yorisel. *Discursos transgresores: Rupturas en el canon musical cubano.* Santiago, Cuba: Ediciones Santiago, 2015.

Andrade, Mário de. *Ensaio sobre a música brasileira.* 3rd ed. São Paulo: Livraria Martins, 1972.

Ángel, Roberto. "Defensa de lo local en Nuestra América y Coney Island de José Martí: El ensayo como un espacio para la ideología dentro de las raíces hispanoamericanas." *Arbor* 191, no. 774 (August 30, 2015): a254, 2–8. https://doi.org/10.3989/arbor.2015.774n4009.

Angeli, Caue, and Hernani Ramos, dirs. *Triunfo.* Canal Aberto, 2014. https://vimeo.com/115718252.

Apter, Andrew. "Recasting Ifá: Historicity and Recursive Recollection in Ifá Divination Texts." In *Ifá Divination, Knowledge, Power, and Performance,* edited by Jacob K. Olupona and Rowland O. Abiodun, 43–49. Bloomington: Indiana University Press, 2016.

Aristide, Jean-Bertrand. *Haiti-Haitii?: Philosophical Reflections for Mental Decolonization.* Translated by Mildred Aristide. Boulder, CO: Paradigm Publishers, 2011.

———. *Haïti-Haitii? Pwezi filozofik pou dekolonizasyon mantal.* Port-au-Prince: Henri Deschamps, 2011.
Aristide, Jean-Bertrand, and Christophe Wargny. *Tout moun se moun: Tout homme est un homme.* Paris: Editions du Seuil, 1992.
Auden, W. H. *Selected Poems.* Edited by Edward Mendelson. New York: Vintage Books, 1979.
Austin, J. L. *How to Do Things with Words.* Oxford, UK: Oxford University Press, 1962.
Avelar, Idelber. *The Letter of Violence: Essays on Narrative, Ethics, and Politics.* New York: Palgrave Macmillan, 2006.
Averill, Gage. *A Day for the Hunter, A Day for the Prey: Popular Music and Power in Haiti.* Chicago, IL: University of Chicago Press, 1997.
Averill, Gage, and Yuen-Ming David Yih. "Militarism in Haitian Music." In *African Diaspora: A Musical Perspective,* edited by Ingrid Monson, 263–89. New York: Routledge, 2004.
Baer, Ben Conisbee. *Indigenous Vanguards: Education, National Liberation, and the Limits of Modernism.* New York: Columbia University Press, 2019.
Baker, Geoffrey. *Buena Vista in the Club: Rap, Reggaetón, and Revolution in Havana.* Durham, NC: Duke University Press, 2011.
———. "Cuba Rebelión: Underground Music in Havana." *Latin American Music Review / Revista de Música Latinoamericana* 32, no. 1 (2011): 1–38.
———. "¡Hip Hop, Revolución! Nationalizing Rap in Cuba." *Ethnomusicology* 49, no. 3 (2005): 368–402.
Bakhtin, Mikhail M. "Discourse in the Novel." In *The Dialogic Imagination: Four Essays,* 259–422. Austin: University of Texas Press, 1981.
Balibar, Etienne. "The Nation Form: History and Ideology." Translated by Immanuel Wallerstein and Chris Turner. *Review, A Journal of the Fernand Braudel Center* 13, no. 3 (1990): 329–61.
Bandeira, Manuel. "Meninos Carvoeiros." In *This Earth, That Sky: Poems by Manuel Bandeira,* translated by Candace Slater, 58. Berkeley: University of California Press, 1989.
Baraka, Amiri. *Selected Poetry of Amiri Baraka / LeRoi Jones.* New York: Morrow, 1979.
———. "what does nonviolence mean?" In *Home: Social Essays,* 155–78. New York: Akashic Books, 2009.
Barbosa dos Santos, Fabio Luis. "Fundamentos políticos de Nuestra América." In *José Martí y Nuestra América,* edited by Adalberto Santana, 123–52. Mexico City: Universidad Nacional Autónoma de México, 2013.
Barcia Paz, Manuel. *West African Warfare in Bahia and Cuba: Soldier Slaves in the Atlantic World, 1807–1844.* Oxford, UK: Oxford University Press, 2014.
Barret, Julien. *Le rap ou l'artisanat de la rime: Stylistique de l'egotrip.* Paris: L'Harmattan, 2009.

Barthélemy, Gérard. *Le pays en dehors: Essai sur l'univers rural haïtien.* Montreal: CIDIHCA, 1989.
Bartlett, Andrew. "Airshafts, Loudspeakers, and the Hip Hop Sample: Contexts and African American Musical Aesthetics." In *That's the Joint!: The Hip-Hop Studies Reader,* edited by Mark Anthony Neal and Murray Forman, 393–406. New York: Routledge, 2004.
Batista, Tarlis. "Os Blacks no embalo do soul." *Manchete,* September 11, 1976.
Baucom, Ian. *Specters of the Atlantic: Finance Capital, Slavery, and the Philosophy of History.* Durham, NC: Duke University Press, 2005.
Bauer, William R. "Scat Singing: A Timbral and Phonemic Analysis." *Current Musicology,* nos. 71–73 (2001): 303–23.
Belt, Cynthia B. "Rap Music as Prophetic Utterance." In *The Black Church and Hip Hop Culture: Toward Bridging the Generational Divide,* edited by Emmett G. Price III. Lanham, MD: Scarecrow Press, 2011.
Benjamin, Walter. "Critique of Violence." In *Reflections: Essays, Aphorisms, Autobiographical Writing,* edited by Peter Demetz, translated by Edmund Jephcott, 277–300. New York: Schocken Books, 1986.
———. *Illuminations.* New York: Schocken Books, 2007.
Bernstein, Charles. "Hearing Voices." In *The Sound of Poetry, the Poetry of Sound,* edited by Marjorie Perloff and Craig Douglas Dworkin, 142–48. Chicago, IL: University of Chicago Press, 2009.
———. "Introduction." In *Close Listening: Poetry and the Performed Word,* edited by Charles Bernstein, 3–28. New York: Oxford University Press, 1998.
Béthune, Christian. *Le rap: Une esthétique hors la loi.* Paris: Autrement, 1999.
Beverley, John. *Testimonio: On The Politics of Truth.* Minneapolis: University of Minnesota Press, 2004.
Bilby, Kenneth. "'Sonorous Vestiges': Stanley Stein's Brazilian Recordings in Hemispheric Perspective." In *Cangoma Calling: Spirits and Rhythms of Freedom in Brazilian Jongo Slavery Songs,* edited by Pedro Meira Monteiro and Michael Stone, 99–106. Luso-Asio-Afro-Brazilian Studies and Theory 3. Independently published, University of Massachusetts Dartmouth, 2013. https://www.umassd.edu/media/umassdartmouth/portgrad/Monteiro-Stone.CangomaCalling.OneFileBook.margin0.8in.1.7mb.pdf.
Bloom, Joshua, and Waldo E. Martin. *Black against Empire: The History and Politics of the Black Panther Party.* Oakland: University of California Press, 2016.
Boal, Augusto. *Teatro do oprimido.* 6th ed. Rio de Janeiro: Civilização Brasileira, 1991.
Bocafloja. "Collective Amnesia." In *La Verdad: An International Dialogue on Hip Hop Latinidades,* edited by Melissa Castillo-Garsow and Jason Nichols, 125–32. Columbus: The Ohio State University Press, 2016.

Bocskay, Stephen. "Undesired Presences: Samba, Improvisation, and Afro-Politics in 1970s Brazil." *Latin American Research Review* 52, no. 1 (July 19, 2017): 64–78. https://doi.org/10.25222/larr.71.

Borge, Jason. *Tropical Riffs: Latin America and the Politics of Jazz*. Durham, NC: Duke University Press, 2018.

Borges-Triana, Joaquín. "Yo creo que Los Aldeanos. . . . " *El Caimán Barbudo*, January 24, 2013. http://www.caimanbarbudo.cu/musica/2013/01/yo-creo-que-los-aldeanos/.

Botelho, Guilherme, Walter Garcia, and Alexandre Rosa. "Três raps de São Paulo: 'Política' (1994), 'O menino do morro' (2003) e 'Mil faces de um homem leal (Marighella)' (2012)." *Nuevo mundo mundos nuevos*, December 1, 2015. https://doi.org/10.4000/nuevomundo.68717.

Boym, Svetlana. *The Future of Nostalgia*. New York: Basic Books, 2008.

Bradley, Adam. *Book of Rhymes: The Poetics of Hip Hop*. New York: Civitas Books, 2009.

Brown, Calvin S. "The Relations between Music and Literature as a Field of Study." *Comparative Literature* 22, no. 2 (1970): 97–107. https://doi.org/10.2307/1769755.

Brown, Jacqueline Nassy. "Black Liverpool, Black America, and the Gendering of Diasporic Space." *Cultural Anthropology* 13, no. 3 (1998): 291–325.

Brown, Timothy S. "'Keeping It Real' In a Different 'Hood: (African-)Americanization and Hip Hop in Germany." In *The Vinyl Ain't Final: Hip Hop and the Globalization of Black Popular Culture*, edited by Dipannita Basu and Sidney J. Lemelle, 137–50. London: Pluto, 2006.

Buarque de Hollanda, Heloisa. *Impressões de viagem: CPC, vanguarda e desbunde, 1960/70*. 5th ed. Rio de Janeiro: Aeroplano, 2005.

Buck-Morss, Susan. *Dreamworld and Catastrophe: The Passing of Mass Utopia in East and West*. Cambridge, MA: MIT Press, 2000.

———. *Hegel, Haiti, and Universal History*. Pittsburgh, PA: University of Pittsburgh Press, 2009.

Burton, Justin Adams. *Posthuman Rap*. New York: Oxford University Press, 2017.

Butler, Judith. *Excitable Speech: A Politics of the Performative*. New York: Routledge, 1997.

———. *Gender Trouble: Feminism and the Subversion of Identity*. New York: Routledge, 2006.

Butler, Kim D. *Freedoms Given, Freedoms Won: Afro-Brazilians in Post-abolition São Paulo and Salvador*. New Brunswick, NJ: Rutgers University Press, 1998.

Caldeira, Teresa Pires do Rio. *City of Walls: Crime, Segregation, and Citizenship in São Paulo*. Berkeley: University of California Press, 2000.

Camacho Moreira, Juanito. "Confluencias del funk y rap en Cuba." In *Contar el rap*, edited by Grizel Hernández Baguer and Malcoms Junco Duffay, 545–57. Havana: Ediciones Cidmuc, 2017.

Camargos, Roberto. *Rap e política: Percepções da vida social brasileira.* São Paulo: Boitempo Editorial, 2015.
Campt, Tina. "The Crowded Space of Diaspora: Intercultural Address and the Tensions of Diasporic Relation." *Radical History Review* 2002, no. 83 (April 1, 2002): 94–113. https://doi.org/10.1215/01636545-2002-83-94.
———. *Listening to Images.* Durham, NC: Duke University Press, 2017.
Cândido, Antônio. "Dialética da malandragem." *Revista do Instituto de Estudos Brasileiros,* no. 8 (1970): 67–89. https://doi.org/10.11606/issn.2316-901X.v0i8p67-89.
———. "O direito à literatura." In *Vários Escritos,* 5th ed., 171–93. Rio de Janeiro: Oura sobre Azul, 2011.
Cano, Rubén López. "Music and Post-Communist Subjectivities in Cuba." In *Music and Youth Culture in Latin America: Identity Construction Processes from New York to Buenos Aires,* edited by Pablo Vila, 132–56. Oxford, UK: Oxford University Press, 2014.
Caramante, André. "Os quatro pretos mais perigosos do Brasil." *Rolling Stone,* December 6, 2013. https://rollingstone.uol.com.br/edicao/edicao-86/racionais-mcs-quatro-pretos-mais-perigosos-do-brasil/.
Carneiro, Édison. *O quilombo dos Palmares.* São Paulo: Companhia Editora Nacional, 1958.
Carpentier, Alejo. "La música popular cubana." *Signos* 2, no. 3 (August 1971): 7–12.
Carvalho, Bruno. *Porous City: A Cultural History of Rio de Janeiro (From the 1810s Onward).* Liverpool: Liverpool University Press, 2013.
Cascardi, Anthony J. "'Orphic Fictions': Poesía and Poiesis in Cervantes." In *Poiesis and Modernity in the Old and New Worlds,* edited by Anthony J. Cascardi and Leah Middlebrook, 19–42. Nashville, TN: Vanderbilt University Press, 2012.
Casimir, Jean. *La cultura oprimida.* Mexico City: Nueva Imagen, 1980.
castillo, constanzx alvarez. *La cerda punk: Ensayos desde un feminismo gordo, lésbiko, antikaptialista y antiespecista.* Valparaíso: Trío, 2014.
Castillo-Garsow, Melissa, and Jason Nichols, eds. *La Verdad: An International Dialogue on Hip Hop Latinidades.* Columbus: The Ohio State University Press, 2016.
Castro Ruz, Fidel. "Conclusión de las reuniones con los intelectuales cubanos, efectuadas en la Biblioteca Nacional el 16, 23 y 30 de junio de 1961." Speech. Departamento de Versiones Taquigráficas del Gobierno Revolucionario, June 16, 1961. http://www.cuba.cu/gobierno/discursos/1961/esp/f300661e.html.
———. "En conmemoración del XXI aniversario del Ataque al Cuartel Moncada, efectuado en la explanada frente al estado mayor del ejército central." Speech. Departamento de Versiones Taquigráficas del Gobierno Revolucionario, July 26, 1974. http://www.cuba.cu/gobierno/discursos/1974/esp/f260774e.html.

Cave, Alfred A. "Thomas More and the New World." *Albion: A Quarterly Journal Concerned with British Studies* 23, no. 2 (1991): 209–29. https://doi.org/10.2307/4050603.
Césaire, Aimé. *Lettre à Maurice Thorez*. 3rd ed. Paris: Présence Africaine, 1956.
———. *Notebook of a Return to the Native Land*. Edited by Clayton Eshleman and Annette Smith. Translated by Annette Smith, Annie Pritchard, Clayton Eshleman, and Mireille Rosello. Middletown, CT: Wesleyan University Press, 2001.
Césaire, Suzanne. "Misère d'une poésie: John Antoine-Nau." *Tropiques*, no. 4 (1942): 48–50.
Cestaro, Lucas Ricardo. "A SAGMACS e o estudo da 'Aglomeração Paulistana.'" *URBANA: Revista Eletrônica do Centro Interdisciplinar de Estudos Sobre a Cidade* 5, no. 1 (July 10, 2013): 6–24. https://doi.org/10.20396/urbana.v5i1.8635085.
Chang, Jeff. *Can't Stop Won't Stop: A History of the Hip-Hop Generation*. New York: Picador, 2005.
———. "It's a Hip-Hop World." *Foreign Policy*, no. 163 (December 2007): 58–65.
Chuck D. *Fight the Power: Rap, Race, and Reality*. New York: Dell, 1998.
Clark, Kenneth Bancroft. *Dark Ghetto: Dilemmas of Social Power*. New York: Harper and Row, 1965.
Clausewitz, Carl von. *On War*. Edited by Beatrice Heuser. Translated by Michael Howard and Peter Paret. New York: Oxford University Press, 2006.
Clifford, James. "Diasporas." *Cultural Anthropology* 9, no. 3 (1994): 302–38.
Cohen, J. M., César Calvo, José Lezama Lima, José Z. Tallet, and Manuel Díaz Martínez. "Dictamen del jurado del concurso UNEAC," 1968. http://www.habanaelegante.com/Spring2001/Barco.html.
Cohen, Steven. "When Castro Came to Harlem." *New Republic*, March 21, 2016. https://newrepublic.com/article/131793/castro-came-harlem.
Condry, Ian. *Hip-Hop Japan: Rap and the Paths of Cultural Globalization*. Durham, NC: Duke University Press, 2006.
Contreras, Felix. "The Meteoric Rise of Latin Urban Explained." Podcast. *Alt.Latino* (NPR), February 28, 2020. https://www.npr.org/2020/02/28/810303100/the-meteoric-rise-of-latin-urban-explained.
Cornejo Polar, Antonio. *Escribir en el aire: Ensayo sobre la heterogeneidad sociocultural en las literaturas andinas*. Edited by Mabel Moraña and Jesús Díaz Caballero. Lima: Centro de Estudios Literarios Antonio Cornejo Polar, 2003.
Cover, Robert M. "Nomos and Narrative." *Harvard Law Review* 97, no. 1 (November 1983): 4–68.
Crawley, Ashon T. *Blackpentecostal Breath: The Aesthetics of Possibility*. New York: Fordham University Press, 2017.
Crenshaw, Kimberlé. "Demarginalizing the Intersection of Race and Sex: A Black Feminist Critique of Antidiscrimination Doctrine, Feminist Theory and

Antiracist Politics." *University of Chicago Legal Forum*, no. 1 (1989). https://chicagounbound.uchicago.edu/uclf/vol1989/iss1/8.

Crook, Larry. *Focus: Music of Northeast Brazil.* New York: Routledge, 2009.

Crosbie, John. "Medieval 'Contrafacta': A Spanish Anomaly Reconsidered." *Modern Language Review* 78, no. 1 (1983): 61–67. https://doi.org/10.2307/3728326.

Cross, Peter. "Soviet Perestroika: The Cuban Effect." *Third World Quarterly* 13, no. 1 (1992): 143–58.

Culler, Jonathan. *Theory of the Lyric.* Cambridge, MA: Harvard University Press, 2015.

Cunha, Euclides da. *Os sertões.* Rio de Janeiro: Fundação Darcy Ribeiro, 2014.

Davis, Angela Y. *Women, Race and Class.* New York: Vintage Books, 1983.

Davis, Mike. *Planet of Slums.* New York: Verso, 2006.

Dayan, Joan. *Haiti, History, and the Gods.* Berkeley: University of California Press, 1998.

Debray, Régis. *¿Revolución en la revolución?* Havana: Casa de las Américas, 1967.

de la Fuente, Alejandro. *A Nation for All: Race, Inequality, and Politics in Twentieth-Century Cuba.* Chapel Hill: University of North Carolina Press, 2001.

Delany, Samuel R. "About 5,750 Words." In *The Jewel-Hinged Jaw: Notes on the Language of Science Fiction*, 1–15. Middletown, CT: Wesleyan University Press, 2011.

Dennis, Christopher. *Afro-Colombian Hip-Hop: Globalization, Transcultural Music, and Ethnic Identities.* Lanham, MD: Lexington Books, 2012.

Deodoro, Juliana. "O funk ostentação está à beira da morte. E já tem um substituto." *Veja São Paulo*, January 30, 2015. https://vejasp.abril.com.br/cidades/funk-ousadia-ostentacao-livinho-pedrinho-bin-laden/.

Derraik, Márcia, and Simplício Neto. *Onde a coruja dorme.* Antenna/TvZERO, 2012. http://www.imdb.com/title/tt6419382/.

Derrida, Jacques. "Che cos'è la poesia?" In *A Derrida Reader: Between the Blinds*, edited and translated by Peggy Kamuf, 223–37. New York: Columbia University Press, 1991.

———. "The Law of Genre." Translated by Avital Ronell. *Critical Inquiry* 7, no. 1 (1980): 55–81.

Díaz Frene, Jaddiel. "Música popular y nacionalismo en los campamentos insurgentes. Cuba (1895–1898)." *Historia Crítica*, no. 57 (2015): 19–36.

Dittmar, Jeremiah E. "Information Technology and Economic Change: The Impact of the Printing Press." *Quarterly Journal of Economics* 126, no. 3 (2011): 1133–72.

Douglas, Rachel. *Frankétienne and Rewriting: A Work in Progress.* Lanham, MD: Lexington Books, 2009.

Drummond de Andrade, Carlos. *Antologia poética.* São Paulo: Companhia das Letras, 2012.

Dubois, Laurent. *Haiti: The Aftershocks of History.* New York: Metropolitan Books, 2012.
Dudley, Shannon. "Judging 'By the Beat': Calypso versus Soca." *Ethnomusicology* 40, no. 2 (1996): 269–98. https://doi.org/10.2307/852062.
———. *Music from behind the Bridge: Steelband Aesthetics and Politics in Trinidad and Tobago.* New York: Oxford University Press, 2007.
Dumesle, Herard. *Voyage dans le nord d'Hayti, ou, Révélations des lieux et des monuments historiques.* Aux Cayes: Impr. du Gouvernement, 1824.
Dunn, Christopher. *Contracultura: Alternative Arts and Social Transformation in Authoritarian Brazil.* Chapel Hill: University of North Carolina Press, 2016.
Duval, Frantz. "Barikad Crew, Respect!" *Le Nouvelliste,* June 16, 2008. https://lenouvelliste.com/public/article/188881/barikad-crew-respect.
Dyson, Michael Eric. *Holler If You Hear Me: Searching for Tupac Shakur.* New York: Basic Civitas, 2001.
Edwards, Brent Hayes. "Diaspora." In *Keywords for American Cultural Studies,* edited by Bruce Burgett and Glenn Hendler, 2nd ed., 76–78. New York: New York University Press, 2014. http://www.jstor.org.ezproxy.princeton.edu/stable/j.ctt1287j69.22.
———. *Epistrophies: Jazz and the Literary Imagination.* Cambridge, MA: Harvard University Press, 2017.
———. *The Practice of Diaspora: Literature, Translation, and the Rise of Black Internationalism.* Cambridge, MA: Harvard University Press, 2003.
Edwards, Paul. *How to Rap: The Art and Science of the Hip-Hop MC.* Chicago, IL: Chicago Review Press, 2009.
Epstein, Dena J. *Sinful Tunes and Spirituals: Black Folk Music to the Civil War.* Urbana: University of Illinois Press, 2003.
Eshun, Kodwo. *More Brilliant than the Sun: Adventures in Sonic Fiction.* London: Quartet Books, 1998.
Evaristo, Conceição. "Da grafia-desenho de minha mãe, um dos lugares de nascimento de minha escrita." In *Representações Performáticas Brasileiras: Teorias, práticas e suas interfaces,* edited by Marcos Antônio Alexandre, 16–21. Belo Horizonte: Mazza Edições, 2007.
Eyerman, Ron. "False Consciousness and Ideology in Marxist Theory." *Acta Sociologica* 24, nos. 1–2 (1981): 43–56.
Fairley, Jan. "'Ay Díos, Ampárame' (O God, Protect Me): Music in Cuba during the 1990s, the 'Special Period.'" In *Island Musics,* edited by Kevin Dawe, 77–98. New York: Berg, 2004.
———. "How to Make Love with Your Clothes On: Dancing *Regeton,* Gender, and Sexuality in Cuba." In *Reggaeton,* edited by Raquel Z. Rivera, Wayne Marshall, and Deborah Pacini Hernandez, 280–93. Durham, NC: Duke University Press, 2009.
Fanon, Frantz. *Black Skin, White Masks.* Translated by Richard Philcox. New York: Grove Press, 2008.

———. *The Wretched of the Earth*. Translated by Richard Philcox. New York: Grove Press, 2004.
Farber, Samuel. *Cuba since the Revolution of 1959: A Critical Assessment*. Chicago: Haymarket Books, 2011.
Faria, Alexandre, João Camillo Penna, and Paulo Roberto Tonani do Patrocínio. *Modos da margem: Figurações da marginalidade na literatura brasileira*. Rio de Janeiro: Aeroplano, 2015.
Fayer, Joan M. "African Interpreters in the Atlantic Slave Trade." *Anthropological Linguistics* 45, no. 3 (2003): 281–95.
Feld, Steven. "From Ethnomusicology to Echo-Muse-Ecology: Reading R. Murray Schafer in the Papua New Guinea Rainforest." *Soundscape Newsletter*, no. 8 (June 1994): 4–6.
Feltran, Gabriel de Santis. "O legítimo em disputa: As fronteiras do 'mundo do crime' nas periferias de São Paulo." *DILEMAS Revista de Estudos de Conflito e Controle Social*, no. 1 (2008): 93–126.
———. "Sobre anjos e irmãos: Cinquenta anos de expressão política do 'crime' numa tradição musical das periferias." *Revista do Instituto de Estudos Brasileiros*, no. 56 (June 1, 2013): 43–71.
Fernandes, Sujatha T. *Cuba Represent!: Cuban Arts, State Power, and the Making of New Revolutionary Cultures*. Durham, NC: Duke University Press, 2006.
Fernández Olmos, Margarite, and Lizabeth Paravisini-Gebert. *Creole Religions of the Caribbean: An Introduction from Vodou and Santería to Obeah and Espiritismo*. 2nd ed. New York: New York University Press, 2011.
Ferreira da Silva, Denise. "Toward a Black Feminist Poethics: The Quest(ion) of Blackness toward the End of the World." *Black Scholar* 44, no. 2 (2014): 81–97.
Ferreira de Souza, Pedro H. G., Rafael G. Osorio, Luis Henrique Paiva, and Sergei Soares. "Os efeitos do programa Bolsa Família sobre a pobreza e a desigualdade: um balanço dos primeiros 15 anos." In *Bosla Família 15 Anos (2003–2018)*, edited by Tiago Falcão Silva, 155–90. Brasília: Enap, 2018.
Fick, Carolyn E. *The Making of Haiti: The Saint Domingue Revolution from Below*. Knoxville: University of Tennessee Press, 1990.
Figueroa Gómez, María Claudia. "Maferefún, Orishas." In *Contar el rap*, edited by Grizel Hernández Baguer and Malcoms Junco Duffay, 270–82. Havana: Ediciones Cidmuc, 2017.
Fischer, Sibylle. *Modernity Disavowed: Haiti and the Cultures of Slavery in the Age of Revolution*. Durham, NC: Duke University Press, 2004.
Fisher, Mark. *Ghosts of My Life: Writings on Depression, Hauntology and Lost Futures*. Winchester, UK: Zero Books, 2014.
Fix, Mariana, Pedro Arantes, and Giselle Tanaka. "The Case of São Paulo, Brazil." São Paulo: Laboratorio de Assentamentos Humanos de FAU-USP, 2003.
Flores, Juan. *From Bomba to Hip-Hop: Puerto Rican Culture and Latino Identity*. New York: Columbia University Press, 2000.

Forman, Murray. *The 'Hood Comes First: Race, Space, and Place in Rap and Hip-Hop*. Middletown, CT: Wesleyan University Press, 2002.

———. "Introduction." In *That's the Joint!: The Hip-Hop Studies Reader*, edited by Mark Anthony Neal and Murray Forman, 1–8. New York: Routledge, 2004.

———. "'Represent': Race, Space, and Place in Rap Music." In *That's the Joint!: The Hip-Hop Studies Reader*, edited by Mark Anthony Neal and Murray Forman, 201–22. New York: Routledge, 2004.

Fornet, Jorge. *El 71: Anatomía de una crisis*. Havana: Letras Cubanas, 2013.

Foucault, Michel. "Des espaces autres." *Architecture, Mouvement, Continuité*, no. 5 (1984): 46–49.

Fowler, Víctor. "De Cimafunk, reparterismo y temas aledaños." *Magazine AM:PM: Descarga de música cubana* (blog), January 26, 2019. https://www.magazineampm.com/de-cimafunk-reparterismo-y-temas-aledanos/.

Frankétienne. *Rapjazz: Journal d'un paria*. Port-au-Prince: Spirale, 1999.

Freire, Paulo. *Pedagogia do oprimido*. Rio de Janeiro: Paz e Terra, 2005.

Freyre, Gilberto. *Casa-grande e senzala: Formação da família brasileira sob o regime da economia patriarcal*. Edited by Fernando Henrique Cardoso, Edson Nery da Fonseca, and Gustavo Henrique Tuna. São Paulo: Global Editora, 2006.

Friol, Roberto. *Suite para Juan Francisco Manzano*. Havana: Editorial Arte y Literatura, 1977.

Frye, Northrop. "Introduction." In *Sound and Poetry: English Institute Essays, 1956*, edited by Northrop Frye, ix–xxvii. New York: Columbia University Press, 1967.

———. "Varieties of Literary Utopias." *Daedalus* 94, no. 2 (1965): 323–47.

Fukuyama, Francis. "The End of History?" *National Interest*, no. 16 (1989): 3–18.

Gago, Verónica. *La razón neoliberal*. Madrid: Traficantes de Sueños, 2015.

Gámez Torres, Nora. "Hearing the Change: Reggaeton and Emergent Values in Contemporary Cuba." *Latin American Music Review / Revista de Música Latinoamericana* 33, no. 2 (2012): 227–60.

———. "'Rap Is War': Los Aldeanos and the Politics of Music Subversion in Contemporary Cuba." *TRANS*, no. 17 (2013): 1–23.

Garabís, Juan Otero. *Nación y ritmo: "Descargas" desde el Caribe*. San Juan, PR: Ediciones Callejón, 2000.

García, José Luis Rodríguez. "A economia cubana: Experiências e perspectivas (1989–2010)." *Estudos Avançados* 25, no. 72 (January 1, 2011): 29–44.

Garcia, Michael, dir. *Coming Home: Haiti*. Crazy Hood Film Academy, 2015. https://vimeo.com/209989202.

Garcia, Walter. "Elementos para a crítica da estética do Racionais MC'S (1990–2006)." *Idéias* 4, no. 2 (December 20, 2013): 81–108. https://doi.org/10.20396/ideias.v4i2.8649382.

———. "Ouvindo Racionais MC's." *Teresa*, no. 4–5 (December 8, 2003): 166–80. https://doi.org/10.11606/issn.2447-8997.teresa.2003.116377.

———. "Sobre uma cena de 'Fim de semana no Parque', do Racionais MC's." *Estudos Avançados* 25, no. 71 (April 1, 2011): 221–35. https://doi.org/10.1590/S0103-40142011000100015.

———. "Um mapa das relações entre o rap das periferias de São Paulo e o samba." *Revista do Instituto de Estudos Brasileiros*, no. 70 (August 31, 2018): 208–29. https://doi.org/10.11606/issn.2316-901X.v0i70p208-229.

García Amorós, Susana. "Agencia Cubana de Rap." *Movimiento: La Revista Cubana de Hip Hop*, no. 1, 2002, 49.

García Canclini, Néstor. *Consumidores y ciudadanos: Conflictos multiculturales de la globalización*. Mexico City: Grijalbo, 1995.

García-Ruiz, Jesús, and Patrick Michel. "El neo-pentecostalismo en América Latina: Contribución a una antropología de la mundialización." *Sociedad y Religión: Sociología, Antropología e Historia de la Religión en el Cono Sur* 24, no. 41 (May 2014): 43–78.

Gaspar, Belkis Delcarmen. "G-Shytt, le nouveau feu du BPC." *Le Nouvelliste*, July 26, 2017. http://www.lenouvelliste.com/article/173890/g-shytt-le-nouveau-feu-du-bpc.

Gates, Henry Louis, Jr. *The Signifying Monkey: A Theory of Afro-American Literary Criticism*. New York: Oxford University Press, 1988.

Gaunt, Kyra D. "Translating Double-Dutch to Hip-Hop: The Musical Vernacular of Black Girls' Play." In *That's the Joint!: The Hip-Hop Studies Reader*, edited by Mark Anthony Neal and Murray Forman, 251–63. New York: Routledge, 2004.

Gee, John. "Notes on the Egyptian Motifs in Mozart's 'Magic Flute.'" *Brigham Young University Studies* 43, no. 3 (2004): 149–60.

Gell, Alfred. *The Anthropology of Time: Cultural Constructions of Temporal Maps and Images*. Providence, RI: Berg, 1992.

Geoffray, Marie Laure. "Juan Carlos Flores, OMNI-Zona Franca, and the Reinvention of Alamar." *Chicago Review* 61, nos. 3–4 (June 2018): 41–51.

George, Nelson. *Hip Hop America*. New York: Penguin, 2005.

———. *The Hippest Trip in America: Soul Train and the Evolution of Culture and Style*. New York: William Morrow, 2014.

Gilroy, Paul. *The Black Atlantic: Modernity and Double Consciousness*. Cambridge, MA: Harvard University Press, 2000.

———. "It's a Family Affair." In *That's the Joint!: The Hip-Hop Studies Reader*, edited by Mark Anthony Neal and Murray Forman, 87–94. New York: Routledge, 2004.

Glick, Jeremy Matthew. *The Black Radical Tragic: Performance, Aesthetics, and the Unfinished Haitian Revolution*. New York: New York University Press, 2016.

Glissant, Édouard. *Caribbean Discourse: Selected Essays*. Translated by J. Michael Dash. Charlottesville: University Press of Virginia, 1989.

———. *Le discours antillais*. Paris: Gallimard, 2008.
Gómez, Sara. *De cierta manera*. Havana: Instituto Cubano del Arte e Industria Cinematográficos, 1974.
Govain, Renauld. "Créolophonie et identité dans la Caraïbe multilingue et multiculturelle?" *Archipélies* 9 (June 20, 2020). https://www.archipelies.org/699.
Graham, Sandra Lauderdale. "Writing from the Margins: Brazilian Slaves and Written Culture." *Comparative Studies in Society and History* 49, no. 3 (2007): 611–36.
Grear, Maxwell. "El Paquete Semanal: Informal Networks and Emerging Infrastructures in Digital Cuba." Undergraduate thesis, Princeton University, 2018.
Guadarrama González, Pablo. "El pensamiento integracionista y latinoamericanista de José Martí." In *José Martí y Nuestra América*, edited by Adalberto Santana, 83–122. Mexico City: Universidad Nacional Autónoma de México, 2013.
Guerra, Lillian. *Visions of Power in Cuba: Revolution, Redemption, and Resistance, 1959–1971*. Chapel Hill: University of North Carolina Press, 2012.
Guevara, Ernesto Che. "El socialismo y el hombre en Cuba." In *El socialismo y el hombre en Cuba*, 53–72. New York: Pathfinder, 1992.
Guillén, Nicolás. "Benny." In *Yo conocí a Benny Moré*, edited by Félix Contreras, 79–81. Havana: Ediciones Unión, 2002.
———. *Obra poética*. Vol. 2. Havana: Editorial Letras Cubanas, 1980.
Guillory, John. *Cultural Capital: The Problem of Literary Canon Formation*. Chicago, IL: University of Chicago Press, 1993.
Guridy, Frank Andre. *Forging Diaspora: Afro-Cubans and African Americans in a World of Empire and Jim Crow*. Chapel Hill: University of North Carolina Press, 2010.
Gutiérrez, Pedro Juan. *El Rey de la Habana*. Barcelona: Editorial Anagrama, 2005.
Hale, Thomas A. *Griots and Griottes: Masters of Words and Music*. Bloomington: Indiana University Press, 1998.
Hall, Michael R. *Historical Dictionary of Haiti*. Lanham, MD: Scarecrow Press, 2012.
Hall, Stuart. "Cultural Identity and Diaspora." In *Identity: Community, Culture, Difference*, edited by Jonathan Rutherford, 222–37. London: Lawrence and Wishart, 1990.
Hallward, Peter. *Damming the Flood: Haiti, Aristide, and the Politics of Containment*. New York: Verso, 2007.
Halstead, Jill, and Randi Rolvsjord. "The Gendering of Musical Instruments: What Is It? Why Does It Matter to Music Therapy?" *Nordic Journal of Music Therapy* 26, no. 1 (January 1, 2017): 3–24. https://doi.org/10.1080/08098131.2015.1088057.
Hamberg, Jill. "The 'Slums' of Havana." In *Havana beyond the Ruins*, edited by Anke Birkenmaier and Esther Whitfield, 73–105. Durham, NC: Duke University Press, 2011. https://doi.org/10.1215/9780822394426-005.

Hamilton, Njelle W. *Phonographic Memories: Popular Music and the Contemporary Caribbean Novel.* New Brunswick, NJ: Rutgers University Press, 2019.

Hanchard, Michael George. *Orpheus and Power: The Movimento Negro of Rio de Janeiro and São Paulo, Brazil, 1945–1988.* Princeton, NJ: Princeton University Press, 1994.

Hankin, Charlie D. "Contrapunteo de Los Orishas y Los Aldeanos: El hip hop cubano dentro y fuera de la revolución." *1616: Anuario de Literatura Comparada,* no. 4 (2014): 201–19.

———. "'Enraizados da Letra': Lyrics and the Letter in Brazilian, Cuban, and Haitian Rap." *Journal of Latin American Cultural Studies* 30, no. 4 (2021): 619–40. https://doi.org/10.1080/13569325.2021.2017270.

———. "*La Aldea:* Martí, McLuhan y marginalidad en el hip-hop habanero." In *Isla diseminada: Ensayos sobre Cuba,* edited by Justo Planas, Reynaldo Lastre, Alex Werner, and Jorge Alvis, 45–68. Editorial Hypermedia, 2022.

———. "The (Latin) American Underground: Havana and Marginocentric Hip Hop." *Atlantic Studies* 14, no. 1 (January 2, 2017): 82–98. https://doi.org/10.1080/14788810.2016.1233485.

———. "Rap e conscientização: O legado de Paulo Freire no hip-hop cearense." *Entrelaces* 1, no. 10 (2017): 132–45.

Harney, Stefano, and Fred Moten. *The Undercommons: Fugitive Planning and Black Study.* New York: Minor Compositions, 2013.

Hartman, Saidiya. "Venus in Two Acts." *Small Axe: A Caribbean Journal of Criticism* 12, no. 2 (June 1, 2008): 1–14. https://doi.org/10.1215/-12-2-1.

———. *Wayward Lives, Beautiful Experiments: Intimate Histories of Social Upheaval.* New York: W. W. Norton, 2020.

Hartog, François. *Regimes of Historicity: Presentism and Experiences of Time.* Translated by Saskia Brown. New York: Columbia University Press, 2015.

Harvey, David. *A Brief History of Neoliberalism.* New York: Oxford University Press, 2005.

Hattemer, B., and R. Showers. "Heavy Metal Rock and Gangsta Rap Music Promote Violence." In *Violence in the Media,* edited by Carol Wekesser, 150–58. San Diego, CA: Greenhaven Press, 1995.

Hays, Terence E. "Sacred Flutes, Fertility, and Growth in the Papua New Guinea Highlands." *Anthropos* 81, nos. 4–6 (1986): 435–53.

Hebblethwaite, Benjamin. "French and Underdevelopment, Haitian Creole and Development: Educational Language Policy Problems and Solutions in Haiti." *Journal of Pidgin and Creole Languages* 27, no. 2 (2012): 255–302. https://doi.org/10.1075/jpcl.27.2.03heb.

Hebblethwaite, Benjamin, and Joanne Bartley. *Vodou Songs in Haitian Creole and English.* Philadelphia, PA: Temple University Press, 2011.

Hebdige, Dick. *Cut 'n' Mix: Culture, Identity and Caribbean Music.* New York: Routledge, 2003.

———. *Subculture: The Meaning of Style.* New York: Routledge, 1991.

Hegel, G. W. F. *Phenomenology of Spirit*. Translated by A. V. Miller. Oxford, UK: Oxford University Press, 1977.
Henle, Michael. *A Combinatorial Introduction to Topology*. New York: Dover, 1994.
Hernández Baguer, Grizel, and Liliana Casanella Cué. "Hora de abrir los ojos . . . ¡El rap cubano existe!" In *Contar el rap*, edited by Grizel Hernández Baguer and Malcoms Junco Duffay, 301–26. Havana: Ediciones Cidmuc, 2017.
Hernández Baguer, Grizel, and Malcoms Junco Duffay, eds. *Contar el rap*. Havana: Ediciones Cidmuc, 2017.
Hernandez-Reguant, Ariana, ed. *Cuba in the Special Period: Culture and Ideology in the 1990s*. New York: Palgrave Macmillan, 2009.
———. "Havana's Timba: A Macho Sound for Black Sex." In *Globalization and Race: Transformations in the Cultural Production of Blackness*, edited by Kamari Maxine Clarke and Deborah A. Thomas, 249–78. Durham, NC: Duke University Press, 2006.
Herrera Veitía, Pablo D. "Producir rap afrocubano: una historia a saltos." In *Contar el rap*, edited by Grizel Hernández Baguer and Malcoms Junco Duffay, 85–104. Havana: Ediciones Cidmuc, 2017.
Hickmann, Hans. "The Egyptian 'Uffāṭah Flute." *Journal of the Royal Asiatic Society of Great Britain and Ireland*, nos. 3–4 (1952): 103–4.
Holbraad, Martin. "The Power of Powder: Multiplicity and Motion in the Divinatory Cosmology of Cuban Ifá (or *Mana* Again)." In *Thinking through Things: Theorising Artefacts Ethnographically*, edited by Amiria J. M. Henare, Martin Holbraad, and Sari Wastell, 189–225. New York: Routledge, 2007.
———. *Truth in Motion: The Recursive Anthropology of Cuban Divination*. Chicago, IL: University of Chicago Press, 2012.
Hollander, John. "Music and Poetry." In *Princeton Encyclopedia of Poetry and Poetics*, edited by Alex Preminger, Frank J. Warnke, and O. B. Hardison, 533–36. Princeton, NJ: Princeton University Press, 1975. https://doi.org/10.1515/9781400872930-018.
Hooker, Juliet. *Theorizing Race in the Americas: Douglass, Sarmiento, Du Bois, and Vasconcelos*. New York: Oxford University Press, 2017.
hooks, bell. *Belonging: A Culture of Place*. New York: Routledge, 2009.
———. *Yearning: Race, Gender, and Cultural Politics*. Boston, MA: South End Press, 1999.
Horace. *The Art of Poetry: To the Pisos*. Edited by Theodore Alois Buckley. Translated by Christopher Smart. Perseus. New York: Harper and Brothers, 1863. http://data.perseus.org/citations/urn:cts:latinLit:phi0893.phi006.perseus-eng1:1-43.
Howe, Susan. *My Emily Dickinson*. Berkeley, CA: North Atlantic Books, 1985.
Hughes, Langston. *The Collected Works of Langston Hughes*. Edited by Arnold Rampersad, Dolan Hubbard, and Leslie Catherine Sanders. Vol. 14. Columbia: University of Missouri Press, 2001.

Hurston, Zora Neale. *Tell My Horse: Voodoo and Life in Haiti and Jamaica.* New York: Harper Perennial Modern Classics, 2008.

Ianni, Clara, and Débora Maria da Silva. "Apelo." In *Esperar não é saber: Arte entre o silêncio e a evidência,* edited by André Luiz Mesquita, 186–87. São Paulo, 2015.

Ibrahim, Awad. "Arab Spring, *Favelas,* Borders, and the Artistic Transnational Migration: Toward a Curriculum for a Global Hip-Hop Nation." *Curriculum Inquiry* 47, no. 1 (January 2017): 103–11. https://doi.org/10.1080/03626784.2016.1254498.

———. "*Languages of Global Hip Hop* Edited by Marina Terkourafi." *Journal of Sociolinguistics* 16, no. 4 (September 2012): 547–52. https://doi.org/10.1111/j.1467-9841.2012.00545_1.x.

Ivan 13P, dir. *Sabotage: O maestro do Canão.* 13 Produções / Elixir Entretenimento, 2015. https://www.youtube.com/watch?v=59CJ4Be48xc.

Jaguaribe, Beatriz. "Favelas and the Aesthetics of Realism: Representations in Film and Literature." *Journal of Latin American Cultural Studies* 13, no. 3 (December 1, 2004): 327–42. https://doi.org/10.1080/1356932042000287053.

Jakobson, Roman. "Closing Statement: Linguistics and Poetics." In *Style in Language,* edited by Thomas A. Sebeok, 350–77. New York: MIT Press, 1960.

———. "The Metaphoric and Metonymic Poles." In *Metaphor and Metonymy in Comparison and Contrast,* edited by René Dirven and Ralf Pörings, 41–47. New York: Mouton de Gruyter, 2003. https://doi.org/10.1515/9783110219197.

James, C. L. R. *The Future in the Present.* London: Alison and Busby, 1977.

Junco Duffay, Malcoms. "Esencia y presencia del rap cubano." In *Contar el rap,* edited by Grizel Hernández Baguer and Malcoms Junco Duffay, 105–35. Havana: Ediciones Cidmuc, 2017.

Kajikawa, Loren. *Sounding Race in Rap Songs.* Oakland: University of California Press, 2015.

Katz, Mark. *Groove Music: The Art and Culture of the Hip-Hop DJ.* New York: Oxford University Press, 2012.

Kauss, Saint-John. "Le spiralisme de Franketienne." *Le Nouvelliste,* October 18, 2010. https://lenouvelliste.com/article/83699/le-spiralisme-de-franketienne.

Kehl, Maria Rita. "Radicais, raciais, racionais: A grande fratria do rap na periferia de São Paulo." *São Paulo em perspectiva* 13, no. 3 (1999): 95–106.

Kelley, Robin D. G. "Kickin' Reality, Kickin' Ballistics: 'Gansta Rap' and Postindustrial Los Angeles." In *Race Rebels: Culture, Politics, and the Black Working Class,* 119–36. New York: The Free Press, 1994.

———. "Looking for the 'Real' Nigga: Social Scientists Construct the Ghetto." In *That's the Joint!: The Hip-Hop Studies Reader,* edited by Mark Anthony Neal and Murray Forman, 87–94. New York: Routledge, 2004.

Kellner, Douglas. *Media Culture: Cultural Studies, Identity, and Politics between the Modern and the Postmodern.* New York: Routledge, 1995.

Kennedy, Ian McColl. "Cuba's Ley Contra La Vagancia: The Law on Loafing." *UCLA Law Review* 20 (1972–1973): 1177–268.

Kilomba, Grada. *Plantation Memories: Episodes of Everyday Racism*. Münster: Unrast, 2008.

Kitwana, Bakari. *Why White Kids Love Hip-Hop: Wankstas, Wiggers, Wannabes, and the New Reality of Race in America*. New York: Basic Civitas Books, 2005.

Kivland, Chelsey. "Street Sovereignty: Power, Violence, and Respect among Haitian Baz." In *Who Owns Haiti? People, Power, and Sovereignty*, edited by Robert E. Maguire, Scott Freeman, and Amy Wilentz, 140–65. Gainesville: University Press of Florida, 2017.

Kojève, Alexandre. *Introduction to the Reading of Hegel: Lectures on the Phenomenology of Spirit*. Edited by Allan Bloom. Translated by James H. Nichols. Ithaca, NY: Cornell University Press, 1980.

Kolbe, Athena R., and Robert Muggah. "Haiti's Urban Crime Wave? Results from Monthly Household Surveys." Rio de Janeiro: Igarapé Institute, 2012. https://igarape.org.br/wp-content/uploads/2015/05/Haitis-Urban-Crime-Wave.pdf.

Krims, Adam. *Music and Urban Geography*. New York: Routledge, 2007.

———. *Rap Music and the Poetics of Identity*. New York: Cambridge University Press, 2000.

Kutzinski, Vera M. "Fearful Asymmetries: Langston Hughes, Nicolás Guillén, and Cuba Libre." *Diacritics* 34, no. 3 (2004): 112–42. https://doi.org/10.1353/dia.2006.0040.

Lacerda, Daniel S. "Rio de Janeiro and the Divided State: Analysing the Political Discourse on Favelas." *Discourse & Society* 26, no. 1 (January 1, 2015): 74–94. https://doi.org/10.1177/0957926514541346.

Lamazares, Alexander. "São Paulo's Pixação and Street Art: Representations of or Responses to Brazilian Modernism?" In *Graffiti and Street Art: Reading, Writing and Representing the City*, edited by Konstantinos Avramidis and Myrto Tsilimpounidi, 197–215. New York: Routledge, 2017.

Lapassade, Georges, and Philippe Rousselot. *Le rap, ou, la fureur de dire: Essai*. Paris: L. Talmart, 1990.

Larose, Sandy. "Représentation de la femme projetée par les rappeurs." Undergraduate thesis, Université de l'État d'Haïti, 2010.

Lefebvre, Henri. *Rhythmanalysis: Space, Time, and Everyday Life*. Translated by Stuart Elden and Gerald Moore. New York: Continuum, 2004.

———. "The Right to the City." In *Writings on Cities,* edited by Eleonore Kofman and Elizabeth Lebas, 147–59. Cambridge, MA: Blackwell Publishers, 1996.

Lenzi, Simone. *Per il verso giusto: Piccola anatomia della canzone*. Venice, Italy: Marsilio, 2017.

Lerner, Ben. *The Hatred of Poetry*. New York: Farrar, Straus and Giroux, 2016.

Lerner, Michael, and Cornel West. *Jews and Blacks: A Dialogue on Race, Religion, and Culture in America*. New York: Plume, 1996.

Levin Becker, Daniel. *What's Good: Notes on Rap and Language*. San Francisco, CA: City Lights Books, 2022.
Levine, Mike. "Sounding El Paquete: The Local and Transnational Routes of an Afro-Cuban Repartero." *Cuban Studies*, no. 50 (2021): 139–60.
Lévi-Strauss, Claude. *Tristes tropiques*. Paris: Plon, 1955.
Lewis, R. Anthony. "Language, Culture and Power: Haiti under the Duvaliers." *Caribbean Quarterly* 50, no. 4 (2004): 42–51.
Librandi, Marília. *Writing by Ear: Clarice Lispector and the Aural Novel*. Buffalo, NY: University of Toronto Press, 2018.
Loitero, Wagner, and Fernando Ripol. "Hino do Samba do Congo." In *Nossa Quebrada: Prosas em cantos e histórias em versos*, 3. São Paulo: Samba do Congo; Prefeitura de São Paulo, 2016.
Lolo, Eduardo. *Lo que quede de aldea: Más sobre José Martí*. Miami, FL: Alexandria Library, 2011.
López Lemus, Virgilio. *La décima constante: Las tradiciones oral y escrita*. Havana: Fundación Fernando Ortiz, 1999.
Lord, Albert Bates. *The Singer of Tales*. Cambridge, MA: Harvard University Press, 2000.
Lorenz, Aaron. "Embodying the Favela: Representation, Mediation, and Citizenship in the Music of Bezerra da Silva." In *Brazilian Popular Music and Citizenship*, edited by Idelber Avelar and Christopher Dunn, 172–88. Durham, NC: Duke University Press, 2011.
Löwy, Michael. *Fire Alarm: Reading Walter Benjamin's "On the Concept of History."* Translated by Chris Turner. New York: Verso, 2016.
Makalani, Minkah. "The Politically Unimaginable in Black Marxist Thought." *Small Axe: A Caribbean Journal of Criticism* 22, no. 2 (56) (July 1, 2018): 18–34. https://doi.org/10.1215/07990537-6985654.
Mane, Gucci, and Neil Martinez-Belkin. *The Autobiography of Gucci Mane*. New York: Simon and Schuster, 2017.
Manuel, Peter, and Michael Largey. *Caribbean Currents: Caribbean Music from Rumba to Reggae*. Philadelphia, PA: Temple University Press, 2016.
Manzano, Juan Francisco. *Autobiografía del esclavo poeta y otros escritos*. Edited by William Luis. Madrid: Iberoamericana, 2007.
Marcus, Greil. *Lipstick Traces: A Secret History of the Twentieth Century*. 2nd ed. Cambridge, MA: Belknap Press, 2009.
Maria de Jesus, Carolina. *Quarto de Despejo: Diário de uma favelada*. São Paulo: Editora Ática, 1995.
Marrow, Tracy Lauren ("Ice-T"), and Andy Baybutt, dirs. *Something from Nothing: The Art of Rap*. Indomina Releasing, 2012.
Marshall, Wayne. "From Música Negra to Reggaeton Latino: The Cultural Politics of Nation, Migration, and Commercialization." In *Reggaeton*, edited by Raquel Z. Rivera, Wayne Marshall, and Deborah Pacini Hernandez, 19–76. Durham, NC: Duke University Press, 2009.

Martí, José. *Martí: Cuba. 1900–1901*. Vol. 2. Havana: Gonzalo de Quesada, 1900.

———. *Nuestra América*. Edited by Juan Marinello, Hugo Achúgar, and Cintio Vitier. Caracas: Biblioteca Ayacucho, 2005.

Martin, Randy. *Financialization of Daily Life*. Philadelphia, PA: Temple University Press, 2002.

Maxwell, Ian. *Phat Beats, Dope Rhymes: Hip Hop Down Under Comin' Upper*. Middletown, CT: Wesleyan University Press, 2003.

Mbembe, Achille. *Critique of Black Reason*. Translated by Laurent Dubois. Durham, NC: Duke University Press, 2017.

McAlister, Elizabeth. "From Slave Revolt to a Blood Pact with Satan: The Evangelical Rewriting of Haitian History." *Studies in Religion / Sciences Religieuses* 41, no. 2 (June 1, 2012): 187–215. https://doi.org/10.1177/0008429812441310.

———. *Rara! Vodou, Power, and Performance in Haiti and Its Diaspora*. Berkeley: University of California Press, 2002.

McCarthy, Jesse. "Notes on Trap." *n+1*, 2018. https://nplusonemag.com/issue-32/essays/notes-on-trap/.

McEnaney, Tom. *Acoustic Properties: Radio, Narrative, and the New Neighborhood of the Americas*. Evanston, IL: Northwestern University Press, 2017.

McGrath, Brian. "Island as Urban Artifact / Archipelago as Urban Model." *Island Studies Journal*, 2020. https://doi.org/10.24043/isj.140.

McLuhan, Marshall. *Understanding Media: The Extensions of Man*. Cambridge, MA: MIT Press, 1994.

McNulty, Tracy. "The Commandment against the Law: Writing and Divine Justice in Walter Benjamin's 'Critique of Violence.'" *Diacritics* 37, nos. 2–3 (2007): 34–60.

Meconi, Honey. *Early Musical Borrowing*. New York: Routledge, 2003.

Mendes de Leon, Mimi. "Poetic Justice: Hip-Hop and Black Liberation Theology." *Denison Journal of Religion*, no. 14 (June 16, 2017): 25–39.

Michelino, Matheus Sant'Ana, and Elizeu Coutinho Macedo. "Consciência fonológica, nomeação automática rápida e leitura em adultos analfabetos funcionais." *CoDAS* 33, no. 1 (2021): 1–8. https://doi.org/10.1590/2317-1782/20202019206.

Mintz, Sidney W. *Caribbean Transformations*. New York: Columbia University Press, 1989.

Miranda, Fernanda R. *Carolina Maria de Jesus: Literatura e cidade em dissenso*. São Paulo: Editora da Cidade, 2017.

Moore, Allan F. *Rock, the Primary Text: Developing a Musicology of Rock*. 2nd ed. Brookfield, VT: Ashgate, 2001.

Moore, Robin D. *Music and Revolution: Cultural Change in Socialist Cuba*. Berkeley: University of California Press, 2006.

———. *Nationalizing Blackness: Afrocubanismo and Artistic Revolution in Havana, 1920–1940*. Pittsburgh, PA: University of Pittsburgh Press, 1997.

Morgan, Marcyliena H. *The Real Hiphop: Battling for Knowledge, Power, and Respect in the LA Underground*. Durham, NC: Duke University Press, 2009.

Morgan, Marcyliena, and Dionne Bennett. "Hip-Hop and the Global Imprint of a Black Cultural Form" 140, no. 2 (April 1, 2011): 176–96. https://doi.org/10.1162/DAED_a_00086.

Morucci, Bérengère. *Alamar, un quartier cubain*. Paris: Harmattan, 2006.

Moten, Fred. *In the Break: The Aesthetics of the Black Radical Tradition*. Minneapolis: University of Minnesota Press, 2003.

Muñoz, José Esteban. *Cruising Utopia: The Then and There of Queer Futurity*. New York: New York University Press, 2009.

Murray, G. F. "The Wood Tree as a Peasant Cash-Crop: An Anthropological Strategy for the Domestication of Energy." *National Agricultural Library*, 1988. http://agris.fao.org/agris-search/search.do?recordID=US8855088.

Murrell, Nathaniel Samuel. *Afro-Caribbean Religions: An Introduction to Their Historical, Cultural, and Sacred Traditions*. Philadelphia, PA: Temple University Press, 2010.

Nakassis, Constantine V. *Doing Style: Youth and Mass Mediation in South India*. Chicago, IL: University of Chicago Press, 2016.

Nascimento, Abdias do. *O quilombismo: Documentos de uma militância panafricanista*. Rio de Janeiro: Vozes, 1980.

———. "Teatro experimental do negro: Trajetória e reflexões." *Estudos Avançados* 18, no. 50 (April 2004): 209–24. https://doi.org/10.1590/S0103-40142004000100019.

Nash, Jennifer C. *Black Feminism Reimagined: After Intersectionality*. Durham, NC: Duke University Press, 2019.

Nava, Alejandro. *In Search of Soul: Hip-Hop, Literature, and Religion*. Oakland: University of California Press, 2017.

Neal, Mark Anthony. "Post-Industrial Soul: Black Popular Music at the Crossroads." In *That's the Joint!: The Hip-Hop Studies Reader*, edited by Mark Anthony Neal and Murray Forman, 363–87. New York: Routledge, 2004.

Neff, Ali Colleen. "Roots, Routes and Rhizomes: Sounding Women's Hip Hop on the Margins of Dakar, Senegal: Ali Colleen Neff." *Journal of Popular Music Studies* 27, no. 4 (December 2015): 448–77. https://doi.org/10.1111/jpms.12157.

———. "Senegalese Hip-Hop." In *The Cambridge Companion to Hip-Hop*, edited by Justin A. Williams, 271–79. Cambridge, UK: Cambridge University Press, 2015. https://doi.org/10.1017/CCO9781139775298.025.

Nesbitt, Nick. "Turning the Tide: The Problem of Popular Insurgency in Haitian Revolutionary Historiography." *Small Axe* 12, no. 3 (2008): 14–31.

Nixon, Rob. *Slow Violence and the Environmentalism of the Poor*. Berlin: De Gruyter, 2011.

Nunes, Andréa. "Life in the Dominican Republic's Sugar Fields: Resistance from the Bateyes." *Journal of Pedagogy, Pluralism, and Practice* 1, no. 8 (2016): 204–24.

Ochoa, Todd Ramón. *Society of the Dead: Quita Manaquita and Palo Praise in Cuba*. Berkeley: University of California, 2010.
Ochoa Gautier, Ana María. *Aurality: Listening and Knowledge in Nineteenth-Century Colombia*. Durham, NC: Duke University Press, 2014.
Ojeda, Jorge Pavez. "Territorios e identidades en la ciudad de La Habana, Cuba: El caso de El Vedado (1860–1940)." Culturas e identidades en América Latina y el Caribe. Programa Regional de Becas CLACSO, 2001. http://bibliotecavirtual.clacso.org.ar/ar/libros/becas/2000/pavez.pdf.
Okiji, Fumi. *Jazz as Critique: Adorno and Black Expression Revisited*. Redwood City, CA: Stanford University Press, 2018.
Oliveira, Ana Claudia de. "Visibilidade e identidade de São Paulo." *Interin* 23, no. 1 (June 2018): 146–66.
Oliveira, Jane Souto de. "Repensando a questão das favelas." *Revista Brasileira de Estudos de População* 2, no. 1 (1985): 9–30.
Oliveira, Roberto T., and João Wainer, dirs. *Pixo*. Roberto T. Oliveira, 2009. https://vimeo.com/29691112.
Ong, Walter J. *Orality and Literacy: The Technologizing of the Word*. New York: Routledge, 2002.
Orta Ruiz, Jesús. *Décima y folclor*. Havana: Ed. Unión, 2004.
Ortiz, Fernando. *Contrapunteo cubano del tabaco y el azúcar: Advertencia de sus contrastes agrarios, económicos, históricos y sociales, su etnografía y su tranculturación*. Edited by Enrico Mario Santí. Madrid: Cátedra, 2002.
———. *La africanía de la música folklórica de Cuba*. Havana: Ministerio de Educación, 1950.
Osumare, Halifu. *The Africanist Aesthetic in Global Hip-Hop: Power Moves*. New York: Palgrave Macmillan, 2007.
Padilla, Heberto. *Fuera del juego*. Miami, FL: Ediciones Universal, 1998.
Padrón, Francisco Morales. "El requerimiento." In *Teoría y leyes de la conquista*, 338–40. Madrid: Ediciones Cultura Hispánica, 1979.
Padura, Leonardo. *El hombre que amaba a los perros*. Mexico City: Tusquets Editores, 2013.
———. *The Man Who Loved Dogs*. Translated by Anna Kushner. New York: Farrar, Straus and Giroux, 2014.
Palmié, Stephan. *Wizards and Scientists: Explorations in Afro-Cuban Modernity and Tradition*. Durham, NC: Duke University Press, 2006.
Palomino, Pablo. *The Invention of Latin American Music: A Transnational History*. New York: Oxford University Press, 2020.
Pardue, Derek. *Ideologies of Marginality in Brazilian Hip Hop*. New York: Palgrave Macmillan, 2008.
Parry, Milman. "Studies in the Epic Technique of Oral Verse-Making. I. Homer and Homeric Style." In *The Making of Homeric Verse: The Collected Papers of Milman Parry*, edited by Adam Parry, 266–324. Oxford, UK: Clarendon Press, 1971.

Pasmanick, Philip. "'Decima' and 'Rumba': Iberian Formalism in the Heart of Afro-Cuban Song." *Latin American Music Review / Revista de Música Latinoamericana* 18, no. 2 (1997): 252. https://doi.org/10.2307/780397.
Pate, Alexs D. *In the Heart of the Beat: The Poetry of Rap*. Lanham, MD: Scarecrow Press, 2010.
Patterson, Orlando. "Ecumenical America: Global Culture and the American Cosmos." *World Policy Journal* 11, no. 2 (1994): 103–17.
Paz, Octavio. *Los hijos del limo: De romanticismo a la vanguardia*. 4th ed. Barcelona: Seix Barral, 1993.
Pedrero, Mayckell, dir. *Revolution*. Q'Bolá?, 2010. https://vimeo.com/17236980.
Peixoto, Luiz Felipe de Lima, and Zé Octávio Sebadelhe. *1976 Movimento Black Rio*. Rio de Janeiro: José Olympio, 2016.
Pellek, Richard. "Combating Tropical Deforestation in Haiti." *Journal of Forestry* 88, no. 9 (September 1, 1990): 15–19. https://doi.org/10.1093/jof/88.9.15.
Pereira, Alexandre Barbosa. "Funk ostentação em São Paulo: Imaginação, consumo e novas tecnologia da informação e da comunicação." *Revista Estudos Culturais* 1, no. 1 (2014).
———. "Quem não é visto, não é lembrado: sociabilidade, escrita, visibilidade e memória na São Paulo da pixação." *Cadernos de Arte e Antropologia* 1, no. 2 (December 1, 2012): 55–69. https://doi.org/10.4000/cadernosaa.631.
Pereira, Claudiney. "Brazil: Fiscal Policy and Ethno-Racial Poverty and Inequality." In *Commitment to Equity Handbook: Estimating the Impact of Fiscal Policy on Inequality and Poverty*, edited by Nora Lustig, 554–67. Washington, DC: Brookings Institution Press, 2018.
Perloff, Marjorie, and Craig Douglas Dworkin, eds. "Introduction." In *The Sound of Poetry, the Poetry of Sound*. Chicago, IL: University of Chicago Press, 2009.
Perna, Vincenzo A. "Selling Cuba by the Sound: Music Tourism in Cuba in the 1990s." In *Sun, Sea, and Sound: Music and Tourism in the Circum-Caribbean*, edited by Timothy Rommen and Daniel T. Neely, 44–69. New York: Oxford University Press, 2014.
———. *Timba: The Sound of the Cuban Crisis*. Burlington, VT: Ashgate, 2005.
Perry, Imani. *Prophets of the Hood: Politics and Poetics in Hip Hop*. Durham, NC: Duke University Press, 2004.
Perry, Keisha-Khan Y. "Geographies of Power: Black Women Mobilizing Intersectionality in Brazil." *Meridians* 14, no. 1 (June 1, 2016): 94–120. https://doi.org/10.2979/meridians.14.1.08.
Perry, Marc D. *Negro Soy Yo: Hip Hop and Raced Citizenship in Neoliberal Cuba*. Durham, NC: Duke University Press, 2015.
Pettway, Matthew. *Cuban Literature in the Age of Black Insurrection: Manzano, Plácido, and Afro-Latino Religion*. Jackson: University Press of Mississippi, 2020.
Pignarre, Philippe, and Isabelle Stengers. *Capitalist Sorcery: Breaking the Spell*. Translated by Andrew Goffey. New York: Palgrave Macmillan, 2011.

Pinn, Anthony B. *Noise and Spirit: The Religious and Spiritual Sensibilities of Rap Music*. New York: New York University Press, 2003.
Pires, Thula Rafaela de Oliveira. "Estruturas intocadas: Racismo e ditadura no Rio de Janeiro." *Revista Direito e Práxis* 9, no. 2 (June 2018): 1054–79. https://doi.org/10.1590/2179-8966/2018/33900.
Robinson, Cedric J. *Black Marxism: The Making of the Black Radical Tradition*. Chapel Hill: University of North Carolina Press, 2000.
Poole, Lizette, and Brian Chu, dirs. *Reggaeton Revolución: Cuba in the Digital Era*. Werehaus, 2016. https://vimeo.com/173759040.
Pope, Alexander. *An Essay on Criticism*. London, 1758.
Potter, Russell A. *Spectacular Vernaculars: Hip-Hop and the Politics of Postmodernism*. Albany, NY: SUNY Press, 1995.
Pravaz, Natasha. "Hybridity Brazilian Style: Samba, Carnaval, and the Myth of 'Racial Democracy' in Rio de Janeiro." *Identities* 15, no. 1 (January 22, 2008): 80–102. https://doi.org/10.1080/10702890701801841.
Preto, Fred Ouro. *Emicida: AmarElo—É Tudo Pra Ontem*. Netflix, 2020.
Price, Richard, ed. *Maroon Societies: Rebel Slave Communities in the Americas*. Baltimore, MD: Johns Hopkins University Press, 1996.
Price-Mars, Jean. *Ainsi parla l'oncle suivi de revisiter l'oncle*. Montreal: Mémoire d'encrier, 2009.
———. *La vocation de l'élite*. Port-au-Prince: Les Éditions Fardin, 2013.
Prieto, José Manuel. "Heberto Padilla, the First Dissident (of the Cuban Revolution)." In *Caviar with Rum: Cuba-USSR and the Post-Soviet Experience*, edited by Jacqueline Loss and José Manuel Prieto, translated by Jorge Castillo, 119–30. New York: Palgrave Macmillan, 2012.
Putnam, Lara. *Radical Moves: Caribbean Migrants and the Politics of Race in the Jazz Age*. Chapel Hill: University of North Carolina Press, 2013.
Quijano, Aníbal. "Colonialidad del poder, cultura y conocimiento en América Latina." *Dispositio* 24, no. 51 (1999): 137–48.
Quintero Rivera, Ángel G. *Salsa, sabor y control! Sociología de la música "tropical."* Mexico City: Siglo Veintiuno Editores, 1999.
Quiroga, José. *Cuban Palimpsests*. Minneapolis: University of Minnesota Press, 2005.
Rama, Ángel. *La ciudad letrada*. Montevideo: Arca, 1998.
Ramazani, Jahan. *Poetry and Its Others: News, Prayer, Song, and the Dialogue of Genres*. Chicago, IL: University of Chicago Press, 2014.
———. *A Transnational Poetics*. Chicago, IL: University of Chicago Press, 2009.
Ramos, Julio. *Desencuentros de la modernidad en América Latina: Literatura y política en el siglo XIX*. Mexico City: Fondo de Cultura Económica, 1989.
Ramsey, Kate. *The Spirits and the Law: Vodou and Power in Haiti*. Chicago, IL: University of Chicago Press, 2011.
Reed, Anthony. *Freedom Time: The Poetics and Politics of Black Experimental Writing*. Baltimore, MD: Johns Hopkins University Press, 2014.

———. *Soundworks: Race, Sound, and Poetry in Production.* Durham, NC: Duke University Press, 2021.

Reilly, Matthew J. "The Nocturnal Negotiations of Youth Spaces in Havana." PhD diss., University of North Carolina at Chapel Hill, 2009.

Rensoli Medina, Rodolfo A. "Visiones paridoras." In *Contar el rap,* edited by Grizel Hernández Baguer and Malcoms Junco Duffay, 23–61. Havana: Ediciones Cidmuc, 2017.

Ribeiro, Raquel. "'Seremos (otra vez) como el Che'? Angola as an 'Alternative Narrative' to Cuba in the 1970s." In *Cuba's Forgotten Decade: How the 1970s Shaped the Revolution,* edited by Emily J. Kirk, Anna Clayfield, and Isabel Story, 209–26. Lanham, MD: Rowman and Littlefield, 2018.

Richard, Nelly. *Masculino/femenino: Prácticas de la diferencia y cultura democrática.* Santiago, Chile: Francisco Zegers Editor, 1993.

Richman, Karen E. *Migration and Vodou.* Gainesville: University Press of Florida, 2005.

Risério, Antonio. *A cidade no Brasil.* São Paulo: Editora 34, 2012.

Rivera, Raquel Z. *New York Ricans from the Hip Hop Zone.* New York: Palgrave Macmillan, 2006.

Rivera-Rideau, Petra R., Jennifer A. Jones, and Tianna S. Paschel. "Introduction: Theorizing Afrolatinidades." In *Afro-Latin@s in Movement: Critical Approaches to Blackness and Transnationalism in the Americas,* edited by Petra R. Rivera-Rideau, Jennifer A. Jones, and Tianna S. Paschel, 1–29. New York: Palgrave Macmillan, 2016.

Rivero Nordet, Balsey. "Crónica de una lengua raspada." In *Contar el rap,* edited by Grizel Hernández Baguer and Malcoms Junco Duffay, 62–68. Havana: Ediciones Cidmuc, 2017.

Robbins, Dylon Lamar. *Audible Geographies in Latin America: Sounds of Race and Place.* Cham, Switzerland: Palgrave Macmillan, 2019.

Rocha, Renato Oliveira. "A dialética da marginalidade em Paulo Lins e Bezerra da Silva." *Revista Crioula,* no. 14 (2014). https://doi.org/10.11606/issn.1981-7169.crioula.2014.74037.

Rodríguez, Jorge Enrique "761." "La aldea, Los Aldeanos, el aldeanismo." In *Contar el rap,* edited by Grizel Hernández Baguer and Malcoms Junco Duffay, 261–69. Havana: Ediciones Cidmuc, 2017.

Roig de Leuchsenring, Emilio. "Bailando junto al abismo." *Espacio Laical* 10, no. 1 (2014): 129–31.

Rojas, Rafael. "The Illegible City." In *Havana beyond the Ruins,* edited by Anke Birkenmaier and Esther Whitfield, translated by Eric Felipe-Barkin, 119–34. Durham, NC: Duke University Press, 2011. https://doi.org/10.1215/9780822394426-005.

Rondón, César Miguel. *El libro de la salsa: Crónica de la música del Caribe urbano.* Caracas: Ediciones B, 2007.

Rose, Tricia. *Black Noise: Rap Music and Black Culture in Contemporary America*. Hanover, NH: University Press of New England, 1994.

———. *The Hip Hop Wars: What We Talk about When We Talk about Hip Hop—and Why It Matters*. New York: BasicCivitas, 2008.

Roth-Gordon, Jennifer. "Conversational Sampling, Race Trafficking, and the Invocation of the *Gueto* in Brazilian Hip-Hop." In *Global Linguistic Flows: Hip Hop Cultures, Youth Identities, and the Politics of Language*, edited by H. Samy Alim, Awad Ibrahim, and Alastair Pennycook, 63–77. New York: Routledge, 2009.

———. *Race and the Brazilian Body: Blackness, Whiteness, and Everyday Language in Rio de Janeiro*. Oakland: University of California Press, 2017.

Rotman, Brian. *Signifying Nothing: The Semiotics of Zero*. Basingstoke, UK: Macmillan, 1987.

Roumain, Jacques. "Is Poetry Dead?" *New Masses*, January 7, 1941.

Rudinow, Joel. *Soul Music: Tracking the Spiritual Roots of Pop from Plato to Motown*. Ann Arbor: University of Michigan Press, 2010.

Sá, Lúcia. *Life in the Megalopolis: Mexico City and São Paulo*. New York: Routledge, 2007.

Salles, Ecio. *Poesia revoltada*. Rio de Janeiro: Aeroplano, 2007.

Saunders, Tanya L. *Cuban Underground Hip Hop: Black Thoughts, Black Revolution, Black Modernity*. Austin: University of Texas Press, 2015.

Saussy, Haun. *The Ethnography of Rhythm: Orality and Its Technologies*. New York: Fordham University Press, 2016.

Scherzinger, Martin. "Mathematics of African Dance Rhythms." Video presented at the Library of Congress, May 4, 2017. https://www.loc.gov/item/webcast-7988/.

Schuller, Mark. *Humanitarian Aftershocks in Haiti*. New Brunswick, NJ: Rutgers University Press, 2016.

Scott, Julius Sherrard. *The Common Wind: Afro-American Currents in the Age of the Haitian Revolution*. New York: Verso, 2018.

Scott, Rebecca J., and Jean M Hébrard. *Freedom Papers: An Atlantic Odyssey in the Age of Emancipation*. Cambridge, MA: Harvard University Press, 2012.

Seabrook, William. *The Magic Island*. Mineola, NY: Dover, 2016.

Segato, Rita Laura. *La guerra contra las mujeres*. Madrid: Traficantes de Sueños, 2016.

Seide, Jean Gardy, Emmanuel Steeve Réginald Badiau, and Hébreux Alexis. "Les causes de l'implantation du Rap en Haïti." Undergraduate thesis, Université de l'État d'Haïti, 2017.

Shaw, Lisa. "São Coisas Nossas: Samba and Identity in the Vargas Era (1930–45)." *Portuguese Studies*, no. 14 (1998): 152–69.

Shilliam, Robbie. *The Black Pacific: Anti-colonial Struggles and Oceanic Connections*. London: Bloomsbury Academic, 2015.

Simas, Luiz Antonio, and Luiz Rufino. *Fogo no mato: A ciência encantada das macumbas.* Rio de Janeiro: Mórula, 2018.
Simmons, David. "Structural Violence as Social Practice: Haitian Agricultural Workers, Anti-Haitianism, and Health in the Dominican Republic." *Human Organization* 69, no. 1 (March 2010): 10–18. https://doi.org/10.17730/humo.69.1.8271r0j17372k765.
Simoni, Valerio. *Tourism and Informal Encounters in Cuba.* New York: Berghahn Books, 2016.
Siskind, Mariano. *Cosmopolitan Desires: Global Modernity and World Literature in Latin America.* Evanston, IL: Northwestern University Press, 2014.
Siwi, Marcio. "Pixação: The Story behind São Paulo's 'Angry' Alternative to Graffiti." *Guardian,* January 6, 2016. https://www.theguardian.com/cities/2016/jan/06/pixacao-the-story-behind-sao-paulos-angry-alternative-to-graffiti.
Smith, Barbara, Beverly Smith, and Demita Frazier. "The Combahee River Collective Statement." In *How We Get Free: Black Feminism and the Combahee River Collective,* edited by Keeanga-Yamahtta Taylor, 15–27. Chicago, IL: Haymarket Books, 2017.
Smith, Duncan. "The Truth of Graffiti." *Art & Text,* no. 17 (April 1985): 84–90.
Smith, Jennie M. *When the Hands Are Many: Community Organization and Social Change in Rural Haiti.* Ithaca, NY: Cornell University Press, 2001.
Smith, Macklin, and Aurko Joshi. *Rhymes in the Flow: How Rappers Flip the Beat.* Ann Arbor: University of Michigan Press, 2020.
Smitherman, Geneva. "'The Chain Remain the Same': Communicative Practices in the Hip Hop Nation." *Journal of Black Studies* 28, no. 1 (1997): 3–25.
———. *Talkin and Testifyin: The Language of Black America.* Detroit, MI: Wayne State University Press, 1986.
Sneed, Paul. "Bandidos de Cristo: Representations of the Power of Criminal Factions in Rio's Proibidão Funk." *Latin American Music Review / Revista de Música Latinoamericana* 28, no. 2 (2007): 220–41.
Sobrevilla, David. "El surgimiento de la idea de Nuestra América en los ensayistas latinoamericanos decimonónicos." *Revista de Crítica Literaria Latinoamericana* 25, no. 50 (1999): 147–63. https://doi.org/10.2307/4531066.
Sosin Martínez, Eileen. "El rap es muchas cosas. Entrevista con Papá Humbertico." In *Contar el rap,* edited by Grizel Hernández Baguer and Malcoms Junco Duffay, 172–78. Havana: Ediciones Cidmuc, 2017.
Spady, James G., Samir Meghelli, and H. Samy Alim. *Tha Global Cipha: Hip Hop Culture and Consciousness.* Philadelphia, PA: Black History Museum Press, 2006.
Span, Christopher M. "Learning in Spite of Opposition: African Americans and Their History of Educational Exclusion in Antebellum America." *Counterpoints,* no. 131 (2005): 26–53.
Stam, Robert, and Ella Shohat. *Race in Translation: Culture Wars around the Postcolonial Atlantic.* New York: New York University Press, 2012.

Staniski, Stanley, dir. *Viva El Vedado: The Story of a Neighborhood*. Ebrahimi Family Foundation, 2019.
Steingo, Gavin. *Kwaito's Promise: Music and the Aesthetics of Freedom in South Africa*. Chicago, IL: University of Chicago Press, 2016.
Stephens, Michelle Ann. *Black Empire: The Masculine Global Imaginary of Caribbean Intellectuals in the United States, 1914–1962*. Durham, NC: Duke University Press, 2005.
Sterling, Cheryl. *African Roots, Brazilian Rites: Cultural and National Identity in Brazil*. New York: Palgrave Macmillan, 2016.
Sterne, Jonathan. *The Audible Past*. Durham, NC: Duke University Press, 2003.
———. "The Theology of Sound: A Critique of Orality." *Canadian Journal of Communication* 36, no. 2 (June 28, 2011): 207–25. https://doi.org/10.22230/cjc.2011v36n2a2223.
Stewart, Garrett. *Reading Voices: Literature and the Phonotext*. Berkeley: University of California Press, 1990.
Stewart, Susan. "Letter on Sound." In *Close Listening: Poetry and the Performed Word*, edited by Charles Bernstein, 29–52. New York: Oxford University Press, 1998.
———. "Rhyme and Freedom." In *The Sound of Poetry, the Poetry of Sound*, edited by Marjorie Perloff and Craig Douglas Dworkin, 29–48. Chicago, IL: University of Chicago Press, 2009.
Stoever, Jennifer Lynn. *The Sonic Color Line: Race and the Cultural Politics of Listening*. New York: New York University Press, 2016.
Suárez de Armas, Lourdes. "El hip-hop desde y con los del barrio." In *Contar el rap*, edited by Grizel Hernández Baguer and Malcoms Junco Duffay, 136–50. Havana: Ediciones Cidmuc, 2017.
Sublette, Ned. *Cuba and Its Music: From the First Drums to the Mambo*. Chicago, IL: Chicago Press Review, 2004.
Taylor, Mark Lewis. "Bringing Noise." In *Noise and Spirit: The Religious and Spiritual Sensibilities of Rap Music*, edited by Anthony B. Pinn, 107–30. New York: New York University Press, 2003.
Temple, Christel N. "The Emergence of Sankofa Practice in the United States: A Modern History." *Journal of Black Studies* 41, no. 1 (2010): 127–50.
Teperman, Ricardo. *Se liga no som: As transformações do rap no Brasil*. São Paulo: Claro enigma, 2015.
Terkourafi, Marina, ed. *The Languages of Global Hip Hop*. New York: Continuum, 2010.
Thompson, Krista A. *Shine: The Visual Economy of Light in African Diasporic Aesthetic Practice*. Durham, NC: Duke University Press, 2015.
Tomashevsky, Boris. "Literary Genres." In *Formalism: History, Comparison, Genre*, edited by L. M. O'Toole and Ann Shukman, translated by L. M. O'Toole, 52–93. Oxford, UK: Holdan Books, 1978.

Tomlinson, Gary. *The Singing of the New World: Indigenous Voice in the Era of European Contact*. New York: Cambridge University Press, 2007.
Tonani do Patrocínio, Paulo Roberto. *Escritos à margem: A presença de autores de periferia na cena literária brasileira*. Rio de Janeiro: FAPERJ, 2013.
Toop, David. *Rap Attack 2: African Rap to Global Hip Hop*. New York: Serpent's Tail, 1994.
Travis, Raphael. *The Healing Power of Hip Hop*. Santa Barbara, CA: Praeger, 2016.
Treece, David. *Brazilian Jive: From Samba to Bossa and Rap*. London: Reaktion Books, 2013.
Treitler, Leo. *With Voice and Pen: Coming to Know Medieval Song and How It Was Made*. New York: Oxford University Press, 2003.
Trouillot, Michel-Rolph. *Haiti, State against Nation: The Origins and Legacy of Duvalierism*. New York: Monthly Review Press, 1990.
———. *Silencing the Past: Power and the Production of History*. Boston, MA: Beacon Press, 1995.
Tryon, Thomas. "Friendly Advice to the Gentleman-Planters of the East and West Indies." In *Caribbeana: An Anthology of English Literature of the West Indies, 1657–1777*, edited by Thomas W. Krise, 51–76. Chicago, IL: University of Chicago Press, 2009.
Tsing, Anna Lowenhaupt. "Inside the Economy of Appearances." *Public Culture* 12, no. 1 (2000): 115–44.
———. *The Mushroom at the End of the World: On the Possibility of Life in Capitalist Ruins*. Princeton, NJ: Princeton University Press, 2015.
Valladares, Licia do Prado. *A invenção da favela: Do mito de origem a favela.com*. Rio de Janeiro: FGV, 2005.
Vaughan, Umi. *Rebel Dance, Renegade Stance: Timba Music and Black Identity in Cuba*. Ann Arbor: University Michigan Press, 2012.
Vaz, Sérgio. "Centralidades Periféricas: Reflexões Sobre Literatura Periférica e Universidade." Lecture presented at Universidade de São Paulo, June 18, 2018.
Vazquez, Alexandra T. *Listening in Detail: Performances of Cuban Music*. Durham, NC: Duke University Press, 2013.
Viana, Elizabeth do Espírito Santo. "Lélia Gonzalez e outras mulheres: Pensamento feminista negro, antirracismo e antissexismo." *Revista da ABPM* 1, no. 1 (June 2010): 52–63.
Vianna, Hermano. *O mistério do samba*. Rio de Janeiro: Zahar, 1995.
———. *O mundo funk carioca*. Rio de Janeiro: Zahar, 1988.
Victorin, Chancy. "Master Dji, plus que le père du Rap Kreyòl." *Le Nouvelliste*, June 6, 2020. https://lenouvelliste.com/article/216847/master-dji-plus-que-le-pere-du-rap-kreyol.
Voegelin, Salomé. *The Political Possibility of Sound: Fragments of Listening*. New York: Bloomsbury Academic, 2019.

Vurkaç, Mehmet. "A Cross-Cultural Grammar for Temporal Harmony in Afro-Latin Musics: Clave, Partido-Alto and Other Timelines." *Current Musicology*, no. 94 (Fall 2022): 37–65. https://doi.org/10.7916/CM.V0I94.5234.

Walser, Robert. "Clamor and Community in the Music of Public Enemy." In *Generations of Youth: Youth Cultures and History in Twentieth-Century America*, edited by Joe Austin and Michael Nevin Willard. New York: New York University Press, 1998.

Weaver, Matthew. "US Agency Infiltrated Cuban Hip-Hop Scene to Spark Youth Unrest." *Guardian*, December 10, 2014, sec. World News. https://www.theguardian.com/world/2014/dec/11/cuban-hip-hop-scene-infiltrated-us-information-youth.

Weheliye, Alexander G. "'Feenin': Posthuman Voices in Contemporary Black Popular Music." *Social Text, 71* 20, no. 2 (Summer 2002): 21–47.

Welsh, Andrew. *Roots of Lyric: Primitive Poetry and Modern Poetics*. Princeton, NJ: Princeton University Press, 1978.

West, Cornel. "The New Cultural Politics of Difference." In *Out There: Marginalization and Contemporary Cultures*, edited by Russell Ferguson, Martha Gever, Trinh T. Minh-ha, and Cornel West, 19–36. Cambridge, MA: MIT Press, 1999.

———. *Prophetic Fragments*. Trenton, NJ: Africa World Press, 1988.

Whitfield, Esther Katheryn. *Cuban Currency: The Dollar and "Special Period" Fiction*. Minneapolis: University of Minnesota Press, 2008.

Williams, Eric. *Capitalism and Slavery*. Chapel Hill: University of North Carolina Press, 1994.

Williams, Raymond L. *Marxism and Literature*. Oxford, UK: Oxford University Press, 2009.

Wilson, James Q., and George L. Kelling. "Broken Windows: The Police and Neighborhood Safety." *Atlantic Monthly*, March 1982.

Wimsatt, W. K. "One Relation of Rhyme to Reason: Alexander Pope." *Modern Language Quarterly* 5, no. 3 (September 1, 1944): 323–38. https://doi.org/10.1215/00267929-5-3-323.

Winn, James Anderson. *Unsuspected Eloquence: A History of the Relations between Poetry and Music*. New Haven, CT: Yale University Press, 1981.

Wittrock, Mary Cobb. "Franketienne's Spirals: Chaos Theory, Minor Literature and Generic Limits." *International Journal of Francophone Studies* 13, no. 1 (June 1, 2010): 103–29. https://doi.org/10.1386/ijfs.13.1.103/7.

Wood, Brent. "Understanding Rap as Rhetorical Folk-Poetry." *Mosaic: An Interdisciplinary Critical Journal* 32, no. 4 (1999): 129–46.

Wynter, Sylvia. "Unsettling the Coloniality of Being/Power/Truth/Freedom: Towards the Human, after Man, Its Overrepresentation–an Argument." *CR: The New Centennial Review* 3, no. 3 (2003): 257–337. https://doi.org/10.1353/ncr.2004.0015.

Yoshinaga, Gilberto. *Nelson Triunfo: Do Sertão ao Hip-Hop*. São Paulo: Shuriken Produções; LiteraRUA, 2014.
Yúdice, George. *The Expediency of Culture: Uses of Culture in the Global Era*. Durham, NC: Duke University Press, 2003.
Zalamea Traba, Fernando. *Filosofía sintética de las matemáticas contemporáneas*. Bogotá: Editorial Universidad Nacional de Colombia, 2009.
Zamora Montes, Alejandro. *Rapear una Cuba utópica: Testimonios del movimiento hiphopero*. Sevilla: Guantanamera, 2017.
Zhdanov, A. A. "On Music: Concluding Speech at a Conference of Soviet Music Workers, 1948." In *On Literature, Music and Philosophy*, 76–112. London: Lawrence and Wishart, 1950.
Zukofsky, Louis. *A*. Berkeley: University of California Press, 1978.
Zumthor, Paul. *Oral Poetry: An Introduction*. Translated by Kathryn Murphy-Judy. Minneapolis: University of Minnesota Press, 1990.
Zurbano Torres, Roberto. "'¡Mami, no quiero más reguetón!' O el nuevo perre(te) o intelectual." In *Contar el rap*, edited by Grizel Hernández Baguer and Malcoms Junco Duffay, 517–44. Havana: Ediciones Cidmuc, 2017.
———. "Se buscan: Textos urgentes para sonidos hambrientos." *Movimiento: La Revista Cubana de Hip Hop*, no. 3. Havana: Instituto Cubano de la Música, 2004.

Index

Italicized page numbers refer to figures.

Abakuá, 205n69
Abiodun, Nehanda, 82, 86
acoustemology, 65–66
African diaspora, 4, 7–8, 72, 73, 92, 94; cultural exchange of, 9–10, 15, 89–90, 94, 128, 135; music of, 16, 21, 49, 54–55; performance of, 36, 51; poetics of, 22, 24, 49, 59, 112–13, 115, 121; and US Black culture, 10, 72, 89
Afrocubanismo, 73
Agencia Cubana de Rap, 86, 171, 176, 181, 185n10, 215n138
Ahearn, Charlie, 179, 204n47
Alamar, 84, 86, 102–3, 181, 205n81, 206n95
aldea, 16, 92–93, 102, 106–8, 109. *See also* global village
Aldeano, El. *See* Aldo
Aldeanos, Los, 1, 3, 114–15, 173, 175, 176; implications of name, 105–8; and improvisation, 130–32; lyrics of, 5, 56–57, 114–15; on protest, 63, 105, 153–54; use of USB drives, 93, 107. *See also* aldea
Aldo (Al2), 56–57, 105–8, 130–32, 150, 173, 175, 224n73. *See also* Aldeanos, Los
Alexey ..el tipo este.., 83–84, 173
alfabetização, 132. *See also* literacy
Alim, H. Samy, 11, 111, 147
A lo cubano (Los Orishas), 84, 185n11
Amenaza, 84
Anderson, 150
Andrade, Mário de, 75, 77, 208n11

Andrade, Oswald de, 203n33, 208n129
Aninha, 149
Anónimo Consejo, 155, 173
antropofagia, 203n33
apologia ao crime, 158–59
apostrophe, 15, 48, 63, 65, 115
Aristide, Jean-Bertrand, 4, 27, 94, 157–58, 162–64, 180
Armstrong, Louis, 136
ars poetica, 15, 48, 56–66. *See also* raplove
Ars Poetica (Horace), 57
Asap Fresh, 39–40, 173, 195n148
assonance, 58, 72, 84, 114, 125, 131
Atitude Feminina, 149
aurality, 17, 113, 136–38, 169; in rap, 121, 123, 128, 130, 135, 140, 168
Austin, J. L., 135, 143
Autobiografía del esclavo poeta (Manzano), 50, 112–13, 128
Auto-Tune (autotune), 36, 37
ayibobo, 39, 40, 60, 195n152

B, El, 9, 56, 106, 150, 175, 216n31; lyrics of, 114–15, 122, 145–46; protest of, 107–8. *See also* Aldeanos, Los
babalawo, 51
background (instrumental), 72
bailes black, 3, 18, 75–80, 179
bailes funk. *See* bailes black; funk carioca
Bakhtin, Mikhail, 126
Baleiro, Zeco, 147
Bambaataa, Afrika, 78, 179, 182
Bandeira, Manuel, 127
Baraka, Amiri, 156

Barbaram, 1
Bárbaro "El Urbano," 16, 72–74, 73, 84, 91, 109, 173, 224–25n73
Barbosa Lima, Francisco Velto. *See* Padêro MC
Barbosa Sales, Erivan. *See* Erivan "Produtos do Morro"
Barikad Crew (BC), 4, 94–95, 174, 175, 181, 182; lyrics of, 142, 158, 163–64
barrios insalubres, 102
batalla, 108, 124
Batalla de los Gallos, 108
batey, 164–65, 228n155
Batista, Fulgencio, 179
Battle of Vertières, 30
baz, 16, 92–95, 109, 157–58. *See also* gangs; marginality
Beastie Boys, 100
Belafonte, Harry, 182
Benjamin, Walter, 26, 143–44, 158
Bergeaud, Emeric, 208n8
Bezerra da Silva, José, 118–19, 122
BIC, 116–17, 174
bildungsroman, 76
Billboard, 37, 39, 100
Black Arts Movement, 156
Black Atlantic, 7–8, 14
Black August Collective, 181, 206n94
Black feminism, 15, 144, 148, 172, 192n46; militancy of, 147–51; and subjunctivity, 24–25; and world-building, 22, 25, 27; and yearning, 15, 22–23, 25, 44
Black Juniors, 78, 204n52
Black Liberation Army, 82
Blackness, 7–13, 36, 44, 46–47, 94, 130, 162; in Brazil, 44–47, 75–79, 117–19, 121, 148–49, 159–62; in Cuba, 33–35, 72–73, 84, 86, 103, 124, 129, 131; in Haiti, 29–30, 60–62, 89, 163–67; and hip hop, 11, 59, 115, 143–44, 168, 202n8; in US, 10, 81, 147, 150, 156. *See also* Black Atlantic; Black feminism; Black Power
Black Power, 21, 41, 60, 62, 76, 77
Black Rio, 77, 203n41
blanqueamiento, 9. *See also* whitening
Blay'Z, 5, 174
Blaze One, 9, 67, 164–65, 174, 186n25
bling-bling, 34. *See also* surfacism
bloqueo, 81

BNegão, 186n25
boasting, 59, 60, 115
Bolsonaro, Jair, 69, 109
bomba, 55
bonches, 82
bossa nova, 4, 127, 189n86
Boukman, Dutty, 30, 165. *See also* Haitian Revolution
Boukman Eksperyans, 62
braggadocio, 117. *See also* boasting
branqueamento, 9. *See also* whitening
Brasília, 99, 102, 181
Brazil, 6, 11, 20, 24–25, 41, 69, 110, 119, 211n53; Afro-Brazilian practices, 12, 55, 75–76, 98, 128, 148; author's fieldwork in, 3–4, 41, 111, 123, 196n169; dictatorships of, 3, 4, 74–75, 78; history of hip hop in, 3, 74–81, 97–102; literacy of, 132; music of, 14, 40–47, 125; racial democracy of, 4, 9, 75; urban periphery of, 97–102, 121; urban violence of, 144, 158. *See also* bailes black; funk carioca; literatura periférica; Palmares; periferia; quilombismo; rap nacional; samba; São Paulo; *individual artists and groups*
Brazilian funk. *See* funk carioca
breakbeat, 2, 5, 6, 13, 55, 123, 187n26; in other genres, 36, 194n127, 195n157; in rap instrumentals, 42, 49, 62, 72, 79, 123, 125, 136, 140, 171; in rap lyrics, 55, 59, 129–30, 153, 168
breakdance, 2, 7, 13, 71, 142, 179, 180, 204n52; in Brazil, 20–21, 77–78, 179; in Haiti, 88. *See also* bailes black; breakbeat; moña
Brebaje Man, 129–30, 174
Brisa Flow, 68–69, 174
Brisant, Ni, 132–35
Bronx, 18, 179
Brown, James, 77, 79, 179
Brown, Mano. *See* Mano Brown
Brown, Nino, 76–77
Buena Vista Social Club (Cooder), 72, 181
bwa, 96–97, 164
bwa kayiman, 30, 165

Cahiers d'Haïti, 142
Caimán Barbudo, 108
Calle 13, 154
Cándida, Yanelis. *See* Nono
cantoria, 125

Index 267

Canudos, 97
capitalism, 9, 17, 22–23, 44; in rap lyrics, 39, 121–22. *See also* neoliberalism
Cardi B, 35–36
Caribbean, 4, 35, 87, 94, 144, 181, 195n8; music of, 13, 15, 54, 74, 81; poetics of, 7, 20, 49, 89–90, 124, 140
Carnival, 61, 95, 157
Carpentier, Alejo, 74, 75
Cassiano, 75
Castillo Pérez, Maykel, 186n12
Castro, Fidel, 19, 33, 81–82, 107, 151, 153, 179, 182, 204n64. *See also* Cuban Revolution
Castro, Raúl, 179, 182. *See also* Cuban Revolution
Cazuza, 14
censorship, 144; of Brazilian rap, 69, 159, 175; of Cuban rap, 105, 155, 213n105; during Cuban Revolution, 34, 74, 81, 104, 153–54, 213n107
Césaire, Aimé, 8, 94, 167, 209n16
Césaire, Suzanne, 90
Chamie, Mário, 223n40
chan pwen, 129
Chante Nwel, 95, 182
Chéreau, Patrice, 14, 126–27, 219n93
Child of the Dark (Maria de Jesus), 98, 147–48
chimè, 94
Chocolate MC, 103
Christian rap, 63
Chuck D, 21, 189n82
Cidinho e Doca, 40, 158, 174
100% Original, 49
cimarronaje, 66. *See also* marronage
citation. *See* intertextuality; sampling
ciudad letrada, La (Rama), 6, 110, 113, 140
clave, 4, 13, 33. *See also* son
Cold War, 24, 74
Colón (city in Matanzas, Cuba), 124
colorblindness, 4, 9, 33, 73–74, 82
Combahee River Collective, 149–50
comisión depuradora, La (Los Aldeanos), 105, 153–54, 182
commercialization: of hip hop, 33–35, 60, 67, 86, 95, 143, 185n8; of other genres, 73, 85, 87, 152
commodification, 21–22, 34–36, 44–46, 168, 172

community-building, 2, 17, 48, 60, 70, 113, 127–28, 144
community writing, 7, 15, 16–17, 70, 112, 128, 132–34, 140–41, 143, 148, 169
Consciência Black (Racionais MC's), 79, 177
Consciência Humana, 158, 174
consciousness-raising, 16, 17, 60, 79, 87, 115, 155, 204n54
conscious rap, 60, 88, 169
Conselheiro, Antônio, 97
Contino, Gabriel. *See* Gabriel "o Pensador"
contradanza, 4
Cooder, Ry, 72, 181
cortiço, 97
Cosmic Race, The (Vasconcelos), 73
cosmopolitanism, 16, 39, 79, 85, 93, 96, 109, 203n33
Coup, The, 168
crack (drug), 36, 144, 176
Creoles, 89–90, 140. *See also* Kreyòl
creolization, 88, 89, 96, 203n23
Criolo, 63, 126–27, 174, 219n93
crónica, 115
Cross Bronx Expressway, 2
Cuba: Afro-Cuban religions, 51, 65; history of hip hop in, 3, 81–87, 102–8; music of, 4, 33–38, 72–74, 81, 115, 124, 130; and race, 4, 9–10, 73–74. *See also* Alamar; Cuban Rap Agency; Cuban Revolution; Havana; hip hop cubano; Martí, José; Special Period; *individual artists and groups*
CubaDisco, 154
Cuban Counterpoint (Ortiz), 73
Cuban hip hop festivals, 84–87, 182, 186–87n25, 205n81, 206nn94–100, 213n98
Cuban Hip Hop Symposium, 73, 154, 185n10
Cuban Institute of Music, 181
Cuban Missile Crisis, 131–32
Cuban Rap Agency, 86, 171, 176, 181, 185n10, 215n138
Cuban Revolution, 19, 24, 73, 102, 151, 152–53; censorship during, 34, 74, 81, 104–5, 153–54, 155, 213n105, 213n107; housing during, 82; racial politics of, 9, 73–74, 81–82; religion during, 65

cuentapropismo, 34
Cuesta, Odaymara, 150, 175
cultural imperialism, 10, 16, 75, 77, 90
cultural nationalism, 72, 75, 88, 90, 92, 130

da Cunha, Euclides, 97
Dade, 95, 206n26
dance: in Brazil, 16, 40, 55, 75, 128, 179; in Cuba, 32–35, 82, 103, 104, 152, 155, 179; in Haiti, 87, 88, 139–40; repression of, 140. *See also* bailes black; break-dance; moña
Dandara, 160. *See also* Palmares
Dantas, Konrad, 42–43, 45
danzón, 4
David "D'Omni," 212n89, 213n107. *See also* OMNI-ZonaFranca
Davis, Angela, 149
dead prez, 84, 181, 206n95
Debray, Regis, 153
dechoukaj, 16, 18, 28, 71, 88, 90, 180. *See also* uprooting
décima, 73, 113, 124–25, 128, 218n78, 218n80
decolonization, 90, 142, 144, 156, 162–67, 174
deforestation, 96–97
deixis, 20, 22, 48, 67, 71, 80, 117, 121
de la Cordillera, Brisa, 68–70
del Monte, Domingo, 112
del Rio, Soandres, 64, 67
desafio, 125
despelote, 34. *See also* timba
Dessalines, Jean-Jacques, 30–31, 193n83, 208n132. *See also* Haitian Revolution
desviaciones ideológicas, 81
Detentos do Rap, 159, 174
D-Fi Powèt Revòlte, 5, 91, 128–29, 174, 187n25; lyrics by, 17, 25–26, 48, 95–96, 166–67
Dia a dia da periferia (GOG), 99, 122
Díaz, Telmary, 49
Díaz Ayala, Cristóbal, 81
Dina Di, 26, 79, 80, 146, 175
Discípulo, El, 150
disc jockey (DJ), 7
DJ Hum, 55, 76–77, 177
Djonga, 46, 91, 127, 146, 175
DMN, 127, 175
Doble Filo, 162, 206n97

Dominican Republic, 165, 202n22, 227n155
doudouisme, 87, 207n108
Doxum, Bia, 117, 118, 132–35, 174, 217n39
drugs, 36–37, 40. *See also* crack; lean
Drummond de Andrade, Carlos, 127
Dukes, 12, 145, 175
Duvalier, François, 87–88, 157, 179. *See also* Duvalier dictatorship
Duvalier, Jean-Claude, 27, 89, 157, 179. *See also* Duvalier dictatorship
Duvalier dictatorship, 3, 9, 16, 27, 28, 71, 87–88, 95, 137, 157, 227n155
dyaspora (of Haitians), 89, 227n155. *See also* African diaspora

Echu-Eleguá, 119
ecocriticism, 97, 165
Edi Rock, 79, 177, 189n80
Edwards, Brent Hayes, 7, 8, 135–36
Ellington, Duke, 136
embargo, 81
embolada, 125, 219n86
embromation, 122–23, 128, 131, 132, 140
Emicida, 197n199
empresa mixta, 34
enraizados da letra, 16
epic poetry, 130
epistrophe, 49, 50, 55, 66, 67, 136, 138
Erivan "Produtos do Morro," 125, 175
Escalona Carrillo, David. *See* David "D'Omni"
escrevivência, 148
Escuadrón Patriota, 155–56, 186n25, 213n107, 225n73
Eshun, Kodwo, 36
Esquivel, Alexis, 31
"Essay on Criticism" (Pope), 57–59
Eud, Princess, 25–26, 139–40, 171, 176
Eudomination (Princess Eud), 25, 139–40, 171
Exu, 119. *See also* Echu-Eleguá
Ezili, 25, 192n61

Facção Central, 159, 175
Fanon, Frantz, 90, 156
Fantom, 29–31, 41, 91, 175
favela, 9, 40, 93, 97, 118–19, 158, 210n49, 211n52, 211n68; in Carolina Maria de Jesus, 98, 147–48; in lyrics,

40–44, 92, 99–100, 159; origins of, 97–98
Feld, Steven, 65–66
Feliú, Vicente, 224n73
Fernandes, Lenny, 142, 175
Ferreira, Tula Pilar, 148
Ferréz, 101, 102
festivals, 105, 125, 181–82; of Cuban hip hop, 84–87, 186–87n25, 205n81, 206nn94–100, 213n98; Petrúcio Maia, 196n169; Potaje urbano, 124–25; Rap'Rocher Haiti, 94, 182
fèy blanch, 25, 167, 169
Filosofia de Rua, 63, 175
financialization, 23, 24, 25, 44, 45. See also neoliberalism; speculation
Five Percenters, 63
flow, 5, 6, 13–14, 36, 122–23, 168; in Brazilian rap, 55, 59, 125–26, 136, 147; in Cuban rap, 37, 130–31; in Haitian rap, 60; in hip hop circulation, 10, 14, 70, 94
Floyd, George, 147
Fortaleza, 3, 41, 119, 125, 132, 142, 174–77, 196n169. See also individual artists and groups
Frankétienne, 48, 135, 137–39. See also spiralisme
freestyle, 5, 50–52, 58, 108, 128–32, 140, 175, 187n26, 220n133. See also improvisation
free trade, 34–35. See also neoliberalism
Freire, Paulo, 141, 144
Frente Negra Brasileira, 75
Frères Parent, Les, 88, 180
Fugees, the, 178
funk (US musical genre), 2, 7, 13, 82, 88, 207n115; in Brazil, 3, 16, 76, 99, 179, 203n38; in Cuba, 3, 16, 82, 104; in Haiti, 71, 88. See also funk carioca
funk carioca (Brazilian funk), 2, 78–79, 81, 180

Gabriel "o Pensador," 100–101, 175
Gaceta del Caribe, 142
Galeano, Eduardo, 68
gangs, 40, 95, 142, 174
gangsta rap, 21, 95, 103, 145
Garcia, Débora, 149
Gardy, Seide Jean. See Kameleyon
Garner, Eric, 147
Garoute, Niska, 61–62, 175

Gates, Henry Louis, Jr., 49, 112
gender, 14, 17, 86, 149, 171–72, 224n65
Gerson King Combo, 75
ghetto, 94–102; as archipelago, 52, 100; in Brazilian rap, 46, 52, 98–99, 111, 118; in Haitian rap, 95–97; racialization of, 95, 168
Gil, Gilberto, 211n65
Gilroy, Paul, 7–8, 21, 93, 94
Ginen, 62, 203n27
Glissant, Édouard, 20, 24, 30, 48, 71, 89
globalization, 2, 5, 9, 10, 15, 23, 43, 78, 82, 89, 92–94, 109; of music, 4, 21, 24, 109, 180, 182. See also global village
Global South, 21, 92, 143
global village, 102, 107–8
GOG, 9, 21, 44, 111–12, 119–22, 147, 175, 181; and periferia, 99, 101–2; and writing, 16
Gómez, Sara, 225n81
Gómez, Tito, 130
Gonçalves, Genival Oliveira. See GOG
Gonzalez, Lélia, 77
González, Sara, 152
gordofobia, 150
graffiti, 2, 17, 134, 143
Grandes Ligas, 212n94
Grandmaster Caz, 48
Grandmaster Flash, 68
Granma, 115, 212n89
gran moun, 62, 163–64
griot, 187n35
G-Shytt, 39–40
Guarany, Horacio, 68–69
Gucci Mane, 189n82
guerreira, 148–49, 224n53. See also Black feminism
guerrera, 148, 150. See also Black feminism
Guerreros de la tinta (Los Aldeanos), 5
Guevara, Ernesto "Che," 102–3, 105, 154, 179, 212n89
Guillén, Nicolás, 73, 208n11
Gutiérrez, Pedro Juan, 31–32

Haiti, 24, 27–31, 40, 74, 200n74, 202n22, 227n155; author's fieldwork in, 3–4, 11, 128; constitutions of, 8, 30; earthquake of, 227n151; history of hip hop in, 3–4, 87–90, 94–97; music of, 3–4, 59, 62, 87–88, 95, 109, 116, 162, 180; rural

270 Index

Haiti *(continued)*
 communities of, 165. *See also* Duvalier dictatorship; Haitian Revolution; Kreyòl; rap kreyòl; *individual artists and groups*
Haitian Creole, 3, 28, 88–89, 137–40, 180
Haitian Revolution, 4, 8, 18, 24, 162; in rap lyrics, 28, 30–31, 60, 89, 164–65
Hall, Stuart, 8, 14
Hansen, Luana, 186n25
Harlem, 74
hate speech, 143
Hathaway, Donny, 99
Havana, 2, 32, 74; author's fieldwork in, 3, 91, 108, 129; East Havana, 82, 102, 122; urban space of, 16, 114, 129, 212–13n94. *See also* Alamar; Cuban hip hop festivals; *individual artists and groups*
Hegel, Friedrich, 162, 195n145
Hérard, Antoine Rodolphe, 88
Hérard, Georges Lys, 27, 41, 88, 94, 176, 180
Hermanos de Causa, 63, 175
Herrera, Pablo, 82, 83
hetereoglossia, 126
heterotopia, 47, 198n205
Hills, Ieda, 79
hip hop: circulation of, 4–5, 9–11, 14, 21, 23, 76, 78, 142; culture of, 54, 61, 77–78, 87, 89, 112, 134; elements of, 2, 13, 206n99; origins of, 2–3, 7, 71; poetics of, 6–7, 20, 48–49, 53–55, 70; and religion, 63; in universities, 11; world hip hop, 93, 109. *See also* hip hop cubano; Hip Hop Nation Language; rap kreyòl; rap nacional
hip hop cubano, 15, 19, 51, 81–87; *individual artists and groups*
Hip Hop Nation Language, 5, 72, 89, 96, 122
hombre nuevo, 102, 155, 212n89. *See also* Guevara, Ernesto "Che"
Homer, 22
Horace, 57
Hughes, Langston, 9
hypermasculinity, 15, 47, 79, 95, 145, 148, 150, 172

Ice Blue, 79
Ifá, 51

illocutionary force, 135, 137, 143. *See also* speech act theory
imperialism, 9–10, 12, 68, 72, 74, 77, 81, 82, 86, 159, 164, 204n63. *See also* cultural imperialism
improvisation, 12–13, 15, 50, 51, 73, 82, 84, 113, 132, 136, 218n76, 218n80; in rap, 50, 122–23, 129, 187n26; in repente, 17, 124–25, 128. *See also* freestyle
Indigenism, 74
Inquérito, Renan, 149–50
intermediality, 135, 140
intertextuality, 14, 68, 122–28, 135, 140, 197n199. *See also* sampling
invasão, 158–59. *See also* violence
Izolan, 158, 175, 175, 209n26

Jakobson, Roman, 20, 57, 146
James, C. L. R., 22
jazz, 49, 74, 75, 87, 88, 202–3n23; influence on rap, 17, 109, 113, 128, 135–40. *See also* rapjazz; Vodou-jazz
Jazz des Jeunes, 74
Jean, Wyclef, 3, 178, 185n8
Jobim, Tom, 14, 126–27
Jodeci, 36
Jor, Jorge Ben, 55
Jornal do Brasil, 77
José Martí Anti-Imperialist Platform, 85
José Martí National Library, 81
journalism, 113, 114–22, 135
Juan y Junior, 153
Junco Duffay, Malcoms "Justicia," 66–67, 81, 123, 171, 176, 224n65; as producer, 1, 91, 122–23, 129; as rapper, 31–32, 38, 41, 105

Kameleyon, 189n82
Kanis, 61–62, 175
kata, 62
kilti libètè, 87
King, Martin Luther, Jr., 27, 29
King rete king (Wendyyy), 59–60
Kitchener, Lord, 54–55
KL Jay, 79
Knight, Jean, 76
kokorat, 116–17
KondZilla, 42–43, 45
konpa-dirèk (konpa), 59, 87
Kool and the Gang, 75

Index

Kool Herc, 13
koudyay, 87
Kreyòl, 3, 28, 88–90, 137–40, 180
Krudas, Las, 150, 175
K-Tafalk, 142, 174
kwaito, 85

La Fina, 186n25
Lathan, Stan, 179, 204n47
Lavalas, 93, 163. *See also* Aristide, Jean-Bertrand
lean (drug), 36–37
lettered city, 6, 110, 113, 140
Lévi-Strauss, Claude, 110
Lezama Lima, José, 104
literacy, 6, 16, 42, 110–14, 132–35, 140 143; in rap, 121, 123, 127–28
literatura periférica, 3, 102, 117
Lolo, 62
Lord, Albert, 130
Lord Kitchener, 54–55
Los Angeles, 21
lòt dimansyon, 15, 25. *See also* yearning
Loups Noirs, Les, 88
Louverture, Toussaint, 193n86
Lula da Silva, Luiz Inácio, 41, 111, 182
Lunes de Revolución, 104
lwa, 25, 30, 61–62. *See also* Vodou
lyric poetry, 17, 52, 57–58, 113, 115, 124, 159, 221n163; apostrophe in, 48, 65. *See also* ars poetica

machismo, 34, 224n65. *See also* hypermasculinity
Macoutes, 157–58
Macumba, 12, 119
magic, 12, 43, 46, 129, 161; in Haitian Vodou, 39; in lyric poetry, 65; in rap lyrics, 100
Maia, Tim, 161
Maikel Extremo, 224n73
Makandal, François, 157
malandragem, 118–19, 160–61
Malcoms "Justicia," 66–67, 81, 123, 171, 176, 224n65; as producer, 1, 91, 122–23, 129; as rapper, 31–32, 38, 41, 105
mambo, 61, 62. *See also* oungan
Mano Brown, 79, 98–99, 100, 145, 160–62, 168, 175, 176, 177, 189n80. *See also* Racionais MC's
Manzano, Juan Francisco, 50, 112–13

maracatú, 55
Marcelo D2, 117–18
marginality, 9, 11, 35, 82, 92–93, 109, 119, 148, 150; in Brazilian rap, 92, 97–102, 121, 134, 159; in Cuban rap, 37, 103–8, 124, 156. *See also* baz; periferia
Maria da Silva, Débora, 69
Maria de Jesus, Carolina, 98, 147–48, 210–11n51
Marín, Rubén, 52
Marley, Bob, 7, 88
marronage: in Brazil, 158–59; in Cuba, 66; in Haiti, 30, 157, 165
Martí, José, 73, 74, 106–8, 115, 152, 208n132
Martineau, Jean-Claude, 96
Marxism, 22, 44, 45, 102, 142
Master Dji, 27, 41, 88, 94, 176, 180
master of ceremony (MC), 2
Matanzas, Cuba, 107
Mateus dos Santos, Mauro, 92, 102, 127, 141, 177, 181
Matos, Flora, 44, 175
mawonaj, 157, 165. *See also* marronage
Mbembe, Achille, 162
MC Boy do Charmes, 43–44, 176
MC Fioti, 45–46, 197n196
MC Guimê, 43, 176
McLuhan, Marshall, 107
MC Solaar, 207n115
MC White, 49–51, 57
Médico de la Salsa, El, 190n4
Mejías, Yamay, 186n25
mereng, 74, 88
merengue, 87
messianism, 21, 26–30, 97
mestiçagem, 9, 75
mestizaje, 9, 73
metonymy, 2, 66, 146–47
Miami bass, 78
Migos, 39
Milanés, Pablo, 105, 152
militarism, 17, 144, 145, 158; in Brazil, 158–59; in Cuba, 132, 152, 155–56, 225n81; in Haiti, 3, 30, 157
Mirville, Ernst, 112
mizik angaje, 88, 116
mizik rasin, 62, 88, 109, 162, 208n11
modernity, 8, 93, 106, 110, 213n94
Moïse, Jovenel, 109

Index

moña, 3, 18, 82–83, 179
Money Honey Mike, 89–90
montuno, 73, 84
Moore, Jessica Care, 206n95
Moré, Benny, 83
More, Thomas, 21
Mos Def, 181, 206n95
Moses, Robert, 2, 71
Moten, Fred, 12, 46, 69, 131, 135–36
mouchwa, 95
Movimiento San Isidro, 186n12
MP3, 5, 17, 56, 107
MTV, 42, 100, 180, 181
Mucharrima, Charly, 224n73
mundo do crime, 100
MV Bill, 5, 121, 176

Nambikwara, 110
nan tèt mwen, 128–29, 132, 140
Nas, 67, 69
Nascimento, Abdias do, 159
nationalism, 4, 71, 90, 106, 208n132. See also cultural nationalism
negritude, 7, 8, 75, 87
neighborhood, 3, 7, 90, 92, 100–102, 103, 114–15, 124; belonging in, 15–16, 37, 41, 71, 81; community dances of, 3, 20–21, 78, 82; placemaking of, 92–93, 100–102, 106; and race, 7, 143; scalability of, 81, 90–100. See also aldea; baz; ghetto; marginality; periferia
Nelson "Triunfo," 77–78, 179, 180
neoliberalism, 2, 15, 23–25, 34–36, 42–43, 93, 98, 196n172; and financialization, 24; and speculation, 23, 43–44. See also yearning
Neruda, Pablo, 65
new man, 102, 155, 212n89. See also Guevara, Ernesto "Che"
New Masses, 142
New York City, 2, 7, 71, 89, 179, 181, 193n103, 204n64; hip hop in, 69, 86, 100, 122, 206n94, 207n118; violence in, 142, 144, 147, 222n20. See also Bronx; Harlem
NG La Banda, 33–34
noirisme, 9
Nono, 1, 12, 176
nostalgia, 21–22, 67–69, 71
nouvèl jenerasyon, 27
Nouvelliste, Le, 95

"Nuestra América" (Martí), 106–7
nueva canción, 68, 152
nueva trova, 5, 105, 152
Nuevo Vedado, 1, 106, 114–15

Obá, 55
Obsesión, 176, 182
Ochoa Gautier, Ana María, 6, 113
Ogou Desalin, 30
OMNI-ZonaFranca, 212n89
onè ak respè, 96
Ong, Walter, 111, 130, 215n10
onomatopoeia, 59, 131, 137, 158
Operation Baghdad, 94
oraliture, 112, 215n12
orality, 6, 51, 110–13, 121, 129–30, 145, 187n35. See also Ong, Walter
oricha, 84. See also Orishas, Los
Original Rap Staff, 89, 163, 176
Orishas, Los, 84–85, 176, 181, 185n11
orixá, 55, 128
Ortiz, Fernando, 73
ostentação, 25, 42–44
oudjenikon, 116
oungan, 39, 61, 200n74
ousadia, 25, 45
Oye Habana, 86

pachanga, 154–55
Padêro MC, 41–42, 119, 176
Padilla, Heberto, 104
Padura, Leonardo, 81
Palmares, 159–60, 162. See also quilombismo
pan (music genre), 54
Pan-Africanism, 75, 77
pancadão, 78
Pando, Joel, 4
Papá Humbertico, 66, 150–51, 176, 206n100
Papa Legba, 119
Papash, 28–29
Papo Record, 49, 52
paquete semanal, 214n128
Parra, Violeta, 68
Parry, Milman, 130
Partido Alto, 78
Paz, Issa, 79–80
peña, 105
periferia, 16, 92–93, 97–102, 109. See also favela; marginality; neighborhood

peripheral literature, 3, 102, 117
perreo, 35. *See also* reggaeton
Pétion, Alexandre, 30, 192n86
peyi andeyò, 165
PIC, 116
Pickett, Wilson, 75
pie forzado, 124, 150, 218n80. *See also* décima
Pilar Ferreira, Tula, 148
Pinheiros River, 100
Pinochet, Augusto, 23
pixação, 17, 113, 133–35. *See also* graffiti; literacy
placemaking, 16, 92, 95–96, 100–101, 104–7, 169
Plano de Avenidas, 97
Plaza de la Revolución, 33
P.M., 155
poetics: of the Caribbean, 7, 20, 49, 89–90, 124, 140; and gender, 17, 172; of hip hop, 2–7, 13, 20–25, 90–94, 167–72, 192n46; and recursion, 14–15, 20, 49–57, 66, 129–30, 168. *See also* ars poetica; deixis; freestyle; improvisation; lyric poetry
poet warrior, 152–55. *See also* guerreira; guerrera
ponto (Brazilian verbal game), 128
Pope, Alexander, 57–59
Port-au-Prince, 2, 11, 71, 74, 116–17; author's fieldwork in, 3–4, 11, 128; Castro neighborhood of, 95–96; urban space of, 16, 138, 193n86; and violence, 94, 144. *See also* baz; *individual artists and groups*
Potaje Urbano, 124–25
prayer, 15, 30, 59, 63–65, 120, 121, 133, 135. *See also* apostrophe; raplove
Presley, Elvis, 99
Price-Mars, Jean, 74
Prieto, Abel, 85
Princess Eud, 25–26, 139–40, 171, 176
Prófugo, 129
proibidão, 25, 40, 174
Projota, 59, 91, 177
Proyecto Chardo, 153, 177
Public Enemy, 21, 41, 78, 79, 84, 180, 204n56
pwen, 113, 129
pwezi filozofik, 162–67. *See also* Aristide, Jean-Bertrand

Quarto de despejo (Maria de Jesus), 98, 147–48
queerness, 29, 44, 45, 47, 175, 197n196
Quijano, Aníbal, 165
quilombismo, 159–62. *See also* marronage; Nascimento, Abdias do

racial democracy, 4, 9, 75
raciocínio, 161. *See also* Racionais MC's
Racionais MC's, 3, 11, 79, 145, 168, 176, 177, 180, 181, 189n86; lyrics of, 41, 99–100, 101, 160–62
radio, 32–33, 73, 75, 82, 84, 88, 105, 176, 179, 180
Radio Planèt Kreyòl, 94
Radyo Pòtoprens, 88
ragamuffin, 88
ragga, 71
rak bwa, 164–65
Rama, Ángel, 6, 110, 140
R & B, 36
RAPadura Xique-Chico, 125–26, 177
rap cubano, 81, 90. *See also* hip hop cubano
rap es guerra, 1–2, 150–52
rapjazz, 135–40. *See also* Frankétienne
rap kreyòl, 9, 24, 27, 60, 87–90, 94–97, 180, 189n86, 221n163. *See also* individual artists and groups
raplove, 15, 20, 48–51, 53, 69–70, 71, 76, 96, 115, 169; and ars poetica, 56–59, 66; and improvisation, 50; raplove songs, 63–70, 79, 83; and religion, 51, 63
rap nacional, 80, 90. *See also* individual artists and groups
rappers. *See* individual artists and groups
Rappin' Hood, 127, 159, 177
Rap Plus Size (Paz and Donato), 79
rara, 3, 88, 109, 116, 157
rasin, 62, 88, 109, 162, 208n11
Rastafarianism, 7, 88
Reação Hip Hop, 117, 118
Reagan, Ronald, 35
realismo sucio, 31
Realismo sucio y arte pop (Malcoms "Justicia"), 31–33
Rebouças, Carolina, 119, 174
recursion, 14–15, 19–20, 38, 48–58, 65–66, 71, 115, 129, 168
Rede Globo, 100
reggae, 7, 71

reggaeton, 2, 24, 25, 38, 72, 103, 104, 178, 181, 182; and dance, 35, 37; vs. rap, 56–57, 81, 155
Regla de Ocha, 2, 34–35, 84, 194n114
Reis, Tássia, 135, 136–37, 145, 177
Relatos de Fortaleza, 119, 177
remix, 39–40, 49, 173, 182
Rensoli, Rodolfo, 205n81
reparterismo, 103–4, 205n81, 213n98
repente, 17, 113, 124–26, 135, 219n86
Requerimiento, 110
Rev ak plim (D-Fi Powèt Revòlte), 5
Rey de la Habana, El (Gutiérrez), 32
rhyme, 13, 36, 49–51, 57–58, 72, 125, 129–31
Riley, Boots, 168
Rincon Sapiência, 123, 160, 177
Rio de Janiero, 40, 59, 75, 78–79, 97, 100–101, 118, 175–80
Rockfam, 29, 91, 177
rodas de jongo, 128
Rodríguez, Silvio, 5, 152–53
Roots, the, 48, 181, 182, 206n95, 206n97
Rose, Tricia, 22, 130, 143, 168
Roumain, Jacques, 142, 208n11
Rousseff, Dilma, 41, 46, 69
rumba, 1, 33
Run-DMC, 180, 204n56

Sabotage, 92, 102, 127, 141, 177, 181
Saint-Domingue, 4, 8
salsa (musical genre), 33, 81, 128
samba, 4, 17, 55, 74–75, 79, 90, 109, 208n11; as precursor to rap, 17, 117–19, 122, 127. *See also* malandragem
Samba do Congo, 122
sampling, 45, 46, 91, 95, 96, 115, 123–30, 197n199; antecedents of, 218n76; of lyrics, 14, 62, 68–69, 83–84, 101, 119, 123, 126–27, 128, 216n31; of music from the US, 63–64, 76, 84, 99; of slogans, 153, 163; of space, 93; of traditions, 17, 57, 59, 107, 125, 128, 136, 144. *See also* intertextuality
sanba, 88, 116
Sánchez, Erick, 69
Sankofa, 24
Santería, 2, 34–35, 84, 194n114
santo: in Afro-Brazilian religions, 76–77; in Afro-Cuban religions, 34, 35. *See also* Macumba; Santería

Santos, Marcelo, 49, 61, 178
São Paulo, 2, 43, 75, 78–79, 181; author's fieldwork in, 3–4, 111, 123; urban space of, 9, 16, 78, 97–100, 134, 222n20; and violence, 9, 92, 144, 158–69, 222n20; zona leste, 117, 222n20; zona sul, 111, 126, 222n20. *See also* periferia; *individual artists and groups*
sarau, 101, 102, 212n81
Sarmiento, Domingo Faustino, 107
scat, 136–37. *See also* jazz
Scott-Heron, Gil, 206n95
sede de hoje, 25, 41
self-referentiality, 48–49, 57–59, 100, 122. *See also* raplove
Sentimientos desafinados (Malcoms "Justicia"), 91, 105
sertão, 125, 177
sertões, Os (Cunha), 97
Shakur, Assata, 82, 86
Shakur, Tupac, 63, 167
Sharylaine, 5, 53–54, 79, 160, 177
signifying, 59, 115, 220n113
Silver, Tony, 179
Silvito "El Libre," 56–57, 108, 177, 224n73
slavery, 8–9, 10, 26, 29, 44, 71, 89; abolition of, 24, 30; contemporary legacies of, 12, 112, 164, 167; resistance to, 4, 9, 12, 66, 87, 97, 112, 159–60
slums, 9, 92–98, 102. *See also* ghetto; neighborhood; periferia
Soandres, 64, 67
Só Balanço, 99, 181
Sobrevivendo no inferno (Racionais MC's), 3, 11, 181
socialism, 33, 74, 82, 85, 102–4
Solis, 30
son, 4, 35, 72–74, 84, 90, 208n11
son montuno, 73, 84
soul (US musical genre), 2, 7, 13, 63, 88; in Brazil, 3, 16, 75–77, 99, 179; in Cuba, 3, 16, 82–83, 104; in Haiti, 71, 88
Soul Train, 82–83, 205n81
SoundCloud, 5, 190n114
sound system, 7
South Africa, 85
Soviet Union, 9, 19, 103, 104, 180, 209n16
Soy Cuba (Yevtushenko), 104

Index 275

Special Period, 3, 19, 32–35, 38, 103, 153, 180, 212n89. *See also* Cuban Revolution
speculation, 15, 23, 25, 37, 40, 43–45. *See also* financialization; neoliberalism
speech act theory, 135, 137, 143, 145
spiralisme, 49, 137. *See also* Frankétienne
steel pan, 54
subjunctivity, 15, 22, 24, 26–33, 38, 41, 46. *See also* Black feminism
superação, 41, 42–45, 196n172
surfacism, 44
syncopation, 6, 13, 33, 36, 38, 55, 195n157

Tabou Combo, 88
Taylor, Cecil, 136
Teddy Fresh, 207n118
Télémaque, Rhod D'Jyvens. *See* D-Fi Powèt Revòlte
Telemax, 95, 182
tembleque, 34. *See also* timba
Temer, Michel, 46
testimonio, 216–17n38
tèt ansanm, 27. *See also* Aristide, Jean-Bertrand
Thaíde, 55, 75–77, 119, 177
Thatcher, Margaret, 23
Tietê River, 100
timba, 33–35, 72, 103, 109, 115
Tim Maia Racional (Maia), 161
Tommy Boy Records, 78
Tony Touch, 181
tourisim, 9, 19, 32–34, 85, 87, 194n114
traficando informação, 5, 121
transculturación, 9
translation, 5, 7–8, 33, 142, 149, 185n1
translocal, 16, 91, 93–94, 97–100, 108–9
trap, 2, 24, 25, 35–37, 39–40, 59, 60, 72, 109, 173, 177, 178, 182, 194n124
traptón, 24, 25, 37–38
35 Zile, 60, 173
Tribe Called Quest, 127, 149, 155
Tribu Mokoya, 154
Tropicália, 211n65
Trouillot, Michel-Rolph, 10
Trujillo, Rafael, 227n115
turntabling, 2, 13. *See also* sampling
twoubadou, 88, 116

Ubuntu, 162
underground, 5, 35, 86, 107

United States Agency for International Development (USAID), 105, 108, 132, 182, 220n135
uprooting, 16, 71. *See also* dechoukaj
urbano music, 2, 24
USB, 93, 107, 214n128
utopia, 20–23, 31, 102, 106, 107, 198n205

Van Winkle, Robert Matthew "Vanilla Ice," 100
Vargas, Bárbaro, 16, 72–74, 84, 91, 109, 173, 224–25n73
Vargas, Getúlio, 74
Vasconcelos, José, 73
Vaz, Sérgio, 41
Vedado, El, 103, 212–13n94
Veja São Paulo, 44
Veloso, Caetano, 211n65
Venas abiertas de América Latina (Galeano), 68
versioning, 49. *See also* remix; sampling
Vertières, Battle of, 30
vèvè, 61, 61–62. *See also* Vodou
Villegas, Aldo "Bocafloja," 86
violence, 17, 141, 142–47; in Brazil, 40–41, 69, 92, 97, 99, 147–50, 174, 175, 222n20; critique of, 14, 143–44, 157–58, 159–62, 167; in Cuba, 147–50, 156; in Haiti, 24, 30, 71, 87, 94, 95, 137, 157; of language, 143, 145–47, 151, 152; and militarism, 155–58; and misogyny, 149, 168; and race, 9, 156, 162–67; slow violence, 165; of urban space, 9, 40–41, 92, 148. *See also* hate speech
violin, 3, 29, 91, 129
Visão de rua, 177
Vodou, 25, 39–40, 60–62, 116, 140, 165, 173, 203n27; music of, 74, 87, 200n68; repression of, 87; rituals of, 61, 61–62, 129, 195nn152–53, 200n68, 200n74. *See also* lwa; vèvè
Vodou-jazz, 87
Vodou rap, 60
von Clausewitz, Carl, 158

War (band), 99
Warhol, Andy, 31
War of Canudos, 97
Wenders, Wim, 72, 181

Wendyyy, 59–60, 91, 177
White, MC, 49–51, 57
whitening, 9, 73
Whodini, 180
Williams, Robert Franklin, 156
Wonder Mike, 48
Worker's Party, 111
World Bank, 92
world literature, 93
world music, 93
Wyclef Jean, 3, 178
Wynter, Sylvia, 36

Xis, 49, 61, 178

yearning, 3, 22–25, 41, 67–70, 71, 191–92n46; and Black feminism, 15, 22, 24, 172; in Glissant, Édouard, 20, 24; and Haitian Revolution, 28; and neoliberalism, 15, 23
Yevtushenko, Yevgeny, 104
Yomil y el Dany, 37–38, 178
Yoruba, 84, 89, 119, 128, 150
YouTube, 5, 17, 18, 39, 43, 45, 60, 173, 182, 185n1, 195n148

zam kongo, 157
Zamora, Alejandro, 81
Zhdanov, Andrei, 104
Zimbabwe Records, 79
zombie, 40, 195n154
zona leste, 117, 222n20. *See also* São Paulo
zona sul, 111, 126, 222n20. *See also* São Paulo
Zukofsky, Louis, 122
Zumbi, 159–60. *See also* Palmares

Recent books in the series
New World Studies

Looking for Other Worlds: Black Feminism and Haitian Fiction
Régine Michelle Jean-Charles

The Epic of Cuba Libre: The Mambí, *Mythopoetics, and Liberation*
Eric Morales-Franceschini

The Mambi-Land, or Adventures of a Herald Correspondent in Cuba
James J. O'Kelly, edited by Jennifer Brittan

Fictions of Whiteness: Imagining the Planter Caste in the French Caribbean Novel
Maeve McCusker

Haitian Revolutionary Fictions: An Anthology
Edited and with translations by Marlene L. Daut, Grégory Pierrot, and Marion C. Rohrleitner

Rum Histories: Drinking in Atlantic Literature and Culture
Jennifer Poulos Nesbitt

Imperial Educación: Race and Republican Motherhood in the Nineteenth-Century Americas
Thomas Genova

Fellow Travelers: How Road Stories Shaped the Idea of the Americas
John Ochoa

The Quebec Connection: A Poetics of Solidarity in Global Francophone Literatures
Julie-Françoise Tolliver

Comrade Sister: Caribbean Feminist Revisions of the Grenada Revolution
Laurie R. Lambert

Cultural Entanglements: Langston Hughes and the Rise of African and Caribbean Literature
Shane Graham

Water Graves: The Art of the Unritual in the Greater Caribbean
Valérie Loichot

The Sacred Act of Reading: Spirituality, Performance, and Power in Afro-Diasporic Literature
Anne Margaret Castro

Caribbean Jewish Crossings: Literary History and Creative Practice
Sarah Phillips Casteel and Heidi Kaufman, editors

Mapping Hispaniola: Third Space in Dominican and Haitian Literature
Megan Jeanette Myers

Mourning El Dorado: Literature and Extractivism in the Contemporary American Tropics
Charlotte Rogers

Edwidge Danticat: The Haitian Diasporic Imaginary
Nadège T. Clitandre

Idle Talk, Deadly Talk: The Uses of Gossip in Caribbean Literature
Ana Rodríguez Navas

Crossing the Line: Early Creole Novels and Anglophone Caribbean Culture in the Age of Emancipation
Candace Ward

Staging Creolization: Women's Theater and Performance from the French Caribbean
Emily Sahakian

American Imperialism's Undead: The Occupation of Haiti and the Rise of Caribbean Anticolonialism
Raphael Dalleo

A Cultural History of Underdevelopment: Latin America in the U.S. Imagination
John Patrick Leary

The Spectre of Races: Latin American Anthropology and Literature between the Wars
Anke Birkenmaier

Performance and Personhood in Caribbean Literature: From Alexis to the Digital Age
Jeannine Murray-Román

Tropical Apocalypse: Haiti and the Caribbean End Times
Martin Munro

Market Aesthetics: The Purchase of the Past in Caribbean Diasporic Fiction
Elena Machado Sáez

Eric Williams and the Anticolonial Tradition: The Making of a Diasporan Intellectual
Maurice St. Pierre

The Pan American Imagination: Contested Visions of the Hemisphere in Twentieth-Century Literature
Stephen M. Park

www.ingramcontent.com/pod-product-compliance
Lightning Source LLC
Chambersburg PA
CBHW030611230426
43661CB00053B/1936